OLD WORLD HISTORY & GEOGRAPHY

IN CHRISTIAN PERSPECTIVE

Fourth Edition

A Beka Book® Pensacola, FL 32523-9100
an affiliate of PENSACOLA CHRISTIAN COLLEGE®

Elementary History and Geography Series in Christian Perspective

(Support materials and Grades 7–12 materials also available.)

Old World History & Geography
Fourth Edition

Staff Credits
Author: Laurel Hicks
Managing Editor: Corinne Sawtelle
Editorial Staff: Marion Hedquist
Contributors: Dawn Mereness, Denis McBride, Judy Moore, Kim Joseph, Rachel Hozey
Designer: Tim Keenan
Illustrators: John Ball, Omar Garcia, Sara Hewitt, Steven Hileman

A Beka Book, a Christian textbook ministry affiliated with Pensacola Christian College, is designed to meet the need for Christian textbooks and teaching aids. The purpose of this publishing ministry is to help Christian schools reach children and young people for the Lord and train them in the Christian way of life.

Credits appear on page 361 which are considered an extension of copyright page.

Cataloging Data
Hicks, Laurel
Old world history and geography / Laurel Hicks.—4th ed.
vi, 361 p. : col. ill., col. maps; 26 cm. + geography handbook. (A Beka Book history and geography program in Christian perspective)
Includes index.
1. History—Study and teaching (Elementary)
2. Geography—Study and teaching (Elementary) I. A Beka Book, Inc.
Library of Congress: D21 .5 .H5 2009 gr. 5
Dewey System: 909

CONTENTS

UNIT 2 ✠ AFRICA Continent of Natural Wonders

UNIT 3 ✠ EUROPE Birthplace of Western Civilization

UNIT 4 AUSTRALIA, OCEANIA, & ANTARCTICA

GEOGRAPHY HANDBOOK

DOCUMENT MEMORIZATION

TIM THE TRAVELER

Join Tim as he travels to interesting places across the Eastern Hemisphere.

Leaning Tower of Pisa, Italy

Great Wall of China

Panda in China

African elephant

Sydney Opera House Australia

An Introduction to HISTORY & GEOGRAPHY

1.1 Getting Started

History is the written record of mankind. It is a story—the true story of what man has done with the time God has given him. Some have called history *His story*. **Geography** is the study of the earth's surface—the continents, oceans, rivers, mountains, islands, and other features that are God's gift to mankind. Studying world history and geography is an adventure—an opportunity to learn more about God's world and the people who live in it.

During this study we will be learning about the **Old World**—the continents of Asia, Africa, Europe, Australia, and Antarctica. Asia is the continent where history began. By studying Asia first, and then the other continents of the Old World, we will gain an understanding of the events that led to the discovery and settlement of the New World—North and South America.

1.2 The Importance of Understanding Geography

An understanding of geography is very important when studying world history. For instance, we can understand God's plans for His people, the Jews (chapter 3), much better when we notice the central location of the land of Israel. The history and culture of ancient Egypt (chapter 7) are much clearer once we learn how the Nile River influenced much of Egypt's culture. Generally, *where* something happened in history is just as important as *when* it happened and *who* was involved.

Geography affects our lives every day. Can you imagine what world travel would be like if airplane pilots and ships' captains didn't know which countries are beside each other or where the oceans are in relation to the countries? On your next visit to the store, look closely at the labels on clothing and other items. Products you see in the store on a regular basis were made all over the world. Have you ever watched the news with your parents or read articles from the newspaper? Did you notice how many news events happen in other countries and how much the countries affect one another? Knowledge of geography is important in government, in business, and in daily life. With so much going on in the world around us, it is important that we know where other countries are located and where events are taking place in order to understand how those events affect us.

A Geography Handbook is included at the back of this text to help us learn about the continents, countries, oceans, mountains, rivers, deserts, climates, and other geographical features of the world. By studying world geography alongside world history, we will gain a clearer understanding of the people and events that make up the history of the Old World.

Comprehension Check 1A

1. What do we call the written record of mankind?
2. What is the study of the earth called?
3. Which continents make up the Old World?

1.3 The Beginnings of Human History

The Creation of Man

God's creation of Adam and Eve, the first man and woman, marks the **beginning of human history.** God gave man some special abilities that He gave to no other creature on earth—the ability to speak and think, the ability to choose right from wrong, and the ability to communicate with God. God told Adam and Eve to *"be fruitful, and multiply, and replenish the earth, and subdue it: and have dominion over [it]"* (Gen. 1:28).

Man's sin nature. The Bible gives us the true account of Adam and Eve's sin and of the Flood that God sent over 1,600 years later to destroy all the people on the earth except Noah and his family. These two events are very important in the history of the world. They tell us that since the fall of man, every human being is a sinner. Because of this, history is filled with stories of war, sickness, poverty, crime, hunger, and death. But because God has chosen to use man to work His will in this world, history is also filled with stories of the building of great nations and empires, the making of books and scientific instruments, the creation of great works of art and music, and many other human acts of reason, beauty, order, and design that reflect the wise, orderly Creator of man.

The promise of a Savior. Another important part of history is the promise God gave that He would send a Savior to take away the sins of the world. As you study history, you will see why this promise and its fulfillment made a big difference in the history of the world.

The coming of Jesus Christ to earth was such an important event in history that our dating system is centered on it. The letters **B.C.** with a date mean "Before Christ." The date 3000 B.C. means "three thousand years before Christ." The letters **A.D.** with a date stand for "anno Domini" [ăn′ō dŏm′ə·nī], which is Latin for "in the year of our Lord." The date A.D. 2000 means "in the year of our Lord 2000," or "two thousand years after the birth of Christ."

CONCEPTS TO CONSIDER

Man Did Not Evolve

In our modern world, many people make up imaginary stories about early man. They teach that man is a product of **evolution,** the false idea that man began as an animal and slowly changed (evolved) into man. Evolutionists scoff at the truth that God created the earth and man. But the more man tries to disprove the Bible, the more proof he finds that the Bible is true. The Bible gives us the only true and reasonable record of where we came from and what our first ancestors were like.

The questions and answers in this section will help you to understand some of the ideas about early man and how we can know the truth about our origin.

1. Did man evolve from animals?

Some people who choose not to believe the Bible say that the first men were monkeylike creatures who gradually developed the ability to stand upright, think, talk, choose between right and wrong, and use tools. People who say this do not have any real evidence that their idea is true, but they choose to believe it because they do not want to accept the Bible. As they move farther away from the Bible in their thinking, their ideas about early man get more and more fanciful. People who believe that man came from animals often argue among themselves about their ideas, because each of them has a different story of what early man was "really" like. There is no scientific evidence that man evolved from animals, and all the evidence we have shows that the idea of evolution is not true.

2. Were there really "ape men"?

Perhaps you have seen drawings in books of hairy, half-man, half-ape creatures standing around a fire, hunting for food, caring for their young, or eating berries and raw flesh. The caption on the picture may have said that this is what early man looked like. There is no evidence at all that the first men were hairy "ape men" and that after many centuries they gradually lost their hair and started to wear clothes. These pictures come from the imaginations of men who do not wish to believe the Bible. Some people have found fossil bones of what they thought were "ape men," but these were later discovered to be hoaxes or mistakes.

Adam and Eve did not look like apes. Adam at his creation was undoubtedly the most handsome man who has ever lived, and Eve the most beautiful woman, for they were the direct product of God's handiwork. The Bible says that as soon as Adam and Eve sinned they recognized their need for clothing and made themselves clothes from fig leaves (Gen. 3:7). Because God knew that this was not good enough, He made them clothes of animal skins (Gen. 3:21). Our first ancestors were not apelike creatures. They were highly intelligent human beings created in the image of God.

3. Did men ever live in caves?

There have been many groups of people in history who have lived in caves. Some people live in caves even today. Adam and Eve may have lived in a cave after they were sent out of the garden. Their descendants may have lived like this for many years until they could develop tools and build other kinds of shelters for protection.

Noah and his family may also have lived in caves after they left the Ark, and certainly many of the people who left the area of the Tower of Babel took advantage of the natural protection of caves until they could build up cities in their new lands. These are just a few examples of people who may have been "cave dwellers."

Caves that have been inhabited by people have been discovered in many parts of the world. Some of these caves are decorated with skillfully drawn pictures. No apelike creature could have done such artwork. The caves also carry evidence that their inhabitants believed in life after death. Yes, men have lived in caves. But that does not mean they were "ape men."

4. How long did it take men to learn to farm and herd animals?

Evolutionists often say that early men lived by gathering berries and roots for food and killing small animals with stones. Then they gradually, over hundreds of years, learned to plant and cultivate seeds and to tame animals for work and food. This is not true, of course. The Bible says that God gave Adam, the first man, the job of dressing and keeping the Garden of Eden (Gen. 2:15). Before the fall of man, there were no weeds to pull up, but Adam kept busy trimming the flourishing plants and keeping them in the best condition for providing food. After Adam sinned, he learned to "till the ground from whence he was taken" (Gen. 3:23). This means that he learned to raise crops. Adam and Eve's first son, Cain, was a "tiller of the ground," and their second son, Abel, was a "keeper of sheep" (Gen. 4:2). The first people in the world were well acquainted with farming and keeping sheep.

5. How did human language originate?

Some evolutionists say that men learned how to speak by listening to the animals and trying to imitate them. This is not true. The first man in the world, Adam, was so good at language that he was able to name all the animals (Gen. 2:20). This was undoubtedly a classifying of the animals such as scientists do today, and it took a great deal of intelligence to do this. As soon as God made Eve, Adam spoke words which showed his understanding of what God had done and the importance of it. *"And Adam said, This is now bone of my bones, and flesh of my flesh: she shall be called Woman, because she was taken out of Man"* (Gen. 2:23).

People who choose not to believe the Bible have tried for years to think of a "better" explanation for human language. Some of their fanciful "better" ideas about the development of human language have been called by evolutionists the "bow-wow" theory, the "ding-dong" theory, and the "yo-he-ho" theory. Most people realize that these ideas are very silly.

The only reasonable explanation for human thought and language is that they are direct gifts of God, not products of evolution.

6. Is human progress the same as evolution?

We can trust the Bible as giving the only true account of early man, because it was written by the Creator of man. Since God made Adam and Eve and put into their brains knowledge and abilities, we can suppose that they were probably the smartest, most perfect man and woman ever to live on this earth. Man has learned many new things since the time of Adam and Eve, of course. This is because God gave man great abilities that He did not give to the animals. Among other things, God gave man the ability to acquire skills and knowledge and to pass them on to others. God did not provide cities and tools for man. Instead, He gave man the ability to *develop* these things for himself.

The human development of new knowledge and greater skills throughout history is called **progress.** Human progress is possible because man was made in the image of God. One of God's first commands to man was the command to progress in his understanding of the earth and his ability to use its resources. *"And God blessed them, and God said unto them, Be fruitful, and multiply, and replenish the earth, and subdue it: and have dominion over the fish of the sea, and over the fowl of the air, and over every living thing that moveth upon the earth"* (Gen. 1:28). Throughout history, the people who have progressed the most have been those who have been most influenced by the Bible. When people get away from the Bible, they start to go backward instead of forward.

It is true that people have used crude tools, gathered food from the wild, and lived in caves. "Stone Age" cultures have existed all down the ages, and they exist even today in remote areas of South America, Africa, and Australia. Many of the people of these primitive cultures have the same level of intelligence and the same capabilities as people living in the most civilized places on earth. They are certainly not in the early stages of an evolutionary process.

Human progress is not the same as evolution. Progress is possible because man was made in the image of God, not because he evolved from the animals. The greatest progress has always been seen in societies influenced by the Bible. ⌘

Comprehension Check 1B

1. What marks the beginning of human history?
2. What does "B.C." mean?
3. What is evolution?
4. What gives us the only true and reasonable record of our beginnings?
5. What is progress?
6. Which people have progressed most throughout history?

The Beginning of Human Government

After the Flood, God instructed men to set up systems to govern themselves and to hold back evil. Therefore, **government** is the setting up of authorities to rule a city, state, or nation. Men have set up many different forms of government throughout history. In the end, however, the power and authority that government has comes from God.

Some **tribes** have rulers known as chiefs. A chief usually has absolute (complete) power over his people.

The rulers of some nations are as absolute in their power as chiefs. They make the laws and enforce them. Often, they are born into their office and rule until their death. A nation ruled in this way is an **absolute monarchy** [mŏn′ər·kē]. The rulers, or monarchs, are called by various names, including king, sultan, czar [zär], and shah [shä].

Similar to an absolute monarchy is a **dictatorship,** which is rule by one man who usually comes to power by force. Dictators are often military leaders.

A government in which the ruler is born into his office but is limited in power is called a **constitutional monarchy.** In constitutional monarchies, the most powerful leaders are usually the prime minister, premier, cabinet, or members of Parliament. Most nations that have kings or queens today are constitutional monarchies rather than absolute monarchies.

A government that is run by representatives of the people and in which no particular group has all the power is

Elizabeth II, queen of England

Hugo Chavez, dictator of Venezuela

Nicolas Sarkozy, president of France

called a **republic.** The ruler is called a president, and the people are actively involved in the process of government. Republics have developed more recently than other forms of government. The United States has a form of republican government under our Constitution.

The Beginning of Nations

After the Flood, man disobeyed God's command to fill the whole earth and subdue it. Instead of spreading out over the earth to take control of the different parts of it, the people all stayed in one area, called **Shinar** [shī′nər] or **Sumer** [so͞o′mər]. At that time, everyone spoke the same language. They all banded together to build the **Tower of Babel** to keep them from being "scattered abroad upon the face of the whole earth" (Gen. 11:4).

Since the people had not obeyed God, He did something to *make* them obey His command—He confused their languages so they could not understand each other. This was the beginning of the different languages of mankind.

After that there were family groups of people each speaking a different language from all the other family groups. One group stayed in the area of Sumer, and the other groups began to spread out over the earth to form separate nations, each with a common language, and each able to live and work together within their own nation. This was exactly what God had wanted them to do in the first place.

Tower of Babel

A large body of people who think of themselves as one and are united under one ruler and subject to the same general laws is called a **nation.** The land in which a nation dwells is called a **country.** When people cannot communicate with one another, they cannot live and work together in harmony. A common language is important to provide the people of a nation with a sense of unity. Because of their unity, the people are able to help each other and, if needed, to defend themselves against other nations.

CONCEPTS TO CONSIDER

Humanism: Man Rebels against God

The Tower of Babel illustrates one expression of man's rebellion against God: **humanism,** man's attempt to put himself in place of or above God. The humanist tries to build man up by ignoring God. Since the Tower of Babel, humanism has appeared in many civilizations around the world. Its consequences are always the same: decline and ultimate ruin. Only when men acknowledge their Creator and honor Him can they succeed and progress as a people. *"Blessed is the nation whose God is the Lord"* (Psa. 33:12).

The Beginning of Cultures

As groups of people left the Tower of Babel and settled around the world, they began to develop their own unique way of life or **culture.** These groups developed into the races we are familiar with today. During our study of world history and geography, we will learn about many different cultures. Culture involves religion, family life, clothing, food and drink, occupations, arts, entertainment, and other things that identify a group of people. It is culture that makes a group of people unique and interesting.

It is important to remember, however, that although the people of the world differ greatly from culture to culture, they all have a common origin: *"God that made the world and all things therein . . . hath made of one blood all nations of men for to dwell on all the face of the earth"* (Acts 17:24–26). All the people of the world have the same human nature, because all were created in the image of God and have descended from Adam and Eve. All are descendants of one of Noah's sons, Ham, Shem, or Japheth. Each person in every culture is a sinner and can be saved only through the blood of Jesus Christ. God loves each person in every culture; with God there is no respect of persons.

Comprehension Check 1C

1. When did God establish human government?
2. What is government?
3. What kind of ruler has absolute authority over his subjects?
4. What is the ruler of a constitutional monarchy commonly called?
5. What is a republic? Name one large country that has a republican form of government.
6. What is a nation?

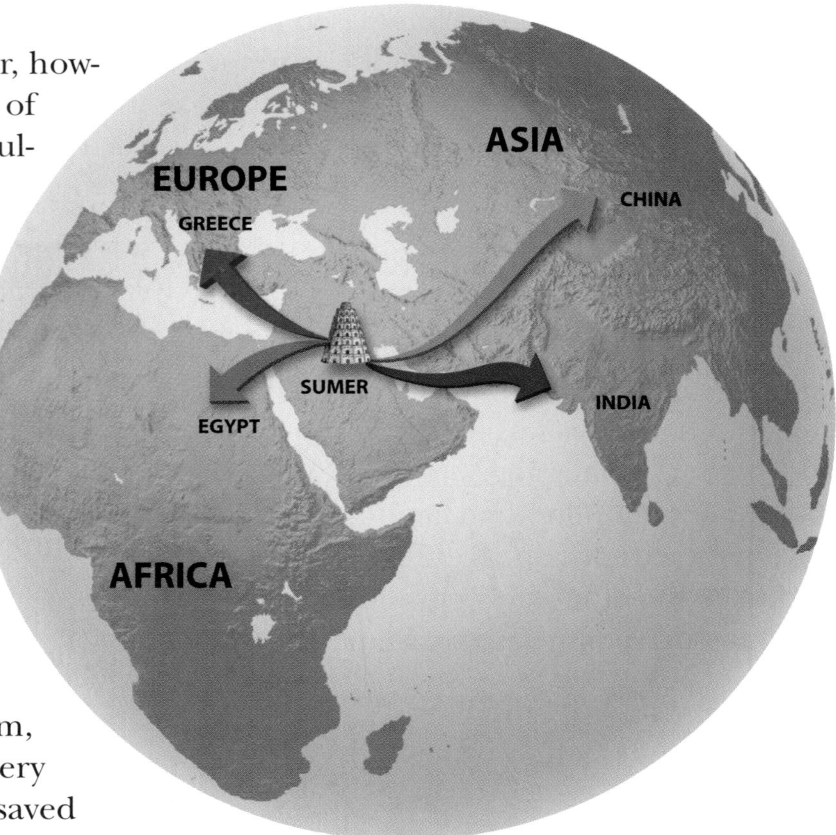

After God confused the languages at the Tower of Babel, groups spread out over the earth and formed separate nations.

CHAPTER 1 CHECKUP

A Define each term.

1. history
2. geography
3. evolution
4. government
5. nation
6. country
7. culture
8. humanism

B Give the ruler for each type of government.

1. tribe
2. absolute monarchy
3. dictatorship
4. constitutional monarch
5. republic

C Answer each question.

1. What event marks the beginning of history?
2. What event marks the beginning of human government?
3. What event marks the beginning of different languages?
4. What is the most important event in all of history?
5. What does "B.C." mean? "A.D."?

UNIT 1 ASIA THE LARGEST CONTINENT

CHAPTER 2

FERTILE CRESCENT
Cradle of Civilization

2.1 The Land of Beginnings

Like all good stories, history has a beginning, middle, and end. What we learn about the beginning of history helps us to understand why the middle of history is the way it is and what the end of history will be.

To begin history's story, we must go back in time to the creation of man in the **Garden of Eden.** We must go to a long, curved strip of land in Asia known for its rich soil and historic past. The combination of its **fertile soil** and its **crescent shape** (like a moon) gave the area its name—the **Fertile Crescent.** Because earth's earliest people lived in the Fertile Crescent, it is often called the "Cradle of Civilization."

Asia

- Asia is the world's largest continent.
- The country of Tibet (now part of China) is known as "The Roof of the World" because it contains the world's tallest mountains, including Mt. Everest.
- Houses and other buildings in the ancient city of Petra, in Jordan, were carved into rocky cliffs. Because many of the cliffs are red, Petra was known as the "rose-red city."
- Lake Baikal in Russia, more than a mile deep at its deepest point, is the deepest lake in the world. During the winter when the lake is frozen, cars can drive over it.
- At a traditional "floating market" in Thailand, merchants sell their goods from small boats.

The Two Rivers

Two rivers in the Fertile Crescent have been known to man from the earliest pages of history. They are the **Tigris** [tī′grĭs] and the **Euphrates** [yo͞o·frā′tēz]. These rivers begin high in the mountains of modern Turkey and Armenia, where melting snows flow down in streams.

The name "Tigris" means "arrow." This river runs a straight course just as an arrow does when it is shot from a bow. "Euphrates" means "that which makes fruitful." This winding river brings much water to the thirsty land around it.

As the rivers flow down the mountains to the south, they pick

Euphrates River near the border between Syria and Iraq

up rich, fertile soil. When they reach the plains below, the rivers deposit the soil creating excellent farmland.

The Land between the Rivers

The part of the Fertile Crescent between the Tigris and Euphrates Rivers was called **Mesopotamia** [mĕs′ə·pə·tā′mē·ə], which means "between the rivers." The Bible names four rivers that came together at the Garden of Eden (Gen. 2:10–14), which was probably located in Mesopotamia where the country of Iraq is today. One of the four rivers was the Euphrates. Another, the Hiddekel [hĭd′ə·kĕl′], is believed to be the modern Tigris. The other two rivers, which have never been found, may have disappeared during the Flood of Noah's day.

For a long time, the Bible was our only record of what early life in Mesopotamia was like. In recent years, men have found other records of early times there, but none is as accurate as **the Bible,** our only completely accurate record of ancient (very old) history.

Comprehension Check 2A

1. Why is the Fertile Crescent called the "Cradle of Civilization"?
2. What two rivers flow through the Fertile Crescent?
3. What does Tigris mean? Euphrates?
4. What does Mesopotamia mean?
5. Where can we find the only completely accurate record of ancient history?

2.2 Sumer: A Civilization of Southern Mesopotamia

Surroundings

To the north of Mesopotamia are mountains, the most famous of which is **Mount Ararat.** In Genesis God tells us that Noah's Ark came to rest "upon the mountains of Ararat." The mountain we call Mount Ararat today may be the very mountain upon which Noah's Ark came to rest. Directly south lies the **Persian Gulf.**

The Land

In the northern part of Mesopotamia, where the mountains are high, there is some rain and the weather is cool. In the south, the land is very flat and dry. There is little or no rain in this area, and the temperature sometimes reaches as high as 120°–140°F. Yet some of the earliest known civilizations were located in southern Mesopotamia. (A **civilization** is a country or a people who have developed to a great extent the natural abilities that God has given to

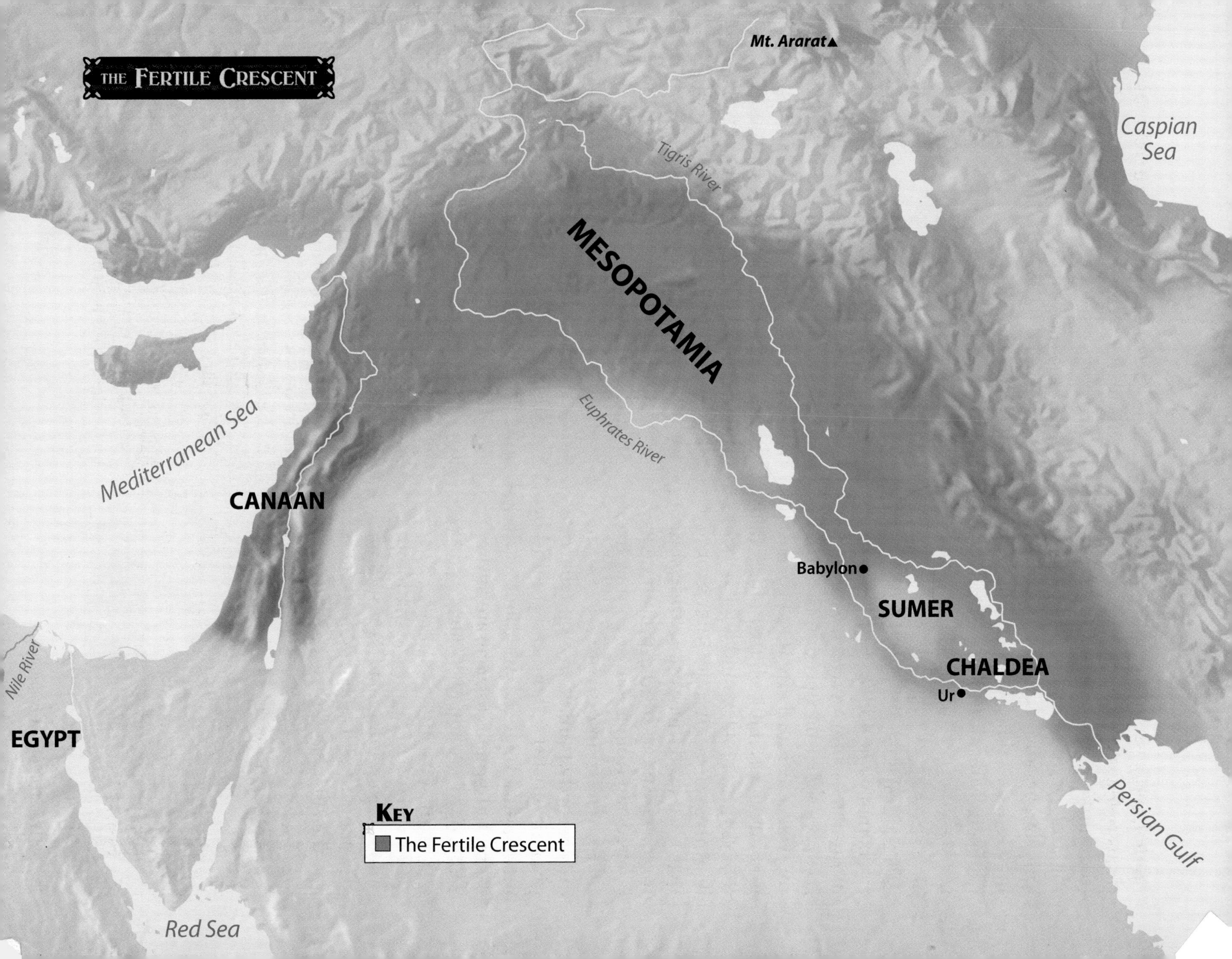
THE FERTILE CRESCENT
Mt. Ararat
Caspian Sea
Tigris River
MESOPOTAMIA
Euphrates River
Mediterranean Sea
CANAAN
Babylon
SUMER
CHALDEA
Ur
Nile River
EGYPT
Persian Gulf
Red Sea
KEY
The Fertile Crescent

man. People who make good use of their God-given abilities, such as talking, thinking, reading, writing, inventing, discovering, treating people kindly, enjoying art and music, and worshiping God are said to be civilized.) One of these civilizations was in the land of **Sumer.**

The Sumerians and Their Work

The people of Sumer were called Sumerians. They were the descendants of the people who stayed in the area of the Tower of Babel after God confused the languages. One of their cities, **Babylon,** was probably named after Babel. The Sumerians and the other groups may have lived in caves or crude shelters for a while after the Flood until they could build homes, but soon they had a well-developed way of life.

The Sumerians were an intelligent people who worked tirelessly to find better ways of living. They became skillful at their jobs and were very inventive. Their hard work made Sumer a wealthy and impressive area.

Farmers. The main occupation in Sumer was farming. Farmers in Sumer grew wheat, barley, vegetables, dates, and figs.

yoke of oxen pulling a plow

examples of Sumerian craftsmanship

Sumer was located in the southern part of Mesopotamia, where the land was very hot and dry. **Irrigation** (supplying land with water by means of ditches, channels, or sprinklers) was extremely important to the Sumerian way of life. The Sumerians dug a system of ditches from the Tigris and Euphrates Rivers to make the water flow from the rivers to their thirsty lands. Without irrigation, most of Sumer would have been a dry wasteland, unable to grow food for all of its people. As time passed, the Sumerians made their irrigation canals wider and larger in order to produce more crops. Sumer became a wealthy area in the Fertile Crescent. But irrigation brought troubles as well as wealth. Many wars were fought over who had the right to build or use certain canals.

Herdsmen or shepherds. Some Sumerians were herdsmen or shepherds, caring for large groups of animals. They raised animals, such as sheep, goats, donkeys, and some oxen, that could stand a hot, dry climate. The sheep provided wool as well as meat; goats provided milk and meat; donkeys were needed to carry heavy loads. When the plow was invented, the Sumerians began raising oxen to pull their plows.

Skilled workers. Many Sumerians were skilled workers. Some made cloth from wool. Some worked at making armor, spears, swords, and chariots for their soldiers. There were some who worked with astronomy, medicine, and law. Others were skilled craftsmen, such as **sculptors,** men who made statues of people and the gods they worshiped. Priests led the people in the worship of many false gods. There were **metalsmiths,** men who worked with gold, silver, copper, and bronze. And of course, there were soldiers for the army.

Inventions from Sumer

Writing. History owes much to the Sumerians, for as far as we know, they were the first people after the Flood who developed and used writing. (No one knows for sure if man used writing before the Flood.) At first, their writing looked more like pictures of what the writer was trying to represent, called **pictographs.**

Gradually their writing became wedge-shaped, each mark standing for a syllable of a word. This form of writing became known as **cuneiform** [kyo͞o·nē′ə·fôrm′]. With a reed or with a sharp instrument, the writers made their marks on a smooth piece of soft clay. If they wanted to keep their writing as a record, they baked the clay until it was hard. In this way, they kept permanent written records, thousands of which have been found by modern day **archaeologists** [är′kē·ŏl′ə·jĭsts: people who dig up and study the remains of ancient civilizations]. Among these are bills, tax records, and records of work that was accomplished by individuals. The Sumerians were quite amazing in their orderly way of conducting business.

Many poems and stories were also written on these baked pieces of clay. Some of the writings were about Creation and the Flood; however, these Sumerian writings included many legends along with some Bible truth.

The wheel. Another invention credited to the Sumerians was the wheel. They were the first people known to

cuneiform writing

The invention of the wheel is credited to the Sumerians.

use it. We are so used to seeing wheels today on our cars, trains, and buses as well as in the workings of clocks and other machines that it is hard to imagine what life must have been like without wheels. For the armies of Sumer, the invention of the wheel meant building chariots for war. For builders and farmers, the wheel meant being able to move heavy loads.

Comprehension Check 2B

1. What is civilization?
2. What city was probably named after Babel?
3. Name two important Sumerian inventions.
4. What was the early form of Sumerian writing called? The later form?
5. What do archaeologists do?

CONCEPTS TO CONSIDER

How Archaeologists Study History

Archaeology is the study of ancient people by means of recovering, preserving, and evaluating remains from the past. Ancient written records, tools, weapons, jewelry, coins, and pottery, as well as remains of ancient buildings, are among the buried treasures that archaeologists find. These **artifacts** give archaeologists their most helpful clues to what life may have been like in some ancient cities.

An archaeologist begins his search by studying historical records, maps, and previous archaeological finds. He then locates a place that looks promising for his **dig,** or excavation site. There are many archaeological digs in the Middle East because that is the location of some of the oldest civilizations.

At the site, the archaeologist and his team begin digging, becoming more and more careful the closer they get to what they are looking for. The workers cautiously uncover objects they find, using small sticks, soft brushes, and sometimes spoons to move the dirt away from their discoveries. Great care has to be taken that nothing is overlooked or destroyed. These ancient objects are very fragile.

Finding artifacts at his dig is just the beginning of the archaeologist's task. When an object is found, it is photographed before it is moved, and a report is made of the object's description and its exact location. After the object is examined to find out its age, it is classified,

archaeologist using a soft brush to gently move dirt

packed, and sometimes shipped to a museum or other location. Quite often, articles are found broken and have to be carefully pieced together. When you consider that hundreds of objects can be found at one site, you can imagine the time and expense put into each ancient city that is studied. Even more time consuming is the fact that sometimes several cities are found stacked in layers. Each one has to be excavated as carefully as the city on top.

The findings of archaeologists are often valuable to students of history. Although the Bible is the world's only completely accurate written record of ancient history, the discoveries of archaeologists have supported the accuracy of biblical descriptions of historic events. This is exactly what those who believe the Bible would expect.

Archaeologists may never find proof for all the events that the Bible describes, but that does not mean that the events never happened. Thousands of years have passed since some of these events took place. With the passing of time, it is only normal that physical evidence has decayed or has been destroyed. Yet beyond a doubt, archaeologists' findings prove the reliability of God's Word. ⌘

Religion in Sumer

Superstition. Although they were an intelligent people who left an impressive culture for men to study, the Sumerians were not wise about one very important thing. They turned away from the one true God. They chose to mix God's truth with their own false ideas. They became very superstitious. **Superstition** is a belief that is based on fear and ignorance rather than on the truth. Superstition often keeps people from learning all the new things that God intended for man to learn, because it makes them afraid to study God's creation.

The Sumerians worshiped what God had created and gave no thought to God Himself. They thought that thunder, wind, and storms were gods. It is no wonder that their superstition brought them fear!

Ziggurats. The Sumerians built tall temples called **ziggurats** [zĭg′ə·răts′] for worshiping their gods. Each ziggurat was built in layers. The bottom layer was the largest. The next layer was a little smaller, and each higher layer was smaller yet. On top of the last and smallest layer, the people built an altar on which to offer sacrifices to their gods. They felt that the taller the ziggurat, the more successful they would be in reaching up to heaven and communicating with their gods.

ziggurat

What a difference between our God and theirs! Ours is the Creator, not something that has been created. Our God can be reached anywhere at any time, not just from the top of a high building. Our God is the living, loving God of Heaven Who is able to hear and answer the prayers of His children. He is not a frightening part of our imagination or of nature.

Education in Sumer

The people in ancient cities realized the importance of education, especially of reading and writing. School was held in the temples, but usually only the wealthy attended. In most cities only boys went to school. The teachers were priests who taught the boys reading, writing, and arithmetic, as well as a trade for later in life.

The boys sat on flat stone benches. Each student was given soft clay that he used as a tablet for practicing his writing. When his tablet was full, he most likely smoothed out the marks on it and began again.

In some schools, there were dictionaries and grammar books. In most cities there were libraries as well as schools.

Homes in Sumer

The Sumerian builders were very skillful. They were the first to build the **arch** and the **dome.**

Prosperous families usually lived in two-story homes built around a courtyard. Less prosperous people lived in one-story homes. The homes were constructed of brick made from clay. The walls were thick to keep out the summer heat. Nearly everyone enjoyed the flat roofs. After a hot day, the people would often go up to their roof to enjoy a cool evening. If the night was hot, the people would even sleep on their roofs.

The Importance of the Seal

The **seal** was an instrument used to stamp an article or document. Nearly everyone had and used his own individual seal; it was a mark of identification because it was different from everyone else's seal.

There were different kinds of seals. People in some areas used rings as stamps to make seals. The most common type of seal in Sumer was the **cylinder.** Each person chose the pictures and words he wanted on his seal and had them engraved on a cylinder. When the cylinder was rolled over a piece of wet clay, it left a raised picture or pattern of the words and pictures. This cylinder mark on a piece of clay was the same as someone signing his name to a piece of paper today.

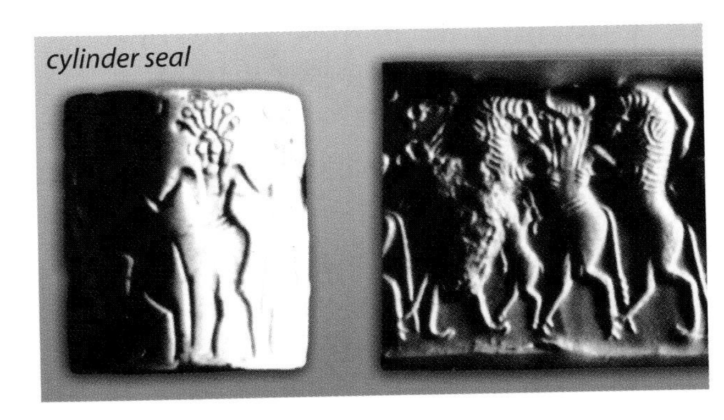
cylinder seal

The Sumerian kept his cylinder seal and clay as handy as we keep our pen and paper. There was a hole in each cylinder through which a cord was strung so the Sumerian could wear the cylinder around his neck.

Laws were written on a clay tablet that bore the ruler's seal. When the people saw the ruler's seal, they realized they must obey the law. Letters were also sealed (1 Kings 21:8) as well as some books (Isa. 29:11).

Comprehension Check 2C

1. What is archaeology?
2. What were tall Sumerian temples called?
3. What two types of architecture did the Sumerians originate?
4. What was the most common kind of seal in Sumer?

2.3 Ur of the Chaldees

The southern part of Sumer was called **Chaldea** [kăl·dē′ə]. **Ur,** the most important Sumerian city, was in Chaldea. It was the largest and wealthiest city on the west bank of the Euphrates River. Remains of the **ziggurat of Ur** can still be seen today. It is considered the best preserved example of a ziggurat in all Mesopotamia.

Life in Ur. The city of Ur itself is considered the best preserved example of an ancient city in Mesopotamia. From the remains of this city, archaeologists can give us some idea of what life was like at that time. The king who ordered the ziggurat built at Ur was named **Ur-Nammu** [ər′näm′o͞o′]. He was a powerful ruler who ruled Ur about 2100 B.C., just before Abraham lived, or 2,100 years before the birth of Christ. This was about two hundred years after the Flood. It is estimated that at this time about 24,000 people lived in Ur.

The residential area. During the rule of Ur-Nammu, Ur was divided into two main areas, a sacred area and a residential area. The residential area was where most of the people lived. Shops, schools, and libraries were also inside the residential area. Ur was luxurious, and many of its people were wealthy. Many had beautiful gardens with man-made fish ponds.

The sacred area. The oval-shaped city was completely enclosed by a great wall. One fourth of the entire city was enclosed by another strong wall. Inside this wall were rooms that were stocked with weapons. The area enclosed by the second wall was the sacred area reserved for the worship and service of **Nanna,** the moon god. The ziggurat was inside this area. Magnificent **stone temples** were also in this area between the walls, as well as a **marketplace** where the people brought their gifts to the moon god. It was here that the people paid their taxes to Nanna. Someone had the job of recording on clay tablets the gifts brought and the taxes paid. These tablets were kept in one of the temples. Archaeologists have found many of these records.

A famous citizen of Ur. The people of Ur and of the Fertile Crescent were an intelligent people. From their inventions, businesses, trades, and crafts, we can see that they were highly creative. Yet they were idolatrous in their religion.

There was one citizen of Ur who did not worship idols. He was **Abraham,** the father of the Jewish nation. God led Abraham out of Ur to a land that He promised to him and his descendants—the land of **Canaan.** For many years, Abraham and his descendants were strangers in the land of Canaan and later in the land of Egypt in northern Africa. On the map of the Fertile Crescent area (p. 13), trace the route one would take to get from Ur to Canaan and from Canaan to Egypt. Move your finger through the Fertile Crescent, for that is the best way to get from Ur to Canaan.

The findings of an archaeologist. Beginning in 1922, Sir Leonard Woolley, a British archaeologist, led excavations to uncover the city of Ur. For twelve years, he led a team of about 200 men, working during the winter months to uncover the time-buried secrets of Ur.

They found that Ur was a number of cities. As one city fell into ruins, another city was built on top of its ruins. The city that Abraham was familiar with was near the bottom.

As the men removed layers of dirt and clay from the various cities of Ur, they usually found objects, such as pottery, tablets, and jewelry, which gave them some idea of the life from the period in which that city was built. Suddenly, in 1927, the men came to an 8-foot layer of clay that had been laid down by water. They could find no objects in this layer. The men kept digging below the water-laid clay and again found objects of city life.

Woolley and his workmen knew that such a deep layer of water-laid clay could only be laid by a great flood. Could this be the great Flood that the Bible says covered the whole earth? Woolley believed that it was.

Shortly afterward, Woolley and his men discovered some of the royal tombs of ancient Ur. The most amazing of the tombs was that of **Lady Shubad** (also known as Queen Puabi). It is from such discoveries that we have learned something of what the ancient people believed about death.

For her burial, Lady Shubad wore a headdress of gold leaves and precious stones. When archaeologists opened her tomb, they discovered this headdress and other treasures. Among the gold and jewels, they found piles of human bones. The pagan priests of Ur had sacrificed young men and women to serve as "soldiers" and "servants" to attend to Lady Shubad in the afterlife. An entire choir of talented musicians had also been murdered to "entertain" the dead. God's servant Abraham refused to follow the cruel religion of the Sumerians. God led him out of a city that had great riches but no respect for human life.

Lady Shubad's burial headdress

CHAPTER 2 CHECKUP

A Know these locations.

1. Fertile Crescent
2. Mesopotamia
3. Tigris
4. Euphrates
5. Mt. Ararat
6. Babylon
7. Ur

B Define each term.

1. civilization
2. irrigation
3. pictographs
4. cuneiform
5. archaeologists
6. superstition
7. ziggurats
8. altar
9. cylinder seal
10. Tower of Babel

C Who am I?

1. a famous citizen of Ur; God promised the land of Canaan to him
2. a queen whose tomb was discovered in ancient Ur
3. the Sumerian moon god
4. the king who ordered the ziggurat at Ur to be built
5. the archaeologist who discovered evidence of a great flood

D Identify the term described by each clue.

1. the only completely accurate record of ancient history
2. the mountain upon which Noah's ark came to rest
3. the river whose name means "arrow"
4. the place where history began
5. the land "between the rivers"
6. the "Cradle of Civilization"
7. the teachers in Sumerian schools
8. the pupils in Sumerian schools
9. another name for an archaeological excavation
10. the southern part of Sumer
11. the most important Sumerian city

E Answer each question.

1. What were the most common occupations in ancient Sumer?
2. What architectural details were the Sumerians first to use?
3. What were the two most important Sumerian inventions?

CHAPTER 3

ANCIENT MIDDLE EAST

3.1 Where History Began

The Fertile Crescent, where history began, and the land of Mesopotamia are located in the **Middle East,** in the center of the Eastern Hemisphere. Three continents, **Africa, Asia,** and **Europe,** come together there; and most of the events in the Bible took place there—in the land that has been called the Crossroads of the Ancient World.

3.2 Homes of Ancient Times

Tent Dwellers

What was it like to live in the Middle East in Bible times? If you could fly to the Arabian Peninsula today and spend some time with a Bedouin [bĕd′o͝o·ĭn] family, you would get a good idea of how many of the people in ancient times lived. **Bedouins** are Arabs who wander from place to place with their herds of camels, sheep, and goats. Because they are wanderers, they live in tents, the way many ancient people did. (People who constantly move from one place to another are called **nomads.**)

In ancient times, as today, tents were pitched in a spot that had both the shade of trees and a nearby water supply. The tents were made of black goat hair cloth. The rains would shrink the goat hair cloth and make it waterproof. During the summer heat, the sides of the tent were lifted, providing the occupants with shade and ventilation. In the winter, the sides were down for protection from cold winds.

Inside, the tent was divided by goat hair curtains into two or more apartments. One apartment was for men, and the other was for women and children.

a Bedouin caravan

Many of the early families were wandering shepherds. When grass became scarce for their flocks and herds to feed on, they packed up and moved to a greener area. The furnishings of the tent had to be light and easy to pack. Rugs made up the floor of the tent. Mats were unrolled at night for beds and rolled up during the day.

Among the usual pots and clay dishes in the tent were goatskin bags for drinking water, a pitcher for carrying water from the well, a leather bucket for drawing water from the well, sacks for storing grain, and stones for grinding the grain. For a table, a piece of leather was spread out on the floor of the tent. The oven was no more than a hole in the ground.

For light, the tent dwellers as well as those who lived in houses lit their olive oil lamps. These lamps were simply clay saucers containing olive oil. A pinched lip in the saucer held the wick, which drew the oil up to be burned. Whether they lived in a tent or a house, most ancient people kept a lamp burning both night and day. This insured them of a means of starting a fire if the fire in their hearth happened to go out.

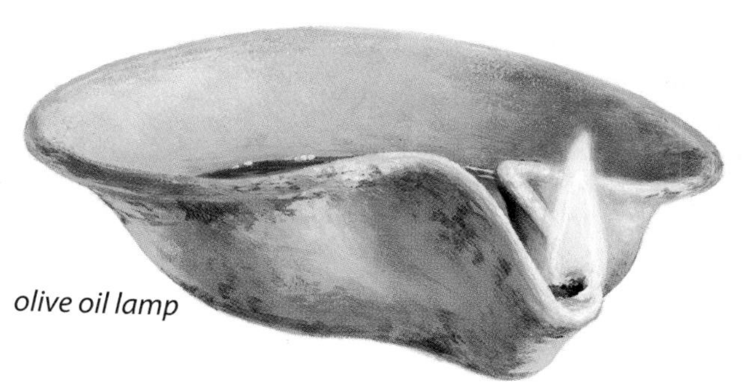
olive oil lamp

Houses in Ancient Cities

Not everyone lived in tents. Many people lived in houses. The houses of the ancient Middle East were similar to some houses that you could see in the Middle East today. Poorer families, who lived in villages, usually had one-room houses. Those who had more money lived in the city and owned bigger homes with more rooms.

The one-room houses were usually made of sun-dried bricks. The floors were hard-packed dirt. The flat roof was covered with dirt and pebbles that were smoothed over with a stone roller. After a rain, a freshly made dirt roof might suddenly sprout grass, because grass seeds were in the soil. Then the heat would cause the grass to wither until the next rain.

The furnishings of the one-room houses were mostly the same as those of the tents. The furniture increased with the wealth of the household. In wealthier homes of more than one room, there were couches, cushions, beds, and a roof made of tile instead of dirt.

Middle Eastern homes with flat roofs

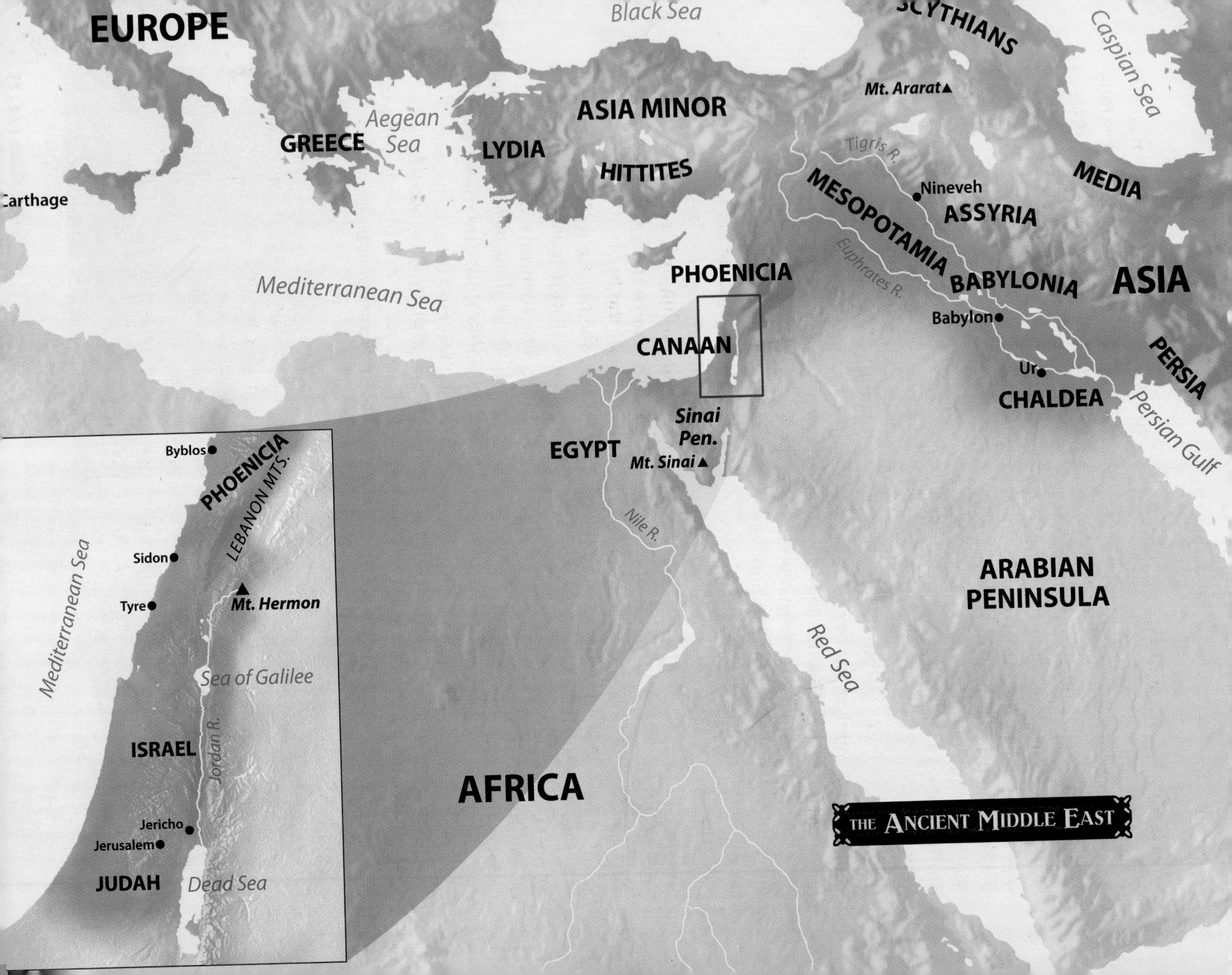
THE ANCIENT MIDDLE EAST
EUROPE
Black Sea
SCYTHIANS
Caspian Sea
Mt. Ararat
ASIA MINOR
Aegean Sea
GREECE
LYDIA
HITTITES
Carthage
Tigris R.
Nineveh
MEDIA
MESOPOTAMIA
ASSYRIA
Euphrates R.
BABYLONIA
ASIA
Babylon
PHOENICIA
Mediterranean Sea
CANAAN
Ur
PERSIA
CHALDEA
Persian Gulf
Sinai Pen.
EGYPT
Mt. Sinai
Nile R.
ARABIAN PENINSULA
Red Sea
AFRICA
Byblos
PHOENICIA
LEBANON MTS.
Sidon
Tyre
Mt. Hermon
Mediterranean Sea
Sea of Galilee
ISRAEL
Jordan R.
Jericho
Jerusalem
JUDAH
Dead Sea

Because most families enjoyed the coolness of their roofs on summer evenings, there were stairs leading to the flat roof. Some families had an upper room built on their roof.

The rooms of the houses were built around open courtyards that were planted with beautiful trees, shrubs, and flowers. In the very center of the courtyard was usually a fountain or cistern for storing rainwater. Meals were usually eaten in the courtyards. In hot weather, an awning was placed over the courtyard to protect the people from the direct heat of the sun. In cold weather, a fire was built for warmth.

3.3 Daily Life in an Ancient City

Early morning. Daily activities in ancient lands began early in the morning, even before dawn. In the city or village, craftsmen such as potters, woodcarvers, carpenters, embroiderers, dyers of cloth, and workers in metals such as copper and gold skillfully worked with their hands. Women might be found busily plunging the family laundry up and down in the water of a nearby stream.

Grinding grain. Other women would have already begun the endless job of making bread for the day. If we could walk down the street of an ancient city at dawn, we would hear the hum of **millstones** as they rubbed against each other, grinding grain into flour.

millstones

The millstone was built from two flat, round stones, one on top of the other. Some measured as much as two feet across the center. The upper stone had an upright handle and a hole to pour grain through. Usually, two women sat on the ground facing each other. Each used one hand to turn the mill and the other to drop grain into the hole. You can imagine what hard work it was to turn the one large, heavy stone against the other. As the heavy stones rubbed together, the grain was ground into flour that fell on an animal skin beneath the millstone.

Baking bread. Bread was a very important part of the diet in Bible times. Sometimes the oven used for baking bread was merely a hole dug in the sand and lined with pebbles or stones. A fire was built at the bottom of the hole. When the stones around the sides of the hole had become very hot, a very thin bread, which looked something like a pancake, was placed directly on them. Because the bread was so thin and the stones so hot, the bread cooked very quickly.

Another type of oven was a large earthenware jar, about three feet high, most likely found in village and city homes. This jar or oven was open at the top and gradually became wider toward the bottom. There was a hole near the bottom of the jar for the fire to be built.

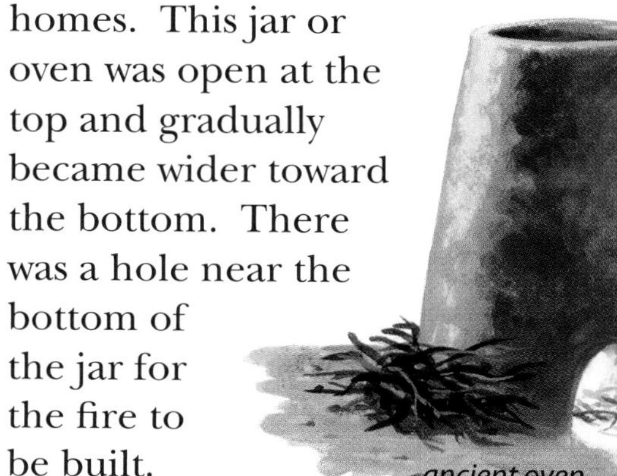
ancient oven

Once the sides of the jar were hot, a very thin bread was placed all over the sides of the jar, inside and out. This kind of bread also cooked very quickly.

Shepherds and husbandmen. Early in the morning, shepherds would lead their flocks from their night shelter to a place where they could watch them graze. The husbandmen, or farmers, went to their fields. The season of the year determined what job a husbandman would begin each morning. Perhaps it was time to take his plow to the field to prepare the ground for seeds. Or perhaps it was time to harvest his crops. Fruits and vegetables were picked and stored. Grain would be cut with a **sickle** and tied into **sheaves.**

The job of separating grain from the husk of the plant in which it grew is called **threshing.** The most common way of threshing grain was to beat the grain with a stick and turn it over and over again. The grain would fall to the ground while the husk was blown aside by the wind. This was a hot and dusty job. Another method of threshing made use of animal power. Sheaves of grain were placed on a hard floor. Cattle or other large animals were driven over it, pulling a rough board. The board was designed to knock the grain out of its husk. On another day, the grain would be ground to make flour.

When the olives were ready to harvest, workers shook the olive branches or beat them with sticks until the ripe olives fell to the ground. The ripe olives were gathered and taken to an olive press. Here the valuable oil was pressed out of the olives so it could be used for cooking and as fuel for lamps. Sometimes the olives were emptied into a vat to be pressed with a beam. At other times the oil was squeezed out simply by stomping on the olives with the feet.

Mealtime. The people usually ate two meals and a snack each day. Before they ate, they had someone pour water over their hands to wash them. Because they ate with their hands, the people washed their hands again after the meal.

Time for rest. As the hottest time of the day approached, the people took a break from their work. Even today in many Eastern countries, most activity stops at noon and the people rest. That is why we read in Genesis 18:1 that Abraham "sat in the tent door in the heat of the day."

Evening activities. After a few hours of rest, the daily activities resumed. As the evening approached, women brought their earthenware pitchers to the well or to a spring to draw water. Then they placed their pitcher on their head or shoulder and walked home.

girls carrying water

This was strictly a woman's job; rarely would a man bring a pitcher to a well.

When the shadows of the evening made it difficult to work, men stopped their jobs. For most people, it was now time for the main meal of the day. If we could wander back through time and be near one of the village homes at a mealtime, we would most likely be asked to stay as guests. To refuse would be to insult our host. Though we would be strangers, we could expect to be treated with great hospitality. As we entered the house, we would remove our sandals. A servant would offer us water to wash our feet. This would feel good since our feet would be hot and dusty from the roads that we had traveled. We would be given a drink and served a meal. Our host would then offer us a place to sleep. We could rest assured that if our host asked us to be his guests, he would see to it that our needs would be met and that we would be protected as long as we were his guests.

Comprehension Check 3A

1. What three continents come together in the Middle East?
2. What has the Middle East been called?
3. What is a Bedouin?
4. Describe a millstone. What was its purpose? How did it work?
5. What was the most common way of threshing grain?
6. How did the people cope with the extreme heat in the middle of the day?

3.4 The Phoenicians: A Seafaring People

Location

Phoenicia [fĭ·nĭsh′ə], north of modern Israel, was made up of many cities, each with its own king. It was located on a narrow coastal plain, two hundred miles long and only about 12 miles wide. To the west was the **Mediterranean Sea,** and to the east were the **Lebanon Mountains.** Locate Phoenicia on the map of the Ancient Middle East (p. 24). Notice **Tyre** [tīr] and **Sidon** [sīd′ʼn] on the seacoast. They were two of Phoenicia's most important cities. To the north was another important city, **Byblos** [bĭb′ləs].

Gifts of Nature

The seacoast gave the Phoenicians a place to build excellent harbors. The great forests in the Lebanon Mountains, especially noted for their firs and cedars, gave the Phoenicians strong wood from which they made fine, fast boats. Using these natural gifts, the Phoenicians became the first great sea traders of the ancient world.

Trade with Many Nations

Byblos. **Byblos** was an important seaport and shipbuilding center. With the ships made at Byblos, the Phoenicians carried on trade with many countries. One trade item from the land of Egypt to the south was **papyrus,** a paper-like material made from the papyrus plant. The Phoenicians began to use the Egyptian papyrus for writing and also traded it with **Greece.** People who carry one country's goods to another country, as the Phoenicians did, are called **middlemen.** (Check the map, p. 24, to see how the Phoenicians would get to Greece.)

Because the Greeks got their papyrus from ships that came from the Phoenician city of Byblos, they called papyrus and the books that were made from it **"biblos."** Since the Bible is the greatest of all books, people simply called it "the Book," or *Biblos.* We get our English word *Bible* from the Greek word *biblos.*

Tyre and Sidon. Both Tyre and Sidon were famous for their manufacturing of a beautiful purple dye and blown glass. The purple dye was made from the **murex** [myo͝or′ĕks], a kind of sea snail that was plentiful along the Phoenician coast. This dye's purple was so rich and beautiful that for a time only kings and royalty were allowed to buy it. Many rulers from other lands were eager to trade with the Phoenicians for their purple dye, which they used to make their royal garments. It has been said that just a pound of silk dyed in this purple color cost the equivalent of nearly thirty thousand dollars.

murex

Some historians say the Phoenicians were the first people to make **blown glass** from the fine, white sands of their sea coast. Pendants and necklaces were manufactured in Phoenicia and were among the trade goods that went to various ancient cities. It became the style for many women in other countries to wear beautiful jewelry made of the blue, white, or yellow glass.

Bold and Fearless Sailors

Phoenicia was known for its bold and fearless sailors. The Phoenicians were among the first people in world history to send explorers through-

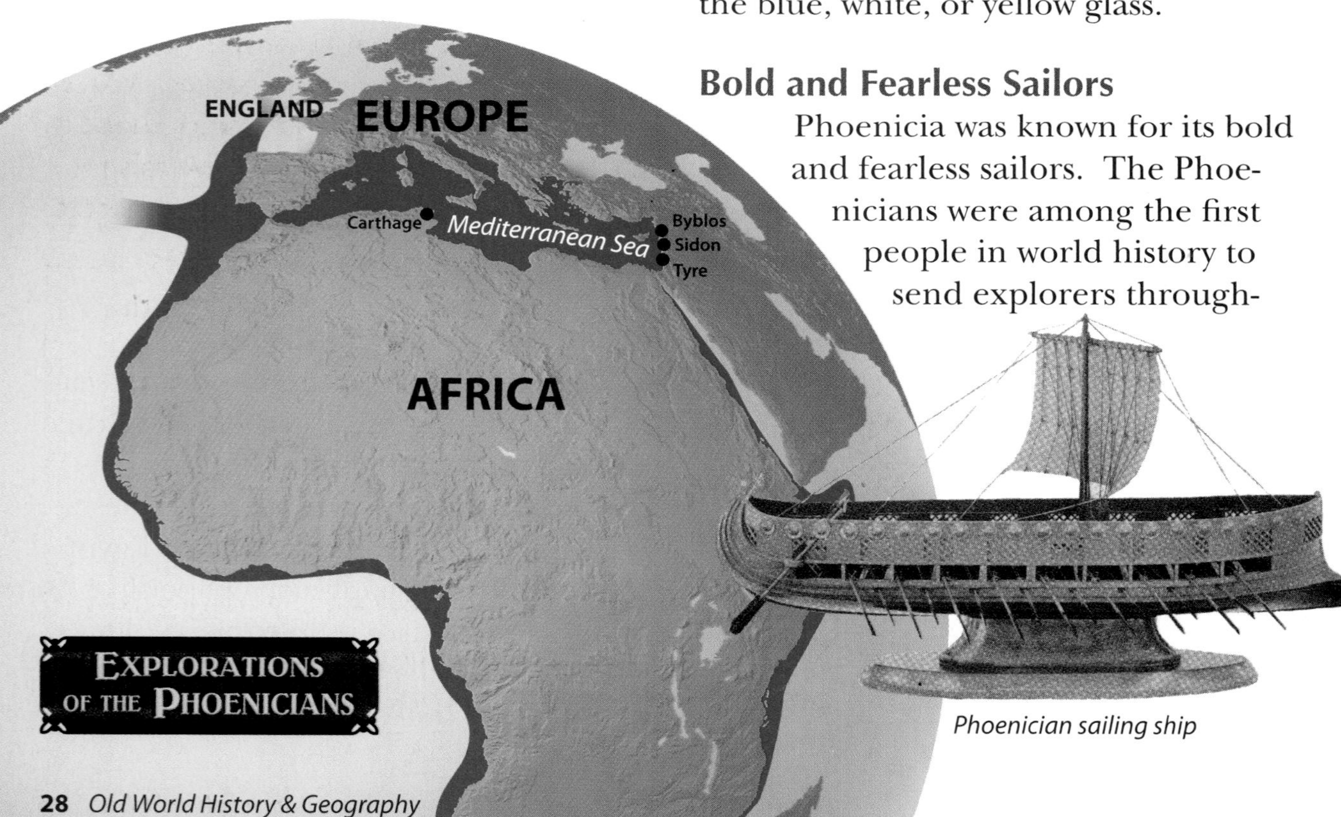

Phoenician sailing ship

out the Mediterranean Sea area. It is known that they sailed along the west coast of Europe and up to England. Some historians even give them credit for being the first to sail around the continent of Africa.

Trading Posts

In the area of the Mediterranean Sea, the Phoenicians built many trading posts that later became important cities. Perhaps the most important of these cities was **Carthage** [kär′thĭj] in North Africa, one of the greatest cities of ancient times.

The Phoenician Alphabet

The Phoenicians developed an **alphabet,** their most valuable contribution to the world, by inventing their own signs that stood for the twenty-two basic consonant sounds in their language. Their alphabet was easier to use than the alphabets from other countries. Yet, despite this important contribution, they wrote no lasting piece of literature.

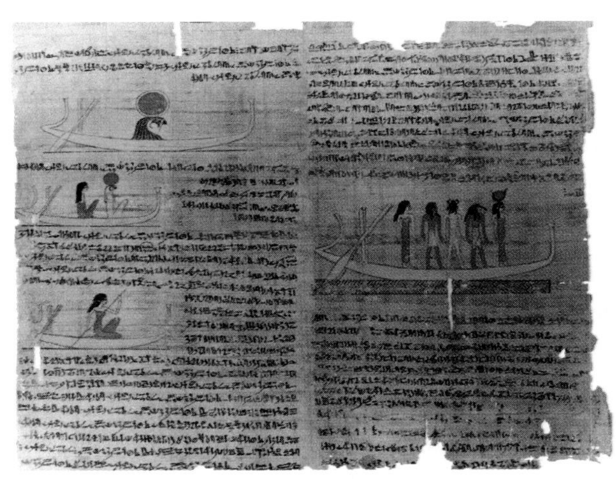

Egyptian papyrus

As the Phoenicians sailed both far and near, they took their alphabet with them. The Greeks further developed the Phoenician signs to form their own alphabet, which was the written language of the world when Christ lived on earth. This Greek language greatly contributed to the spread of the gospel, for the New Testament was first written in Greek. Our word *alphabet* comes from the names of the first two letters of the Greek alphabet, **alpha** and **beta.**

Worshipers of False Gods

Phoenicia had been a part of the land of Canaan before the children of Israel returned from their captivity in the land of Egypt. While still a part of Canaan, the Phoenicians had learned to worship the many false gods of the wicked Canaanites. To satisfy their gods, the Canaanites would sacrifice human beings, sometimes even their own babies. When the Phoenicians began new settlements they spread the worship of these false gods to the peoples they had conquered.

Comprehension Check 3B

1. What two natural gifts made the Phoenicians the first great sea traders of the world?
2. The Phoenicians were _?_; they carried one country's goods to another.
3. Name an important city in Africa with which the Phoenicians traded.
4. What was the Phoenicians' most valuable contribution to the world?

3.5 ✠ The Hittites: Empire Builders

Fierce conquerors. **Asia Minor** (modern Turkey) is a large peninsula that sticks out of the northern Middle East into the Mediterranean and Black Seas. (A **peninsula** is a body of land that is surrounded by water on three sides.) The earliest known inhabitants of Asia Minor were the **Hittites,** who settled there around 2000 B.C. They fought and conquered many peoples until they controlled most of Asia Minor. By fighting and conquering, they built a great and powerful empire for themselves that was feared for many years. Yet later the Hittites became almost a forgotten people.

Hittite warrior

Evidence of Bible truth. By 500 B.C., the name of the Hittites had practically vanished from anyone's memory. The Bible mentions the Hittites several times, but because no other evidence of them could be found, people who did not believe the Bible claimed that there never was a group of people known as the Hittites. It was over 2,400 years before people rediscovered the Hittites.

As always, the Bible speaks the truth. In the A.D. 1800s, men began finding evidence that led them to believe in the existence of the Hittites. In the 1900s, even greater discoveries were found that gave archaeological proof that the Hittites were a real people and that the Bible spoke the truth.

Empire builders. The Hittites are remembered as great empire builders. An **empire** is a group of countries or kingdoms that are under the control of a more powerful ruler. The powerful ruler who controls the empire is called an **emperor.** The Hittites were among the first to build an empire. Before 1500 B.C., the Hittites were at the height of their power. They had conquered a fantastic amount of land that was made up of more than a dozen kingdoms. Their neighbors, afraid of the swords and fast-moving iron chariots of the Hittites, sometimes surrendered before there was any fighting in order to avoid being destroyed.

The Hittite empire was so large that the Hittite king could not personally rule over each kingdom his army had conquered. Therefore, he usually let the king of the conquered kingdom continue to rule over his own people. Of course, there was one big change. The king of that conquered kingdom had to obey the words and laws of the Hittite king. This included sending men to fight in the Hittite army if it became necessary. In return, the Hittite king protected all of those he conquered.

Wicked practices. Most ancient kingdoms and countries had their own gods, but the Hittites borrowed most of their gods from the kingdoms they conquered. As the Hittite empire grew, so did their number of gods. There were so many wicked practices involved in their religious worship and in their everyday life that God ordered His people, the Israelites, to destroy the Hittites upon entering the land of Canaan—the Promised Land.

3.6 ⌘ The Lydians: Makers of Money

Small but prosperous. Another country in Asia Minor was **Lydia** [lĭd′ē·ə], very small but prosperous. Its fertile soil grew good crops, and its land was rich in gold and other minerals.

Lydia was just across the Aegean [ĭ·jē′ən] Sea from Greece, where the first great European civilization grew up. Because of its location between Greece and Mesopotamia, Lydia was a great trading center. Boats carried goods across the sea, and **caravans** (people traveling in groups with their pack animals) carried goods to other parts of the Middle East.

Trade by barter. Lydia, like most of the ancient countries of that time, traded by giving some of its own goods for the goods that it needed. This kind of trade is called **barter.** If a country needed to trade its extra wheat for the copper or iron it needed, it would first have to find someone who needed the wheat and then hope that they also had copper or iron to trade. You can see why trading in this manner could be difficult.

Systems of money. It soon became clear that trading would be easier and more profitable using a system of money. At first, bars or lumps of precious metals such as gold, silver, and bronze were used to pay for goods. However, there were problems involving the bars. Not everyone involved in trading was honest. Someone could make a bar less valuable by cutting a piece from it. Thus, every time someone traded his goods for a bar of precious metal, it had to be carefully weighed. Part of this problem was solved by stamping a seal on each bar telling the weight of the bar and the type of metal from which it was made. This made buying goods somewhat easier than before, but the bars were still very heavy and awkward to carry around.

The world's first coins. About 700 B.C., the Lydians came up with an even better idea than trading with bars. Lydia **minted** (or made) the world's first coins. Instead of bars of metal, the Lydians made rough, rounded coins of the same metals with seals stamped on both sides of them. The seals nearly covered the sides of the coins. A dishonest person would have a harder time cutting a piece of metal from a coin than he would from a bar. The coins encouraged honesty on the part of both

ancient gold and silver coins

the buyer and the seller. They were also much easier to handle than bars.

Slowly, other countries began to see the advantages of having coins and began making their own. By 500 B.C., most ancient countries used coins.

"As rich as Croesus." The last king of Lydia was named **Croesus** [krē′səs]. He raised his country to the peak of its power just before it was taken over by the Persian Empire. Croesus was so wealthy that the saying "as rich as Croesus" became common in many lands.

Comprehension Check 3C

1. Who were the earliest known inhabitants of Asia Minor?
2. They were known for building a great _?_, a group of countries or kingdoms under the control of a more powerful ruler.
3. Giving some of your own goods for the goods you desire is called _?_.
4. What replaced this system of trade?
5. Which group of people minted the first coins?

Jordan River

3.7 The Israelites: God's Chosen People

The Geography of the Holy Land

Important location. The nation of Israel inhabited the narrow strip of land between the Mediterranean Sea and the Jordan River. Small as it was, Israel became the center of the ancient world. Over this strip of land, trade goods passed to and from the world's two oldest cultures, Mesopotamia and Egypt. Israel also became a "road" on which the ancient armies traveled to battle. Because of its important location, Israel was often invaded by enemies.

Land of beauty. Still today, Israel is a beautiful land with mountains and hills, valleys and plains, and fertile well-watered farmland as well as areas of dry, barren desert. Even the water scenery is varied with seas, lakes, rivers, waterfalls, rapids, and streams.

A variety of water. The Mediterranean Sea, which runs along Israel's coast, affects Israel's climate; land closest to the sea is coolest and land farthest from it is desert. Israel has a Mediterranean climate, with mild, rainy winters and hot, dry summers.

To the north of Israel is **Mount Hermon,** where there are many cool, fresh springs of mountain water. These springs are the source of the longest and most important river in Israel, the **Jordan River.** The Jordan River runs through the middle of the deepest-known **fault** (crack in the earth's surface) in the world. This

Sea of Galilee

crack lies in the middle of the Jordan River Valley and goes beyond the country of Israel into the continent of Africa.

From Mount Hermon, the Jordan flows south for 100 miles. In ancient days it flowed into a small body of water called Lake Hula [hōō′lə]. (Today Lake Hula does not exist, since it was completely drained to make more farmland available.) The Jordan left Lake Hula and continued its journey south for ten more miles. The Jordan falls nearly 700 feet over waterfalls, making dangerous rapids that are impossible for boats to travel over.

The next stop was the **Sea of Galilee,** which is about 700 feet **below sea level.** The Sea of Galilee is a lake that is nearly fourteen miles long and eight miles across at its widest point. The Sea of Galilee was and still is an excellent place to fish.

From the Sea of Galilee, the Jordan winds and twists its way south toward its last stop—the **Dead Sea,** the lowest place on the earth's land surface (about **1,300 feet below sea level**). If we flew on a straight course between the Sea of Galilee and the Dead Sea, the distance would be only sixty-five miles. But if we walked along the Jordan's twists and turns, making our way to the Dead Sea, we would walk over two hundred miles. Along the way, we would see other small rivers flowing into the Jordan.

The Jordan River empties tons of water into the Dead Sea each day. There is no outlet from the Dead Sea, yet the Dead Sea keeps the same level of water from day to day. Because the climate around the Dead Sea is hot and dry, the same amount of water is evaporated from the sea that is emptied into it by the Jordan River. As you know from your study of science, when the water evaporates, the salt and other minerals remain in the sea. You can imagine how salty the Dead Sea is as day after day, year after year, the water evaporates and the salt remains. In fact, the Dead Sea is the saltiest body of water in the world. (It is nine times saltier than ocean water.) The Old Testament refers to it as the **Salt Sea** (Gen. 14:3).

The Dead Sea itself is about fifty miles long and ten miles wide. It reaches the greatest depth in the northern part—1,349 feet. In the south, however, it is only from five to twenty feet deep. No fish have ever been found in the Dead Sea, because it is too salty. Even birds avoid flying over it, because there are no fish for them to catch and there is no water that they could drink. The water of the Dead Sea contains 24 percent minerals, mostly salt. That is close to one fourth of the sea! These mineral solids do not lie on the bottom. They are suspended throughout the water of the Dead Sea. Therefore, people float when they try to swim in the Dead Sea.

God's People in Egypt

God had promised the land of Canaan to Abraham and his descendants. Abraham had believed God, left his home in Ur, and traveled to this new land. Many years later, however, a great famine caused Abraham's descendants to leave Canaan and enter Egypt, one of the oldest civilizations in the world, located in northeastern Africa.

At the time the Israelites entered Egypt, the pharaoh (ruler) was friendly toward foreigners. As time passed, however, other pharaohs were not as friendly. When the children of Israel or the **Hebrews,** as the descendants of Abraham were called, first entered Egypt, they numbered only seventy. During their stay, they increased to possibly three million people. The pharaohs now feared that the Hebrews were a threat to their power. In an effort to keep the Hebrews from growing more powerful, they made slaves of them and forced them to make bricks and build cities.

Though they were slaves, God was still with His people. With fearful cruelty and hatred, the Egyptian pharaoh did his best to destroy the Hebrews. He even ordered that all the Hebrew male infants be killed, but God spared a baby boy named **Moses.** He was rescued by the pharaoh's daughter, who raised him in pharaoh's court. He could have been

crossing the Red Sea

called "the son of Pharaoh's daughter," but when he became old enough, he refused the honor. God had chosen Moses to lead His people, the Hebrews, out of slavery in Egypt, back to the land that God had promised them—Canaan, which would one day be called Israel.

The Hebrews miraculously crossed the Red Sea and traveled into the wilderness of the **Sinai Peninsula,** a triangular peninsula between Egypt and the Promised Land. From **Mount Sinai,** God gave the Hebrews the **Ten Commandments,** God's basic rules for right and wrong. The children of Israel became known as the **Israelites.**

The Israelites Return to Their Land

After the Israelites had wandered in the wilderness of Sinai for forty years under Moses' leadership, God gave them a new leader—**Joshua.** With Joshua in command, God allowed them to miraculously cross the Jordan River into Canaan, the land that God had promised to Abraham and his descendants.

God had told Abraham long before, *And I will make of thee a great nation, and I will bless thee, and make thy name great; and thou shalt be a blessing: And I will bless them that bless thee, and curse him that curseth thee: and in thee shall all families of the earth be blessed.*

Gen. 12:2–3

What a tremendous promise! The descendants of Abraham would become a great nation. Through Abraham's family, which included Isaac, Jacob, Joseph, and many others, all nations would be blessed. Hundreds of years later, God gave His Son, the Lord Jesus Christ, through the descendants of Abraham.

Today, we call the land of Canaan **Israel** or the **"Holy Land"** (because many events recorded in the Bible took place there, and because Jesus lived there when He was on earth). The people are called **Israelites, Hebrews, Jews,** or **Israelis.**

Comprehension Check 3D

1. Between what sea and what river does Israel lie?
2. Why was Israel often invaded by enemies?
3. What is the longest and most important river in Israel?
4. What is a crack in the earth's surface called?
5. What is unusual about the Dead Sea? What is its other name?
6. What did God promise Abraham?

The Canaanites

Canaan was the name of one of Noah's grandsons (Gen. 9:18). The Canaanites whom the Hebrews were told to conquer were the descendants of Canaan. There were also settlers from other countries in the land of Canaan because of the land's favorable location.

The Canaanites' religion. The Canaanites worshiped many false gods, but their religious ceremonies were far from what we would consider worship. Their religion encouraged them to do horrible, wicked deeds. They held wild dances and rituals that included the sacrifice of human beings. Even children and helpless babies were sacrificed to the idols. The most well-known of the Canaanite gods was **Baal** [bā′əl]. He was considered the god of war and storms.

On many of the hills in Canaan were places of worship called **high places.** There were also wooded areas called **groves.** Both high places and groves were outdoor places where the Canaanites worshiped their gods and made their sacrifices.

Perhaps you remember the Bible account of Lot and the destruction of Sodom, a very wicked Canaanite city. The Canaanites' wickedness had a powerful influence on those who were around them. Although Lot and his family believed in the one true God, they found themselves attached to the wicked city of Sodom.

Canaan's importance in world history. Sadly, the Canaanites did not leave any important deed to be written in the pages of world history. They were so involved in their wicked practices that they had no time for great accomplishments. Is it any wonder that God wanted to take this land away from them and give it to the descendants of Abraham? The Canaanites were not important to history, but the land of Canaan became extremely important because of the plans that God had for Abraham's descendants and the entire world.

The Conquest of Canaan

God, as Judge of the universe, brought judgment upon the wicked practices of the heathen people in the land of Canaan. He ordered the Israelites to destroy all of the Canaanites and their neighbors. The Israelites obeyed only partly, and the wicked nations that were left caused them many problems in the years to come.

God fought for the Israelites many times as they sought to conquer the land. He allowed them to take the walled city of **Jericho** with no other weapons than shouts and trumpet blasts. He made the sun stand still as they fought and conquered a great alliance (union or joining together) of kings in Canaan. In about seven years, much of Canaan was under Israel's control, and the land was divided among the twelve tribes of Israel.

conquest of Jericho

Israel as a Nation

The period of judges. Because the Israelites failed to drive all the Canaanites out of the land, many Israelites began worshiping the false Canaanite gods. Whenever they did this, God allowed the enemies in the surrounding areas to come in and do the Israelites much harm. Then the Israelites would cry out to God in repentance, and God would send a leader called a **judge** to deliver them. The **judges** were chosen by God, Who was the true King of Israel. This cycle of idolatry, conquest, repentance, and deliverance was repeated again and again in the first three hundred years after Israel returned to Canaan.

The kings of Israel. As the Israelites looked around them and saw that the other nations had earthly kings, they wanted an earthly king, too. God warned them that a king would force them to pay high taxes and serve his every whim.

The first king, **Saul,** was a great military leader. He disobeyed God, however, and his son was not allowed to rule after him. God then chose **David,** a man after His own heart, to be king. King David was beloved of God and the people. Under the leadership of David, Israel defeated almost all its enemies.

David's son **Solomon** became the third king of Israel. King Solomon was the richest and wisest man who ever lived. At the time of his reign, Israel reached the peak of its glory as probably the most powerful and richest country in the world.

During Solomon's reign, godly justice prevailed in Israel. It was a time of peace, righteousness, and material wealth. Solomon built the magnificent Temple at **Jerusalem** and undertook other great building projects during his reign.

the Temple at Jerusalem

The kingdom falls. Despite the great glory that God had allowed the Israelites to experience, they forgot God again and fell into sin. Upon Solomon's death, Israel was split into two kingdoms. The Northern Kingdom, made up of ten tribes, was still called Israel, and the Southern Kingdom, where Jerusalem was located, was called **Judah.** The two kingdoms continued to turn away from God. First Israel and then Judah fell into the hands of new empires that were rising in the east.

Israel had forgotten God, but God had not forgotten Israel. He kept His promise to bless all nations of the earth through the seed of Abraham and continued to watch over His people, even when they were captives in strange lands.

Comprehension Check 3E

1. Who was the best-known Canaanite god, the god of war and storms?
2. Did the Canaanites leave many important gifts to civilization? Why or why not?
3. God chose the first leaders of the Israelites and called them _?_.
4. After Saul, Israel's first king, disobeyed God and failed, whom did God appoint?
5. King Solomon built the great _?_ at Jerusalem.
6. Israel again fell and was split into two kingdoms. The Northern Kingdom was called _?_. The Southern Kingdom was called _?_.

Tiglath-pileser III of Assyria

3.8 The Assyrian Empire

In the rolling hill country near the source of the Tigris River, about five hundred miles northeast of Canaan, lived the **Assyrians.** Assyria was not a large area, but it was located on fertile, well-watered land. Its capital, **Nineveh,** was a great city (Jonah 1:2).

Feared conquerors. Around 750 B.C., Assyria became very powerful under **King Tiglath-pileser III** [tĭg′lăth·pə·lē′zər]. The Assyrians conquered a land area greater than any people had ever ruled before. Soon Assyria controlled nearly all the Fertile Crescent, part of Asia Minor, and the land of Egypt. The very name of the Assyrians brought fear to the people in Mesopotamia. Even the Egyptians sought to keep the Assyrians happy by sending **tribute money** to the Assyrian kings. Why? Assyrian soldiers were fierce and brutal. They not only set out to conquer nations, but they destroyed them as well. They burned cities and tortured or killed men, women, and children. They uprooted entire populations and moved them to other cities.

The Assyrian army was heavily armed. Soldiers wearing iron helmets and armor drove fast-moving chariots. Their iron weapons were sharper than the bronze ones used by their opponents. The conquered people, too terrified to fight back, were expected to send tribute to their Assyrian conquerors.

The conquest of Israel. The Assyrians conquered the ten tribes of the Northern Kingdom of Israel, whose people had fallen into great wickedness. They carried the ten tribes away to scattered parts of the empire, and the northern tribes never returned to their land.

The defeat of Sennacherib. Twenty years later, the Assyrian king **Sennacherib** [sĭ·năk′ər·ĭb] attempted to destroy the two tribes of Judah. He boasted that the God of the Jews had no power to save them. The vast Assyrian army camped outside the walls of Jerusalem, holding the people in fear. But then, during the night, God sent His angel to kill 185,000 Assyrian soldiers. Sennacherib and the other survivors fled in shame to Nineveh, and Sennacherib was slain by his own sons.

Sennacherib of Assyria

The prophecy of Jonah. God sent the Jewish prophet **Jonah** to warn the wicked city of Nineveh that He was going to judge them. For a while, the people of Nineveh repented and believed in God. Eventually, however, the Assyrians resumed their wicked ways. Meanwhile, the Assyrian Empire had grown so large that it became difficult for the rulers to control the people. As God had prophesied in the Book of Nahum, Nineveh and many other Assyrian cities were destroyed by the **Babylonians.**

3.9 The Babylonian Empire

Babylon

In the middle of Mesopotamia, on the banks of the Euphrates River, stood the very ancient city of **Babylon.** It was probably near where the Tower of Babel had been built. The name *Babylon* came from "Babel." Babylon was one of the chief cities of ancient days and was considered a world power. An important highway began in Babylon and led to many other cities. This highway played an important part in making Babylon a center for world trade.

The large city of Babylon was built from bricks made of clay. The whole city was surrounded by two thick walls built apart from each other. The double walls provided an extra measure of protection from enemies. If enemies were able to get over one wall, they would get trapped between the walls. The top of each wall was so wide that two chariots could be driven side by side on it. As an added protection, a large moat, fed by the waters of the Euphrates River, was built around the entire outer wall of the city.

One hundred bronze-plated gates with iron bars were set in the walls. Babylon was a planned city. Its streets were well laid out with a wide street or highway passing through the middle of the city. Lining the streets were well-built houses, three and four stories high.

The city of Babylon was divided into two sections by the Euphrates River. A bridge was built across the river and a tunnel was built under it to connect the two sections of the city. Thus there were two ways of crossing the Euphrates in ancient Babylon—over it or under it!

The First Babylonian Empire

Babylonia was the region around and including the city of Babylon. One of the great leaders of Babylonia was **Hammurabi** [hăm′ə•rä′bē]. About 3,700 years ago, before the Israelites went down to Egypt, Hammurabi ruled Babylon. (This was about 1,700 years before the birth of Christ.) Hammurabi ruled for forty-three years.

Hammurabi conquered the cities around Babylon and placed them under his rule. His empire is known as the **First Babylonian Empire.** He also gathered the laws of his land, put them in order, and commanded that the laws be written on columns of black stone. This set of laws became known as the **Code of Hammurabi.** It contained nearly 300 laws that governed the everyday life of the Babylonians. There were laws about marriage, business, and farming. Not everyone was dealt with in the same manner. A slave received a different punishment from a free man for the same crime.

The New Babylonian Empire

About two hundred years after Hammurabi, the First Babylonian Empire fell, and Babylon was destroyed. A thousand years after Hammurabi, Babylon was rebuilt, and became God's instrument for the destruction of the wicked Assyrian Empire and for the punishment of the people of Judah.

As discontent grew among the Assyrians, the **Chaldeans** from southern Mesopotamia (around the site of Ur) were establishing themselves at the site of old Babylon, under the leadership of **King Nabopolassar** [năb′ə•pə•lăs′ər]. The Chaldeans, with help from the Medes and Scythians, overthrew the Assyrian Empire and established the **Second** or **New Babylonian Empire.**

King Nabopolassar, who ruled from 625 to 605 B.C., rebuilt the city of Babylon. When he died, his son **Nebuchadnezzar II** [nĕb′ə•kəd•nĕz′ər] became king. He continued the rebuilding of Babylon that his father had started. His hope was to make Babylon the most beautiful city in the world.

code of Hammurabi

The Hanging Gardens of Babylon

King Nebuchadnezzar ruled around 600 B.C. One of his many wives came from the mountains. Babylon is flat and dry, quite different from the mountains where she had grown up. It is said that she missed the beautiful mountains so much that Nebuchadnezzar decided to build high, terraced gardens to remind her of her old home.

The gardens were planted on a square that rested seventy-five feet above the ground on pillars. The square was then covered with soil that was built into wide steps or terraces. Each step was a little smaller than the one below it. A waterfall was built into the terraces. Men worked constantly to carry water from the Euphrates River up to the gardens. Trees, vines, and flowers, some of which were brought from other countries, were planted on the terraces. To the people standing in the city streets, the beautiful gardens looked as if they were hanging in the air. The Hanging Gardens looked so beautiful that the Greeks listed them among the **Seven Wonders of the Ancient World.**

Hanging Gardens of Babylon

Daniel in Babylon

The Babylonian captivity. Under Nebuchadnezzar's command, the Chaldean army attacked the city of Jerusalem and destroyed it. They carried most of the people away to Babylon as prisoners. When the Jews arrived in Babylon, King Nebuchadnezzar commanded that the best young men be brought to his palace. Among those chosen was a boy named **Daniel.** God had given to Daniel the rare ability of interpreting dreams and visions. After three years in the king's court, the captive young men were brought before the king. King Nebuchadnezzar found Daniel to be ten times wiser than any of the wise men of Babylon.

Nebuchadnezzar's dream. One night, Nebuchadnezzar had a strange dream that he forgot by morning. This troubled him so much that he ordered his wise men to tell him both the dream and its meaning. Although they were unable to do so, Daniel, with God's help, told the king that the dream foretold future events. The dream represented the four great kingdoms of the earth. The grateful king made Daniel ruler of all the provinces of Babylon and chief of the governors over all the wise men of Babylon.

Nebuchadnezzar's pride. Like Hammurabi hundreds of years before him, Nebuchadnezzar was a proud and boastful king. He had rebuilt Babylon. He had made great improvements and built the Hanging Gardens. Not giving God any credit, he boasted, *"Is not this great Babylon, that* ***I*** *have built for the house of the kingdom by the might of* ***my*** *power, and for the honor of* ***my*** *majesty?"* (Dan. 4:30)

The judgment of Nebuchadnezzar. While Nebuchadnezzar was boasting of his accomplishments, God interrupted and foretold that Nebuchadnezzar would become insane. His insanity lasted for seven years, during which he lived and ate grass like an ox (Dan. 4:30–33). After those seven years, Nebuchadnezzar repented and recognized God as the One Who is able to make the proud humble and Who is truly the King of the whole world.

King Belshazzar. While Babylon did become one of the greatest and wealthiest of all ancient cities, it also became one of the most wicked. One night, **King Belshazzar** [bĕl·shăz′ər: Nebuchadnezzar's grandson] held a wild and drunken feast. He drank to the Babylonian gods from golden cups that had been taken from the Temple in Jerusalem.

Suddenly a hand appeared and began writing a message on the wall. Can you imagine the fearful silence that followed? The message was God's prophecy that Babylon would fall. That same night, in 539 B.C., the Medes and Persians under **Cyrus the Great** invaded Babylon. Belshazzar was killed; Babylon was captured; and the Chaldean Empire (New Babylonian Empire), which had conquered the Middle East, fell.

Cyrus the Great was a mighty and powerful conqueror. He was also very cunning and clever. In order to defeat the Chaldeans at Babylon, his men had used shovels to redirect a river. The people of Babylon had felt safe behind their strong walls. Little had they known that Cyrus the Great would bring his army across an empty river bed that led under the very walls that they thought protected them. You can imagine the Chaldeans' complete surprise when Cyrus's army suddenly appeared inside the walls of Babylon.

Daniel becomes a ruler. At the time of Belshazzar's death, Daniel had been in Babylon for seventy years. Another Persian ruler, **Darius,** was impressed by his wisdom and strength of character; he chose Daniel to be the first and most important of three presidents who would rule his kingdom. Daniel's godly life led Darius to make a decree, *"that in every dominion of my kingdom men tremble and fear before the God of Daniel: for He is the living God, and stedfast for ever, and His kingdom that which shall not be destroyed, and His dominion shall be even unto the end"* (Dan. 6:26).

Daniel was greatly used of God. He foretold what would be written in the pages of history after his death, and by his sincerity and daily faithfulness to his God, he affected those rulers who had the power to influence history.

Darius of Persia

Certainly, the influence of Daniel demonstrates that one person who walks with God can affect the events of history.

Daniel had influenced the Chaldean Empire. Now with the coming of Cyrus the Great and the destruction of Babylon, he would influence the **Persian Empire.**

Comprehension Check 3F

1. Which group of people conquered the ten tribes of Israel (the Northern Kingdom)?
2. In what great Assyrian city did the prophet Jonah preach?
3. What did the great highway leading from Babylon to several other cities help Babylon to become?
4. Whose empire was known as the First Babylonian Empire?
5. Name one of the Seven Wonders of the Ancient World and tell why it was built.
6. How was Babylon defeated?

3.10 The Persian Empire

Cyrus the Great (ruled 559–529 B.C.)

Clever Cyrus. Cyrus the Great, leader of the Persians, was known for his cleverness. When he went to war against the country of Lydia, he realized that horses were frightened of camels. Thus he had his men ride camels. The Lydian army, mounted on very frightened horses, was not able to defeat the cunning Cyrus the Great.

Once he had conquered a country, Cyrus showed wisdom in the way he treated the people. Instead of fear and terror, Cyrus treated them with kindness, allowing them to follow their old customs as long as they obeyed him. For example, old officials kept their same jobs. The conquered people could keep their gods and follow their old religious practices. Given such freedoms, the newly conquered people were more apt to give their loyalty to their new ruler.

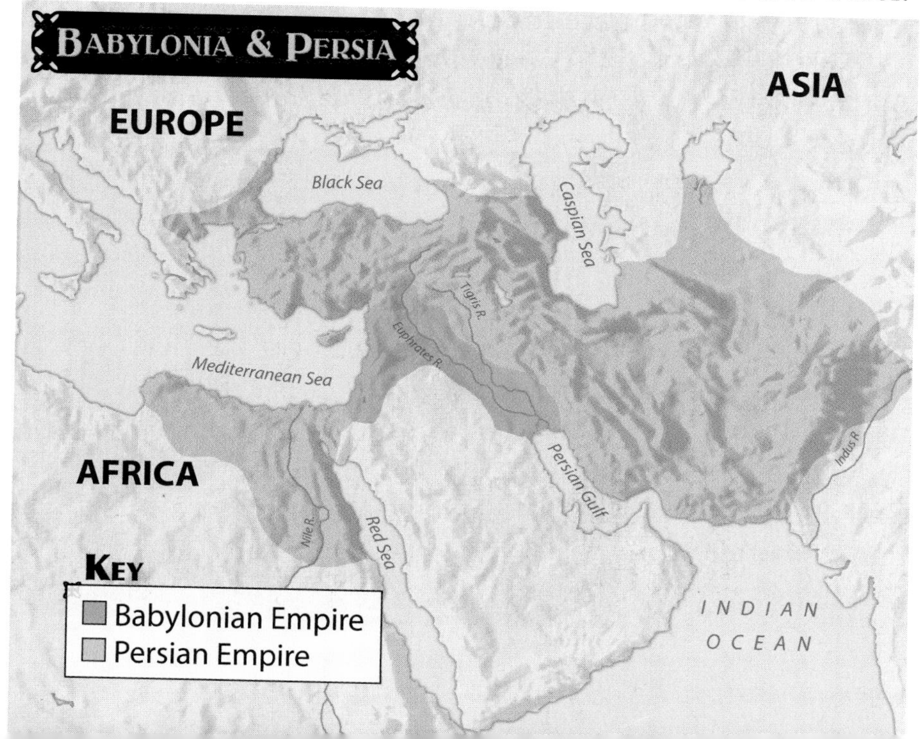

Such clever tactics were to make Persia one of the largest empires the world was ever to see. Eventually the conquests of Cyrus as well as his successors included the land that now makes up the countries of Egypt, Israel, Jordan, Lebanon, Syria, Iraq, Turkey, Afghanistan, and part of Pakistan.

Concepts to Consider

The Bible as History

The Bible, the most important source for the knowledge of history, is the only completely reliable source because God told the men who wrote it exactly what to say. The Bible is the Word of God and therefore contains no mistakes, something that can be said of no other book.

The Bible provides us with invaluable information about ancient cultures. Only the Bible, for example, records the moments when the empires studied in this chapter were briefly in a right relationship with God. Read the books of Jonah and Daniel to learn more about these events in history.

The book of Esther is another good book to read. It records the life of a brave and beautiful Israelite girl who helped save her people from disaster. This Bible book contains some of the best information available anywhere about the daily life of Persian kings and how some people misused the rule that a Persian king's commandment could never be changed.

The Bible has also been the source for many of the most important things you have learned about Sumer, Canaan, and Israel, and will later be learning about Egypt. If you want to do further reading about ancient history, you could do no better than to read the Old Testament!

Cyrus lets the Jews return to their land. Shortly after Cyrus had become king of Persia, the Lord placed in his heart the desire to let the captive Jews return to Jerusalem and also to help them rebuild their Temple. Did Cyrus realize that over one hundred years before he was born, God had prophesied through Isaiah that Cyrus would help rebuild the city of Jerusalem and the Temple?

> *That saith of Cyrus, He is my shepherd, and shall perform all my pleasure: even saying to Jerusalem, Thou shalt be built; and to the temple, Thy foundation shall be laid.* Isa. 44:28
>
> *Thus saith the Lord to his anointed, to Cyrus, whose right hand I have holden, to subdue nations before him . . . I will go before thee.* Isa. 45:1–2

Perhaps through these words Cyrus realized that he had become a great conqueror through the power of almighty God. It is no wonder that Cyrus gave this command:

> *Thus saith Cyrus king of Persia, All the kingdoms of the earth hath the Lord*

ruins of Darius I at Persepolis

God of heaven given me; and He hath charged me to build Him an house in Jerusalem, which is in Judah. Who is there among you of all His people? The Lord his God be with him, and let him go up. 2 Chron. 36:23

After Cyrus died in 529 B.C., some people around Judah tried to stir up trouble against the Jews who had returned to Jerusalem. However, the Persian kings who ruled afterward were reminded of Cyrus's commandment and kept it, even though they had different religious beliefs. One king even added that tax money would be used to help rebuild the Temple.

The Persian Empire Falls

The Persian Empire, which lasted about 200 years, slowly weakened, and was eventually conquered by the **Greeks.**

CHAPTER 3 CHECKUP

A Know these locations.

1. Phoenicia
2. Canaan
3. Lydia
4. Hittite Empire
5. Assyria
6. Persia
7. Byblos
8. Tyre
9. Sidon
10. Carthage
11. Jerusalem
12. Nineveh
13. Jordan River
14. Dead Sea
15. Sea of Galilee
16. Sinai Peninsula
17. Mt. Sinai
18. Asia Minor

B Define each term.

1. Bedouins
2. papyrus
3. murex
4. alphabet
5. middleman
6. biblos
7. peninsula
8. empire
9. caravan
10. barter
11. mint
12. fault
13. Judges

C Identify the people described by each clue.

1. developed the first alphabet
2. built an early empire
3. minted the world's first coins
4. first great sea traders
5. were so involved in wickedness that they left no great accomplishments
6. took the Northern Kingdom (Israel) into captivity

(cont.)

7. took the Southern Kingdom (Judah) into captivity
8. made the beautiful purple dye, murex
9. their re-discovery by archaeologists is evidence of the truth of the Bible
10. descendants of Abraham
11. defeated the New Babylonian Empire
12. defeated the Persians

D Who am I?

1. the last king of Lydia; my great riches led to the common saying, "as rich as __?__"
2. led the Hebrews out of Egypt; received the Ten Commandments on Mt. Sinai
3. led the Israelites to victory at Jericho
4. first king of Israel; lost my throne because of disobedience
5. second king of Israel; a man after God's own heart
6. third king of Israel; built the Temple in Jerusalem
7. prophet who warned Nineveh to repent
8. gathered the laws of the First Babylonian Empire
9. built the Hanging Gardens of Babylon
10. prophet who served in the government of Babylon and Persia
11. the clever Persian ruler who allowed the Jews to return to Jerusalem

E Answer each question.

1. Where do we find God's basic rules for right and wrong?
2. Which three continents meet at the Middle East?
3. What did ancient Middle Easterners often do in the middle of the day?
4. What is the lowest place on the earth's land surface?
5. What is the largest and most important river in Israel?
6. What peninsula is the home of Turkey today?

CHAPTER 4

MIDDLE EAST TODAY

Study the map of the Middle East (p. 49). Some modern geographers include African countries, such as Egypt and Sudan, in the Middle East because of cultural and religious connections in the area. However, for this study only the following Asian countries are included: Israel, Lebanon, Syria, Jordan, Iraq, Turkey, Cyprus, Iran, and Saudi Arabia and the smaller countries that surround it. (Turkey is mostly in Asia, but it has a small section in Europe.)

What tropic line runs through Saudi Arabia? On the physical map of the world (pp. 314–315), find through what North American country this same tropic line runs. Find the equator on the same map. Where are North America and the Middle East in relation to the equator? Then, compare the size of the Middle East with the size of the United States.

4.1 Geographical Features

Seas and Gulfs

Many seas and gulfs surround the Middle East, giving it an irregular shape. Locate the following seas on the map (p. 49)—the Black Sea, the Aegean Sea, the Mediterranean Sea, the Red Sea, the Arabian Sea, and the Caspian Sea. Then locate the Gulf of Aden, the Gulf of Oman, and the Persian Gulf.

Peninsulas

Three peninsulas reach out into the water from the Middle East. The **Arabian Peninsula** is the largest peninsula in the world. What bodies of

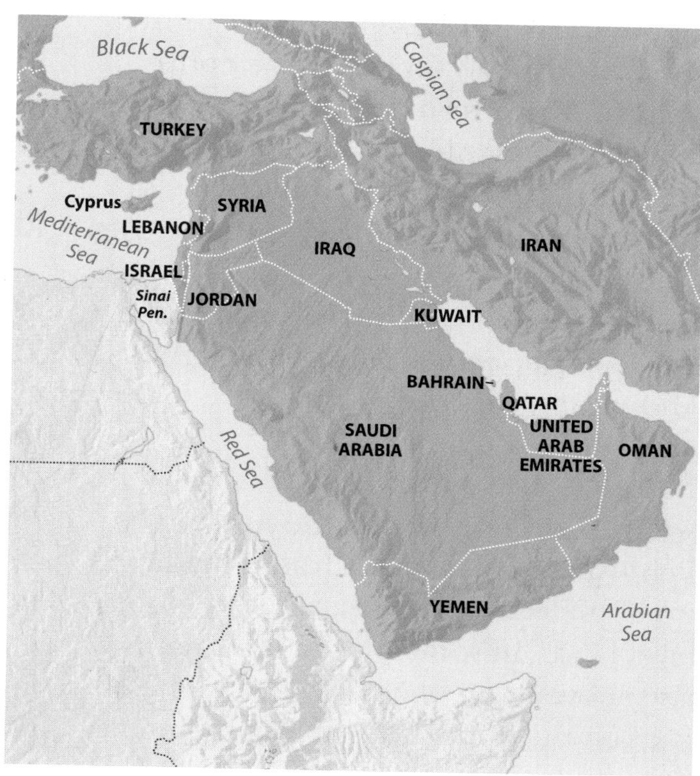

WONDERS OF WORLD GEOGRAPHY

Peninsulas of the Middle East

Name	Interesting Facts
Arabian Peninsula	This peninsula, the largest in the world, is almost entirely desert. However, because of its rich oil deposits, it is one of the wealthiest and most important areas in the modern world.
Sinai Peninsula	The tribes of Israel spent forty years wandering through the wilderness of this peninsula before they entered the Promised Land. Mt. Sinai, where Moses received the Ten Commandments, is located here. Today, the Suez [so͞o′ĕz] Canal separates the Sinai Peninsula from the continent of Africa, making a waterway from the Red Sea to the Mediterranean Sea.
Asia Minor	This mountainous peninsula is the home of modern-day Turkey. For many centuries, the term *Asia* was used to refer to the western part of this peninsula. When the Bible refers to cities in Asia, it is referring to cities in Asia Minor.

water surround it? The **Sinai Peninsula** is triangular in shape. It reaches into the Red Sea and separates the continent of Africa from the Arabian Peninsula. The peninsula of **Asia Minor** (modern Turkey) is surrounded by the Black Sea, the Aegean Sea, and the Mediterranean Sea. Israel, or the Holy Land, and other countries are located between the Sinai Peninsula and Asia Minor.

Plateaus and Mountains

Much of Asia Minor, the Arabian Peninsula, and modern Iran is made up of **plateaus** [plă·tōz′], areas of high, level land. In some places, mountains rise above these plateaus. The highest peak in the Middle East is Damavand, a dormant volcano in Iran. The second highest mountain peak, **Mount Ararat,** is located in Turkey, near the borders of Iran and Armenia. Can you remember what important Bible event took place at this spot?

Rivers

Three rivers have been important to the Middle East since ancient times. They are the Tigris and Euphrates Rivers, which flow into the Persian Gulf; and the Jordan River, which the tribes of Israel crossed when they entered the Promised Land.

The Arabian Peninsula has no rivers that flow all year long. Temporary rivers called *wadis* [wä′dēz] appear when an occasional downpour occurs, but these rivers quickly dry up in the intense heat.

THE MIDDLE EAST
EUROPE
Black Sea
Istanbul
ASIA MINOR
Ruins of Troy
Ankara
Aegean Sea
TURKEY
GEORGIA
ARMENIA
Mt. Ararat
AZERBAIJAN
Caspian Sea
Mediterranean Sea
Cyprus
SYRIA
LEBANON
Euphrates R.
Tigris R.
Tehran
Damavand
IRAN
Baghdad
IRAQ
ISRAEL
SYRIAN DESERT
JORDAN
Suez Canal
Sinai Pen.
Nile R.
EGYPT
Mt. Sinai
Basra
KUWAIT
ASIA
Persian Gulf
ARABIAN PENINSULA
BAHRAIN
Medina
QATAR
Gulf of Oman
Riyadh
UNITED ARAB EMIRATES
Tropic of Cancer
SAUDI ARABIA
Mecca
OMAN
RUB AL KHALI
Red Sea
YEMEN
Arabian Sea
Gulf of Aden
AFRICA
SUDAN
Byblos
LEBANON
Beirut
Sidon
Damascus
Tyre
SYRIA
Sea of Galilee
Jordan R.
Tel Aviv
Amman
Jerusalem
Dead Sea
ISRAEL
JORDAN
NEGEV DESERT
N
NW
NE
W
E
SW
SE
S

4.2 ⌘ Climate

If one word describes the climate of the Middle East, it is *dry*. Many areas have only a very little winter rain, while the vast **desert regions** have almost no rain at all. The Syrian Desert and the Rub al Khali [ro͞ob′ ăl·kä′lē: the Empty Quarter], along with deserts in Northern Africa, make up the world's greatest desert area.

The land along the coasts of the Black Sea, the Caspian Sea, and the Mediterranean Sea receives the most rain. These areas have a **Mediterranean climate,** with hot, dry summers and cool winters with some rain. If the winter rains are not abundant enough, drought comes, and areas that were once green and fertile become desert.

Between the desert regions and the Mediterranean lands are areas with a **steppe** [stĕp] **climate,** dry grassy plains with little rainfall. The steppes receive more rainfall than the desert but less than the coastal areas.

date palms

The Middle East has not always been as dry and barren as it is today. In Bible times, there was much **fertile** (able to grow crops) farmland, and much of the land near the coast and in the mountains was covered with forests. God promised His people, the Jewish nation, that as long as they obeyed Him, He would send abundant rain, but that when they disobeyed (Deut. 28:12, 24), He would hold back the rain.

Comprehension Check 4A

1. Name the three peninsulas of the Middle East.
2. Which peninsula is the largest in the world? Which is called Turkey today?
3. Name the second-highest mountain in the Middle East where Noah's ark is believed to have settled after the great Flood.
4. What type of climate dominates the Middle East?

4.3 ⌘ Plants and Animals

Plants

The Mediterranean areas and mountains of the Middle East are home to a variety of trees. Olive trees, fig trees, date palms, almond trees, and pomegranate trees are important sources of food. Other trees are the cedar, fir, pine, myrtle, oak, poplar, and willow. In the past, many trees were cut down; however, in recent years Middle Eastern nations, such as Israel, have begun planting trees again.

The **date palm** has always been important to the people of the Middle

East. In ancient days, every part of the date palm was used—the date itself was important for food, the wood could be used for building, and a very strong rope could be made from fibers of the wood.

Some people used the leaves of the date palm to cover the frames of huts they made from the branches. They kept the floors of the huts clean with brooms they made by tying palm leaves together. They also made mats and baskets from palm leaves.

The stones (seeds) from the dates were dried and used as fuel, ground up and pressed for oil, or ground up as food for camels. If the buds and the palm sprout (new growth at the top of the tree) were picked at just the right time, they could be eaten as a vegetable.

Other useful plants of the Middle East are flax, whose fibers are used to make linen cloth; and papyrus, which was used for making a paperlike material. Food crops include grapes, beans, lentils, barley, wheat, and millet.

Animals

Dromedaries (one-humped Arabian camels), horses, and donkeys have carried men and their burdens in the Middle East for many centuries. Cattle, sheep, and goats have long been important sources of milk and meat, and oxen were once used to pull plows, carts, and wagons.

Still living in the woods and mountainous areas of the Middle East are such familiar wild animals as the wolf, deer, fox, and brown bear. Leopards and lions were once common, and in some places there were even elephants. Bees have always been important for their honey, which is one of the few foods that will not spoil.

Many varieties of birds—such as eagles, owls, ravens, quails, doves, sparrows, partridges, cranes, and storks—can be seen throughout the Middle East. Some of these birds stop along the coast of the Mediterranean Sea while following one of the world's main migration routes. Others make the Middle East their home.

4.4 ⌘ People

Most people in the Middle East are Arabs who speak the **Arabic language** and practice the religion of **Islam.** For many years, the majority of the people lived in small towns and villages and grew crops or tended livestock for a living. In recent times, however, with the growth of the oil industry, many have moved to large cities much like those in the United States, France, or Japan.

dromedaries carrying burdens

Bedouin sheik washes hands for dinner

Some cities still resemble the ancient circular cities that were divided into sections called **quarters.** Many of the modern cities still have sections or quarters where different groups of people live and work. A number of the people outside the cities still struggle from day to day to make a living from growing crops or tending animals using old agricultural methods in the dry, desert climate.

Some nomadic Bedouin herdsmen still live in the Middle Eastern deserts. They are organized into tribes, and the head of each tribe is called a **sheik** [shēk]. Bedouin men are allowed to have more than one wife. During the rainy season, they move with their herds to the desert. In the dry summer months, they migrate toward the farmland, though few raise crops. The Bedouins move from oasis to oasis to graze their herds of camels, sheep, goats, and cattle. Despite their simple, nomadic lifestyle, some Bedouins are very rich.

Today, Bedouins are being treated quite differently from ancient times. Countries are no longer as willing for them to freely cross borders in their wanderings. Some Bedouins are being encouraged or even forced to settle in camps.

4.5 Importance to History and Current Events

The Middle East is important because the world's three most influential religions had their beginnings there. **Islam** (the religion of the Muslims) began in Saudi Arabia. **Judaism** (the religion of the Jews) and **Christianity** began in Israel, the land God promised to Abraham and his heirs. The Hebrews settled there after their exodus from Egypt. The great kings David and Solomon ruled there in splendor and glory. Most important, Jesus lived His earthly life there.

The Middle East is also of great importance because of its valuable oil reserves. **Natural resources** are the riches of the earth, including the soil, atmosphere, minerals, water, and fuels. Many natural resources of the Middle East are found in smaller quantities than in earlier years, and others are completely gone. Oil, however, is still abundant. The oil deposits of the Middle East are among the richest in the world. Because many nations desire the oil and the petroleum made from it, the Middle East has great economic and political power in the world today.

The Middle East faces many problems in the modern world. Unstable governments and struggles among the nations are cause for continual unrest. Because of this unrest, the names and borders of countries could change with little warning.

The conflict between the Arabs and Israelis goes all the way back to biblical times. The Israelis are descendants of Abraham's son Isaac, and the Arabs are descendants of his son Ishmael. God promised that Isaac and Ishmael would each be the father of a great nation and that through Isaac all the nations of the earth would be blessed. From the time Isaac and Ishmael were young men, the struggle has existed, and it continues in the Middle East today.

The Bible describes the greatest struggle of all time, the Battle of Armageddon, which will occur in the Middle East when Christ returns to set up His kingdom on earth. (Rev. 16:16; 19:11–21)

Comprehension Check 4B

1. Most Arabs in the Middle East speak __?__ and follow the religion of __?__.
2. What are the three most influential religions in the world?
3. Many modern cities in the Middle East have sections called __?__ that are patterned after the ancient circular cities.
4. What is a natural resource?
5. What is the most important resource in the Middle East today?

4.6 Three Geographical Areas

The Middle East can be divided into three geographical areas: the Fertile Crescent, the Arabian Peninsula, and the Northern Plateaus. In the **Fertile Crescent,** the area that has been called the "Cradle of Civilization," lie the modern countries of Israel, Jordan, Lebanon, Syria, and Iraq. The **Arabian Peninsula** is dominated by the country of Saudi Arabia, but is also home to the six smaller countries of Kuwait, Bahrain, Qatar, the United Arab Emirates, Oman, and Yemen. The countries of Turkey and Iran lie within the **Northern Plateaus** region. The island nation of Cyprus lies off the southern coast of Turkey. Three countries that were under the influence of the former Soviet Union—Georgia, Armenia, and Azerbaijan [ăz′ər·bī·jän′]—can also be included as Middle Eastern countries. Most of these nations were established between 1920 and 1960. Before that, other countries ruled them.

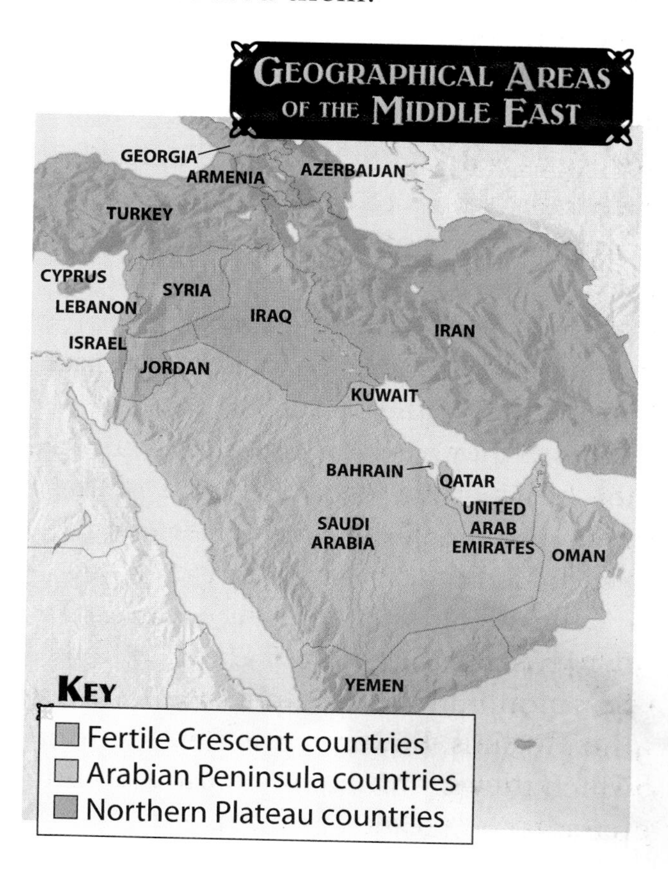

4.7 Fertile Crescent Countries

Israel

The Holy Land stands in great contrast to other countries in the Middle East. Living standards for most Israelis are similar to those in Europe and America and are much higher than those in most other countries of the Middle East. Many well-trained Jews from Europe and other parts of the world have settled there, and the country continues to develop in spite of the ever present Arab-Israeli conflict.

The Jews return to their land. For centuries the Jews were scattered all over the world, many under great persecution. Then, in 1897, a movement called **Zionism** began with the intention of gathering the Jews to form a Jewish nation in the Promised Land (also known in history as Canaan and Palestine). In 1948, the modern state of Israel was formed with the help of leading nations of the West (especially Great Britain and the United States) as a refuge for Jews persecuted during World War II. The first prime minister, **David Ben-Gurion,** was very influential in this process. Soon Jews from all over the world were making their homes in this new nation.

Jerusalem. **Jerusalem,** the "City of Peace," is the largest city in Israel and one of the oldest cities in the world. To the Jews, it is the "City of David" where Solomon built the Temple of God. To the Muslims, however, it is the city from which they say Muhammad went up into paradise.

Jerusalem

Tel Aviv

The eastern part of Jerusalem includes the old walled city of Jerusalem, containing holy places that are precious to the Jewish people. In 1967, Israeli soldiers captured the east side of Jerusalem from the country of Jordan in the **Six-Day War.**

Jerusalem is the capital of Israel. However, because of the Arab-Israeli conflict, many countries carry on their important political business in **Tel Aviv,** one of the most modern cities in the Middle East. The Bible promises that the city of Jerusalem will have much future glory.

young Israeli soldiers

Rebuilding the land. Before the new state of Israel was formed, the land had been damaged by lack of rain, overgrazing of flocks, and the chopping down of forests. In recent years Israelis have planted many trees and irrigated the land. The **National Water Carrier,** the central pipeline of Israel's vast and efficient system of irrigation, has brought water to the Negev [nĕg′ĕv] Desert in the south, transforming parts of the desert into fertile farmland. The Bible says, "The wilderness and the solitary place shall be glad for them; and the desert shall rejoice, and blossom as the rose" (Isa. 35:1). Israelis now actually do grow roses, as well as fruits, grains, and vegetables, in the desert that for centuries was barren land!

For many years, agriculture was the most important part of Israel's economy. Today, however, cut diamonds are Israel's leading export. The Israelis also obtain phosphates and other minerals from the Dead Sea, and use sand from the Negev Desert for making glass. Other exports include computer software, books, chemicals, and citrus fruits such as oranges.

Tourism is another Israeli industry. Many people come to see the biblical sites and to enjoy the sandy beaches and pleasant Mediterranean climate.

Military strength. The Jews in the land of Israel must deal not only with the Arab nations that surround them, but also with the Arabs who live among them. Many **Palestinians,** descendants of the Arab people who occupied Palestine before the Jews returned to the land in 1948, live in the northern part of Israel called **Galilee.** (Galilee, probably the most beautiful part of Israel, is where Jesus spent much of his earthly ministry.)

Because of the Arab disputes, all Jewish men must serve at least three years in the military after they become eighteen years old. Many Israeli women also join. In this way, Israel maintains a large group of trained citizens who can be called upon to defend the nation if needed.

Comprehension Check 4C

1. What was the purpose of the Zionist movement?
2. What year was the modern nation of Israel founded?
3. __?__, the "City of Peace," is Israel's capital city.
4. Israel's important political business is carried on in the city of __?__.

Lebanon

History. In Bible times, the land north of Israel was home to the Phoenicians who lived in a group of independent cities such as Tyre and Sidon and never built a great nation or empire. The ancient cities of Tyre, Sidon, and Byblos still exist in modern Lebanon today.

modern Tyre

The stately **cedars of Lebanon** were treasured in the ancient world for their precious wood. Israel's King Solomon used this wood in building the Temple. Today, most of Lebanon's cedars have been cut down, but a group of these trees is preserved in the mountains.

cedars of Lebanon

Modern Times. Modern **Lebanon,** Israel's neighbor to the north, is slightly smaller than the state of Connecticut. The majority of its population is made up of Arabs, most of whom are Muslims, with a smaller group of Roman Catholics. Since Israel declared its independence in 1948, many Palestinians have taken refuge in Lebanon, adding to its Arab Muslim population.

Beirut

Before 1975, Lebanon served as a center of world banking through which Middle Eastern oil money flowed. But in 1975–1976, a civil war between Catholics and Muslims devastated this once prosperous nation. Many of Lebanon's most educated and skilled workers fled the country during the war. As some of them have begun to return, they have found continuing strife throughout their land. One major cause of this strife is the presence of Hezbollah, an Islamic terrorist group that is supported by Iran. Hezbollah continues to use south Lebanon as a place from which to launch attacks on Israel. Such instability discourages other countries around the world from taking part in Lebanon's economy.

Because of Lebanon's recent instability and strife, schools are unable to operate freely and safely. Hundreds of thousands of children and teenagers are often forced to stay out of schools for extended periods of time. As a result, the level of education in Lebanon, once the highest in the Middle East, has dropped.

The influence of the West can be seen in the diet of the Lebanese people. Along with their flatbread (pita bread), Laban (yogurt), bulghur (crushed whole wheat), and Kebbi (lamb meat), Lebanese eat hamburgers and apple pie.

Today, Lebanon's greatest challenge is to rebuild the capital city of **Beirut** [bā·rōōt′]. Before the civil war, nearly all of the trade of the Middle East passed through this Lebanese port. But when the war destroyed beautiful Beirut, Lebanon's role in international trade declined sharply. The Lebanese hope that the restoration of their capital will revive their role in trade between the Western world and the Middle East.

Syria

Syria, a large country surrounding Lebanon to the north and east, is the site of important trade routes that link the Middle East with Europe, Asia, and Africa. Its capital and largest city, **Damascus,** is one of the oldest cities in the world. It has been an important city in the Fertile Crescent since ancient times. The Old Testament often mentions Syria and Damascus, and in the New Testament, the apostle Paul was converted to Christ as he journeyed on the road to Damascus.

In 1920, France gained control of Syria. Then in 1946, Syria became a republic. The majority of the people in Syria are Arabs who follow the Islamic religion. Syria and Israel have had many conflicts that continue to this day.

Jordan

Jordan is over four times larger than Israel, its neighbor to the west. The British controlled Jordan from 1921 to 1946, when it became an independent kingdom. In 1952, **King Hussein** [hōō·sān′] became the country's leader and ruled until his death in 1999. About half of the Arabs who live in Jordan are Palestinians who fled when Israel became an independent nation in 1948. Most Jordanians follow the Islamic religion.

Damascus

Amman

Baghdad in 2006

The capital city, **Amman** [ä·män′], is located on old trade routes and is still a major trading center. Around 1000 B.C. Amman was the capital city of the Ammonites. King David and Joab led the Israelites in the capture of the city. Later, other groups captured Amman.

Iraq

Mesopotamia, where the Assyrian and Babylonian Empires once raised their proud heads, is now called **Iraq** [ĭ·răk′]. Some Bible scholars believe that the Garden of Eden may have been located in this area. The country's two principal rivers, the Tigris and Euphrates, flow southeast from the mountains of Turkey toward the Persian Gulf providing Iraq with some of the best farmland in the Middle East.

soldier in the Iraqi War

About ⅓ of the Iraqi people are farmers with the other ⅔ living in cities. Over 4 million of the people live in **Baghdad** [băg′dăd′], the capital and largest city. Basra [bäs′rə] is Iraq's most important port near the Persian Gulf. Most of the Iraqi people are Arabs, but there is also a large group of Kurds, a seminomadic people who live in the northeast. The majority of Iraqis follow the Islamic religion.

Since 1980, Iraq has fought three wars. First, the Iran-Iraq War (1980–1988) brought numerous casualties and burdened the Iraqi economy with a large war debt. Then in 1990, the Iraqi dictator, **Saddam Hussein,** directed an invasion of **Kuwait** [ko͞o·wāt′], a small, oil-rich kingdom to the south. In the **Persian Gulf War** (1991), the United States led an international force against Hussein and liberated Kuwait, causing the Iraqi forces to retreat with heavy losses. After the war, Hussein's government remained a source of international tension.

The United States and a coalition of nations invaded Iraq in 2003 to remove dictator Saddam Hussein. Hussein was captured; he was then tried and executed by an Iraqi court. Under American supervision the Iraqis held the first free elections in their country in 50 years. American troops remain in Iraq to maintain stability and order, helping Iraq to establish a democratic society.

Comprehension Check 4D

1. What natural resource from Lebanon was treasured in the ancient world?
2. What is Lebanon's capital?
3. The apostle Paul was converted to Christ as he journeyed to what city in Syria (the modern capital)?
4. Amman, the capital of _?_, is located on old trade routes and is still a major trading center.
5. What is the capital of Iraq?
6. What aggressive action started the Persian Gulf War?

4.8 Countries of the Arabian Peninsula

Saudi Arabia

Three characteristics dominate the culture of the Arabian Peninsula—the **desert, Islam,** and **oil.** At the center of all three is the Kingdom of **Saudi Arabia,** the largest of the Middle Eastern nations. The majority of the people are Arabs, and Islam is the dominant religion.

From desert to city. Until recently, many Saudi Arabians were nomadic herdsmen, wandering through the deserts of the Arabian Peninsula. However, since Saudi Arabia has become the largest producer of oil in the Middle East, the income from **oil exports** (oil sold to other countries) has made it possible for many Saudis to live in modern cities. **Riyadh,** the capital, is one of those cities. Farmers have benefited from new irrigation projects, and modern, privately owned industry is becoming an important part of the Saudi economy.

Muslim religion. The king of Saudi Arabia claims the title "Guardian of the Two Holy Shrines," referring to **Mecca** and **Medina.** Like Jerusalem, from which Muhammad is believed to have gone up to paradise, these cities are regarded as holy by the Muslims—Mecca as the birthplace of **Muhammad,** and Medina as the place where he founded **Islam** around A.D. 600. From Medina, Muhammad's followers spread out to conquer the world for **Allah** (the Arabic word for

throngs of Muslims praying at the holy site in Mecca

god). Today, Muslims are the single largest religious group in the world.

Every year, millions of Muslims from around the world visit Mecca and Medina. Their pilgrimage (or "holy" trip) is one of the religious requirements commanded in the **Koran,** the holy book of Islam. Ritual prayer is another requirement. Five times a day, Muslims stop what they are doing and, wherever they might be, kneel to pray to Allah. In some cities, a man stands at the top of a narrow tower at the local **mosque** (building of worship) and reminds the people to pray.

Under Islamic law, Saudi women may not work outside the home except as teachers and nurses. They may not socialize with the men in public, and they must cover their face with a veil whenever they leave their home. Men may not gamble, smoke tobacco, or drink alcoholic beverages, but they may have more than one wife. In every aspect of life, Islam exerts a powerful influence over the Saudis.

Neighbors

The six smaller countries of the Arabian Peninsula—**Kuwait, Bahrain, Qatar, the United Arab Emirates, Oman,** and **Yemen**—reflect many of the same geographic and cultural influences that characterize Saudi Arabia. The majority of the people are Arabs, most are Muslims, and oil is the basis of each nation's economy (with the exception of Yemen, which still depends on agriculture).

an Islamic mosque

4.9 Countries of the Northern Plateaus

Turkey

Although a small part of modern Turkey is in Europe, the greater part is in Asia on the peninsula of Asia Minor. The Hittites and the Lydians occupied this area in ancient times. Mount Ararat, Turkey's highest point, is identified in the Bible as the place where Noah's ark came to rest after the Flood.

Modern country. In 1923, the republic of Turkey, one of the largest countries in the Middle East, was created. Turkey became strong and increasingly more modern, looking to England, France, and the United States as examples. As a result, Turkey is more like a European country than a country of the Middle East. Because the people speak **Turkish,** Turkey is not considered an Arab country. However, the country does practice the Islamic religion.

Strategic location. The fact that Turkey controls the exit to the Black Sea was a source of tension between Turkey and Russia for centuries. Russia, which lies to the northeast, has often demanded a voice in controlling the route because they have several ports on the Black Sea. The water route is also important to the countries of Europe and to the United States for free trade.

Cities. **Ankara** [ăng′kər·ə] is the capital of Turkey. For hundreds of years, it was called *Angora,* and the long-haired goats raised in the region were named after it. **Istanbul** [ĭs′tăn·bo͞ol′], Turkey's largest city, is also the leading port. The ancient Turkish city of **Troy** was the scene of one of the most famous battles in history, the battle between the Trojans and the Mycenaeans [mī′sə·nē′ənz] that you will be learning about later this year.

Resources and industries. Turkey has some of the best forests in the Middle East. Its dry central plateau, however, does not have enough tree roots to hold moisture in the land. Sheep are raised

bazaar in Istanbul

Angora goats

for their wool and Angora goats for their long silk hair, which is called mohair [mō′hâr′]. Turkey is the world's largest producer of chromium [krō′mē·əm], which is used in the steel industry.

Turkey has a number of prominent lakes and rivers including the Tigris and Euphrates rivers that originate in the mountains of eastern Turkey. Much of the nation's electricity is produced by hydroelectric dams. In recent years, the Turks have built dams along the Tigris and Euphrates in order to irrigate several million acres of farmland.

Turkish rug

On the coast, Turkish farmers grow the world's largest crop of hazelnuts and sultanas (yellow seedless raisins). On the plateau, they tend irrigated fields of cotton for Turkey's large textile industry, which produces beautiful carpets.

Cyprus. The **Republic of Cyprus** is an island forty miles south of Turkey and sixty miles west of Syria. Cyprus is the third largest Mediterranean island. The island is mountainous; yet about one half of the Cypriots [sĭp′rē·əts: citizens of Cyprus] are farmers. Turks occupy the northern part of Cyprus, although Turkey and Greece have long disagreed over who owns this copper-rich island.

Iran

Most of the people in **Iran,** which was called **Persia** until 1935, are Muslims. Because they speak Persian instead of Arabic, Iran is not considered to be an Arab country. It is famous for its Persian rugs and for being the second largest producer of oil in the Middle East.

Formerly the powerful king of Iran was called a **shah.** A revolution in Iran in 1979 dethroned the shah and an ayatollah [ī′ə·tō′lə: Muslim religious leader] became the ruler. The shah had tried to do away with some of the old customs in order to make Iran more modern. The new ruler, **Ayatollah Khomeini** [kō·mā′nē], however, reinstituted Islamic law, effectively stopping Iran's progress as a modern nation. Khomeini died in 1989, but the system of government he established lives on.

Tehran [tĕ·hrän′], Iran's capital city, was the scene of the capture of the American embassy in 1979. There, fifty Americans were held hostage for over a year. In 1980, the Islamic Conference (an official Muslim group) openly disagreed with Iran for holding the hostages. The hostages were returned to America in January of 1981. Iran continues to be a source of instability in the region. The Iranians provide money and supplies for Islamic terrorist groups and have repeatedly called for Israel's destruction.

Tehran

PEOPLE IN HISTORY

Henry Martyn: Missionary to India and the Middle East

When Henry Martyn was a boy in England, he read about the life of David Brainerd, a famous missionary to the American Indians. Even though his health was poor, Henry was filled with a desire to take the gospel to people of other lands.

Henry Martyn had a special talent for languages. He studied diligently as he sailed to his first new country, India, in 1806. By the time he arrived in India, he knew seven different languages! Determined to use his abilities for God's glory, he wrote these famous words in

PEOPLE IN HISTORY *cont.*

his diary: **"Now let me burn out for God."**

Henry Martyn did burn out for God. He translated the Bible into an Indian language and then began translating it into the languages of the Arabs and Persians who often visited India. When his doctor told him that he must return to England or die, he decided to return by way of Arabia and Persia (Iran). He sailed from India to Arabia and then rode on horseback to Persia. Wherever he went in the Middle East, he presented the gospel to Muslims and Jews.

The frigid air of the mountains and the intense heat of the plains made the trip to Persia extremely difficult, and when he arrived he used all his remaining strength to complete his Persian translation of the New Testament. He sent a special gift copy to the shah of Persia, who received it with gratitude.

Henry Martyn's last trip was a 1,300-mile ride by horseback from Persia to Turkey. From there, he planned to sail to England, but his strength was gone. On October 18, 1812, Henry Martyn died in Turkey. He was thirty-one years old. He was a missionary for only six years, yet his memory continues in his translations of God's Word in three different languages: Arabic, Persian, and a language of India.

CHAPTER 4 CHECKUP

A Know the countries and capitals of the Middle East and their locations. (See Continent Study 1, p. 322.)

B Define each term.

1. plateau
2. Mediterranean climate
3. wadi
4. steppes
5. fertile
6. natural resources
7. zionism
8. mosque

C Identify the term described by each clue.

1. a one-humped Arabian camel
2. the most important tree in the Middle East today
3. a section of a city
4. the head of a Bedouin tribe
5. the year that the modern state of Israel was formed
6. the god of Islam
7. the holy book of Islam

(cont.)

D Name the **two** largest oil producers of the Middle East.

E Name **three.**

1. peninsulas of the Middle East
2. important rivers of the Middle East
3. religions that began in the Middle East

F Who am I?

1. the founder of Islam
2. the missionary willing to "burn out" for God
3. the first prime minster of Israel
4. the leader who invaded Kuwait
5. the leader of Iran after it became an Islamic state

G Answer each question.

1. What is the world's largest peninsula?
2. What is the Middle East's second highest mountain?
3. What Tropic line runs through the Middle East?
4. What language is the most common in the Middle East?
5. What is the single largest religious group in the world?
6. What are the two holy cities for Muslims?
7. What is the largest city in Turkey?
8. In what country is the National Water Carrier located?
9. Which modern Israeli city is an important center of business?
10. What island nation is located south of Turkey?
11. What is the Middle East's most valuable natural resource?
12. What is the largest Middle Eastern nation?
13. Which country used to be called "Persia"?

CHAPTER 5

Countries of CENTRAL & SOUTHERN ASIA

Asia's three great river valleys supported three important ancient cultures. (1) The *Tigris-Euphrates Valley* was home to **Mesopotamia,** which we have already studied; (2) **India,** which will be studied in this chapter, rose up in the *Indus* [ĭn′dəs] *Valley;* (3) and the *Huang He* [hwäng′ hə′], or *Yellow River, Valley* was the location of **China,** which will be studied in chapter 6.

5.1 India

The country of **India** has a wonderful variety that few nations can claim. Where else can you find 700 different languages and dialects in one nation? Or travel from snow-capped mountain peaks to tropical jungles in a matter of hours—without crossing a national border? The variety of India makes this country one of the most interesting places in the world. It is the third largest nation in Asia (after Russia and China) and the second most populous country in the world (after China).

A Triangular Peninsula

Find India on the map (p. 67). Notice that the peninsula of India reaches into the **Indian Ocean** and makes this country look like a large

ANCIENT RIVER CIVILIZATIONS

Three of the early river civilizations—Mesopotamia, India, and China—were located in Asia. The fourth—Egypt—rose up in northern Africa.

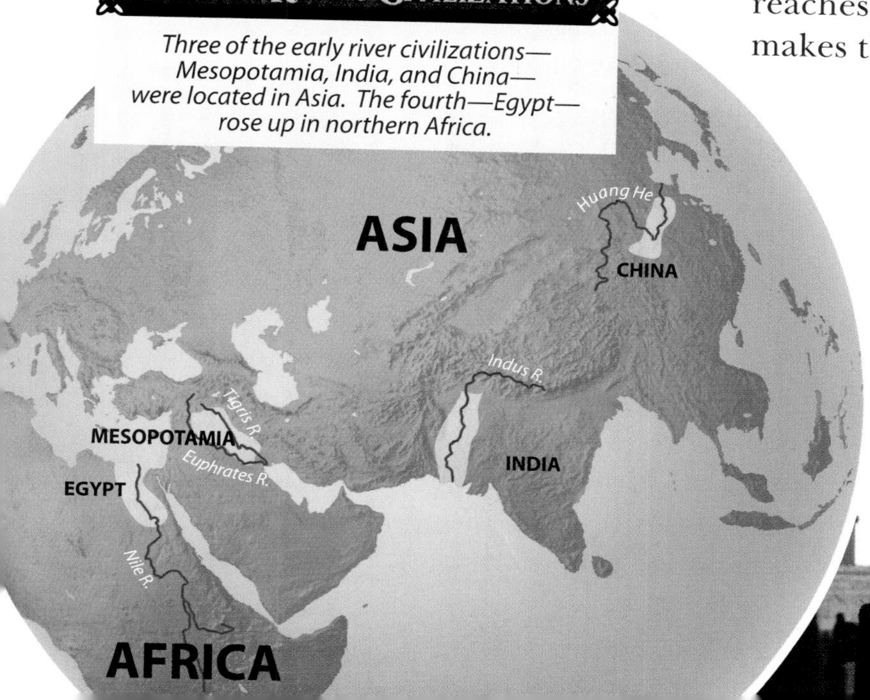

Taj Mahal

triangle. Along the top of the "triangle" are the **Himalayan Mountains.** Mountains, deserts, and rivers divide India into many different land regions.

The Indus River Valley

The **Indus River** flows for nine hundred miles from the northwestern foothills of the Himalayan Mountains down to the coast. Along its banks are very fertile plains. Around 2000 B.C., a great civilization began developing in the Indus River Valley. Towns and cities were built that were more prosperous, had more conveniences, and were more advanced than many towns and villages that exist in India today. The streets were carefully mapped out in a rectangular pattern. The houses were built of sun-dried bricks, and some were two-story homes built around open courtyards. Some of these ancient houses even had bathrooms with pipes that carried away waste water.

The people of these towns evidently carried on trade; items from Mesopotamia have been found in their ruins. Large houses have been found where the people stored their grain. Farmers dug ditches to irrigate the fields, and craftsmen worked with gold, silver, bronze, and copper. The people of the Indus Valley also developed their own system of counting, measuring, and writing.

By 1700 B.C., the Indus River Valley civilization had disappeared. It remained unknown to the world until about 1920, when archaeologists discovered ruins of its great cities.

The Aryans and the Dravidians

Around 1500 B.C., a group called the **Aryans** [âr′ē·ənz] began coming into India through mountain passes. The **Dravidians** [drə·vĭd′ē·ənz], who had lived in India before them, were driven south. The Dravidians were mainly merchants who lived in prosperous cities and traded cotton goods, gold, pearls, and pepper. The Aryans, in contrast, considered the number of cows a man owned to be the measure of his wealth. In fact, the Aryan word for war meant "a desire for more cows."

Although the Dravidians had a more highly developed culture than the Aryans, the Aryans wanted nothing to do with them. Because the Aryans looked down on the Dravidians whom they had conquered, they developed a strict social plan, the **caste** [căst] **system,** to keep the peoples apart from each other.

Cows were important in the Aryan society.

CENTRAL & SOUTHERN ASIA
Black Sea
Mediterranean Sea
TURKEY
GEORGIA
ARMENIA
AZERBAIJAN
Caspian Sea
Aral Sea
KAZAKHSTAN
UZBEKISTAN
TURKMENISTAN
KYRGYZSTAN
TAJIKISTAN
LEBANON
SYRIA
ISRAEL
JORDAN
IRAQ
Tigris R.
Euphrates R.
IRAN
SAUDI ARABIA
KUWAIT
Persian Gulf
BAHRAIN
QATAR
UNITED ARAB EMIRATES
OMAN
YEMEN
Red Sea
23°
AFGHANISTAN
PAKISTAN
Indus R.
Huang He
HIMALAYAS
NEPAL
Mt. Everest
BHUTAN
Brahmaputra R.
Ganges R.
BANGLADESH
New Delhi
Calcutta
INDIA
Mumbai (Bombay)
Calicut
Arabian Sea
Bay of Bengal
INDIAN OCEAN
SRI LANKA
MALDIVES
0°

The Caste System

In the early years there were four traditional castes and thousands of subcastes. The **Brahmins** [brä′mənz: priests] made up the most important caste. The second, less important caste was made up of **princes** and **warriors.** The members of the third caste were **landowners** and **merchants.** The lowest and least important of the four castes was made up of **farmers, laborers,** and **servants.**

The worst thing about the caste system was that a person could never work his way out of the caste into which he was born. For example, if an Indian boy was born on a farm, he could never hope to be a warrior or a merchant. He could only be a farmer, like his father. What might have happened in America if Abraham Lincoln had been forced to be a poor farmer all his life because his father was a farmer? In India there was absolutely no way in which a person could ever rise to another caste.

If a person broke the rules of his caste, he was put out of his caste and considered an **outcaste** for the rest of his life. It was considered a disgrace if an outcaste accidentally touched a person belonging to a caste. For this reason they were called **"untouchables."** Untouchables did not belong to any caste. They could live only with other outcastes, and were given only the hardest kind of work. They were not even allowed to draw water out of the public wells. When Christian missionaries began coming to India, they found the untouchables to be their most eager audience. Thousands of these despised outcastes became Christians.

Although the government of India has abolished the caste system, most Indians still cling to it as their traditional way of life. Caste causes many people in India to live in poverty and guarantees wealth and comfort to only a few.

Family Life in an Indian Village

Ancient India was made up of thousands of villages. Most Indians were farmers who lived in huts made of mud and straw. Early villages were made up of family groups, and very few people ever left their village. Nearly all the farm work, including plowing, planting, and harvesting, was done by hand.

Family life was very important in India, but in a much different way than we think of family ties. Like many ancient peoples, Indians did not consider individuals to be important. A wife was

Untouchables sweep and mop the streets.

often chosen by the elders of the family rather than by the man himself; and no matter who earned something, it was taken and owned by the entire family. All the men from the family would come together to make important decisions. The oldest man ruled, and when he died, the rule passed to the oldest son.

sacred cows lying in the streets

Comprehension Check 5A

1. Name Asia's three ancient cultures and tell the general area where they were located.
2. Who began the caste system? Why?
3. Name the four main castes.
4. What was an outcaste or "untouchable"?

Religion in India

Hinduism. To understand the people of India, one must know something about **Hinduism,** the main religion in India today. Hindus worship many gods that they believe make up one universal spirit called **Brahma.** They believe that man's soul is a part of Brahma, along with animals and even plant life. When someone or something dies, its soul is reborn into some other newborn man or animal in a process called **reincarnation.**

Hindus believe that a person's deeds in this life directly affect his position in the next life. Good deeds result in reincarnation to a higher caste. For example, if a farmer leads a good, honest life, he may become a wealthy businessman in the next life. On the other hand, evil deeds result in a reincarnation to a lower caste or even an animal. A dishonest or selfish person might be reincarnated as a dog or a flea.

Their belief in reincarnation causes Hindus to revere and even worship certain animals, especially sacred bulls and cows. Even today, if you visited India, you might find a cow roaming the streets of a modern city. Because they believe that all life is connected in the universal spirit, they refuse to kill even harmful creatures like rats or insects that destroy crops. Belief in reincarnation has caused India to be overrun with animals.

Today, India is one of the poorest nations in the world. Two major reasons for India's poverty are belief in the false religion of Hinduism and a continued following of the caste system. Hinduism has led to a superstitious regard for animal and plant life that hinder progress. The caste system has caused the people to accept their poverty rather than work to escape it.

The superstition of India's religion keeps the people living in fear, and keeps them from a knowledge of the one true God Who promises to take care of all those who follow and trust Him.

Buddhism. The religion of Buddhism [bo͞o′dĭz′əm] is much like Hinduism. By 550 B.C., some people had become dissatisfied with the Hindu caste system and the Brahmin priests. Among these was Gautama [gô′tə·mə], the son of a ruler of one of the kingdoms that existed in ancient India. According to the ancient story, Gautama, who lived in the palace of his wealthy father, took a walk one day and was shocked to see so many people in need of food and clothes. Distressed by their needs, he sought for an answer to questions about life and death. He felt that in order to find the answers, he must leave his wife and newborn son and torture himself. After nearly dying, he decided to give up self-torture, since it did not answer his questions.

One day, while Gautama was meditating under a tree, he claimed to receive **"enlightenment,"** or a vision that answered his questions. Because he received this vision, his followers gave him the title **Buddha,** which means "Enlightened One."

In his enlightenment or vision, Buddha claimed to have found the way to be free from suffering. He called the state of being free from suffering **nirvana** [nĭr·vä′nə]. How could a person achieve nirvana? According to Buddha, it came through getting rid of all desires and all worldly goods.

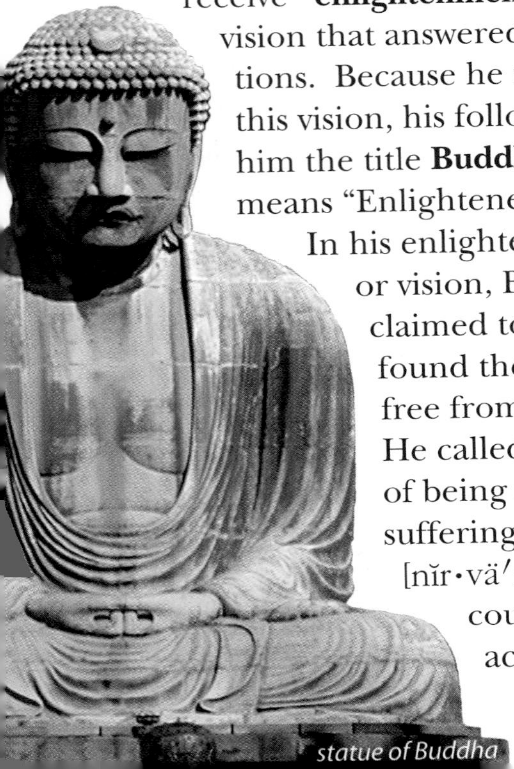

statue of Buddha

When Buddha was about eighty years old, he died, and his followers began spreading his teachings abroad. Soon people had images of Buddha and worshiped him as well as his teachings. With the passing of years, the false religion of Buddhism spread throughout Asia. Although Buddhism is not as widespread as Hinduism, it does survive today in several countries around the world.

Like Hindus, Buddhists worship in temples, but they worship individually, not as part of a congregation. Most of the temples have shrines or images, each devoted to a god or goddess. The images are treated as if they were living, each being cared for and fed daily. How thankful we ought to be that we do not have to take care of our God, but that He will take care of us.

When Buddha died, his body was burned, and the people were taught that his bones had a sacred power. After our Lord Jesus died at Calvary, His body was buried and three days later He arose bodily from the grave. We serve a living Savior, not a dead teacher.

India's Contributions to Civilization

Mathematics. The Indians discovered some very important principles of mathematics. They developed a symbol that meant "not any" that we call **zero.** They also developed **place value,** which is now called the **decimal numeral system** and is used by most nations. Our modern **written numbers** were also created in India. We know them as Arabic numbers because Arabs transmitted them from India to the West.

Cotton. Cotton was grown in many ancient countries, including India. In some countries, the cotton plant grew wild. India, however, had begun to cultivate it very early in their history, even before 2000 B.C. The cotton was used to make clothing, sandals, and harnesses for elephants. When the army of **Alexander the Great** invaded India in the 300s B.C., Alexander took some of India's cotton goods with him. He later introduced them to Europeans for the first time.

Perhaps you have heard of **calico,** a cotton material that usually has a checked or figured print. The name "calico" is taken from **Calicut** [kăl′ĭ·kŭt′], a city in India where the material was first made.

Trade goods. In the southern areas of India, much trade was carried on. Traders spread Indian ideas and culture to other parts of the world. Can you tell by looking at the map of Asia (p. 67) why India would be a good center of trade? As trade developed, India's products became highly treasured in Europe. Among these products were cotton goods, spices (especially pepper), ivory, pearls, perfumes, tea, and dyes. Because these goods were costly, only the very wealthy in Europe could afford to buy them.

Comprehension Check 5B

1. What is the main religion in India today?
2. What do Hindus believe about Brahma?
3. What is reincarnation?
4. What religion was started by a man dissatisfied with Hinduism?
5. What does Buddha mean?
6. What material gets its name from an Indian city? Which city is it named for?

Time of Change

The Mauryan dynasty. During the expansion of his empire, Alexander the Great conquered northwest India. However, since he was occupied in other parts of the world, he never had strong control there. After Alexander's death, the Mauryan [mour′yən] dynasty took over India. (A **dynasty** is a line of rulers that succeed each other in the same family. The ruler's son usually takes control when the ruler dies. Then *his* son will most likely rule when *his* father dies. A new dynasty begins when a ruler who is not related to the currently ruling family takes control.) The rulers of the Mauryan dynasty were in control at the time of Christ. One of the Mauryan emperors, Asoka [ə·sō′kə], converted to Buddhism and did much to spread this belief throughout India.

Dynasties. From 120 B.C. until A.D. 1500, different dynasties controlled India, each invading from the north.

Each one tried to force its own ideas, especially about religion, on the people of India. During this time, some of India's people became Muslims and separated into two groups. One group moved far to the northwest and the other to the northeast.

One of the dynasties' rulers had the beautiful **Taj Mahal** built as a tomb for his favorite wife. (See picture on p. 65) If you were to visit India, you would want to be sure to see this most famous of India's historic sites.

Coming of the Europeans

In 1498, **Vasco da Gama** was the first European to reach India by sailing around Africa. His accomplishment opened up trade with the Western world. European countries were seeking to control trade routes, and the Portuguese seized control of ports on the coast of India. Within India, various rulers retained strong control.

Vasco da Gama with the king of Portugal shortly before sailing for India

English rule. But by the 1700s, the power of these rulers was gone. An English trading company, the **East India Company,** took advantage of this and gained much power and control. Finally the East India Company took over India and used the people to their advantage. The people of India rose up in rebellion. England then realized the problems in India, and the English government took control. The British did much to help improve the conditions in India, but many of India's problems were caused by false religious beliefs. The great pioneer missionary **William Carey** and the missionaries who came after him did much to change the religious practices and evil worship forms by spreading the gospel in India.

Comprehension Check 5C

1. What English company controlled India for a time?
2. What is a dynasty?
3. What empire controlled India at the time of Christ?
4. What European was the first to reach India by sailing around Africa?

Modern India

Independence. Despite the benefits of British rule and the good that had been brought about by English missionaries, many Indians were uneasy. They were afraid that western culture and Christianity were weakening such Indian traditions as the practice of Hinduism and following of the caste system. After 1900, the Indian independence movement grew rapidly. One of the key leaders in the struggle for Indian independence was Mahatma **Gandhi** [mə·hät′mə gän′dē]. Gandhi encouraged the people to refuse to obey laws of the British government of India in order to achieve their goals. Although Gandhi promoted "peace-

Gandhi

PEOPLE IN HISTORY

William Carey: The "Father of Modern Missions"

William Carey was born in England in 1761. Because his family was poor, he went to school only until he was fourteen. At that age, he became an apprentice (learner) to a shoemaker. But having a thirst for reading, he studied languages and science on his own. It wasn't long before he learned Latin, Greek, French, and Dutch. A fellow apprentice shared the gospel with him, and he was saved. William spent all his free time reading the Bible and other books, studying languages, and telling others of Christ. He became a preacher, married, and supported his family by making shoes.

William Carey read in the Bible, "Go ye therefore and teach all nations . . ." (Matt. 28:19). He read of David Brainerd and his great work among the American Indians. He read of the terrible conditions of people without Christ in other lands. He thought, "Someone must go and tell these people of Christ." It took a long time for Carey to find people who were interested in missions. In those days, very few people thought of the needs of people in other lands who had never heard of Christ.

But finally, in 1793, William Carey and his family sailed for India. The Careys settled in Bengal, now a part of the country of Bangladesh [bäng′glə·dĕsh′]. William Carey's ability with languages aided him greatly in his work in India. He learned the Bengali language, and other languages of India, very quickly, and began preaching. Most of the people of Bengal were Hindus, and they were very resistant to new ideas. Carey preached to them for six years before the first Hindu came to Christ.

William Carey served in Bengal for fifty-nine years. He translated the Bible or portions of it into over forty languages and dialects. He helped to encourage education in India, and he was able to help the Indians improve their farming methods. Through his influence, the evil practices of sacrificing children to idols and of killing widows were abolished.

William Carey's motto, "Attempt great things for God; expect great things from God," and his dedication to Christ inspired many people to become missionaries. For this reason, he is called the "Father of Modern Missions."

ful disobedience," the result of his teachings was often violence and bloodshed.

In 1947, India received its independence, and **Nehru** [nā′ro͞o] became the first prime minister of India. Within a year it was decided to separate the northwestern and northeastern sections of land for the Muslims. The result was the divided nation of **East and West Pakistan.** Over the next few years millions of Indian Muslims moved to Pakistan and Hindus moved to India. East Pakistan later became **Bangladesh** and West Pakistan came to be known as **Pakistan.**

The land and climate. India is separated from most of the rest of Asia by the Himalayas. The mountainous parts of India have a highland or alpine climate, but much of the rest of the country has a humid subtropical climate much like that of America's Southeast. The Northern plains area south of the mountains, where most of the Indian people live, has some of the most fertile soil in the world. The **Ganges** [găn′jēz′], the **Indus,** and the **Brahmaputra** [brä′mə· po͞o′trə] Rivers, as well as many small rivers, make the Northern plains good for farming. A low mountain range near the Arabian Sea holds back the moisture from the sea. Thus the coast is a tropical rain forest and the area on the other side of the mountains is almost like a desert. **Monsoons** (seasonal winds) blow in from the sea between May and October, bringing as much as 450 inches of rain to many parts of India. From November to April, the winds blow away from the land, and very little rain falls. The monsoons are vitally important to Indian farmers, since they depend on water from the rains to keep their crops alive.

Agriculture. Agriculture is India's largest source of income and its largest employer. Agricultural advances in recent years have improved harvests, increasing the country's supply of rice, wheat, and other important food crops. Coffee, tea, and rubber are some of the crops grown on large plantations to sell to other countries.

Cities. The capital of India is **New Delhi,** a very modern city. The largest city, **Mumbai (Bombay),** is a busy seaport located on the western coast. **Calcutta,** one of India's most famous cities, is a seaport on the eastern coast.

Many people in cities travel in a **pedicab,** a carriage pulled by a person riding a bicycle. Cities are often so

flooded city street following a monsoon

pedicab in New Delhi

crowded with people and pedicabs that it can be difficult for cars to drive down the narrow streets.

Homes. In the cities, some people live over their shops or in small homes. Some live in the slums where the houses are made of scraps of cloth or metal, and many sleep in the streets because they have no homes. In villages, homes are often mud or clay huts. Few villages have electricity, and even where electricity is available, few people have it in their homes. Most villagers still go to the main well to draw water for their families.

Dress. Although many people in the cities wear western-style clothing, much of the clothing in India is unique to that part of the world. Because of the extreme heat, clothing is often light or bright in color and loose-fitting. Many men wear loose-fitting robes or pants with large jackets. On their heads they wear turbans. Women wear either loose-fitting pants with a tunic, or a **sari,** which is a long piece of cloth wrapped around the body in such a way as to form a long, flowing skirt. The free end can be draped over the shoulder like a shawl.

Most women wear jewelry, some even wearing rings in their noses. Many Indian women wear a **bindi,** or round dot, on their forehead. When it originated in ancient times, the bindi signified that a woman was married. Although the traditional meaning continues today, women around the world have begun wearing bindis for fashion. They can be painted on, or attached with an adhesive, in a variety of colors and styles.

The Himalayas. The **Himalayas** are a system of several chains of mountains that run side by side and form a band that is 1,500 miles long and at times nearly 200 miles wide. They provide a natural barrier between India and China. The Himalayas are the world's highest mountains. Among them is the famous **Mt. Everest,** the highest mountain on earth (29,035 feet). It is located in the kingdom of **Nepal** [nə·pôl′], a small country between India and China. Some of the highest **passes** (narrow passages or openings between mountains) in the world run through the Himalayas. Even today, many of these passes are impossible to cross, especially during the winter when they are covered with snow.

Indian women wearing saris

young Indian girl

Mt. Everest in Nepal

5.2 Other Central and Southern Asian Countries

Afghanistan. *Afghanistan* is located northwest of India. Shortly after America was attacked on September 11, 2001, it became evident that an Islamic terrorist group called al-Qaeda was responsible for the attack. These terrorists were led by a man named Osama bin Laden, and the United States believed he was hiding in the rugged hill country of Afghanistan. In October, 2001, the United States and Great Britain began bombing key locations in Afghanistan, but bin Laden was not captured. Although the government that sheltered bin Laden was quickly driven from power, it has gradually reestablished itself again in many regions of Afghanistan.

Other Asian Countries. Asia is so large that it covers about one third of the world's land area and spreads almost halfway around the earth. Check a world globe to see just how extensive this huge continent is. We have already studied an important part of Asia in Chapter 4—the Middle East. How many Middle Eastern countries can you name? Can you find them on the map (p. 67)? Find the five Asian countries studied in this chapter. How many other central and southern Asian countries can you find? In the next chapter we will be studying the last section of Asia—the Far East.

Comprehension Check 5D

1. Name three missionaries to India.
2. Who was India's first Prime Minister?
3. What two new countries were once part of India?
4. Name the three main rivers of India.
5. What are seasonal winds that bring heavy rains?
6. What is India's capital city?
7. The __?__, the world's highest chain of mountains, contain __?__, the world's highest peak.

People in History

Amy Carmichael: Rescuer of Indian Children

There were big tears in three-year-old Amy's eyes. She had prayed for blue eyes, and God did not seem to answer! Her eyes were still brown. Amy Carmichael was to learn that all of God's answers, whether "yes" or "no," are for our best and for His glory.

Amy Carmichael was born in Northern Ireland in 1867. Her family went to church regularly. Each night they gathered for a special time of prayer. Amy learned about Christ as a young child. She soon accepted the Lord as her Savior and sought to please Him.

Amy Carmichael had a deep concern for others, and she strove to show Christ's love by her actions. She was always assisting the elderly, the poor, or the sick, even though she was sometimes laughed at for her efforts.

The Lord began impressing on her heart the need to become a missionary. Though many family hardships and her own poor health made it difficult for her, she went to India, where she served for 59 years. She worked at learning the language and taught women and children.

Amy saw the big heathen temples and the people worshiping in fear. She wanted to see what strange religion could have such a strong power over the people. Because foreigners were not allowed in the temples, she used a disguise. With coffee, she stained her skin; then she dressed in Indian clothing. How thankful she was now that God had answered "no" to her childhood request for blue eyes! She was able to walk into the temple unrecognized. Inside, it was dark and dirty. There was no sunlight, only torches to make a frightening light on the cold, damp walls. Amy saw some young boys and wondered what they were doing. On another occasion, Amy saw a fancy carriage carrying a huge idol. Around it were little girls whose eyes were full of fear. Amy discovered that these girls were to be slaves in the temple. Amy's heart longed to save the temple children who were treated cruelly and kept in the temple as if it were a prison.

The first temple children she helped were some who had escaped. Later, Amy would buy children from parents who were going to sell them to the temple because they needed the money. When her little home was no longer large enough for her growing "family," Amy purchased a home in Dohnavur [dŏn′ə•vər]. Her home became a place of refuge, because those who accepted Christ in India suffered great persecution. Young girls who accepted Christ often ran away to live at Dohnavur. Soon the home was opened to boys, also.

Amy Carmichael was not financially supported by any individual or group. She trusted the Lord alone to provide, and God never failed her. Through His help she reared over a thousand children. Her first goal was to tell them of Jesus' love and then to care for them and train them to serve Him. She often faced great danger and threats of imprisonment, but she could not say "no" to a child in need.

When Amy Carmichael was 64 years old, she fell and broke her leg. It could not be cared for right away, and when it healed, it was never right again. Amy could not be as active as before, but now she had time to write. Through some of her writings, the people of India saw the evil of allowing children to become temple slaves, and laws were passed to prevent this. Many people were challenged to serve the Lord through reading her books.

Amy Carmichael saw the Christian life as a continual climb up a mountain. She continued to climb for the Lord until her death in 1951 when she was 84 years old. She found the Lord faithful to meet her every need. Many Indian children's lives were saved for this life and for eternity because Amy Carmichael dared to trust God. ⌘

CHAPTER 5 CHECKUP

A Know these locations.

1. Indian Ocean
2. Himalayas
3. Indus River
4. New Delhi
5. Pakistan
6. Bangladesh
7. Mt. Everest

B Define each term.

1. Aryans
2. caste system
3. Brahmins
4. outcaste
5. Hinduism
6. reincarnation
7. Brahma
8. Buddhism
9. nirvana
10. calico
11. dynasty
12. monsoons

C Who am I?

1. the "enlightened one"
2. first to bring India's cotton goods to Europe
3. first European to reach India by sailing around Africa
4. the "Father of Modern Missions"
5. a key leader in India's struggle for independence
6. first prime minister of India
7. the "Rescuer of Indian children"

D Name **three.**

1. ancient river valley civilizations of Asia
2. Indian contributions to mathematics
3. rivers of India

E Answer each question.

1. What dynasty ruled India at the time of Christ?
2. What is India's capital city? Largest city?
3. What structure was built as a tomb for the wife of an Indian ruler?
4. What is the world's highest mountain? In what country is it located?
5. What do we call the cotton material developed in Calicut?
6. What mountain range forms a barrier between China and India?
7. Today, West Pakistan is known as ___?___. East Pakistan is known as ___?___.

List the four castes in order of importance.

CHAPTER 6

Countries of the FAR EAST

6.1 China

China, with a culture rich in tradition, is one of the most fascinating countries in Asia. As the third largest nation in the world, it is just a little larger than the United States. Its borders touch 14 nations, more than any other country in the world. Can you find China's border nations on the map (p. 82)?

China was the largest of the three ancient Asian river valley cultures. Its people were descendants of a group who settled along the **Huang He** after they left the area of the Tower of Babel. The Huang He (formerly called the Hwang Ho or Yellow River because of its yellowish-brown color) is also known as **China's Sorrow,** because it often floods and causes considerable damage.

Tall mountains, vast deserts, and ocean surround China. In ancient times, no one, friend or enemy, could easily enter ancient China, nor could the Chinese easily leave. Without outside influence, the Chinese developed a completely different culture from that of Europe, Africa, or the Americas.

Chinese Dynasties

First dynasty. Like the people of ancient India, the Chinese were ruled by dynasties. During the first dynasty (around 1500 B.C.), the Chinese developed a **system of writing** that involved more than three thousand symbols. With that many symbols to learn, do you suppose very many ancient Chinese learned how to write?

The ancient Chinese were skilled in bronze work, which was used to make vessels for religious ceremonies, weapons, and chariots. They also made beautiful carvings from jade and marble stones.

Chou dynasty. About 500 years later, during the Chou Dynasty, China was divided into many states, each with its own ruler. The strongest state ruled over the others. The Chou Dynasty was the longest-ruling dynasty in Chinese history. A famous Chinese teacher who came to be known in the western world as **Confucius** [kən· fyo͞o′shəs] lived during this dynasty.

China's first emperor. **Shih Huang Ti** [shĭr′hwăng′tē′], ruler of the state called Ch'in [chĭn], invaded and conquered other states. He began a new dynasty (in 255 B.C.) and proclaimed himself to be the first emperor of China. (The

Great Wall of China

Ch'in dynasty got its name from the state of Ch'in; China gets its name from the Ch'in dynasty.)

Shih Huang Ti was a strict ruler who created a strong central government. Other rulers before him had built short walls here and there to keep out bands of wild tribesmen who robbed and killed the Chinese farmers. Shih Huang Ti ordered that all the short walls be joined together to form the **Great Wall of China.**

The Great Wall, built entirely by hand, took hundreds of years to complete. Winding its way over mountains and valleys, it measures more than fifteen hundred miles in length, making it the longest structure ever built by man. It is roughly 25 feet tall, 25 feet thick at the base, and 15 feet thick at the top. The sides of the wall form a shell that is made of brick and stone, filled with earth, and covered with bricks set in lime. Ancient horsemen used the top of the wall as a road. Towers were built every 200 to 300 yards to further fortify the wall.

As in other dynasties, when Ti died, his son came to rule. His son, however, was a poor ruler, and the Chinese rose up against him. As a result, the Ch'in

Great Silk Road

dynasty was one of the shortest dynasties in China's history. Yet the Chinese empire that began with Ch'in lasted for more than 2,000 years.

Han dynasty. During the Han dynasty (206 B.C.–A.D. 220), the Chinese Empire grew to be one of the greatest ancient empires of the world and China grew to its greatest size. The Chinese accomplished many things during this period. For the first time in world history, a land route connected China with Europe. The most famous land route was called the **Great Silk Road,** which allowed trade between China and the Roman Empire. It is possible that the first Christian missionaries to China followed this trade route.

Education became more important, and a university was built. Han writers wrote poetry, literature, and histories of China. The teachings of Confucius became so important that in order to hold a government job, one had to study these teachings and then pass an examination.

Comprehension Check 6A

1. Where does China rank in size with the other nations of the world?
2. Whose teachings did the Chinese have to study to hold a government job?
3. From which dynasty did China get its name?
4. Give three facts about the Great Wall of China.
5. What was the name of the land route that connected China with Europe?

Discoveries and Inventions

Silk. The Chinese were the first people to discover and use **silk.** For thousands of years, they had used silk to make beautiful garments, curtains, and upholstery. Once the Great Silk Road was established, the Chinese traded their silk with other nations, but they kept their knowledge of how to make silk a guarded secret for over three thousand years.

Before the Chinese discovered silk, they noticed that the silkworm has quite

PEOPLE IN HISTORY

Confucius: Chinese Philosopher and Teacher

A man's way of thinking is called his philosophy. **Confucius's** philosophy was so strong that it influenced Chinese history for over 2,000 years. His teachings were based on his own beliefs that a person should be sincere and polite. He believed a person should examine his own life and be a gentleman.

Who is a gentleman? According to Confucius, a gentleman was a man who respected his country's ruler and his family ancestors. A man's father should be highly respected. If rulers were gentlemen, they would inspire their subjects to be gentlemen, also.

Confucius made many rules for good behavior. After he died, the people who had listened to his teachings carried his beliefs throughout China. His teachings became so accepted that they were written in five books called the ***Five Classics.*** These books were taught at the university built during the Han Dynasty. Anyone who mastered the teachings in these books was thought to be a good person. In fact, mastering these books was a must for anyone who wanted a job with the government.

Confucius's teachings have many good points, but they also have weaknesses. It is good to have respect for ancestors, but the Chinese lived strictly as their ancestors lived before them. They thought that accepting new ideas would dishonor their families. There is another major weakness in Confucius's teachings. Although it is right to do what is good, we cannot rely upon ourselves to be good. We must remember that *"There is none righteous, no not one"* (Rom. 3:10). The only way anyone in the world can know true goodness is by believing on the only One Who knew no sin at all, the Lord Jesus Christ.

Some followed Confucius as if his beliefs were a religion. Many people still consider his teachings a religion.

THE FAR EAST
WEST SIBERIAN PLAIN
RUSSIA
Lake Baikal
Caspian Sea
KAZAKHSTAN
MONGOLIA
GOBI DESERT
TURKMENISTAN
UZBEKISTAN
KYRGYZSTAN
TAJIKISTAN
TAKLIMAKAN DESERT
AFGHANISTAN
Indus R.
GREAT WALL
Beijing
Tianjin
Grand Canal
Huang He
CHINA
Nanjing
Shanghai
Hangzhou
Ningbo
Chongqing
Yangtze R.
NORTH KOREA
P'yongyang
Seoul
SOUTH KOREA
JAPAN
Tokyo
Mt. Fuji
Osaka
Hiroshima
Nagasaki
23°
PAKISTAN
HIMALAYAS
NEPAL
BHUTAN
INDIA
Arabian Sea
BANGLADESH
Taipei
TAIWAN
Guangzhou
Hong Kong
PACIFIC OCEAN
MYANMAR (BURMA)
LAOS
VIETNAM
THAILAND
Bangkok
CAMBODIA
Bay of Bengal
PHILIPPINES
Manila
SRI LANKA
BRUNEI
0° Equator
MALDIVES
MALAYSIA
Borneo
SINGAPORE
INDONESIA
INDIAN OCEAN

an appetite for mulberry leaves. In fact, after it first hatches, it eats nothing but mulberry leaves both day and night. It is said that in 2700 B.C., a Chinese ruler noticed that the mulberry trees in his garden were being damaged. His wife found the tiny silkworms eating the leaves. She noticed that when the silkworms stopped eating, each began spinning a cocoon. The cocoons were shiny and beautiful. Then she discovered that threads could be unwound from the cocoon. She had discovered silk, the strongest fiber that nature makes. The Chinese soon learned to twist the fibers into thread and make the thread into a beautiful, shiny cloth.

Paper. The Egyptians, using the papyrus plant, were the first to make a paperlike writing material. However, the Chinese, using the inner bark from the mulberry tree, invented the first real paper in A.D. 105. Paper made from wood was not introduced into Europe until the late 1100s.

Printing. The Chinese were most likely the first inventors of printing. They made **block prints** by carving a picture or a symbol on a piece of wood. The carved side of the block was then coated with

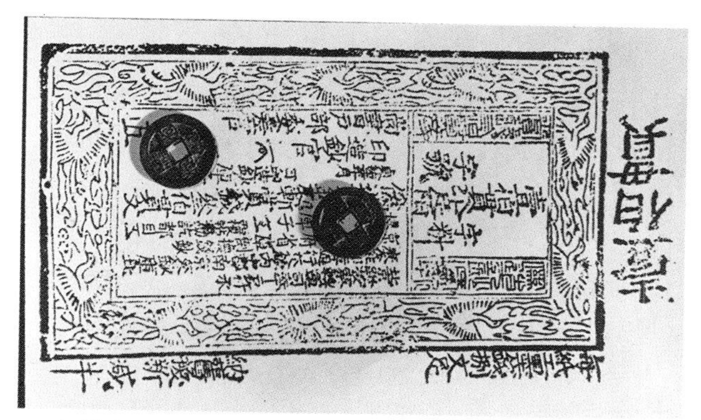

early Chinese paper money and coins

Colorful silk is still manufactured in China today.

ink and stamped on a piece of paper. Although beautiful block prints were made, there was a big disadvantage. If a change needed to be made, the entire wood block needed to be carved again.

About A.D. 1045, a Chinese printer invented the first movable type. Each piece of type was made of baked clay. The movable type was much more practical than the wood block method that required carving a new block of wood for each printed page. The printer who used movable type could use the same pieces of type over and over again by simply rearranging the type for each new page.

Even movable type was not very practical for the Chinese because of their system of writing. A person would have to carve over three thousand different symbols to produce books. The Chinese were able to find at least one practical use, however—the printing of the world's first known **paper money.**

Printing would not become important to the history of the world until the Europeans, who had alphabets, were given movable type around A.D. 1440 by Johann Gutenberg.

Porcelain. The Chinese developed a very fine and delicate type of pottery known as **porcelain.** Porcelain is different from any other type of pottery because of its whiteness. When China began its trade with other countries, porcelain dishes became a much desired item. People who bought these beautiful dishes called them **"china"** after the country they came from. Today, porcelain dishes are made in many countries, especially England, but we still refer to them as "china."

Chinese porcelain

Coal, gunpowder, and the compass. The Chinese were the first people to develop a coal industry. By the A.D. 300s, they were mining coal to heat buildings and to smelt (refine by melting) metals. The Europeans did not mine coal until the 1200s. **Gunpowder** and the **compass** are both ancient inventions. Many people claim the Chinese were the first to invent them, although there is no proof of this.

PEOPLE IN HISTORY

Hudson Taylor: The "Father of Faith Missions"

J. Hudson Taylor was one of the most famous missionaries to go to China. He is remembered for his great faith in God. Before his time, missionaries were supported by a mission society. Hudson Taylor determined that he would trust God alone to meet his needs in answer to his prayers. He did not tell people about his needs; instead, he prayed that God would move many people to give money for his missionary support. Many missionaries after Hudson Taylor began to trust God alone for their needs, and Hudson Taylor became known as the "Father of Faith Missions." His motto was, "To move men through God by prayer."

In 1853, young Hudson Taylor left his home in England to sail to Shanghai [shăng·hī′], China. The trip took five and a half months.

Taylor wanted nothing to keep him from being used of God among the Chinese. He quickly learned the Chinese language and mastered such Chinese customs as eating with chopsticks. He began to dress in the Chinese manner. He had most of his head shaved and wore the remaining hair in one large pigtail, called a queue [kyo͞o], that was worn by all Chinese men at that time. The Chinese, whom he longed to win to Christ, trusted him because of his great interest in them.

Taylor married Maria, a young teacher in a Christian girls' school. Together they worked at Ningpo [nĭng′pō′: modern Ningbo], where he opened a mission hall for preaching and won many to Christ. One of his converts was Mr. Nee, a well-educated Chinese businessman. Mr. Nee was used of God to win many Chinese people to Christ.

In 1865, the Taylors returned to England. There Hudson rested, studied more medicine, and worked on revising the Chinese New Testament. He was very concerned about the millions of people in inland China who had never had a chance to hear of Christ. He began to pray for others who would go back with him to China. He started the China Inland Mission and asked God in faith to send him other missionaries. Soon he returned to China with 22 other missionaries, two for each province in inland China. Hudson Taylor continued to trust God to meet his needs. By the time of his death in 1905 at the age of 73, over 800 missionaries had gone into China's heartland to tell the Chinese people about Christ. God had answered Hudson Taylor's prayer of faith. ⌘

China Becomes Known to the World

In 1271, **Marco Polo,** an Italian trader, left Venice, Italy, with his father and uncle. Their destination was the little-known country of China. They traveled as far as they could by ship, sailing southeast on the Mediterranean Sea. Then they crossed the mountains and deserts of Asia by camel. Three years later they reached China, which they called **Cathay** [kă·thā′].

During their 20-year stay, the Polos were amazed at China's cultural achievements. In 1295, they returned to Venice with many gifts from China's ruler. Among their gifts were ivory, jewels, jade, porcelain, and silk. A few years later, Marco Polo wrote a book that for the first time gave Europeans information about the mysterious land of China. In his book, Polo described to spellbound Europeans China's amazing accomplishments.

Marco Polo before China's ruler

Because Europeans desired the beautiful trade items China had to offer, trade between China and Europe was established. Before long, wealthy European ladies were wearing silk dresses. Although many Europeans desired to own pieces of the beautiful Chinese porcelain, only the very wealthy could afford it.

Trade that began during the time of Marco Polo grew as demands for Asian products increased, and new trade routes were formed. Because China had learned to exist without the influence of the Western world, they accepted the new trade and enjoyed the wealth that came from it, but had little use for most European goods.

Missionary efforts. Once China was opened to European trade, missionaries began going there as well. **J. Hudson Taylor** spent forty years teaching the Chinese about Christ. Other missionaries, such as **John and Betty Stam,** were later to give their lives to tell the Chinese the true way of salvation. Most of the Chinese followed the teachings of Confucius or of Buddha. Slowly some Chinese began to accept Christ. As they realized that they did not need to worship their ancestors and the past, they were free to accept new ways to improve their country.

Comprehension Check 6B

1. The philosophy of what famous Chinese teacher influenced Chinese history for over 2,000 years?
2. What beautiful fabric were the Chinese the first to discover and use?
3. Of what was the first real paper made?
4. What was the first type of printing used?
5. What were the Chinese able to print even though movable type was not practical for their language?
6. Who made China known to the outside world? What was established because of this?
7. Why is Hudson Taylor called the "Father of Faith Missions"?

A Changing Country

The dynasties end. As China prospered during the time of European trade, many people moved there from poorer surrounding countries. The population grew rapidly, and the new wealth was highly taxed by the government. People became more and more discontented. In 1911, the last dynasty was overthrown, and the **Republic of China,** led by **Sun Yat-sen** [so͞on′ yät′sĕn′] and roughly patterned after governments in the West, was established. Free China was now open for many more missionaries.

Problems of a new republic. The new government had many problems to handle. Unrest and revolution continued. Hunger and disease were widespread among the people. In the meantime, some of China's leaders had begun to accept a new idea of government—**Communism.** Communism, which had first been put into practice in Russia, promised to feed the poor and bring peace and prosperity, but in reality sought to take away personal, political, and religious freedoms. Republican government and Communism began a struggle that would last for many years as a civil war broke out between them.

Communists take control. **Mao Tse-tung** [mou′ tsə′to͞ong′, also spelled Zedong] led the Chinese Communists, and **Chiang Kai-shek** [chăng′ kī′shĕk′] led the Nationalists of the Republic of China. During World War II, these two groups joined together to fight against Japan as part of the Allied forces. After the

PEOPLE IN HISTORY

John and Betty Stam: Martyrs in Communist China

John and Betty Stam were American missionaries in China during the time that the Communists were taking over. Betty Stam had grown up in China with her missionary parents, and John Stam was called to be a missionary to China while he was a student at Bible school. After John and Betty Stam had worked together in China for a year, God gave them a baby girl, whom they named Helen Priscilla.

In 1934, when Helen Priscilla was only three months old, Communist soldiers stormed into their town unexpectedly. Before the Stams could leave, the town was surrounded and there was no way to get out. The Communists thought nothing of human life and had already killed many people as they marched across China. Thinking they could get money from the mission, they captured John, Betty, and the baby. When it appeared that they would be of no value to the Communists, the Communists killed John and Betty Stam, who became modern-day martyrs for Christ. Their baby girl was left in the house alone. After the Communists left, missionaries and Chinese Christians who had been hiding in the hills buried the Stams and took little Helen to friends where she would be safe.

John and Betty Stam were able to serve in China for only a few years, but their love for Christ won many to the Lord. Through their deaths, many more Chinese people have been saved and many have dedicated their lives to serve God, even though they know it may mean giving up their earthly lives or freedom because of the Communist control of China. God truly used John and Betty Stam in life and in death to bring glory to Himself.

war, however, the Communists rose up against the Republic and took control of China in 1949. Chiang Kai-shek and his supporters fled to **Taiwan,** a small island off the coast of China. There they maintained the **Republic of China.**

Chiang Kai-shek

The mainland, under Communist control, became known as the **People's Republic of China.** The name is misleading, for the Communists had no interest in having a true republic, and soon took away from the people their land, businesses, and freedoms. Mao and his forces terrorized the people and murdered millions of Chinese for supposed "crimes against the people."

Individual farms were replaced with large collective or communal farms owned by the state but worked by the Chinese people for low wages. Families were also under attack. The Communist Party decided when couples could marry and how many children they could have. Some missionaries lost their lives, and many Chinese fled to other countries, including the United States.

Comprehension Check 6C

1. Who established the first Republic of China?
2. Who was the leader of the Communists in China?
3. Who was the leader of the Nationalists of the Republic of China?
4. Who gained control of mainland China?
5. Where did the Chinese Nationalists go?
6. What young missionary couple was killed when the Communists took over China?

Chinese farmers working by hand

Modern China

Today the People's Republic of China (also called Red China, Communist China, or just China) is one of the most densely populated nations in the world. Over ⅕ of all the people of the world live in China.

The Chinese people are very industrious and have a great sense of family and country pride. They believe that it is very important to be respectful and polite, especially to elderly people. Since the people are hard workers, the country has prospered. However, because of the Communist system, very little of the wealth makes it to the individual who works long, hard hours for little pay.

Agriculture. Many of China's people live and work in rural areas. When the Communists took over China, they took the farms away from individual people and said that the land and the work of the people belonged to the state. However, the Communist system of governmental control does not work well for the prosperity of the nation. Chinese officials have more recently seen the problem, and some land has been given back to individuals, but the Communists still keep a very tight control. Today China is recognized as an economic giant. Manufacturing has increased to the point that China exports many products which previously could be purchased only from Europe or the United States.

ANIMALS AROUND THE WORLD

Giant Pandas in Forests of Bamboo

The **giant panda** is one of the world's rarest animals. Except for a few in zoos, all giant pandas live in the dense **bamboo** forests that grow among the mountains of western China. The pandas live in these forests because they love to eat bamboo, which makes up 99 percent of their diet. A giant panda spends about 16 hours a day eating. Over the course of a year, one giant panda can eat an incredible five tons of bamboo! It is hard to imagine that much bamboo, but it would be something like your eating 13,333 twelve-ounce steaks a year, or 37 steaks every day.

Chinese farming has changed very little from the methods used hundreds of years ago. Water buffalo are still used to pull simple farm machines, and most work is done by hand. **Rice,** the main crop raised, is usually eaten at every meal. Since rice must be grown in two to six inches of water, workers use flooded areas or flood the field purposely. Small ridges, or dikes, are made to hold back the water. The land is drained just before harvest time.

Cities. Although most people in China live in rural villages, China has some large, modern cities. China's capital city, **Beijing** [bā′jĭng′: formerly called Peking], is one of the largest cities in the world. It is well known for its palaces built by the many rulers of China. Other cities are *Shanghai* (a famous and busy seaport), *Tianjin* [tyän′jĭn′], *Guangzhou* [gwäng′jō′], *Chongqing* [chông′chĭng], and *Nanjing* [năn′jĭng′]. The thriving, prosperous colony of **Hong Kong** returned to Chinese rule in 1997.

Many Chinese who live in cities work in manufacturing, China's leading industry. Chinese products, including toys, clothing, and electronics, are sold in countries around the world.

Homes. Some farmers live in simple clay or thatched houses while others live in large dormitory buildings on collective farms. In the cities, many people live in modern apartments or small houses. On rivers and canals, people live in houseboats or on barges.

Art and architecture. The Chinese are known for their beautiful carvings of coral, jade, and teak (a type of wood). Chinese paintings are simple in design and well balanced. They often include mountains, trees or tree branches, flowers, and birds. Paintings are made on silk and on long bamboo or rice mats as well as on paper. The **pagoda** is a common sight in China. It is a building or tower with many stories. Each story has a small roof before the next one begins, and each story is slightly smaller than the one beneath it. Often the top is pointed.

a pagoda

Transportation. China has many rivers and canals that are used for travel. The 1,200-mile **Grand Canal,** which connects Hangzhou [häng′jō] and Beijing, is the longest man-made waterway in the world. People use barges and small boats called **junks** and **sampans** to get their goods to market from farming areas. Trains link the larger cities. The roads are poor, and though some people have cars or trucks, most travel by foot, bicycle, or oxcart.

Communication. Communication in China has improved in recent years, especially in the cities. China has a huge on-line population, and though one telephone used to serve an entire village, many Chinese now have cellular phones. However news is often still posted on a town bulletin board or broadcast from radio or television in the town square with loudspeakers. All the news the Chinese people hear is closely controlled by the Communists, who own all newspapers and all television and radio stations.

a junk

boats in the harbor of Hong Kong

Concepts to Consider

Freedom or Communism?

	Free countries	Communist countries
1	**People are free to worship God in the way they think is right.** This is the most important right guaranteed to Americans by the Constitution of the United States.	**The Communists say that there is no God.** Because Communists do not believe in God, they do not allow religious freedom.
2	**People have the right to free speech and press.** Newspapers, televisions, and radio stations in the United States are free to report the news as they see it and to make their own comments on it.	**Communists control all newspapers, televisions, and radios in the countries they rule.** People are told by the government how to think and what to read and listen to.
3	**Families have the right to privacy in their homes.** In the United States, "a man's home is his castle," and no one can legally interfere with the responsibility parents have to care for their family in the way they believe is best.	**Families have very little privacy.** The Communists can go into homes at any time to make sure families are not listening to a non-Communist radio broadcast, reading the Bible, or speaking against Communism.
4	**People have the right to own private property.** Americans are allowed to own land, houses, businesses, and many other things and to use these things as they see fit.	**According to Communist teaching, property should be held in common, and there should be no private property.** The Communist Party takes homes, farms, businesses, and factories away from the people and forces them to work for the government.
5	**People have the right to move about freely at home or abroad.** Americans have great freedom in traveling within the United States and among other countries.	**People must get permission from the Communist Party to move from one place to another,** and only rarely are they allowed to travel outside the country. The people are like prisoners in their own country.

6	Free countries	Communist countries
	People have the right to petition for grievances and expect fair and honest judgment. If an American thinks he has been wronged or that something in the government needs to be changed, he can present his case to judges and expect to have a fair hearing.	**The benefit of the State is more important than the fair treatment of individuals.** People enslaved by Communism live in fear that the state will treat them harshly, no matter how they behave.
7	**People have the right to trial by jury; a person is innocent until proven guilty.** In America, every caution is taken to make sure a person is not punished for a crime he did not commit. An American is not responsible to prove his innocence; his accusers are responsible to prove his guilt.	**People do not have the right to trial by jury.** A person accused by the State is assumed to be guilty unless he can prove he is innocent. Even if a person is innocent, he can be punished.
8	**People have the right to free elections using personal secret ballots.** Americans have the privilege and responsibility to vote for their leaders without being pressured to vote any certain way.	**The people may sometimes vote, but they can vote only for Communists.** Sometimes they have only one Communist for which to vote. The Communist Party bosses watch them as they vote and punish them if they do not vote the "right" way. In some Communist countries, elections are not held at all.

Continuing Communism

Communist oppression continues in China today. Personal property, family life, and religious beliefs are still under strict Communist control. In the spring of 1989, the world watched as a million Chinese people gathered at **Tiananmen Square** [tyän′än′mĕn′] in Beijing to protest Communism and demand democratic reforms that would allow the citizens to take a more active part in their

soldiers and tanks at Tiananmen Square in 1989

country's government. Would China allow its people some of the freedoms they desired? The Communist government responded by sending tanks and soldiers to Tiananmen Square and killing at least 5,000 Chinese people and imprisoning many others.

Despite the evidence of continuing oppression and abuse of the Chinese people by the Communist government, many nations including the United States continue to favor the People's Republic of China over other countries in matters of trade, technology, etc.

Comprehension Check 6D

1. What is the capital of China?
2. What is a pagoda?
3. What are junks and sampans?
4. The lack of what freedom makes people in Communist countries like prisoners without a jail?
5. What American right helps prevent innocent people from being punished for crimes they did not commit?
6. What happened in Tiananmen Square in 1989?

6.2 The Chinese Sphere

The Far East can be subdivided into three main regions: the Chinese Sphere, Northeast Asia, and Southeast Asia. The Chinese Sphere centers on Communist China and includes Mongolia and the free republic of Taiwan.

Taiwan: The Free Republic of China

The small island of **Taiwan** became a place of refuge for **over one and a half million Chinese people** who fled from mainland China when the Communists took over. Taiwan, which is called the Republic of Nationalist China, has a republican form of government. Its capital is **Taipei.** For many years, the world recognized Taiwan as true China, but since 1970 many countries have begun favoring Communist China and cutting relations with Taiwan. Taiwan has few natural resources and little land for farming. Because they are free to get what they work for, however, the Taiwanese have made great use of the few resources they have. Through free-

Taipei, Taiwan

dom and hard work, the people of this tiny country have developed their land much more than the Communists have developed mainland China.

Mongolia

Mongolia is named for the **Mongols,** a group of nomadic tribes who for centuries wandered northeastern Asia on horseback in search of food for their livestock. They carried their homes—round tents called *gers* or *yurts*—with them. When **Genghis Khan** united the fierce Mongol tribes in the early 1200s, they began conquering many lands. At its height, the **Mongol Empire,** with its capital in China, reached all the way to Europe, making it the largest empire in history. It was during the rule of the Mongol Empire that Marco Polo journeyed to China and revived European interest in the East.

Genghis Khan

yurt

Gobi Desert. Do you think of a desert as being a very hot, dry place? Most deserts are, but some deserts are very cold. The **Gobi** [gō′bē], one of the coldest deserts in the world, lies mostly in Mongolia but extends down into northern China. This vast, sandy, treeless desert, twice as large as the state of Texas, is the world's northernmost desert.

Modern times. Today, many Mongolians continue to live as nomads, tending sheep, goats, cattle, horses, and camels. They depend on their herds for meat and milk, the staple foods, as well as for wool and skins, with which they make boots, clothing, and tents. Yurts are still common sights both in towns and across the countryside.

Gobi Desert

6.3 Northeast Asia

Northeast Asia consists of the Korean peninsula, which is divided into the countries of North Korea and South Korea, and the island nation of Japan.

Korea

The Korean peninsula is located on the northeastern coast of China. The countries of North and South Korea provide a contrast between Communism and free enterprise similar to that of China and Taiwan.

Two Koreas. For centuries, Japan and China fought over the Korean peninsula, each in turn dominating Korea until the end of World War II, when Allied forces liberated Korea from Japanese occupation. In **North Korea,** the Soviet Union set up a Communist government with a capital at P'yongyang [pyŭng′yäng]. In **South Korea,** the United States helped the people establish a free republic with a capital at **Seoul.**

Seoul, South Korea

The people of North Korea were mostly farmers until the Russian Communists took over. They lived in small towns, and families usually lived together in one house. The Communists took away the people's land and took control of their businesses. Today many North Koreans find jobs in the capital or in factories in other large cities. But because the North Korean people have no real freedoms or goals to work toward, they are becoming less prosperous than their South Korean neighbors.

South Koreans have made great advances in industry, standards of living, and government since 1948, even though they have few natural resources. Many South Koreans still live in one-story stone houses and grow rice, their main food. Others, though, have moved into the cities to work at industrial jobs.

The Korean War. As soon as the U.S. troops were withdrawn from South Korea in 1950, North Korea invaded, resulting in the Korean War. Many brave soldiers, especially from the United States, fought to keep South Korea free. In 1953, a truce was signed that allowed South Korea to remain free. This was considered a victory for all the nations of the world that desire to be free from Communism.

Since the war, South Korea has kept a large army to defend herself against Communist aggression from the north. North Korea remains one of the most aggressive and oppressive Communist governments in the world.

Japan: "Land of the Rising Sun"

Japan is an island nation located in the North Pacific Ocean just east of China and Korea. It is made up of four main islands and many smaller ones. In Japanese, the country is called *Nippon,* or the "Land of the Rising Sun."

A closed country. Emperors ruled Japan for about 1,300 years. For centuries, the Japanese were taught that their emperor was a god and that the Japanese were better than any other people. The Japanese killed any outsiders who landed on their islands, including missionaries who tried to take the gospel to the Japanese.

Commodore Perry opens Japan. In 1854, the United States sent a fleet of battleships to Japan under the command of **Commodore Matthew Perry** of the U.S. Navy. He was ordered to open Japan for trade with the nations of the world. The commodore's mission was successful, but while he was in Japan, he saw that there was a great need for the gospel. He himself read the Bible to a large group of Japanese people and taught them a Christian hymn.

When Townsend Harris, a devout Christian, became the first United States ambassador to Japan, he appealed to American Christians to go to Japan as missionaries. Since then, some Japanese people have been saved, but many more still continue to worship their false gods.

Military aggression. At the end of the 1800s and the beginning of the 1900s, Japan became known for its aggression against other nations. It fought successfully against China and Russia, and it made Korea one of its territories. It was a fierce fighter during World War I.

World War II. Before and during World War II, **Hirohito** [hĭr′ ō·hē′tō] was the emperor of Japan, but the army and navy were so strong that the military leaders, especially a general named **Tojo,** became more powerful than the emperor. The plan of Japan's military leaders was to conquer and rule all of Asia and the islands of the Pacific. Japan

Hirohito

Commodore Perry opened Japan for world trade.

bombing of Pearl Harbor

joined with Germany and Italy in World War II in order to reach this goal.

On December 7, 1941, Japan attacked **Pearl Harbor,** an important U.S. military base in Hawaii, and killed over two thousand American men. This surprise attack brought the United States into the war. Japan continued to fight fiercely against the Allies, even after Italy and Germany surrendered. More and more people, including Japanese people, were being killed by Japanese aggression. Finally, in August of 1945, the United States put an end to the terrible war by dropping the world's first atomic bombs on the Japanese cities of **Hiroshima** [hĭr′ə•shē′mə] and **Nagasaki** [nä′gə•sä′kē]. The Japanese surrendered, and for the first time in Japanese history the emperor admitted that he was not a god and the Japanese people were just the same as all other people in the world. The U.S. general, Douglas MacArthur, sent out another plea for Americans to send missionaries to Japan. Many American missionaries answered this call, and a number of Japanese people became Christians.

New ways. After the war, Japan was much more open to Western ways, and the Japanese people were more open to the gospel than ever before. The Japanese were eager to accept any new ideas that would improve their country, and they benefited greatly from the efforts of the Allied troops who were stationed there to help rebuild Japan. The Japanese put their own skillfulness to work to use outside help to better their country.

THAT'S AMAZING!

The Bullet Train

Japan is home to a great deal of modern technology, including the **bullet train.** In the 1970s, Japan began building a high-speed electric train between Tokyo and Osaka, a city to the southwest. The train would move working people to and from their jobs in the big cities. The train resembles the shape of a bullet and travels at speeds of 130 mph and faster. Today, more than 17,000 miles of railroad tracks connect many cities on all four islands of Japan. Perhaps the most unique feature of the Japanese rail system is "pushers," guards hired to push people into the trains until they are crammed into every available inch of space. There are often so many people on the trains that passengers do not have room to raise their arms to hold on to the safety straps.

bullet trains

Modern Japan. Japanese industries—especially steel making, shipbuilding, car manufacturing, and computer technology—have increased greatly since World War II, making Japan one of the most highly industrialized nations in the world. The Japanese are able to produce cameras, televisions, radios, computers, and automobiles cheaply because of the many people available to do factory work and their skillful use of electronics and mechanical "robots" to speed up the process.

Tokyo [tō′kē·ō′], Japan's capital, is the world's largest city (in population). Japan's government is democratic and is very similar to the governments of the United States and England. The country's most famous landmark is the beautiful cone-shaped volcanic mountain, **Fujiyama** [fo͞o′jē·yä′mə] or **Mt. Fuji,** that is still considered sacred by many Japanese.

Japanese who live away from the cities still observe many old customs. They sit on the floor to eat at a low table, and they take off their shoes before they enter a house. At night they sleep on straw mats that can be rolled up and put away. Some Japanese women wear beautiful **kimonos** (long robes) even today. Japanese who have jobs in the cities live and dress very much like Americans.

Mt. Fuji

About 85 percent of Japan's land is mountainous. Since farmers have very little land for growing food, they have learned to use every available foot of land for crops. One method of farming, called **terracing,** plants crops on mountainsides by cutting the slope into a series of steps. The forests that grow on the mountains are also harvested for lumber. Even though Japan is one of the most crowded nations on earth, her people are able to live fairly well because of their industry and inventiveness.

colorful Japanese kimono

Comprehension Check 6E

1. Genghis Khan was ruler of the __?__ Empire, the largest empire in the world.
2. Which desert, located mostly in Mongolia, is one of the coldest and is the northernmost desert in the world?
3. After World War II, who controlled North Korea? South Korea?
4. Who opened Japan for foreign trade?
5. What caused America to enter World War II?
6. What brought the end of World War II and Japanese fighting?
7. What is Japan's most famous landmark?

6.4 Southeast Asia

The region in eastern Asia that is south of China is known as Southeast Asia. It includes the mainland countries of *Myanmar* [myän·mär′: formerly Burma], *Thailand* [tī′lănd], *Laos* [lous], *Cambodia* [kăm·bō′dē·ə], and *Vietnam,* as well as the island countries of *Malaysia* [mə·lā′zhə], *Singapore* [sĭng′gə·pôr], *Brunei* [bro͞o·nī′], *Indonesia* [ĭn′də·nē′zhə], and the *Philippines.*

Vietnam, Cambodia, and Laos

Before World War II, the countries of Vietnam, Laos, and Cambodia were known as French Indochina. After the war, the nations of Europe were forced to give up their colonies, but many of those colonies were not ready for independence. When the French pulled out of Indochina, the young nations they left behind quickly fell prey to Communist aggression.

Like Korea, Vietnam was divided to create a Communist dictatorship in the north and a free republic in the South. Cambodia and Laos, on the other hand, became constitutional monarchies.

Communist attacks. Communist aggression began almost immediately in South Vietnam, leading to the long **Vietnam War.** In 1955, the free nations of Southeast Asia asked the United States to help them combat the Communist threat to their countries. The South Vietnam-

People in History

Adoniram Judson

One of the first foreign missionaries sent out by the United States was **Adoniram Judson** (1788–1850). In 1812, he and his wife Anne, having been denied entrance to India, went to Burma (modern-day Myanmar), a nation in Southeast Asia. Within the first 14 years, Judson was put in prison and tortured several times; he came close to death, and his wife and all of their children died. But God was faithful to him, giving him grace to translate the Bible into the Burmese language. Some have estimated that in addition to his translation work, he led 7,000 people to Christ. He is remembered as the "Father of American Missions."

ese president requested American troops to protect his country from invasion. In 1957, President Eisenhower sent military trainers to help the South Vietnamese army. When both the Soviet Union and Communist China began to help the Communist invaders in the early 1960s, President Kennedy began to send American soldiers to help free the Vietnamese. Eventually, under President Johnson, almost 500,000 Americans were sent to defend freedom in South Vietnam.

Freedom betrayed. A land invasion of North Vietnam was the only way to defeat Communism and preserve the freedom of Southeast Asia. However, some liberal Americans convinced a number of government leaders that the war in Vietnam was unwinnable and that the Communists should be allowed to conquer South Vietnam. Communist China made it known that it would buy goods from the United States if American troops would leave South Vietnam and the United States would cut its relations with Taiwan. At the same time, Congress became convinced that better relations with the Soviet Union would result if we left Vietnam. When Richard Nixon became President in 1968, he began to withdraw American troops from South Vietnam. Soon Congress recognized the Communist government of mainland China and favored it over the Nationalist Chinese government on Taiwan.

South Vietnam falls to Communism. Without American support, the little nation of South Vietnam was soon overrun by the Communists, who were supported by arms from Communist China and the Soviet Union. Not long after, the Communists extended their control to Cambodia and Laos, and began a reign of terror. Millions were murdered, and more than a million Vietnamese fled their country on makeshift rafts and barges. Many of these "boat people" perished at sea, but some found refuge in the United States and Canada. Those left behind lost all freedoms and became the slaves of inefficient state farms and factories. Today, Americans of Vietnamese ancestry are noted for their patriotism and hard work. The United States has worked to establish a normal relationship with Vietnam. President Bill Clinton visited Vietnam in November of 2000 to promote business ties with the Hanoi government.

prosperous Singapore

Thailand

Thailand (formerly Siam) is called by its people "Land of the Free." It is the only Southeast Asian country that has never been under the rule of a European country. The Thai people are very patriotic and are working hard to keep their land free from Communist rule. They are not free in the most important way, however, because most Thais are worshipers of Buddha and spirits. **Bangkok** is the capital city.

Southeast Asian Islands

Malaysia occupies part of the Malay Peninsula as well as part of **Borneo,** the third-largest island in the world. **Singapore,** whose capital is also **Singapore,** is one of the most prosperous countries in the world. It is located on a small group of islands at the tip of the peninsula. **Brunei** [brōō·nī′], rich in oil and natural gas, is a small country on the northern coast of Borneo.

The largest country in Southeast Asia, **Indonesia,** is made up of many islands. Once known to westerners as the "Spice Islands" or "East Indies," Indonesia is one of only two Asian countries that extends south of the equator. (The small island nation of Maldives [môl′dīvz] in Southern Asia is the other.)

The **Philippines,** with their capital at **Manila,** were given to the United States by Spain in 1898. The United States helped these islands to develop schools and a stable government and then gave them their independence in 1946.

Wonders of World Geography

The World's Eight Largest Islands

Island	*Location*	*Island*	*Location*
1. **Greenland**	Atlantic Ocean	5. **Baffin Island**	Arctic Ocean
2. **New Guinea**	Pacific Ocean	6. **Sumatra**	Indian Ocean
3. **Borneo**	Pacific Ocean	7. **Honshu, Japan**	Pacific Ocean
4. **Madagascar**	Indian Ocean	8. **Great Britain**	Atlantic Ocean

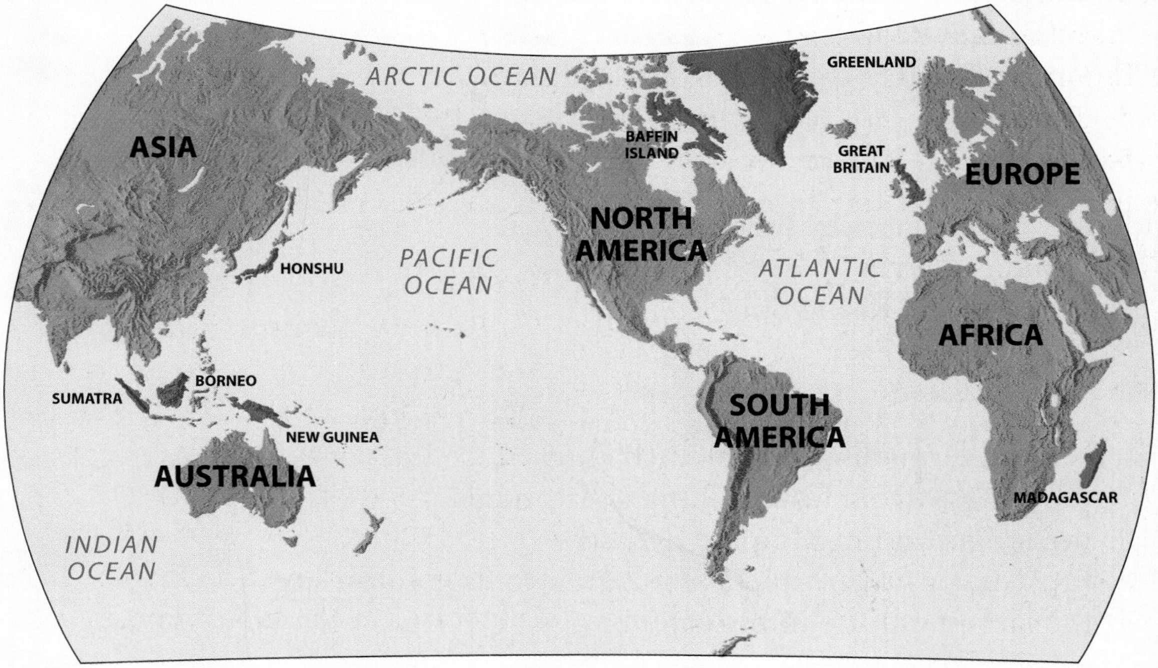

CHAPTER 6 CHECKUP

A Know the countries and capitals of the Far East and their locations. (See Continent Study 1, p. 322.)

B List **six** Chinese inventions or discoveries.

C Who am I?

1. a well-known Chinese philosopher and teacher
2. China's first emperor
3. Italian trader who traveled to China and back
4. the "Father of Faith Missions"
5. missionary martyrs in Communist China
6. leader of China's first republic
7. leader of the Communist Chinese
8. leader of the Chinese Nationalists
9. ruler who united the Mongol tribes
10. opened Japan to foreign trade
11. emperor of Japan during World War II
12. powerful Japanese general during World War II
13. the "Father of American Missions"

D Tell what each place is most famous for.

1. Great Wall of China
2. Great Silk Road
3. Grand Canal
4. Taiwan
5. Tiananmen Square
6. Gobi Desert
7. Pearl Harbor
8. Hiroshima
9. Fujiyama

E Identify these places by their nicknames.

1. "China's Sorrow"
2. "Land of the Rising Sun"
3. "Land of the Free"
4. "Spice Islands"

F Identify the term described by each clue.

1. the dynasty from which China got its name
2. the longest ruling Chinese dynasty
3. the dynasty under which China grew to its greatest size
4. the largest empire in history

5. the world's largest island; second largest; third largest
6. the world's most northern desert
7. the world's largest city
8. the main food crop of China
9. the half of Korea that remained Communist

G Define each term.

1. pagoda
2. junk
3. sampan
4. bullet train
5. kimono

H Answer each question.

1. What is the most important right guaranteed to Americans? Why?
2. Why is the right to free speech and press important?

UNIT 2

AFRICA
CONTINENT OF NATURAL WONDERS

EGYPT
The Gift of the Nile

7.1 Geography of Egypt

Location

Egypt is located in the northeastern corner of the African continent. Almost all of Egypt is in the great **Sahara Desert,** the largest desert in the world. North of Egypt is the Mediterranean Sea. East of Egypt is the **Red Sea.** Between the two fingers of the Red Sea is the **Sinai Peninsula.**

Africa

- Africa is home to some world-record animals. The cheetah is the fastest land animal over short distances. It can run 70 miles per hour for a few hundred yards. The giraffe is the tallest animal, standing at 18 feet. Its legs may be six feet long, and its neck even longer. The elephant is the heaviest animal, weighing up to 12 tons.
- Mt. Kilimanjaro, in Tanzania, is not part of a mountain range. It is an extinct volcano. Even though it is near the equator, it always has snow on top.
- So much water cascades over the Victoria Falls, creating loud noise and heavy mist, that natives of Africa refer to the Falls as "the smoke that thunders."
- The Horn of Africa, a large peninsula that resembles the horn of a rhinoceros, juts eastward from the continent into the Arabian Sea. In the west is a region known as Africa's "hump." Can you find Africa's Horn and "hump"?

The Sinai Peninsula

Land bridge. The Sinai Peninsula is located on the western edge of the continent of Asia where it meets with the continent of Africa. On one side of the Sinai Peninsula is the country of **Israel** (Canaan). On the other side is **Egypt.** You can see why some people refer to this piece of land as a **land bridge.** Many ancient traders crossed the Sinai Peninsula on their way from one of these countries to the other. Included among these travelers were Abraham's great grandson Joseph, and later Joseph's father, Jacob, and Jacob's family. Find the Sinai Peninsula on the map (p. 106). Trace the route that Jacob and his family must have followed from Canaan to Egypt.

Euphrates R.
Mediterranean Sea
Sea of Galilee
CANAAN
Jordan R.
Dead Sea
ASIA
[Rosetta]
Nile Delta
LOWER EGYPT
Heliopolis
[Cairo]
Giza
Memphis
SINAI
PENINSULA
Nile R.
Mt. Sinai
EGYPT
ARABIAN
PENINSULA
UPPER EGYPT
Valley of the Kings
Thebes
SAHARA DESERT
Red Sea
First Cataract
AFRICA
Nile R.
Second Cataract
KEY
fertile land
Cities in brackets are modern, not ancient.
Third Cataract

Rugged wilderness. The Sinai Peninsula is about 140 miles long. The land itself is very rugged and is considered a wilderness. The northern part of the peninsula is desert. The southern part is a very rugged mass of mountains, on which nothing grows. In the mountainous area, there were copper and turquoise mines in which some ancient Egyptians worked. Few people have ever lived in this area, however, for there is very little water. Nomads are usually the only ones who live in this region. They camp where they can find grazing land for their animals and water to drink. When the grass or water is gone, the nomads move to another area.

rugged wilderness of the Sinai Peninsula

The Nile River

Egypt has been called the **"Gift of the Nile."** Without the **Nile River,** the longest river in the world, all of Egypt would be a desert. The Nile is one of the few rivers in the world that flow from south to north. It flows over 4,000 miles from its source high in the mountains of central Africa, near the equator, to its mouth in the Mediterranean Sea.

At its mouth, the Nile forms a **delta,** a piece of land that has slowly built up over the years by the deposit of loose sand and soil at the mouth of a river. A delta gets its name from its fan shape, which looks something like the fourth letter in the Greek alphabet, *delta* (Δ). A river delta keeps growing in size because new soil is continuously deposited there. The many little branches of the Nile that form at the delta empty their waters into the Mediterranean Sea.

Even though most of Egypt is a desert, the land along both sides of the Nile is rich, fertile farmland. The Nile carries dark, rich soil with it as it flows

Nile River

from the mountains of Africa into Egypt. Almost every year until recent times the Nile flooded its banks as the snow on the mountains at its source melted. It deposited the rich soil along the Nile Valley of Egypt.

The width of the Nile Valley varies from two to thirty miles. Where the black, fertile land stops, desert begins. The change is so sudden that you can stand with one foot on black, fertile farmland and the other foot on dry, sandy desert. For this reason, ancient Egyptians called their land **"Red Land, Black Land."** Compared to the thousands of miles of desert located on either side, the black land looks like a thread.

Of course, the black land is greatly prized. All of it is needed to grow crops. For this reason, and also to avoid being carried away by the flooding of the Nile, the Egyptians built their homes on the red land or desert, not very far away from the black land.

How the Desert and the River Protected Egypt

Hot sands and cataracts. The hot, dry red land supplied the people of ancient Egypt with the gift of protection. Few

SPOTLIGHT ON HISTORY

The Three Egyptian Seasons

The seasons in ancient Egypt were dependent upon the cycle of the Nile. The Egyptians carried on a particular kind of work during each season.

1. Flood Season (June–September)

To make sure that what they were building was straight and level, ancient Egyptians used an instrument called a square and plumb line. This square and plumb line was found in the tomb of an Egyptian ruler.

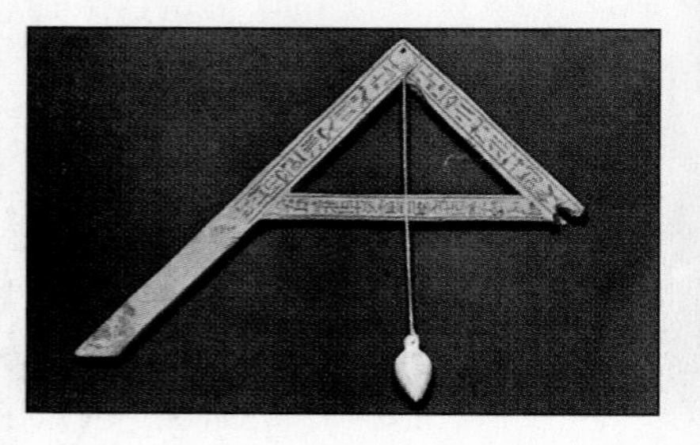

2. Planting Season (October–February)

This painting from an Egyptian tomb shows irrigation canals and agriculture along the Nile. How did the ancient Egyptians plant seeds and plow soil?

3. Harvest Season (March–May)

After the gathering of grapes from the vines, the Egyptians pressed them with their feet to make grape juice.

enemies would dare risk their lives crossing the burning desert sands to approach the fertile region along the Nile. The only other way enemies could approach Egypt was by sailing on the Nile itself. Another natural barrier—cataracts—prevented that. A **cataract** is a large bed of rocks piled in the river that produces small waterfalls. There are six cataracts along the Nile. The longest cataract is 124 miles long with the water falling over 200 feet. You can see why ships could not travel over the cataracts. The only way enemies could attack was from the north by the Mediterranean Sea. Fortunately, this area could easily be protected by forts.

Years of famine. Every year the ancient Egyptians depended upon the flooding of the Nile. And every year with few exceptions, the flooding occurred. But there were years when the Nile was a few feet lower than normal during a flood. Such years were times of **famine,** a period of serious shortage of food, because there was less good, black land on which to plant crops. Occasionally, there were years when the Nile rose higher than normal. This, too, meant destruction because entire villages were covered by flood waters.

Three Seasons

The annual flooding of the Nile was so important to the life of the Egyptians that they based their seasons on it rather than on the position of the sun in the sky. (A season is a part of a year in which the weather conditions are somewhat alike.)

From June through September was the **flood season.** During this time, no work could be done with crops. Men spent their time working on buildings.

During the **planting season,** from October through February, the water slowly left the fields. Men worked on irrigation projects to hold back as much extra water as possible. As the water left the fields, they planted crops.

During the **harvest season,** from March through May, there was no extra water, and the Egyptians harvested their crops. The Nile was so helpful to the Egyptians and so much a part of their daily lives that they worshiped it as if it were a god.

7.2 Egypt's Beginnings

Early River Civilizations

Egypt was one of the four earliest civilizations. Earth's earliest civilizations were all built near life-sustaining rivers, and thus they have been called

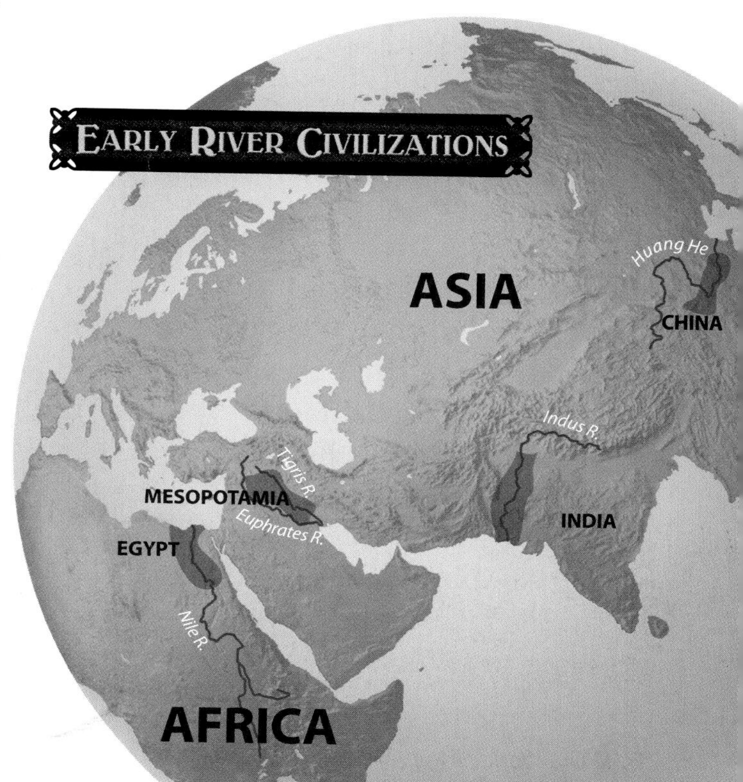

River Civilizations. The oldest was Mesopotamia, in the Tigris-Euphrates Valley. Then came Egypt, along the Nile Valley. Later, very impressive civilizations were built along the Indus River in India and the Huang He in China. People may have lived in most of these areas before the Flood. After the Flood, family groups again migrated (moved) to Egypt, India, and China from Mesopotamia.

Upper Egypt and Lower Egypt

Egypt was a major world power for more than a thousand years. It was settled by Ham's son **Mizraim** [mĭz′rā·ĭm] soon after the Flood, and it quickly developed into a very impressive empire.

Ancient Egypt was divided into two areas known as Upper Egypt and Lower Egypt. **Upper Egypt** was really southern Egypt. It was where the fertile Nile River Valley is located. It began at the Nile's first cataract and ended near the delta. It was called "Upper Egypt" because it was **upstream,** away from the mouth of the Nile. Because the hot, dry climate allows no dampness or moisture to begin decay, archaeologists have found in Upper Egypt the best preserved ancient Egyptian artifacts.

Lower Egypt was the delta area. This area was also known as "Red Land." In ancient days, the area around the delta was very swampy with salty lakes.

At first Upper and Lower Egypt were two separate kingdoms, each ruled by a different king. The king of Upper Egypt wore a **white crown.** The king of Lower Egypt wore a **red crown.** Each kingdom even had its own gods and goddesses.

There were frequent wars between these two kingdoms until the king from Upper Egypt conquered the king from Lower Egypt. Many people think that the king's name was **Menes** [mē′nēz]. From then on, he called himself **"King of Upper and Lower Egypt,"** for even though the two areas became united into one, the Egyptians still called it "Two Lands." Then the king wore a double crown that looked like the white crown and red crown put together. This king ordered the city of **Memphis** to be built. Memphis was the capital of ancient Egypt for a thousand years. Then the capital was moved to **Thebes** [thēbz].

Comprehension Check 7A

1. What is unique about the Sahara?
2. Why is the Sinai Peninsula sometimes referred to as a land bridge?
3. What is the longest river in the world?
4. Why is Egypt called the "Gift of the Nile"?
5. Upon what did the Egyptians base their seasons?
6. Who was considered to be the "King of Upper and Lower Egypt"?

7.3 Dynasties

Menes began the first dynasty in Egypt. All the kings that were related to Menes were in the first dynasty. The second dynasty began when a king who was not related to Menes took the crown. Altogether there may have been thirty dynasties in Egypt over a period of nearly two thousand years.

The Ruler of Egypt

For many years, the rulers of Egypt were called "kings." Later, the king assumed the title **pharaoh**, which means "great house." The Egyptians were taught to believe that their ruler's body was a temple or "great house" where a god lived. The first to take the title of pharaoh was **Akhenaton** [ä′kə•nät′n].

Akhenaton, first pharaoh of Egypt

The Government

The vizier. Next in importance to the king was the **vizier** [vĭz′yər]. The vizier was in charge of everything! He was called "Overseer of All Works of the King." He was considered a companion to the king. He was the overseer of the fields, the farmers, the farmers' animals, and the granaries. He supervised all business that had to do with the Nile River, including the building of canals for supplying water.

The vizier was in charge of collecting taxes throughout the land. He controlled the army and the navy. He inspected the crafts that were made for the king. He was in charge of all major construction work. The vizier was also considered the mayor and the chief of police of the city in which he lived. In all, he had at least thirty different jobs.

Any man who proved to be a wise, capable, hard worker could become a vizier. **Joseph,** a Hebrew who had been sent to Egypt to be a slave, became a vizier of Egypt. Joseph was first a slave and then a prisoner in Egypt. He worshiped the one true God instead of Egypt's many false gods. Joseph impressed the pharaoh with his ability to interpret dreams and with his humbleness in giving God the credit. Then Joseph increased in favor by giving the pharaoh a plan that would save Egypt from seven years of famine. Joseph went from the lowest position as a slave to the highest position as the pharaoh's vizier.

Joseph, a vizier in Egypt

7.4 ✠ The Building Projects of the Pharaohs

Irrigation and Flood Control

Irrigation and flood control projects were necessary for life in Egypt. Walled irrigation ditches or canals were built through Egyptian fields. Water from the Nile was placed in these ditches by men who worked a device called a **shadoof** [shä·do͞of′]. This was simply <u>a long pole with a bucket tied on one end to dip water from the Nile</u>. A weight was fastened to the opposite end. The pole was placed on a crossbeam. After the man filled the bucket with water, he eased his grip on the rope. The weight on the other end helped to lift the bucket, which was then emptied into the walled irrigation ditch. This helped to irrigate the dry land along the river so that better crops might grow. Basins were built in the fields to hold extra floodwater even after the flood was gone.

To help control big floods from the Nile, workers built mud walls for the protection of the villages.

a shadoof

Building "Homes" for Eternal Life

mummy

The Egyptians believed in a life after death. They believed that for life after death they would need not only their bodies but also physical materials such as food, clothing, and articles they used in everyday life. A dead king's body was **mummified** (preserved with chemicals). These **mummies** were placed inside large and costly tombs.

Pyramids. The tombs for the pharaohs got bigger and bigger as time passed. Finally, the Egyptians were building huge structures called **pyramids** for the burial of their rulers. Thirty-five pyramids still stand in Egypt today. Huge stone blocks were used to build the pyramids. Many blocks weighed over two tons each! Some blocks weighed as much as fifteen tons each. These pyramids were so amazing that the Greeks listed them among the Seven Wonders of the Ancient World. They are the only structures given that honor that remain standing today.

The <u>most famous and largest of the pyramids still standing today</u> is the **Great Pyramid,** which is located near the modern city of **Cairo** [kī′rō]. It was built for **King Khufu** [ko͞o′fo͞o]. The base or floor of the Great Pyramid is as large as ten football fields. Although some of the upper stones are gone, at one time this pyramid was *over four hundred eighty feet tall* and contained *over two million stone blocks,* each weighing *two and a half tons.*

The ancient Egyptians had no machinery or iron tools with which to cut the blocks and no wheels to help move the gigantic stones. No one knows for sure how they accomplished their great building task, but we can be sure that they were very intelligent and inventive people to figure out a way to break the stones and move them. Most of the stone for the pyramids came from a site nearly six hundred miles away. Some think that the Egyptians chipped slots into the solid rock walls and then forced wet wooden wedges into the slots. Wood always swells when it is wet. As the wet wood expanded in the rock, large pieces of rock would split away from the stone wall. Groups of men then hammered these large pieces of stone into rough blocks. Once this was done, other workers probably tipped the blocks over onto log rollers and sledges. Teams of workers then dragged the stone blocks on these rollers or sledges to the Nile River. Here they were placed upon barges and floated closer to the site where the pyramid would be built.

The Egyptians devised a means of making sure the ground where they would build the huge pyramid was level. Then they hauled the blocks in and set them tightly together. As work on the pyramids continued, ramps were built on which the blocks could be pulled up on sledges.

Temples. After many of the pyramids were built, the Egyptians began building temples. Probably the most beautiful and famous temple belonged to **Queen Hatshepsut** [hat·shĕp′sōōt′]. She was ancient Egypt's only woman pharaoh. Her temple was built to blend with the cliffs behind it. The pharaohs had their accomplishments written on the walls of their temples. These writings have become valuable to us because they tell some of the history of Egypt.

The Great Sphinx

The hot, dry Egyptian sand drifts easily with each breeze that blows. Many ancient secrets probably still lie unnoticed beneath the sands. The sand did its best to cover one of the most famous monuments in the ancient world. This monument is the **Great Sphinx** [sfĭngks] that stands near the Great Pyramid. It probably would have been lost in the sand if people had not worked from time to time to keep the sand away from its base.

The Sphinx has the head of a man and the body, legs, and paws of a lion. Its head and body are carved of solid rock, and its legs and paws are built of stone blocks. It is 240 feet long and 66 feet high. The Great Sphinx is a mystery. No one knows the history behind it.

Obelisks. The ancient Egyptians worshiped the sun, which they believed was the maker of all their gods. They called their sun god **Ra** [rä]. They built monuments to honor and represent their sun god. These monuments were tall, pointed pillars called **obelisks** [ŏb′ə·lĭsks]. There was even an Egyptian city that was the center of sun worship, the city of **Heliopolis** [hē′lē·ŏp′ə·lĭs].

an obelisk

Valley of the Kings

In a very rocky valley on the west bank of the Nile River near the city of Thebes lies the **Valley of the Kings.** The pharaohs who ruled between 1500 B.C. and 1100 B.C. used this valley as a cemetery. They had elaborate tombs cut into the rocks. Like the pyramids, each tomb had several rooms. One room was for the dead pharaoh's body, and the other rooms were used to store food, furniture, jewelry, and other treasures the pharaoh hoped to enjoy in his life after death.

Over 60 tombs have been found in this valley. The most famous of these was not found until 1922. Perhaps

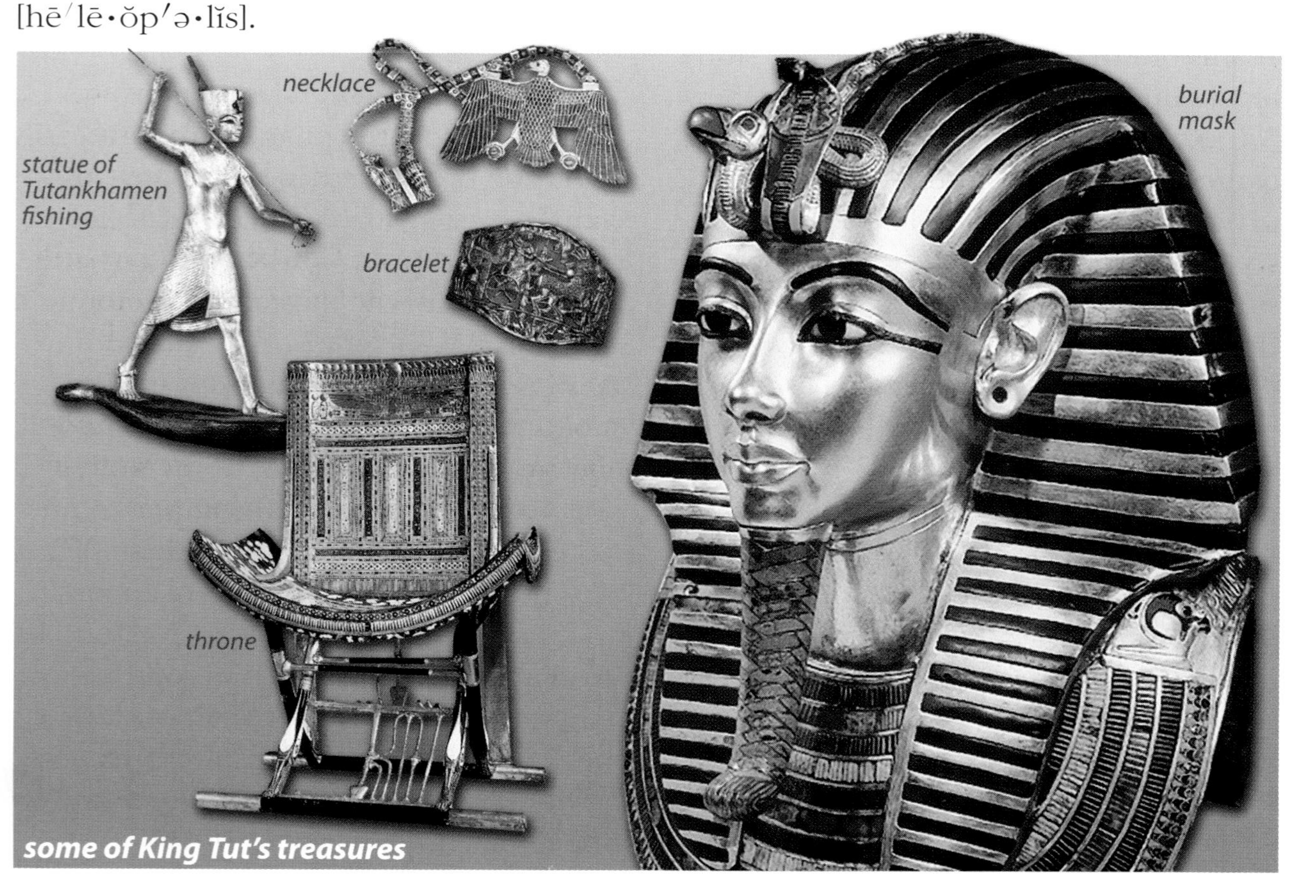

some of King Tut's treasures

you have heard someone refer to **"King Tut."** This is just a short and easy way of saying **King Tutankhamen** [tōōt′äng·kä′mən]. Very little is known about King Tutankhamen. His tomb is more famous than he is. Men who have studied him estimate that he became king when he was 10 years old, that he married a 12-year-old girl, and that he died around the age of 18. He was pharaoh around 1350 B.C. Because he became king at such an early age, King Tut's vizier was more powerful than he was.

Because the pharaohs' tombs were filled with golden treasures, hardly a tomb was left untouched by thieves. Yet King Tut's tomb was hardly touched. It was buried in the drifting Egyptian sands and forgotten. Men found out about King Tut, but they could not find any clues to the location of his tomb. The British archaeologist Howard Carter dug six years in the Valley of the Kings until at last he found the door of the tomb. Inside were four rooms, filled with over 2,000 objects. Among these objects were statues, golden treasures, a chest filled with jewels, chariots, chests of linen, ivory game boards, the king's throne, weapons to protect him, and even a toy box and a paint set that had evidently been his as a child. The treasures of pharaohs such as King Tut help to explain what life must have been like for those who came from ancient royal families.

Comprehension Check 7B

1. What title did Egyptian kings give themselves?
2. Who was next in importance to the king?
3. What were the huge stone structures built as tombs for burying pharaohs called?
4. What is the most famous and largest of these tombs still standing today?
5. What does the Great Sphinx look like?
6. What interesting pharaoh was buried in the Valley of the Kings?

7.5 Everyday Life in Ancient Egypt

The People

Work. Most ancient Egyptians were farmers. Because the farmland was so fertile and the climate so warm, two to three crops could be raised each year. Wheat and barley were the main grains, and flax was grown to make into linen cloth. The farmers also raised peas, beans, cucumbers, cabbage, lettuce, radishes, fruits, and melons. Some Egyptian workers raised cattle, donkeys, geese, ducks, goats, and sheep. Oxen were used to pull their plows. (Horses were not brought into Egypt until later.)

Although the farmers worked hard, they did not own the land on which they lived and worked. The farmers had to give most of their crops to the wealthy men who owned the land.

Clothing. The ancient Egyptians usually wore white linen clothing. The clothing differed according to occupation. Men usually wore a knee-length kilt that wrapped around the waist and fastened in the front. As time passed, the wealthy men chose to wear a robe over the kilt. For comfort while they toiled under the hot sun, the farmer and the average worker wore only kilts. The priests wore animal skins.

The Egyptian women wore ankle-length, straight dresses. As time passed they wore colorful cloaks over their dresses. They colored their lips red, painted their fingernails yellow or orange, and outlined their eyes with green paint. Most women had long hair. The very wealthy wore long, heavy, black wigs.

Most Egyptians wore only white, probably because this color reflects the sun making white the most comfortable color to wear in a hot, dry climate. But many used jewelry to add color to their white outfits. The wealthy people wore fine jewelry crafted in gold. Most people wore jewelry made out of a paste into which ground quartz was mixed. The paste was then molded into different shapes and glazed with different colors.

Collars made of wide rows of beads were popular, as were necklaces, bracelets, earrings, anklets, and rings. Precious stones such as diamonds were unknown in Egypt.

The children dressed quite similarly to their parents, although their hairstyles were quite different. The girls usually wore their hair in two braids. The young boys had all their hair shaved except for one long braid on the side. In Egyptian literature, this is spoken of as the "sidelock of youth." When the boy became a certain age, the sidelock of youth was shaved off, for men kept their heads shaved.

Children at play. The ancient Egyptian children enjoyed many of the same kinds of toys that small children play with today. Some play materials do not change for children of any time in history, such as sticks, puddles, and mud! There were real toys, too. The boys enjoyed playing with tops, toy weapons, and mechanical toys that worked by pulling a string. (There were no batteries, of course.) Ancient Egyptian girls played with paddle dolls. The doll was painted on a piece of wood that looked something like a paddle. For hair, the paddle doll had strings of small clay beads. Just as children today, the Egyptian children liked to play in the water and swim. They also enjoyed foot races and ball games.

Ancient Egyptians wore white to reflect the sun's heat.

Where there are children, there are often pets to play with. The **cat** was considered sacred and worshiped by the Egyptians, and you can be sure pet cats were well treated. Other pets included dogs, monkeys, and baboons.

Cats were considered sacred.

Education

If Egyptian parents desired that their son be more than a craftsman, they sent him to a scribe school. There he learned to read and write. A boy with training in the scribe school could become a scribe, a priest, or a government worker. A **scribe** was like a secretary to the ruler or to leaders in the army, the court, or the temple.

Students sat on the floor or the ground with their legs crossed. School supplies consisted of brushes and blocks of paint to write with, a **palette** [păl′ĭt] to hold the paints, a water pot to moisten the brush, and a piece of cloth to use as an eraser. The older and more advanced students used papyrus scrolls to write on, but these scrolls were too expensive for beginners' mistakes. Beginners practiced their writing on pieces of broken pottery.

Food

Bread and vegetables were the main part of the average ancient Egyptians' diet. Their vegetables included onions, leeks, beans, and lentils. Only the wealthy had a wide variety of foods including meat such as beef, mutton, goose, or duck in their diet. For a sweetener, the Egyptians added honey to their food, because sugar was still unknown. For fruit, they enjoyed figs, dates, and grapes.

Comprehension Check 7C

1. What did most Egyptians do for work?
2. Why did the Egyptians choose mostly white as a color to wear?
3. What pet was considered sacred by the Egyptians?

7.6 The Papyrus Plant

Thousands of years ago, the **papyrus plant** grew in the swampy delta area of Lower Egypt. The papyrus plant, which has a brownish flower, grew from three to ten feet high in the hot and humid climate of that area.

Ancient Egyptians found many good uses for the papyrus plant. The fibers of the papyrus plant could be twisted into an excellent rope. The Egyptians found ways to make clothes, sandals, and mats from the plant as well as medicine and food. Wood was scarce in Egypt; thus the papyrus plant was all the more valuable, for it could be used as fuel for fire.

The First Paper

The Egyptians found another use for the papyrus plant that is far more important to world history. They used it to make the world's first **paperlike material.**

The papyrus plant grows in the water.

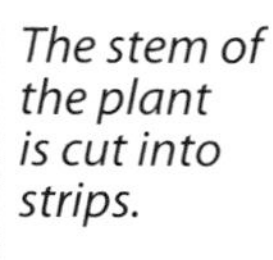

The stem of the plant is cut into strips.

The strips are pounded together with a wooden mallet, and then smoothed with a polishing stone.

Our word "paper" comes from the word "papyrus," but the papyrus scrolls were not what we call paper today. (Our paper was invented by the Chinese much later in history—A.D. 105. Papyrus was in use before 2000 B.C.)

To make paper, the Egyptians first removed the outer bark of the papyrus plant. The inner stem of the plant was then cut into thin strips. These strips were laid in layers on a hard, flat surface and pounded with a wooden mallet until the strips matted together to form one single sheet. The sheet was then smoothed with a polishing stone. The strips of papyrus that formed the paper also formed lines as it became matted together. The front side of the papyrus had horizontal lines that were used to write upon. The back side had vertical lines that could be used after the front was filled. Thus the Egyptians had lined paper to write on.

The papyrus was made into sheets that were glued from end to end. This eventually made a long roll of paper that we call a **scroll.** Most scrolls were made of 20 sheets glued together. The average length of a scroll when it was unrolled was 35 feet. Some were even longer. The longest one known is 133 feet long.

Egyptian Literature and the Rosetta Stone

The early ancient Egyptians wrote using a system of pictures called **"hieroglyphics"** [hī′ər·ə·glĭf′ĭks]. These pictures actually stood for the objects pictured. Later, they developed an Egyptian alphabet of 24 letters. The letters were really pictures, also. Each picture stood for a consonant sound. The reader had to guess what the vowel sound was. The Egyptians wrote on the walls of pyramids and temples as well as on papyrus scrolls.

With the passing centuries and easier methods of writing, the old hieroglyphic writing was no longer used. Soon, it became forgotten. By A.D. 500, even the Egyptians could no longer read the writing of their ancestors. The history of the ancient Egyptians was a mystery, because no one could read their writing.

In A.D. 1799, while the French were invading Egypt to gain control of the land route to India, a French officer discovered a strange, black stone half buried in the mud. On the stone was a message written in three different languages, one of which was hieroglyphics. Named for the town near which it was found, the **Rosetta Stone** became the key to unlocking the meaning of the ancient Egyptian language.

Rosetta Stone

7.7 The Decline of Egypt

The early Egyptians mined copper from the Sinai Peninsula. The copper was made into tools and weapons. Later, they found they could make copper stronger by melting copper and tin together to make **bronze.** However, before 1500 B.C., many countries were beginning to find that **iron** was highly superior to copper and bronze for making tools and weapons. Egypt's enemies began using these strong iron weapons. Although the Egyptians were able to mine their own rich deposits of gold, they had no iron. Bronze and gold would not help them fight against enemies who had iron weapons.

To make matters worse, the Egyptian priests and nobles began to fight among themselves for royal power. Such quarreling hurt them just as much as not having iron weapons did. By 1000 B.C., Egypt was broken into less powerful states. Slowly, the once-powerful Egypt became weak. For the next 2,000 years, one enemy after another invaded and conquered Egypt.

CHAPTER 7 CHECKUP

A Know these locations.

1. Sahara Desert
2. Red Sea
3. Sinai Peninsula
4. Nile River
5. Nile Delta
6. Upper Egypt
7. Lower Egypt
8. Memphis
9. Thebes

B Define each term.

1. delta
2. cataract
3. famine
4. pharaoh
5. vizier
6. shadoof
7. mummy
8. pyramids
9. obelisk
10. scribe
11. palette
12. papyrus
13. scroll
14. hieroglyphics

(cont.)

C Who am I?

1. King of Upper and Lower Egypt
2. the first pharaoh
3. built the Great Pyramid as his tomb
4. a vizier mentioned in the Bible
5. ancient Egypt's only woman pharaoh
6. the pharaoh whose tomb is more famous than he

D Answer each question.

1. What peninsula has been a land bridge between Africa and Asia?
2. What is the world's longest river?
3. Because the Nile is so important, Egypt is often called "the _?_ of the Nile."
4. Because the fertile land in Egypt ends so abruptly, what did the ancient Egyptians call their land?
5. What is the largest of the pyramids standing today?
6. What famous monument has the head of a man and the body of a lion?
7. What do we call the area near Thebes that the pharaohs used as a cemetery?
8. What was the key to understanding the meaning of hieroglyphics?
9. What color clothing did most ancient Egyptians wear? Why?

E List the **three** Egyptian seasons and the type of work done during each season.

AFRICA LONG AGO

Imagine a land of endless variety—a world of rain forests, deserts, volcanoes, waterfalls, primitive villages, modern cities, simple farms, large plantations, oil rigs, diamond mines, and national parks with thousands of fascinating plants and animals. This land is **Africa.** You might want to travel to the snowy summit of **Mount Kilimanjaro** [kĭl′ə·mən·jär′ō], Africa's highest peak. From there you could make a quick stop in the hot, dry Sahara, the world's largest desert. Later you might wander through the steamy jungles of the Congo; but no matter where your travels take you, you will realize that Africa's natural beauty is beyond description.

Africa, the second largest continent (after Asia), reaches almost as far north of the equator as it does south. To the north lies the Mediterranean Sea, which separates Africa from Europe. At the **Strait of Gibraltar** [jĭ·brôl′tər], the two continents are only about 8 miles apart. On the map of Africa (p. 125), locate the Strait of Gibraltar, the Gulf of Guinea [gĭn′ē] under Africa's "hump," and the Gulf of Aden [äd′'n], which separates the Horn of Africa from the Arabian Peninsula. Africa once touched Asia at the Sinai Peninsula, but today, the **Suez Canal** divides the two continents. The Mozambique [mō′zəm·bēk′] Channel separates **Madagascar,** the world's fourth largest island, from the mainland.

Although Africa is three times the size of Europe, it has a shorter coastline. Compare the two continents on the Eastern Hemisphere map (pp. 312–313) to see how this could be. Because the coastline of Africa is very smooth, there are few good harbors.

8.1 ✕ Land of Mystery

Much of Africa was a mystery to Europeans for many centuries. Europeans were familiar with the African civilizations along the Mediterranean Sea, such as Egypt and Carthage, an African city founded by the Phoenicians as a trading post. However, Europeans knew so little about the rest of Africa that they called it the "Dark Continent." Portuguese adventurers tried to establish trading posts along the western coast of Africa in the A.D. 1500s with little success. Early in the 1800s, missionaries from England and Scotland began going to the mysterious interior of Africa, and soon explorers and traders were going there as well. The exciting stories that they took back to Europe made many people want to know more about this interesting continent.

8.2 ✕ Highlights of African History

African history began shortly after the Flood when descendants of three of Ham's sons, **Mizraim, Phut** [fŭt], and **Cush** [ko͝osh], migrated there. The land of Mizraim became Egypt, one of the first great empires in history, and many Egyptian customs, legends, and false religious beliefs spread to the rest of Africa as the continent became more populated.

The Land of Phut

Before the Sahara was a desert. Phut's family probably settled in the area that is now the Sahara Desert. In the Bible, this area is called Phut, Put, or Libya. The Sahara has not always been a desert. In the early days, it was green and fertile. Many rivers flowed through its grassy valleys, and wild animals—elephants, giraffes, hippopotamuses, and ostriches—lived there. The people of the Sahara made their living by hunting, farming, and herding animals.

Skillful workers. These early Africans painted scenes from their everyday life on the rocks of the Sahara's high central plateaus. Their artwork still exists today, and it shows that they made musical instruments, baskets, pottery, and jewelry, and that they domesticated (tamed) cattle, goats, and sheep. They had a well-organized social and political life, and they were especially known for their skill with the bow and arrow. (The name *Phut* means "a bow.") Men from Phut often served in the armies of the Middle Eastern empires. Unfortunately, the descendants of Phut followed a false, pagan religion. As the Sahara dried up and as warriors from the Middle East overcame them, these early people moved to the northern savanna, where tall grasses and some trees grew, and began to grow rice, yams, and other crops. Northern Africa became inhabited mostly by Arabs from the Middle East, and the nomadic Bedouins and Berbers.

early African rock painting

ancient ruins from Kingdom of Cush

39:16–18). The most famous Cushite in history was the servant of Queen Candace whom Philip led to Christ (Acts 8:26–40). This **Ethiopian eunuch** [yo͞o′nək], the first recorded African Christian, took the gospel back to Africa, and founded a Christian church that thrived there for many centuries.

The Land of Cush

A great civilization. The descendants of Cush built the greatest ancient civilization in Africa's interior. The **Kingdom of Cush** (also spelled *Kush*), which lasted about a thousand years, was located along the Nile River south of Egypt, in modern Sudan. The Cushites sent caravans laden with gold, ivory (elephant tusks), precious stones, and works of art to Egypt and the rest of the Middle East for trade. At one time, Cush attacked and overcame Egypt, but Egypt made an alliance with Assyria and won back its land.

Famous Cushites. In ancient times, Cush was often called Ethiopia, though it was located to the west of modern Ethiopia. The Ethiopians mentioned in the Bible were Cushites. Two interesting Bible accounts tell about the kindness and the faith of certain ancient Cushites. A Cushite named Ebed-melech helped the prophet Jeremiah when he was in prison (Jer. 38:6–13 and

The Mountains of Ethiopia

Saba. East of Cush was Saba [sä′bə], modern Ethiopia, one of the most mountainous countries of Africa. Saba was also called **Sheba,** and later it was called the **Kingdom of Aksum** [äk′so͞om′], Africa's first and greatest Christian kingdom. Some of the people who lived there were Cushites, and others had crossed the Red Sea from Arabia. The **Queen of Sheba,** who carried gold, precious stones, and

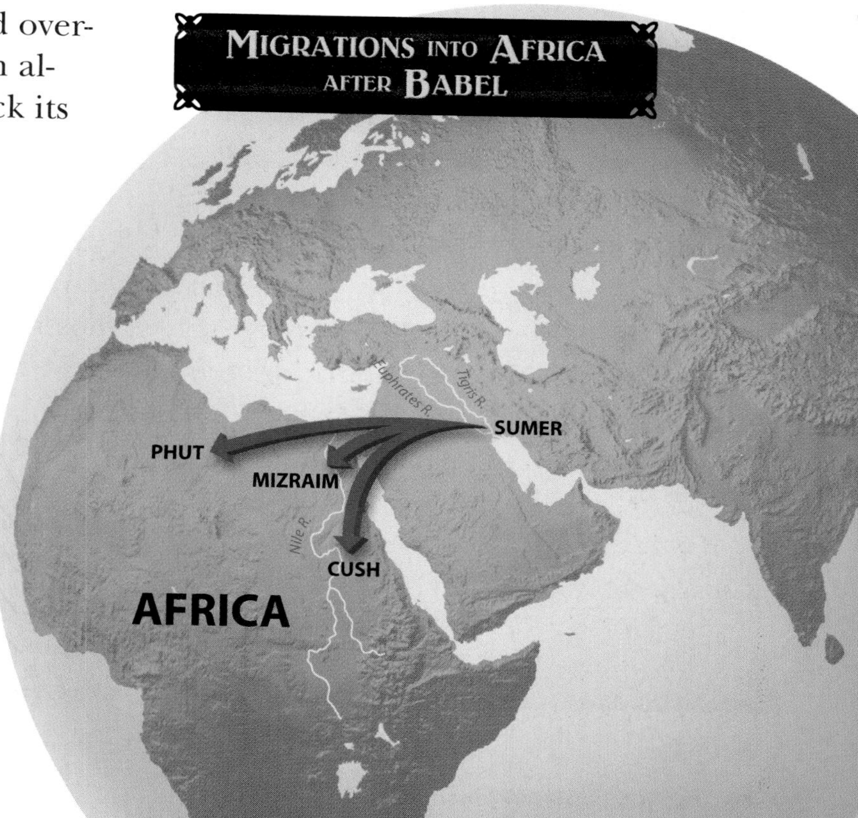

spices to King Solomon in Jerusalem, may have come from Saba. According to Ethiopian tradition, the family who ruled Ethiopia for thousands of years were descendants of King Solomon and the Queen of Sheba.

The Ethiopian Orthodox Church. Around A.D. 300, two Christian boys from the city of Tyre (in modern Lebanon), Aedesius [ĭ·dē′sē·əs] and Frumentius [fro͞o·mĕn′shəs], were shipwrecked and taken to Ethiopia as slaves. They preached the gospel in the court where they served, and so many people came to Christ that **Frumentius** had to go to Egypt to ask other Christians to come and help with the church work in Ethiopia. Frumentius himself was made a leader of the church in Ethiopia, which was called the Ethiopian Orthodox Church. From their mountain strongholds, the Ethiopian Christians bravely defended their faith against Muslim invaders who swept into Africa during the Middle Ages. During the 1200s, Ethiopia's **King Lalibela** [lā′lē·bä·lä] carved ten churches from solid rock; they still stand today in the mountains of central Ethiopia.

one of King Lalibela's churches carved from rock

Comprehension Check 8A

1. What is the highest peak in Africa?
2. What African island is the fourth-largest island in the world?
3. Which kingdom was the greatest ancient civilization in the interior of Africa?
4. What African nation had a strong Christian influence in New Testament times? Why?
5. What special fact do we know about the Ethiopian Eunuch?
6. What was Africa's first and greatest Christian kingdom?
7. Which king had churches carved out of solid rock?

Early Christians in North Africa

Center of Christianity. Northern Africa, along the Mediterranean Sea, became one of the strong centers of the Christian church shortly after the time of Christ. Simon of Cyrene [sī·rē′nē] is remembered as the man who carried the cross for Jesus (Matt. 27:32). Cyrene was an African city just across the Mediterranean Sea from Greece.

Athanasius the Great

One of the leaders of the African church, **Athanasius** [ăth′ə·nā′shəs] **the Great,** boldly proclaimed that Jesus is God when some church people were doubting Christ's deity. He was one of the greatest leaders in all of church history.

Muslim control. During the Middle Ages, Arab Muslims conquered the Christians in northern Africa. Most of the Christians moved to Europe, and by A.D. 700, northern Africa was almost completely occupied by Arab Muslims. The gospel was not taken to Africa again until more than a thousand years later.

Important Centers of Trade

East coast trading cities. Although Europeans knew very little about Africa south of the Sahara until the 1800s, the continent was well known to people from Asia in early times. From a number of cities along Africa's east coast, where Kenya and Tanzania [tăn′zə·nē′ə] are today, ships sailed to Arabia, India, China, and Siam (modern Thailand), carrying cargoes of smelted iron, ivory, and gold. They returned to Africa with silk, porcelain, and precious jewels from the lands in the East. This trade was carried on for five hundred years during the Middle Ages.

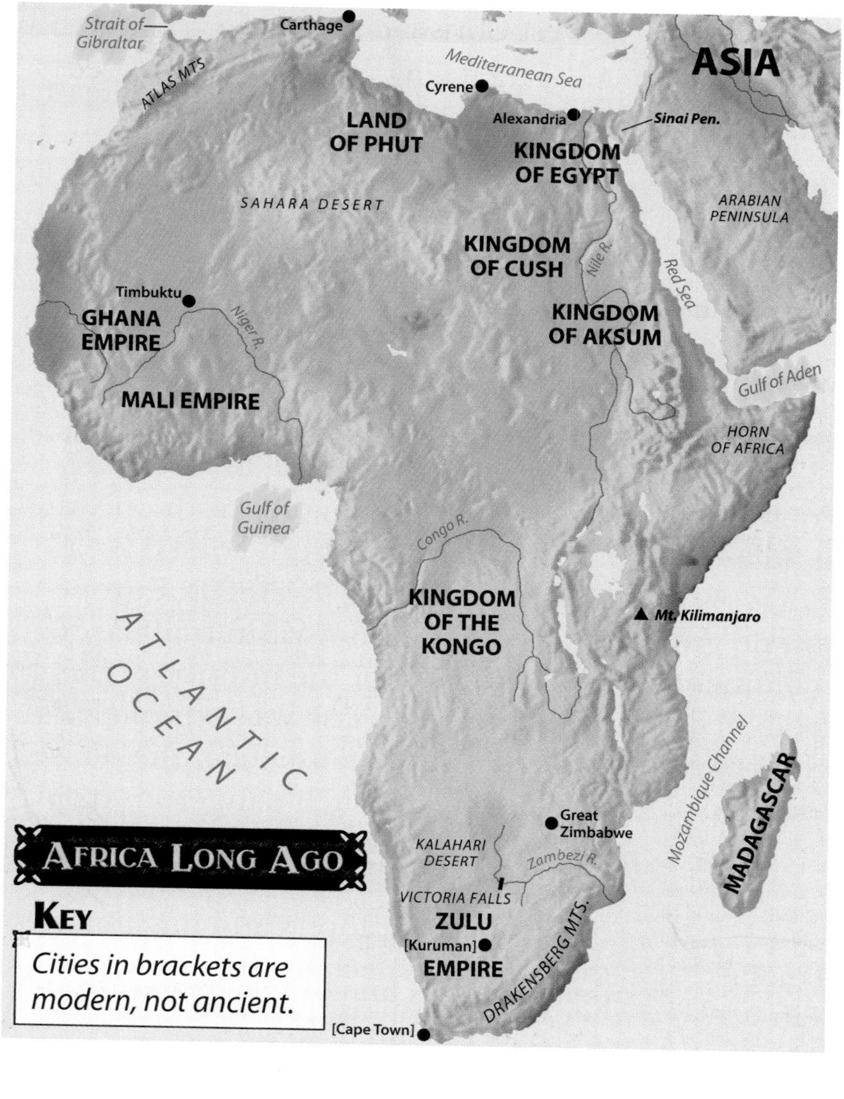

AFRICA LONG AGO

KEY

Cities in brackets are modern, not ancient.

The Ghana Empire. There was also a great deal of overland trade across the Sahara and into the interior of Africa. One of the greatest trading areas from A.D. 300 to 1200 was the Ghana [gä′nə] Empire, which was ruled by black Africans on the west coast, near the Niger [nī′jər] River. Arabs from the Middle East brought salt, copper, and dried fruits to trade for gold, ivory, and slaves. The modern nation of Ghana, which is near the area of the Ghana Empire, looks back to the great empire as an important part of its heritage.

The Mali Empire. Another impressive empire arose in the west after Ghana's fall. The Mali [mä′lē] Empire was known

an ancient mosque from Timbuktu in the Mali Empire

ruins of Great Zimbabwe

for its great wealth in gold and for its famous center of learning, the city of **Timbuktu** [tĭm′bŭk·to͞o′]. Many people traveled to Timbuktu to use its libraries and study at its university.

Southern kingdoms. Huge kingdoms also arose in the south during the Middle Ages. They included the **Kingdom of the Kongo,** the fierce **Zulu Empire,** and the kingdom centered in **Great Zimbabwe** [zĭm·bäb′wē], a city in the modern nation of Zimbabwe. During the time of all the great kingdoms there were also many tribal people who lived simple lives in the deserts, jungles, mountains, and savannas. For over a thousand years, there was almost no gospel witness in the vast African continent. Idol worship and witchcraft, combined with very difficult geographical barriers, kept most of the people from developing a high civilization.

Early Achievements

Early Africans were skilled metalworkers. They invented a smelting furnace and a process for making cast iron. Africa is known as the "home of animal tales." **Aesop,** a Greek slave who wrote the famous fables, is believed by many to have come from Ethiopia.

8.3 The Age of Exploration and Missions

The "White Man's Grave"

Only the courageous. Before 1800, Europeans were familiar with only the northern and southern coastal areas of Africa. During the 1800s, Europeans led by skillful African trailblazers explored most of the interior of the continent. The task was extremely difficult. The intense heat, the dense vegetation, and such dangerous tropical diseases as **malaria, yellow fever,** and **sleeping sickness** took their toll on so many explorers and missionaries that Africa, especially the west coast, became known as the "White Man's Grave." None but the very brave were suited for the exploration of this great land.

Dangers from the slave trade. Another thing that made Africa dangerous was the slave trade. Africans raided other tribes and carried away people to sell to Arab and Portuguese traders. These traders packed the captives onto ships and resold them as slaves to people in Asia and the New World. Many Africans owned slaves themselves and they caught slaves for the traders, but they also despised the foreign slave traders. Because they thought more of money than of people, the slave traders were often extremely cruel. Africans suspected any white men who came to their land of being slavers, and they often made life difficult for the European explorers and missionaries.

Scotland Leads the Way

Some of Africa's greatest missionaries and explorers came from Bible-loving Scotland. The Scottish people combined their love for travel with a desire to share the Scriptures with other people and courageously blazed many paths into Africa's interior.

Bruce and Park, early explorers. The first European explorer of Africa, **James Bruce,** went to Ethiopia and Sudan to try to find the source of the Nile River. His precise descriptions of the wonders that he saw in eastern Africa so amazed the Europeans that many did not believe him. Another Scottish explorer, **Mungo Park,** went to western Africa and explored the Niger River.

Robert Moffat, pioneer missionary. **Robert Moffat,** another Scotsman, was one of the first missionaries to Africa. He sailed to Cape Town, a Dutch settlement in South Africa. From there he made many trips inland by foot or canoe over mountainous terrain, through thick forests, and on to the edge of the **Kalahari** [kä′lə·här′ē] **Desert,** the largest desert region in Southern Africa. On one such trip Moffat met a fierce and violent outlaw chief and led him to Christ.

Robert Moffat

Moffat eventually settled in Kuruman [ko͞or′ə·män′], a town in South Africa, where he and his wife Mary lived and worked for fifty years. For many years, they saw few results. Then, after twelve years of labor, revival broke out among the tribe. Many were saved, and lives were changed. People of other tribes, seeing the change that had taken place, went to Robert Moffat to hear his message. After many people came to Christ, Moffat put their language into a written form and then translated the Bible into it. He taught some of the Africans to read, and they in turn taught others. Soon many people at the edge of the Kalahari Desert were able to read the Bible in their own language and grow as Christians. Moffat also did a translation of *Pilgrim's Progress* for them to read.

Comprehension Check 8B

1. Northern Africa today is inhabited mostly by what group of people?
2. What section of Africa carried on much trade during the Middle Ages?
3. Why was Africa called the "White Man's Grave"?
4. Who was the first European explorer of Africa?
5. What famous Scotsman was one of the first missionaries in South Africa? Near what desert did he minister to the people?

David Livingstone: Africa's Most Famous Explorer

"The smoke of a thousand villages." One time when Robert Moffat was in England for a rest, he met a young Scottish medical doctor named **David Livingstone.** "Do you think I could be of help in Africa?" Livingstone asked.

"Yes," replied Moffat, "but don't go to a place where missionaries already work. From where I live in Kuruman, I can see the smoke of a thousand villages where the name of Christ has never been heard."

Opening up the interior. Dr. Livingstone joined the Moffats in Kuruman. Later he married their daughter, Mary. Then he began traveling north, far into the interior. His goal was to explore the land as he preached the gospel in order to open up the interior for other missionaries. He accomplished the task so well that he is known as the greatest of all African explorers and one of the most famous explorers in history.

The "smoke that thunders." David Livingstone traced the course of the Zambezi [zăm·bē′zē] River, which he called "God's highway to the interior." He became a trusted friend of many African people, some of whom told him about the mysterious "smoke that thunders." When they led him to the "smoke," Livingstone became the first European to see Africa's largest waterfall, **Victoria Falls,** which he named for Queen Victoria. As the water of Victoria Falls crashes 360 feet into the Zambezi River, it makes a thunderous noise, and huge columns of mist rise 3,000 feet into the air like great clouds of smoke. Victoria Falls is one of the greatest natural wonders of the world.

Victoria Falls

Honors in life. Dr. Livingstone's explorations of Africa made him one of the most famous people in the world of his day. On his two trips back to England he was greeted as a great hero. People in England, Scotland, America, and other places eagerly followed the news of his explorations as he pushed deeper and deeper into the "Dark Continent." Suddenly, the news stopped. David Livingstone was lost! This was such an important news event that an American newspaper sent the young reporter **Henry Stanley** to search for him.

"Dr. Livingstone, I presume?" After searching for months, Stanley came upon the village where Livingstone, who was very ill, was resting. He greeted the great missionary explorer with words that have become famous: "Dr. Livingstone, I presume?" Stanley explored parts of the continent with Livingstone, and later he followed in his footsteps as a missionary explorer of Africa. Stanley is most remembered for his trip through the jungles on the great **Congo River,** the world's second-largest river in the volume of water it carries, and for his witness to the king of the Baganda tribe in Uganda [yo͞o·găn′də].

"Dr. Livingstone, I presume?"

Honors in death. Dr. David Livingstone won the hearts of the Africans by his desire to share the gospel with them, his willingness to teach them new ways of growing crops and building homes, and his resolve to introduce commerce into Africa in order to destroy the slave trade. He cheerfully submitted to many dangers in order to help the people of this continent. Once he even had his arm chewed by an attacking lion. One morning, after he had been in Africa for about thirty years, the Africans found him dead. He had died while kneeling beside his bed in prayer. Because the Africans wanted to keep the memory of this great man in their land, they buried his heart in a jungle clearing. They sent his body to the coast, and from there it was taken to London and buried in Westminster Abbey, where the most famous people of Britain are honored.

Comprehension Check 8C

1. Who was Africa's most famous explorer?
2. What was the "smoke that thunders"? Why was it called that?
3. Who went to find and assist Dr. Livingstone?

PEOPLE IN HISTORY

Khama: A Great African Chief

When **Khama** [kă′mă], son of a fierce chief, was fourteen years old, David Livingstone came riding into his town on the back of a hornless ox. Khama's father received Livingstone with interest. Khama's father asked for medicine to change his proud and angry heart. Livingstone held up the New Testament to tell him about the only medicine that can change a sinful heart, but Khama's father would not listen. He wanted medicine that could change his heart at once. When none was given, he arose and went away.

As the years passed, the chief, his heart hardened, became a fierce enemy of Christians, but his son Khama, who would be the next chief of the Batswanas [bŏt·swä′nəz], became a Christian. Khama resolved that he would lead his people according to the standards taught in the Bible. This resolve would not be easy to carry out in a land that was ruled by witchcraft, but Khama was a man of courage and determination, and with God's help he would do right.

One of the first things that Khama did when he became chief was to outlaw liquor. European traders in Africa made much profit by selling brandy to the Africans, and Khama was determined that his people would not be destroyed by drunkenness. Kindly but firmly, he told the traders that they were not to weaken his people with their drink. Anyone who did not cooperate with this rule was sent out of the land. Khama's rules against drink brought him enemies, but his firm stand also helped to win the respect of the people.

For over fifty years, Chief Khama ruled his people in righteousness. He put an end to witchcraft, he outlawed polygamy (the marrying of many wives), and he made a law against the purchase of slaves. He treated the neighboring Kalahari Bushmen and other nearby tribes with kindness and taught the Christian way of life to his people and their neighbors. He did all he could to help the large church that was built in his capital city and to encourage his people to go as missionaries to other tribes.

Not all of the Batswana accepted Christ during Chief Khama's rule, but all of them heard the gospel message, and all enjoyed the benefits that come from having a righteous ruler. Khama even took a trip to England with two neighboring chiefs, whom he had influenced for good, in order to appeal to the British government on the behalf of his people.

The British leaders were so impressed by the high standards and courteous manners of the three chiefs that they gave them their requests. These men were doing a better job of ruling their people than the Englishmen could do, the British realized.

Khama lived to be almost 100 years old. A few months before his death in 1923, his people celebrated his fifty years of rule, and Khama gave a speech that ended with these words:

> *I am an old man, and to the young men I say: "Let these words enter your hearts. The work that has been done here is a work of God. Depart from disputes; think like men; seek to know the Way; let your hearts depart from drink and from the heathen ceremonies. May God bless you, white people, and my people."*

Some of the young men listened. Those who did listen continued, like Khama, to be lights in a dark world. To this day, many of the people of Botswana follow some form of Christianity.

The Power of the Gospel in Africa

Missionary contributions. Thousands of missionaries have gone to Africa in the 1800s and 1900s. These missionaries were the greatest friends that the Africans had. They stood up for them when European governments or traders tried to take advantage of them. They did much of the exploration of the continent. They put many of the African languages into a written form and then translated the Bible and other books into the African tongues. The Bible in whole or in part has been translated into almost 600 of Africa's nearly 2,000 known languages, with over 200 other translations in progress today. The missionaries started almost all of Africa's schools, hospitals, and medical clinics and then trained African Christians to take part in these ministries. They spoke out against the cruelties of the slave trade and helped the Africans learn new ways of farming, building, and preventing disease. Above all else, they led many Africans to Christ and taught them the Christian way of life.

Black missionaries. The greatest numbers of missionaries came from England, Scotland, and the United States, but there were also missionaries from Holland, Germany, Switzerland, Scandinavia [scăn′ də·nā′vē·ə], and other countries. Some of the most effective missionaries were African Christians, including freed slaves who took the gospel back to their people.

Lott Carey was a freed slave from Virginia who worked with his friend **Colin Teague** [tēg] to establish many Baptist churches throughout northwestern Africa. Carey became the governor of **Liberia,** Africa's first black republic. Liberia was founded by an American group as a home for freed American black slaves and later became independent. The British helped to establish another free black republic in Sierra Leone [sē·ĕr′ə lē·ōn′]. People went from Sierra Leone to Nigeria and other coastal nations to tell the people about Christ.

The most famous missionary from Sierra Leone was **Samuel Crowther.** In 1821, when he was just a boy, he was captured by the Portuguese and put on a slave ship, but British warships rescued him and took him to a Christian school at Freetown. Later he went to England for further education. When he returned to Africa, Samuel Crowther became the first black bishop the Church of England had ever had, and he started a mission in Nigeria that was completely staffed by African nationals. He and his staff established churches, elementary schools, high schools, and a college in Africa.

Samuel Crowther

The influence of African Christians. African Christians have done much to bring Christianity and civilization to formerly dark parts of Africa. Samuel Crowther and Chief Khama were just two of many faithful servants of Christ. Without the work of dedicated Africans, exploration and Bible translation would have been impossible. Many Africans today are busy teaching the Bible and other subjects, caring for the sick, preaching the gospel, and in other ways helping to bring the light of the Scriptures to their people. The progress that Africa knows today was brought about by the power of the Word of God in the hearts of the African people.

PEOPLE IN HISTORY

Mary Slessor: Queen of the Cannibals

"Run, Ma, Run!" The cry rang through the village. It was a familiar sound to **Mary Slessor,** who was called the "White Ma" by the natives. She was needed again in a trouble spot. When Mary arrived, several tribes were ready to begin war. Mary walked calmly into their midst and commanded them to sit down. They formed a circle around her and, as she sat knitting, each tribe told their side of the disagreement. With God-given courage and wisdom, Mary handed down her judgment and peacefully settled the argument. The natives respected this little red-haired missionary lady for her boldness, bravery, and wisdom.

Mary Slessor had been well prepared for her hard life as a missionary to Africa. Born in the slums of a town in Scotland in 1848, she was often mistreated by her father, who spent most of his money on liquor and frequently came home in a drunken rage. Mary had to go to work when she was eleven years old to support the family. She worked six hours, went to school six hours, and also helped at home. Her life might have been unbearable had Mary not come to know Christ when she was young.

One day Mary heard about the missionary work in the rain forests of Africa's west coast, and in 1876, she

PEOPLE IN HISTORY *cont.*

sailed for Africa. Mary Slessor went into the interior of Nigeria to a place where missionaries had never been. There she saw a way of life that made her heart sick. The men quarreled and made war. Because twin babies were thought to be a sign of evil, they were killed. The witch doctors used many evil and cruel practices. Some of the people were cannibals. Mary longed to tell these people of Christ.

Mary began taking in the twins and raising them herself. With God-given bravery she would meet tribal warriors and command them not to fight. Strangely enough, they listened to her. She taught by her example as well as by her words how to work hard. Many native people accepted Christ, whole villages were changed through the power of the gospel, and Mary again moved farther into the interior to contact another tribe with the gospel.

During her forty years in Africa, Mary Slessor raised fifty-one African children, most of whom became pastors, teachers, or government officials. She brought Christ to thousands who had never heard of Him. She taught the people to read, to work, to resolve problems, and to respect human life. How could one little Scottish woman bring such change to a savage land? Only through the power of God and a life yielded to Him.

CHAPTER 8 CHECKUP

A Know these locations.

1. Mt. Kilimanjaro
2. Strait of Gibraltar
3. Suez Canal
4. Madagascar

B Who am I?

1. the first recorded African Christian
2. an early leader of the Ethiopian Orthodox Church
3. king who had ten churches carved from solid rock
4. one of the greatest leaders in church history, he boldly proclaimed that Jesus is God
5. Greek slave who wrote famous fables

C Tell the most important fact about each person.

1. James Bruce
2. Mungo Park
3. Robert Moffat
4. David Livingstone
5. Henry Stanley
6. Khama
7. Samuel Crowther
8. Mary Slessor

(cont.)

CHAPTER 8 CHECKUP *cont.*

D Answer each question.

1. What is the second largest continent?
2. What narrow waterway separates Africa from Europe?
3. What man-made waterway separates Africa from Asia?
4. What is the fourth largest island in the world?
5. What is the world's second largest river in water volume?
6. Which country led the way in exploration and evangelization of Africa?

E Identify the place described by each clue.

1. the "Dark Continent"
2. the greatest ancient civilization of Africa's interior
3. the first and greatest Christian kingdom of Africa
4. the city famous as a center of learning in the Mali Empire
5. the largest desert region in Southern Africa
6. Africa's largest waterfall; the "smoke that thunders"
7. Africa's first black republic

F In complete sentences, tell why early exploration and missionary efforts in Africa were so dangerous.

AFRICA IN MODERN TIMES

Europe and Asia had interacted with Egypt and other parts of Northern Africa since ancient times, and European sailors had grown acquainted with the African coastline during the 1400s and 1500s. The center of the continent, however, remained largely unexplored until the 1800s, when missionary-explorer David Livingstone and others began to penetrate the interior. As European explorers discovered Africa's great natural resources, including gold, diamonds, and ivory, the nations of Europe began to scramble for colonies.

European rule. By 1914, most of Africa was ruled by European powers. There were only two independent nations: **Ethiopia,** which had been independent for about two thousand years, and **Liberia** [lī·bĭr′ē·ə], which had been founded by an American group as a home for freed American black slaves and later became independent. The other African nations were ruled by Britain, France, Italy, Germany, Spain, Portugal, and Belgium. The period of European rule was a time of great progress in Africa, especially in the countries that were affected most by the gospel. Schools were started, roads and railroads were built, and new cities were established.

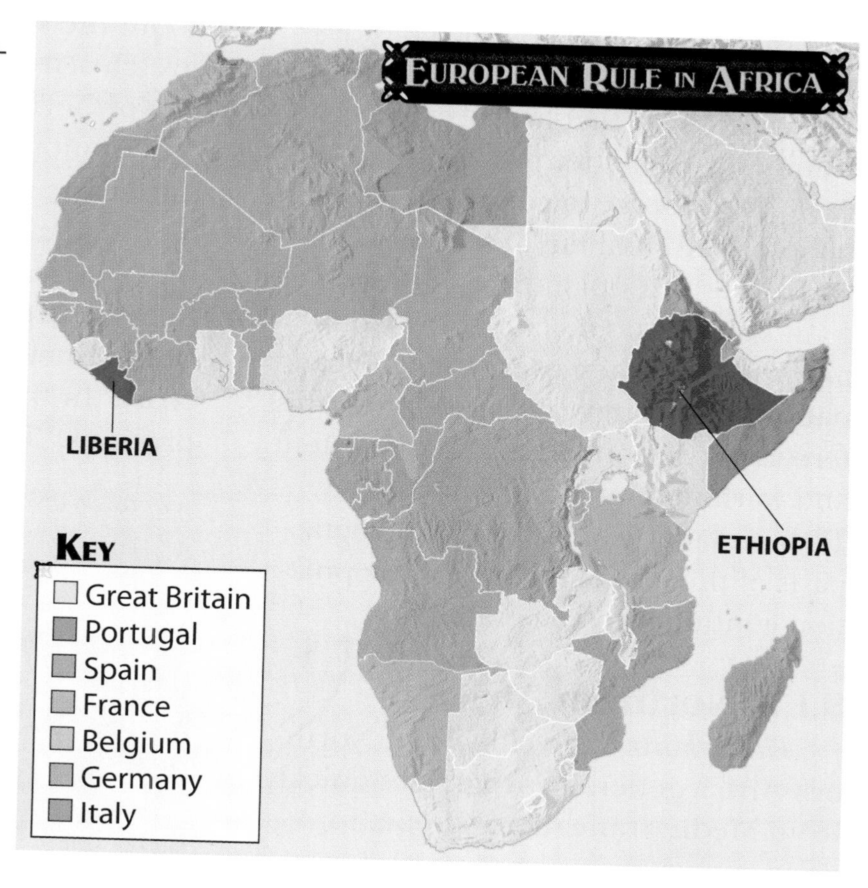

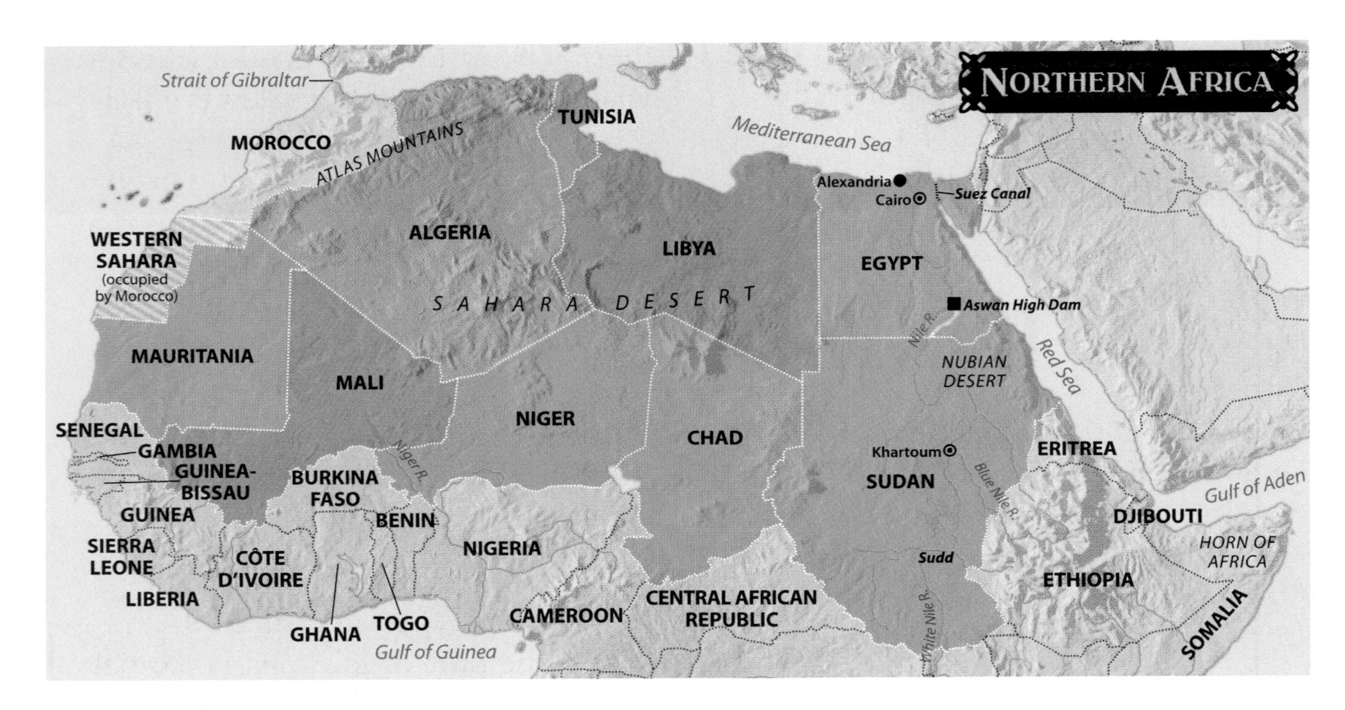

Desire for self-government. After World War II, the nations of Europe began to pull out of Africa, giving the colonies their independence. Some countries, especially those that had been British colonies, were better prepared for self-rule than others. In countries where the people were still held in fear by witchcraft and spirit worship, self-government soon turned into dictatorship. Communists have taken over many African nations in recent years, and Communist terrorists continue to stir up discontent and warfare in much of Africa today. Though famine and war often plague parts of the continent, Africa's population continues to grow rapidly.

9.1 Northern Africa

The Sahara. The climate of Northern Africa generally progresses quickly from Mediterranean, to steppe, to desert as you move from north to south. (See *Climate Zones,* p. 337.) The Sahara, the largest desert in the world, is about the size of the United States. It stretches from the east to the west coast of Northern Africa, and occupies all or part of more than 10 nations. Most of this desert region is unsettled. Only on the Mediterranean coast and in the Nile Valley is the land hospitable to man. Most precipitation falls in the **Atlas Mountains** along the northwestern coast. In the desert, water is rare and precious. Temperatures in the Sahara

an oasis in the Sahara Desert

vary greatly but are generally very hot in the day and cooler at night. Temperatures as high as 136 °F have been recorded in northern Libya.

South of the Sahara. South of the Sahara the land begins to be more varied with the climate ranging from desert, to steppe, to savanna. Precipitation plays an important part in this transitional zone. Drought can transform a steppe into a desert within a year. Agriculture on the steppe is limited and constantly threatened by drought. Livestock such as cattle, sheep, and camels, however, do fairly well since they feed on the low grasses, shrubs, and scattered trees that characterize the landscape. In the savanna, the greater amount of precipitation brings forth a variety of vegetation and wildlife, as well as more human settlement.

Outside influences. Of all Africa, the north had the most contact with the outside world before the 1800s. Jews, Arabs, Greeks, and Romans all played a part in the history of this ancient land. The Old Testament speaks often of Egypt, Libya, and other parts of Northern Africa in its account of Israel's history.

In the A.D. 600s, Muslim Arabs from the east overran Northern Africa, introducing the Arabic language and Islam. The original inhabitants of this area were a nomadic people known as the Berbers. For several hundred years, Arab and Berber Muslims controlled an empire that included most of Northern Africa and part of Europe's Iberian [ī·bĭr′ē·ən] Peninsula (modern Spain and Portugal). Called the **Barbary Coast** after the Berbers, the area became known for pirates who lived there, attacking and looting ships that sailed in the Mediterranean Sea.

Today, the countries of this region share several common characteristics, including the Islamic religion, the Arabic language and culture, and a dry climate. Find all 10 Northern African nations, and Western Sahara, on the map (p. 136).

Comprehension Check 9A

1. At the time of European colonial rule in Africa, what two nations remained independent?
2. What large mountain range is located in northwest Africa?
3. The area of northern Africa known for its fierce pirates was called __?__.

modern Berber from Algeria

Egypt

Like the empires of the Middle East, Egypt eventually declined and came under the domination of Alexander the Great and then Rome. Later, Arabs swept into Egypt bringing the Arabic language and the Muslim religion. Egypt was also briefly under British rule. Since the country achieved independence in 1922, it has played an important role in North Africa and with its neighbors in the Middle East.

Today, most Egyptians are of mixed African and Arab descent. The majority speak Arabic, the official language, and practice Islam, the official religion. Nearly all of the population lives in the Nile valley.

Village life. Almost half of the Egyptian people live in rural areas. Village life in Egypt has remained virtually unchanged for hundreds of years. Farmers live in small, low houses built of sun-dried bricks made the same way the Israelites made them during their captivity in Egypt. Many families keep chickens, goats, and donkeys. Fewer than 50% of all Egyptians are able to read and write, and there are villages where only a few can.

City life. In contrast to rural living is the bustling lifestyle of cities such as **Alexandria** and **Cairo.** Cairo, Egypt's capital and Africa's largest city, is located in the fertile Nile delta. A wide variety of opportunities for employment, education, and entertainment is available in the cities. New arrivals to the cities, seeking better lives, are often unable to compete for jobs with the more educated city dwellers. Unwilling to return to their villages, they live in tents, shanties, and other makeshift housing. This mixture of rural and urban life provides a blend of old and new in Egypt's cities. Only blocks away from modern skyscrapers, apartments, and department stores are traditional Arab open-air markets and hovels made of cardboard.

Aswan High Dam. Since the completion of the **Aswan High Dam** in 1970, farmland in the Nile Valley has been under year-round irrigation, producing two or three crops per year. In addition to controlling the annual flood waters of

village along the Nile in Egypt

Cairo

the Nile, this enormous dam produces enough power to meet more than half of the country's needs. But the dam does have some drawbacks. Among other things, it keeps the Nile from depositing rich, fertile soil on the land the way it did in ancient times, forcing farmers to use costly artificial fertilizers.

Suez Canal. The **Suez Canal** connects the Mediterranean Sea and the Red Sea, giving ships a shorter route of travel between Europe, Asia, and eastern Africa. The 100-mile-long canal was completed in 1869. It had been owned mainly by British and French stockholders, but in 1956 Egyptian President **Nasser** took over the Suez Canal by force and would not allow Israel to use it. Israel, Britain, and France attacked Egypt, but the fighting stopped when Egypt agreed to reopen the canal to all nations.

Aswan High Dam

Suez Canal

Peace with Israel. In 1979, Egypt surprised the world by becoming the first Arab nation to make peace with Israel. This was accomplished when Egyptian President **Anwar Sadat** [än′wär sə·dät′] traveled to Israel to meet with the Israeli prime minister.

Economics. The Egyptian economy depends largely on the export of oil, cotton, and oranges. Egypt's most valuable mineral resources are her reserves of oil and natural gas in the western desert and beneath the Red Sea. Tourism is another important industry. Millions of tourists visit Egypt to see the Sphinx, the pyramids, the museums, and the mosques.

Sudan

South of Egypt lies the largest country in Africa, the Republic of **Sudan.** The White Nile and the Blue Nile meet in northern Sudan near the capital, **Khartoum** [kär·to͞om′: means "elephant's trunk"], forming the great Nile River. The **Sudd** [sŭd], a vast marshy area between the White Nile and the Blue, is the world's largest swamp. From the Nubian [no͞o′bē·ən] Desert in the north to the highlands in the east and south, Sudan has a progression of climate zones from desert, to steppe, to savanna, to rain forest. The tropical rain forest is the home for many African big game animals, including elephants, leopards, and buffalo.

History. Known as Nubia to the ancient Egyptians, Sudan was for many years a thoroughfare for trade caravans passing between Southern Africa and the

camel market in Sudan

Mediterranean. It was here that the Kingdom of Cush arose to become the greatest ancient civilization in the African interior.

The Ethiopians mentioned in the Bible were actually Sudanese or Cushites, as was the Ethiopian eunuch whom Philip led to Christ. This Cushite, the first recorded African Christian, carried the gospel back to his native land, where a thriving church was established. Later, Christians from Egypt came to the Sudan, followed by Muslim Arabs and Turks. After some 50 years as a British protectorate, Sudan came under Egyptian control in 1951 and finally declared independence in 1956.

Modern Times. Today, the Sudanese population is divided between Muslim Arabs and Nubians in the north and non-Muslim tribes in the south. The Muslim government has caused great destruction and persecution for the people in the south. Millions of Sudanese Christians have been killed in Sudan's civil war.

Although the official language is Arabic, more than 100 languages are spoken in Sudan. The majority of Sudanese live in rural villages and make their living by farming. Agriculture is very important to Sudan's economy, with cotton being the chief crop. Though rainfall varies, numerous rivers supply water to irrigated fields. Sudan remains among the poorest countries in the world.

Comprehension Check 9B

1. Cairo and Khartoum are the capitals of which two African countries?
2. What was built in Egypt in 1970 that controlled the flooding of the Nile River and provided power for the people's use?
3. What two bodies of water does the Suez Canal connect?
4. What is unique about Egypt's relationship with the nation of Israel?
5. What is the largest African country?
6. What is the world's largest swamp called? In which African country is it located?

9.2 ✠ Tropical Africa

History

East of the Sudanese kingdom of Cush lay the ancient kingdom of Aksum in the area of modern Ethiopia. Aksum became Africa's first and greatest Christian kingdom around A.D. 300. With the exception of Aksum, however, very little was known before the 1400s about lands south of the Sahara, mainly because those tribal peoples lacked a written history.

Archaeologists have discovered evidence of advanced cultures, however, and historians know from European and Asian sources of several great trading empires that were active during the Middle Ages. The kingdoms of Ghana and Mali each ruled parts of Tropical Africa. Caravans from the Middle East journeyed across the Sahara to cities on the Niger River for gold, ivory, and slaves.

African tribes were involved in the slave trade with Arab merchants long before Europe joined in that degrading practice. When European ships began to stop along Africa's western coast, the center of trade shifted away from the interior. Small coastal states rose to power and gained unprecedented wealth through the slave trade. The coastal people raided interior tribes, capturing and selling men, women, and children to European slave traders who transported them to Europe and the New World. It is estimated that as many as 30 million African people may have been sold into slavery between the 1500s and the 1800s. Fortunately, by the late 1800s, the slave trade had been largely abandoned thanks to the efforts of Christian reformers in Great Britain.

Many African people were sold into slavery between the 1500s and the 1800s.

Geography

Tropical Africa is often studied in three sections—Western, Central, and Eastern Africa. You might have a hard time locating all 28 Tropical African countries on the map p. 142. Some are island countries and some are very small. Can you find them?

Western Africa. The western portion of Tropical Africa is influenced by the desert to the north and the sea to the south. The climate ranges from steppe in the north to rain forest along the coast, with a band of savanna in between. Except in the country of Senegal, which has a drier climate than the other countries, rainfall averages more than 50 inches per year (the average annual rainfall in Atlanta, Georgia), and some areas along the coast receive well over 80 inches (more than the average rainfall in any U.S. state). This tropical climate provides ideal growing conditions for such plantation crops as bananas, coffee, and cacao (the seeds of an evergreen tree that are used to make cocoa and chocolate).

cacao trees

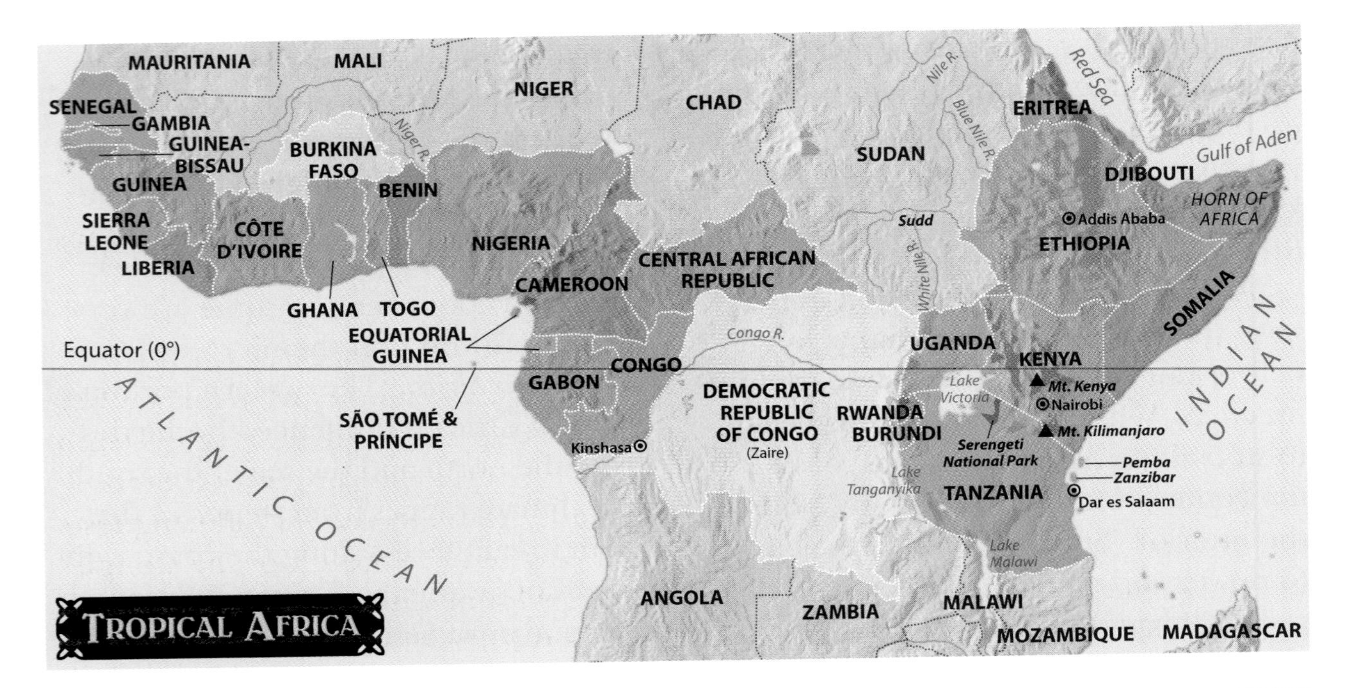

Central Africa. The climate in the central part of Tropical Africa can be described in two words—hot and wet. Located on the equator, most of Central Africa has a tropical rain forest climate. Here the rainy "season" lasts all year long, and dense jungles cover much of the land. Almost every afternoon tremendous thunderstorms drench the rain forest, resulting in an average annual rainfall of over 100 inches. Plants thrive in this moist, warm climate. Biologists have found over 3,000 plant species within a single square mile. In the rain forest, the trees form a dense canopy that blocks out most sunlight. Beneath their shade, thousands of thick, fast-growing vines, ferns, and shrubs compete for space and light. Most animals, including monkeys and snakes, dwell in the trees. One Englishman described the birds as being "bright as butterflies" and the butterflies "as big as birds." Far-

tropical rain forest

green mamba snake

ther south, the forest opens to tropical savanna, where rainfall is more seasonal and some areas experience drought.

Eastern Africa. In the eastern part of Tropical Africa lies the **Horn of Africa,** a large peninsula that resembles the horn of a rhinoceros, that juts eastward from the continent into the Arabian Sea. The Horn occupies a strategic location because it is near the oil supplies of the Middle East and the shipping lanes between the Indian Ocean and the Mediterranean Sea.

Africa's highest peak, Mt. Kilimanjaro, is a volcanic peak that rises abruptly from the surrounding area. **Lake Victoria,** the world's second largest freshwater lake (after Lake Superior) and the major source of the Nile River, was named by David Livingstone for his queen. **Lake Tanganyika** [tăng′ən·yē′kə], the longest and second-deepest (after Baikal [bī′kôl] in Russia) freshwater lake in the world, lies southwest of Lake Victoria.

Lake Victoria

Tropical savanna covers most of Eastern Africa. Rainfall generally depends on elevation, with the mountains receiving more precipitation than the lower coastlands. But in the mountains, a highland climate prevails.

Democratic Republic of Congo

History. Formerly known as the Belgian Congo and Zaire [zī′ĭr], the Democratic Republic of Congo is covered by dense rain forests. The Portuguese first reached the mouth of the Congo River, the world's second-largest river in the volume of water it carries, about 10 years before Columbus's first voyage to America. They established trade, primarily in slaves, with the Kongo kingdom; but they never explored the river.

It was 395 years before the first white man journeyed up the Congo River into the heart of Africa. American explorer **Henry M. Stanley** (who had searched for and found David Livingstone), under orders from the king of Belgium, traced the Congo to its source. The king of Belgium governed the Congo Free State as a personal domain until 1908 when the region became an official colony called the **Belgian Congo.**

Independence. The Belgians established plantations and mining companies in the Congo and sent thousands of Catholic missionaries to the region, but they did little to help the native people develop themselves and failed to prepare them for independence. Thus, when independence came in 1960, the Congo immediately fell into political chaos, with several groups fighting for control.

The United Nations sent "peace-keeping" forces in an attempt to maintain order, but rather than promoting peace the UN only added to the problem. When one province tried to peacefully secede, UN troops crushed the independence movement. Many people of the Congo died in the struggle. Hundreds of Europeans were killed, including many missionaries, as well as thousands of Congolese.

Time of change. Finally, General Joseph **Mobutu** [mŭ·bo͞o′to͞o] emerged as the victor and established a dictatorship in 1965. He immediately began to place the Congo's most important industries, including those owned by foreign companies, under state control. He then tried to remove all foreign cultural influences, including the use of Christian names. Mobutu renamed the country **Zaire** and required all citizens to take African names. Then he ruthlessly maintained power for some 30 years at the expense of his suffering people.

General Joseph Mobutu

African Pygmy hunter

The Democratic Republic of Congo has the potential to be one of Africa's richest countries. It has lush rain forests; large plantations; deposits of copper and cobalt; and reserves of gold, silver, uranium, diamonds, and oil. Yet this country has one of the poorest economies in Africa. During his dictatorship, Mobutu led the nation into debt while he became one of the world's richest men. Although he prospered, his people joined the ranks of the world's poorest.

Civil war. In 1997, a civil war in Zaire forced Mobutu to step down and flee the country. The new leadership immediately abolished the Zairean constitution and changed the name of the country from Zaire to the **Democratic Republic of Congo.** Military rule ended in 2006 when a democratic election took place.

The people today. More than 200 tribes live in the Democratic Republic of Congo today. Almost all of these tribes speak their own dialect, but they communicate with each other in French, the official language. Groups of **Pygmies,** short descendants of the original inhabitants, still roam the forests, living almost entirely by hunting wild animals and gathering wild plants. Most people, however, live in rural villages or in towns and cities, such as **Kinshasa** [kĭn•shä′sə: formerly Leopoldville], the capital and largest city. Many live by working their small farms; others work on plantations or in mines.

Comprehension Check 9C

1. What are the two large lakes located in Eastern Africa?
2. What are these two lakes known for?
3. What dictator took over the country of Congo and renamed it Zaire?
4. After that dictator lost control, what was the country renamed?
5. What are the short descendants of the original inhabitants of this country called?
6. What is the capital of this country?

Ethiopia

History. Unlike most African nations, Ethiopia was never a European colony. For this reason, it has been important to modern Africa as a symbol of independence. You will remember that the ancient kingdom of Aksum accepted Christianity through the influence of Frumentius and Aedesius, and that Frumentius became the first bishop of the Ethiopian Orthodox Church.

The invasion of Northern Africa by Arab Muslims in the 600s isolated Ethiopia from the rest of Christendom for nearly 800 years. During its isolation, the Ethiopian Church continued to thrive, fighting for survival against Muslim invaders until the Portuguese helped the Ethiopians defeat the Muslims in the 1500s. After a time of division, the Ethiopian empire was finally reunited in the late 1800s, and modern Ethiopia was born.

Emperor Haile Selassie I

Progress. In 1930, **Emperor Haile Selassie I** [hī′lē sə•lăs′ē] began a program of modernization in Ethiopia to increase the prosperity and security of his people. By 1970, Ethiopia had a written constitution, a parliament, and a court system; and programs were in motion to improve transportation, education, and agriculture.

Communism. But Ethiopia's progress came to a halt in 1974, when a military revolt overthrew Selassie and set up a Communist dictatorship. The Ethiopians' great emperor died in captivity while his beloved country crumbled around him. As the military confiscated all farmland and forcibly relocated tribal groups, Ethiopia was plunged into a devastating famine that killed millions.

Modern day. In 1991, after 17 years of Communist oppression, the Ethiopians drove their dictator out of the country and began a long struggle to rebuild their land. Years of Communism, civil war, and tribal conflicts have made Ethiopia one of the world's poorest countries. Most Ethiopians today are farmers or herdsmen with some nomads. A small percentage of the people live in cities or towns. **Addis Ababa** [ăd′ĭs ăb′ə·bə], the capital, is the largest city in Ethiopia.

Kenya

Geography. The Republic of Kenya is located on the equator, just south of Ethiopia. Because of its elevation, Mount Kenya is covered with snow all year even though it rests on the equator. In the southwest corner of the country lies Lake Victoria, the world's second-largest freshwater lake and the major source of the Nile River.

History. Most Kenyans live in the highlands of the southwest. Forests and grasslands cover much of this region, especially around Lake Victoria. Tall, thin Masai [mä·sī] herder-warriors migrated to the central highlands, Kenya's most fertile land, in the 1700s and successfully drove out all other tribes except for the Kikuyu [kĭ·ko͞o′yo͞o]. The Kikuyu were able to hold onto their farmland until the arrival of the British in 1895. Soon a railroad was constructed to link the interior with the coast, and European settlers began to set up plantations in the fertile highlands. By 1920, Kenya had become a British crown colony.

Masai herder-warriors

Over the next 30 years, the British developed Kenya, introducing cash crops such as coffee and tea, building hospitals and schools, and establishing trade with other nations in Africa and overseas. The railroad town of **Nairobi** became a modern city as the capital of the colony and later of the country. But native tribes, especially the Kikuyu, resented the British intrusion into their farmlands and declared war on all European settlers in the 1950s. In the fighting, the Kikuyu and other hostile tribes massacred 1,700 Africans and about 100 European settlers and missionaries before British troops were able to subdue the uprising. Afterward, Britain accepted the idea of Kenyan independence and in 1963, Kenya became a republic.

Modern times. A Kikuyu leader of the fighting, Jomo **Kenyatta** [kĕn·yä′tə], became the country's first president. By 1978, Kenya had become one of the most industrialized countries in Africa. Agriculture remains the largest export industry, however, and most Kenyans continue to live in rural areas, where they work on communal farms and plantations. One of the country's most important economic activities is tourism; half a million people visit Kenya every year to see its exotic wildlife.

Tanzania

Geography. The country of Tanzania lies south of Kenya, between Lake Tanganyika, the longest and second-deepest freshwater lake in the world, and the Indian Ocean. With Africa's highest peak, Mount Kilimanjaro, and its three largest lakes, Tanzania has some of the most inspiring scenery in the world. Most of the country consists of a broad plateau. The famous Serengeti [sĕr′ən·gĕt′ē] Plain occupies a portion of this plateau southeast of Lake Victoria. Two islands, Zanzibar [zăn′zə·bär] and Pemba [pĕm′bə], lie off the northeastern coast. Mangrove forests and swamps characterize the coast, and savanna grasslands cover much of the plateau.

ANIMALS AROUND THE WORLD

Elephants and Egrets

Africa is home to many wonderful animals, some of which are not found anywhere else in the world. In the desert, you would see camels. In the grasslands, you would find lions, giraffes, hippopotamuses, zebras, wildebeests, baboons, and elephants.

The elephant is the largest land animal in the world. A full-grown male can weigh 13,000 pounds, almost as much as a school bus! Even a baby elephant is big, weighing close to 200 pounds. That would be as much as you and two or three of your friends. The elephant has very heavy feet, and he is able to trample and crush enemies such as tigers or leopards. An elephant's little toenail can be bigger than your hand. Do you think you'd be afraid to come close to those big feet? At least one animal in the world is not—the egret.

An egret is a small, white bird that makes cattle, elephants, and other grazing animals its companions. Egrets will walk along with the elephants, eating the insects stirred up by the elephants' feet. In return, it helps the elephant by sitting on its back and eating ticks and other insects that can bite and irritate the elephant's skin. When the bird senses danger near, it will fly up and call out, warning the elephant that enemies lurk about. How wonderful the partnership God has designed between this large, heavy beast and small, fragile bird!

giraffes at Serengeti National Park

baboon

lion

Like Kenya, Tanzania is famous for its savanna wildlife. Nearly ⅓ of the country is set aside for national parks or game preserves. **Serengeti National Park,** a large wildlife refuge covering some 5,000 square miles on the Serengeti Plain, is famous for its lions, wildebeests, zebras, rhinoceroses, giraffes, baboons, leopards, elephants, and more than 200 species of birds.

History. Arabs controlled the islands and the coast for centuries, trading ivory and slaves with merchants from Arabia and India. In the late 1800s, Great Britain claimed the island of Zanzibar, and Germany colonized the mainland, called Tanganyika. During World War I, the British acquired the German colony, which they controlled until Tanganyika became independent in 1961. When Zanzibar joined Tanganyika a few years later, the country of Tanzania was born.

Communism. Like many newly independent African countries, Tanzania came under the power of a strong leader, Julius **Nyerere** [nyə·rĕr′ā]. In 1967, Nyerere instituted economic reforms that transformed Tanzania into a Communist state. The government seized profitable British plantations, factories, and land, and forced rural African tribes to work on collective farms.

The results of Tanzania's Communist experiment were disastrous. Farmers refused to grow food because the government's regulated price was too low, and once-profitable plantations became overgrown with tangled vines and trees. Today, the rural landscape is dotted with the remains of abandoned farm equipment, factories, and irrigation systems that the Tanzanians were unable to operate or maintain because they lacked the necessary education, funding, and spare parts. Tanzania's economy collapsed, and the people finally forced Nyerere to resign in 1985.

Modern times. Tanzania, with its capital at **Dar es Salaam,** has many cultural groups and many languages. The majority of the people live in rural villages. Almost ½ of the Tanzanian people consider themselves Christians, and about ⅓ are Muslims. Because Nyerere's Revolutionary Party remains in power, freedoms are still limited, but the government has begun to permit some free enterprise capitalism.

Tanzania's economy depends largely on farming, especially of coffee and cotton. The island of Zanzibar produces ⅓ of the world's cloves. Mineral resources, including oil off the coast of Pemba, await development, and manufacturing is limited.

Comprehension Check 9D

1. Which Tropical African country was never a European colony?
2. What emperor led this country on a program of modernization?
3. What system of government took over the country and led it away from the progress it had seen?
4. What is the capital of this country?
5. What is the capital of Kenya?
6. Which country contains Mount Kilimanjaro and Africa's three largest lakes?
7. What famous national park is also located there?

9.3 Southern Africa

Southern Africa is made up of 10 mainland countries and 4 island nations. Can you find all 14 Southern African countries on the map on p. 150?

The **Cape of Good Hope,** a small peninsula at the southwestern tip of the continent, forms one of the best harbors in Africa and guards a strategic position between the Atlantic and Indian oceans.

The **Drakensberg** [drä′kənz·bûrg′] **Mountains** in the southeast form the only significant mountain range in Africa besides the Atlas Mountains on the western edge of the Sahara.

As it courses eastward across the continent, the Zambezi River forms one of Africa's most spectacular natural formations, Victoria Falls, called the "Smoke that Thunders" because of the cloud of mist that rises up from it. Victoria Falls is Africa's largest waterfall, and is sometimes included among the Seven Natural Wonders of the World.

Drakensberg Mts.

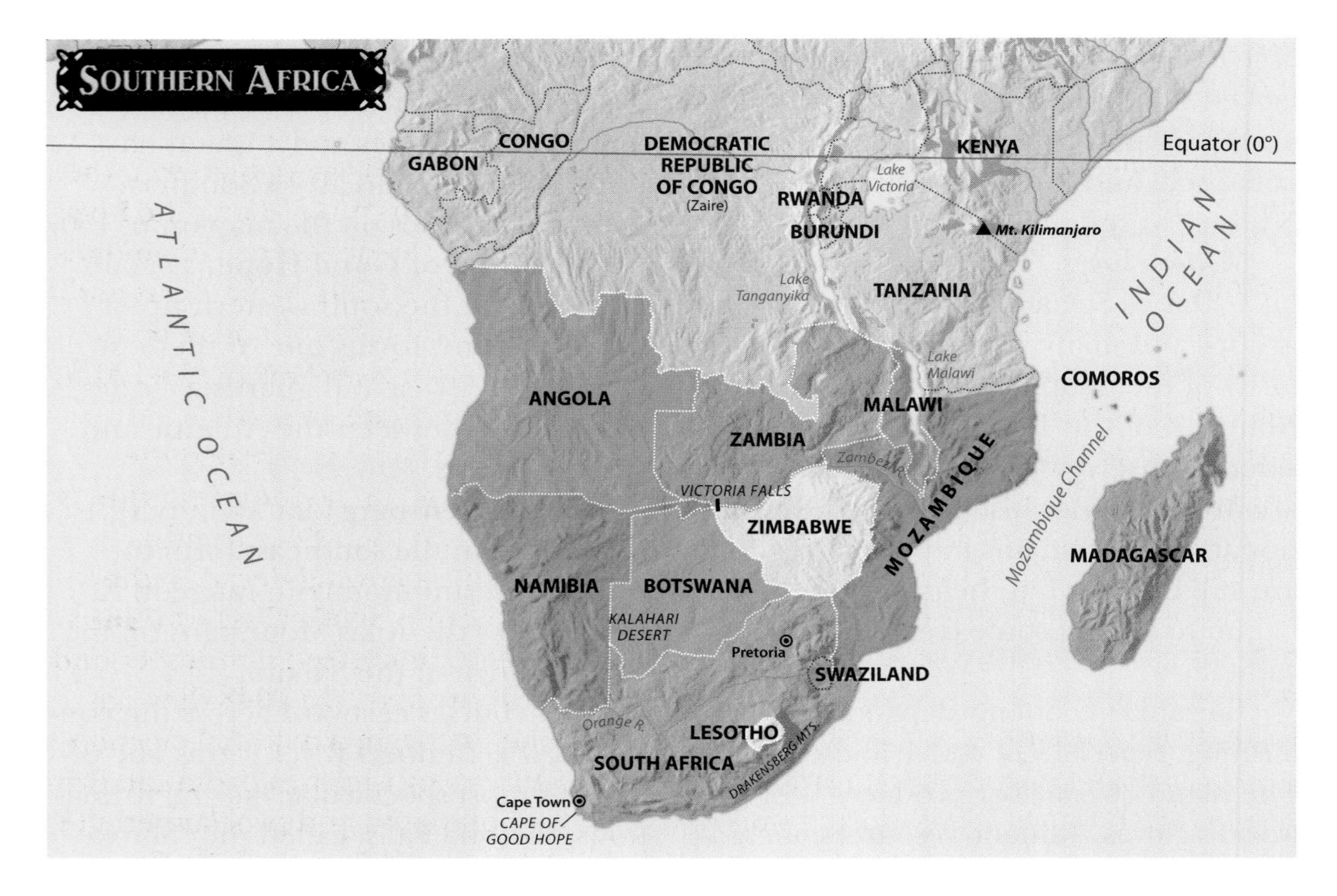

Most of Southern Africa has a steppe or desert climate. Steppe nearly surrounds the Kalahari, Southern Africa's largest desert region, while a savanna climate influences several of the countries. The region's highest annual rainfall is found in the extreme south: the Cape of Good Hope has a Mediterranean climate, and the uplands to the east have a marine west coast climate.

Republic of South Africa

The **Republic of South Africa** has more than one capital city. **Cape Town** is its legislative capital, and **Pretoria** is its executive capital. Although South Africa has suffered from conflict within and opposition without, it is the wealthiest and most highly developed nation in Africa. Part of its success may be attributed to abundant mineral resources, but the hard-working people must be

Cape Town, South Africa

given credit for the great nation they have built at the southern tip of the African continent.

European settlement. In addition to many African tribes, the population of South Africa includes people of European and Asian origin. The first Europeans to arrive in South Africa were Dutch colonists, who founded Cape Town on the Cape of Good Hope in 1652. About that same time, several African tribes settled northeast of the Orange River. As Dutch farmers, called **Boers** [bōrz], moved inland in search of pastureland for their growing herds, they met these African tribes moving southward. Thus began a long struggle over territory.

The British joined this territorial conflict in the early 1800s, during wars against France that were fought in Europe. Because the British feared that the French might use the Cape's strategic location to control trade and travel between Britain and India, they seized the area around Cape Town to keep it out of the hands of the French.

A British colony. After defeating France, the British remained on the Cape and took formal possession of the Dutch colony there. The British ended the fighting south of the Orange River and brought in laborers from India and other parts of Southern Asia to work on plantations. Resenting the British takeover and desiring to govern themselves, several thousand Boers packed up and left the Cape in 1835. As the Boers migrated northeast of the Orange River, they pushed the African tribes into the hills and established two new republics of their own.

Trouble erupted again, however, when British prospectors poured into the Boer republics after the discovery of diamonds (1868) and gold (1886). The Boers and the British finally took up arms against each other in the **Boer War** (1899–1902), which ended in British victory.

By 1910, Britain had created the Union of South Africa, including the Cape Colony and the Boer republics. Over the following decades, the Boers, who came to be called *Afrikaners* [ăf·rĭ·kä′nərz], increased in number and in political strength. In 1948 they defeated the British in a national election, and in 1961 they withdrew from the British Commonwealth and proclaimed the Republic of **South Africa.** (The **Commonwealth of Nations** is an association that includes Great Britain and about fifty-two nations that were once British colonies. The Commonwealth nations and their territories cover about ¼ of the earth's land surface and have about ¼ of the world's population. The king or queen is the symbolic head of the Commonwealth nations, but each has its own government.)

The new republic. To keep control of the country and prevent fighting among rival tribes, the Afrikaners divided South Africa's population into several racial groups—white, black, Indian, and people of mixed ancestry—and established 10 "homelands" for the black African population. The white Afrikaners generally kept for themselves the lands with more fertile soil and mineral wealth. The program of racial divisions also kept black South Africans from political participation and permitted widespread discrimination in employment, education, and housing. Many black Africans obtained permits to work in the cities or in the mines, but they were required to live apart in black communities on the outskirts of the cities.

Throughout the 1960s and 1970s, opposition to the racial divisions grew within South Africa and around the world until the United Nations intervened. World news media focused on the racial conflict, making the Afrikaners' discrimination against black South Africans known. But newscasts did not mention the Afrikaners' struggle against Communist terrorists who were trying to take control of the country. Hundreds of black Africans suffered and died at the hands of Communist guerrillas, but the world blamed the South African government.

Communism. In 1990, South Africa's president began working to end the racial divisions. Black citizens received voting rights in 1992, and in 1994 South Africa held its first multiracial elections, which brought to power **Nelson Mandela** [măn·dĕl′ə], South Africa's first black president.

Mandela's political intentions soon became clear as he appointed Communists to key positions and extended government control over businesses and industries. The growing influence of Communism concerns South Africa's citizens, especially Christians who make up a large part of the population.

The people today. Today, most of South Africa's people are black Africans, some are white descendants of European settlers (mostly Afrikaners and British), and a small group are people of mixed ancestry (called Coloreds).

Nelson Mandela

South African tropical fruits sold at market

Afrikaner farmer inspecting harvest

A small minority of Asians still reside in the country as well.

Resources and industries. In the past century, South Africa has proved to be richer than anyone believed possible, with vast gold fields, diamond mines, uranium deposits, and large supplies of coal, iron, chromium, platinum, and other minerals. Gold and diamonds are still the country's leading exports.

South Africa's agricultural land has also been developed more effectively than anywhere else in Africa. Though about half of the people live in rural areas, relatively few are employed in agriculture because much labor is accomplished by machinery. The majority of the population is employed in mining or manufacturing. South Africa is able to feed its own people without needing to import food from other nations. Farmers grow tropical fruits and sugar cane along the eastern coast, and on the Cape they raise apples, grapes, and wheat. Much of the interior is pastureland. The Afrikaners have raised cattle and sheep since they came to the cape. South Africa is one of the world's leading suppliers of wool.

farmers growing sugar cane

9.4 Modern Africa's Needs

The gospel. Africa is a continent with many needs. It is still in need of the gospel. Many people have gone there as missionaries, but the continent is so vast, and spirit worship and the Muslim religion are so strong, that only a small percentage of Africans claim to be Christians. There is a great need for more Christians to take the gospel to the people of the second-largest continent.

Food, shelter, and education. There have been great famines and wars in Eastern Africa in recent years, and thousands of people are homeless and starving. All over Africa, there is a great need for education. Only about ten percent of Africans can read and write. In some areas, the mission schools have been shut down by the Communists who have taken over the government; thus there may be even more illiteracy (inability to read and write) in coming years.

Stable governments. Many of the new African governments are very unstable, and the threat of Communism is great. Communists promise the people a better way of life, and the people sometimes believe this. In reality, Communism brings a life of misery and terror.

CHAPTER 9 CHECKUP

A Know the countries and capitals of Africa and their locations. (See Continent Study 2, p. 323.)

B Know these locations.

1. Atlas Mountains
2. Cape of Good Hope
3. Drakensberg Mountains
4. Horn of Africa

C Who am I?

1. the Egyptian president who took over the Suez Canal by force
2. the Egyptian president who was the first head of an Arab state to make peace with Israel
3. Ethiopian ruler who tried to modernize his country but was defeated by Communism
4. first president of Kenya
5. first black president of South Africa
6. leader who brought Communism to Tanzania
7. leader who changed the name of his country to Zaire; when he was overthrown it became the Democratic Republic of Congo

D Answer each question.

1. What African nation has been independent for over 2,000 years?
2. What is the largest country in Africa?
3. What is the world's largest swamp?
4. What is the largest city in Africa?
5. What structure was built to control flooding along the Nile?
6. Name the area along the Mediterranean Sea that was famous for its fierce pirates.
7. What is the world's second largest freshwater lake?
8. What is the world's longest and second deepest freshwater lake?
9. What is Africa's highest mountain peak?
10. What man-made waterway connects the Mediterranean Sea and Red Sea?
11. What large national park is located in Tanzania?
12. Who are the very short people descended from the original inhabitants of the Democratic Republic of Congo?

13. Who were the Dutch farmers of South Africa that were later called Afrikaaners?
14. What organization consists of Great Britain and 52 former British colonies?
15. Which Arab nation was the first to make peace with Israel?
16. What mountain range is located along Africa's northwestern coast? Its southeastern coast?

E In complete sentences, tell about three or more of modern Africa's needs.

UNIT 3 EUROPE
BIRTHPLACE OF WESTERN CIVILIZATION

CHAPTER 10

ANCIENT GREECE
Home of Beauty

The ancient Greeks developed one of the most impressive cultures the world has ever known. They produced beautiful works of art and literature, and they developed a system of democracy, giving the people a voice in the government.

10.1 Geography

Greece is located on the **Balkan Peninsula,** which stretches out into the Mediterranean Sea from southeastern Europe. On the east side of Greece is the **Aegean Sea,** and on the west side is the **Ionian** [ī·ō′nē·ən] **Sea.** Ancient Greece also included many islands in the Aegean and Ionian Seas. The mainland of Greece is almost cut in half by the **Gulf of Corinth.**

Europe

- Three of the world's smallest countries are located in Europe. Andorra, covering only 175 square miles, is smaller than New York City. Liechtenstein and San Marino are not even half the size of Andorra. Can you find these tiny European countries on the map?
- A small section of Russia is located just north of Poland and is separated from the rest of the country by Latvia, Lithuania, and Belarus.
- Ruins of the Parthenon, an ancient temple, are a central feature of the Acropolis in Athens, Greece.

Greece has a rugged, rocky seacoast. Inland from the coast the land is very mountainous, making it difficult to farm. Today, crops can be grown on only about one fourth of the land.

10.2 The First Greeks

The Greeks were descendants of one of Japheth's sons. (Japheth was the third son of Noah.) The first settlers that we know of in the region were the **Minoans** [mĭ·nō′ənz], who lived on the island of **Crete,** and the **Mycenaeans,** who had a thriving city on the mainland of Greece. Both had flourishing cultures long before 1000 B.C.

You may be familiar with the legend about the Mycenaeans during the Trojan War. According to the legend, the war ended when the Mycenaeans

Trojan Horse

Homer, the blind poet

pretended to depart from the city of Troy in Asia Minor. They left behind a large wooden horse with soldiers hidden inside. When the curious Trojans brought the **Trojan Horse** inside their city walls, the hidden soldiers came out and opened the gates, allowing their comrades to enter and defeat the city.

10.3 ✠ Greek Alphabet and Writings

In the 700s B.C., the Greeks added vowels to the Phoenicians' alphabet. The new Greek alphabet spread quickly. The alphabet used previously was fine for making lists and for bookkeeping, but it was awkward to use for literature. Now Greek poets and writers could put their poems and stories down in writing instead of just reciting them.

Homer: The Blind Poet

The blind poet **Homer,** a **bard** or singing poet, probably lived about seven hundred years before Christ. Homer turned many old Greek stories and myths into two long poems called the *Iliad* [ĭl′ē·əd] and the *Odyssey* [ŏd′ĭ·sē], which are still read and enjoyed today. Because he was blind, Homer most likely sang or recited his poems to someone who wrote them down using the new Greek alphabet.

The ancient Greeks loved Homer's stories of made-up heroes and their imaginary gods, and much of what Greeks knew about the gods was learned from these works. Supposedly, Zeus [zo͞os] was the king of all the gods. Other gods were associated with nature—Apollo with the sun, Poseidon [pō·sīd′'n] with the sea, and Artemis [är′tə·mĭs] with the moon. There were also gods and goddesses who personified things from everyday life—Athena, the goddess of wisdom; Aphrodite [ăf′rə·dī′tē], the goddess of love and beauty; and Hera [hĭ′rə], the goddess of marriage.

Greek gods and goddesses were far from perfect; they acted in anger and selfishness much like human beings. The major difference between the Greeks and their gods seemed to be that men died and gods lived forever. The imaginary gods that Homer wrote

Aesop, writer of fables

about could give the Greeks no hope of life after death and no encouragement to live purely in this life.

Aesop: Writer of Fables

You have probably read many stories by one famous Greek. He was a freed slave named **Aesop** [ē′səp], who lived about six hundred years before Christ. Aesop, who may have originally come from Africa, became the most famous writer of fables in the world. Aesop's fables are stories that have a moral, or teaching, attached to them. They include the story of the frog that wanted to be as big as an ox, the crow that figured out how to get water from a pitcher, and the boy who learned how to handle nettles. From Aesop's fables come many of our common sayings, such as "sour grapes" and "don't count your chickens before they hatch."

10.4 Greek Philosophers

The word **philosopher** means "lover of wisdom." The Greek men known as philosophers loved to ask such questions as: Why do things happen the way they do? From what is the world made? What is energy? and What is the reason for living?

Most philosophers did not believe in the false Greek gods. For this, they were criticized. Some were even put to death. Still the philosophers demanded truths that could be explained.

Some Greek philosophers turned toward mathematics and science. In the 500s B.C., **Pythagoras** [pĭ·thăg′ər·əs] thought of some very important rules of mathematics that we still use today. Another philosopher, **Democritus** [dĭ·mŏk′rĭ·təs], passed along an atomic theory, which while not completely accurate, is close to our understanding of atoms today.

By the 400s B.C., a group of philosophers called the Sophists [sŏf′ĭsts] argued that something is true only if someone believes it. They taught that since the Greek gods did not exist, men should do whatever they desired. Since there was no god to punish them, they reasoned that there could be no right and no wrong. Thus, according to the Sophists, a man should do whatever he pleased.

Not all philosophers were pleased with this false view. **Socrates** [sŏk′rə·tēz], for one, asked, "What is the best way to live?" He was concerned with doing what was right and good. Yet he was condemned to die because he did not believe in the Greek gods. Two

Plato and Aristotle

other famous Greek philosophers were **Plato** [plā′tō] and **Aristotle** [ăr′ĭ·stŏt′′l].

Later on, philosophers became concerned with what makes man happy. As you can see, the questions and answers of philosophers can differ greatly from person to person. It is important that we as Christians base our understanding of things on the truth of God's Word. The Bible gives us the true answers to questions philosophers ask.

Comprehension Check 10A

1. On which peninsula is Greece located?
2. What early settlers of Greece are remembered for leaving the Trojan Horse outside the city of Troy?
3. What did the Greeks add to the Phoenicians' alphabet to make it usable for literature?
4. Who is a Greek example of a bard? What poems did he compose?
5. Name two famous Greek philosophers or "lovers of wisdom."

10.5 The Greek City

Government

Because over 70 percent of Greece's mainland is made up of mountains and her islands are scattered, transportation and communication from one city to the next were very difficult in ancient Greece. Thus Greece was a country made up of independent cities. Each city had its own government that ruled the people in the surrounding villages as well. This kind of government is called a **city-state.** Ancient Greece had hundreds of city-states; some were wealthy and powerful while others were very weak. The two most important Greek city-states were **Sparta** and **Athens.**

Since each Greek city wanted to rule itself, it had to be prepared to defend itself. Many Greek cities were surrounded by strong walls. Stone towers were often built along these walls from which guards could look for approaching enemies. Strong gates were the only way to enter the city.

Public Places

Each Greek city-state had important public places. The most important were the **acropolis** [ə·krŏp′ə·lĭs], the **agora** [ăg′ə·rə], the **theater,** the **gymnasium,** and the **stadium.**

The Acropolis. The ancient Greeks built their cities around high hills that could easily be defended. These hills became the center of the city and were known as the **acropolis,** which means "upper city." As the city grew, the acropolis also became a religious center, in

PEOPLE IN HISTORY

Archimedes and His Inventions

Perhaps the greatest scientist of ancient Greece was **Archimedes.** One famous story tells how he discovered the concept of volume displacement.

The king gave a mass of gold to a goldsmith to make a crown. When the crown was finished, the king suspected that a cheaper metal, such as silver, had been substituted for some of the gold.

Archimedes knew that gold is heavier than silver, so he reasoned that a crown of pure gold would have less volume than a crown of mixed metals, even though they weighed the same.

One day as he stepped into a full bathtub, Archimedes saw the water begin to overflow. He guessed that the amount of spilled water was equal to the volume of his body. He realized he could measure the volume of the crown by measuring the volume of water it would spill out of a full tub. When Archimedes put the crown into a tub and measured the spilled water, it displaced more water than pure gold did. The goldsmith had cheated!

Archimedes always considered his real work to be in mathematics. He invented an advanced form of mathematics, called calculus. He also discovered the value of *pi.* Among his other inventions are a type of irrigation system and the catapult. Truly, he was a gifted man. ⌘

which temples, shrines, and statues were built to honor the Greek gods. Often these buildings and statues were great works of art, yet sadly they had nothing to do with the one true God. The most famous acropolis whose ruins can still be seen is located in Athens.

The Agora. The **agora** was a marketplace where farmers could sell their produce and shopkeepers could sell their wares. It was also a meeting place for men who needed to do government business. Children gathered at the agora to play.

The Theater. Almost every ancient Greek city had an open **theater.** The earliest theaters were merely wooden seats arranged around a stage. But as people became more enthusiastic about Greek plays, the theaters grew larger. They

ruins of a Greek theater

ruins of the Parthenon, an ancient temple in the Acropolis of Athens

were built of stone around the sides of a hill with rows of seats rising one above the other. The theater was usually the largest gathering place in the city. Sometimes it was used for religious festivals as well as plays.

The Gymnasium. The **gymnasium** was another important place in every Greek city. Here, the young men spent many hours each day practicing their favorite sports, which included boxing, jumping, racing, and throwing the javelin. At first, the gymnasium was merely an open field. In time, the Greeks built large gymnasiums around the sides of open courtyards.

The Stadium. Not all Greek cities had a **stadium.** The stadium was a long racing track, straight at one end and rounded at the other. The most famous ancient stadium was built in the town of **Olympia.** It had room for 40,000 people to watch the races. That made it as large as many of our football stadiums.

Olympia is where the first Olympic games took place in 776 B.C. The Olympic games were religious festivals to honor Zeus, king of the Greek gods. Although there were other games to honor the gods, the Olympics were the most important. When the games first began, the only Olympic sport was a footrace; only men could participate, and only men could watch. Every four years, the Olympic games were held again. By 700 B.C., other sports that were practiced in the gymnasium were added to the Olympic games. Winners of the Olympic games were crowned with wreaths of wild olive leaves.

footrace at the early Olympic games

10.6 A Greek Idea—Democracy

The ancient Greeks were the first to develop **democracy**—the idea that the citizens of a country should take an active part in the government of the country. The word "democracy" comes from two Greek words that mean **people** and **rule.** It meant rule by laws that the people had made.

To the city-state of Athens goes most of the credit for developing this idea. The Greek idea of democracy was far different from today's democracy. In ancient Athens, there were many slaves. Neither slaves nor women had the right to vote. Only free male citizens had the right to vote. These free men were expected to work in the assembly, a group of men who made laws and important decisions about the government. While the free men's time was taken up with passing laws, their slaves were taking care of their homes and businesses.

Comprehension Check 10B

1. Who is known as perhaps the greatest scientist of ancient Greece?
2. What is a city-state?
3. Name five important public places of Greek city-states.
4. What is democracy?

10.7 Two Famous City-States

The two best-known city-states of ancient Greece were Sparta and Athens. They were very different from each other in their way of life and in their governments. Because of these differences, a strong rivalry developed and they often warred against each other.

Sparta

Sparta was the first city-state to become powerful in Greece. The Spartans were known for their **courage, strength,** and **loyalty.**

Dedicated to war. Sparta did not have a democracy like Athens. Sparta expected each citizen to lead a disciplined life dedicated only to the city. No trade was allowed with foreigners, for the rulers thought foreign goods might make life too easy for Spartans. Strangers were not welcome to visit Sparta because they might provide a bad influence on her citizens. The only poets who were appreciated were those who wrote poems on war and hate. Not even philosophers were welcome, for there was only one idea the government of Sparta wanted its people to learn—the art of war.

How babies were judged. From birth, a child was trained to be loyal, not to his family, but to his city. Parents took their newborn baby to a group of judges. If the judges said the baby was weak, it was taken to a lonely mountainside to die. The Spartans thought little of softness or gentleness, even when it came to their own children.

A boy's training. The Spartan government believed that a boy belonged to the city-state as soon as he was born. At the age of seven, he was taken from home, and his education—learning how to fight—began. The first step was to harden the boy. Nothing was made easy for him. He swam in the cold, swift river and slept on reeds pulled up from the river banks with his bare hands. He learned to endure pain without complaining, to despise cowards, and to admire bravery.

The young boys were organized into packs. At mealtime, the boys were purposely not given enough to eat. They were expected to learn how to steal food. If a boy was caught stealing, he was severely whipped, not because he stole but because he was caught.

Soldier and citizen. When a Spartan boy reached manhood, he was usually very strong and nimble, but also ignorant. Most were never taught to read and write. At the age of twenty, a young man became a soldier. At the age of thirty, he received the right to be a citizen. Now he could marry, but he was still a soldier and was away from his home much of the time. At sixty, he was no longer a soldier, but was expected to work either in public affairs or helping to train the young men. From birth to death, the Spartan government owned a man.

The work of the helots. The Spartan soldiers often conquered other Greek people outside their own city-state. These people were called **helots** [hĕl′əts]. The citizens of Sparta had only one occupation—to train and prepare for war. The helots grew the food and did all the other work.

Athens

Cultural center. Athens was located only 100 miles away from Sparta. It became the greatest cultural center of ancient Greece as well as the most famous city-state. Many great philosophers, writers, and statesmen lived there. Our world still enjoys the cultural achievements of those men today. Ruins of the great buildings of Athens can be visited by tourists. Athenian works of drama are still performed in theaters. As you study further in school, you will probably read some of the history, philosophy, and poems that the authors of Athens wrote.

The statesman Pericles [pĕr′ĭ·klēz] became one of the greatest political leaders of ancient Greek history. He worked to make Athens a democracy. Among his changes was allowing the common people as well as the wealthy to serve in government jobs.

Training of children. Although Athenian parents admired the disciplined children of Sparta, they treated their own children with more care. The children of Athens had many toys to play with and were allowed to play games. Rough play was not encouraged as it was in Sparta. Some believe that in the 300s B.C., an Athenian philosopher and mathematician invented the baby rattle. Other toys were much the same as children had in other cultures—dolls, tops, boats, carts, toy animals, and balls. Until they were seven years old, Athenian children stayed with their mother and the other women of the family.

A boy's companion. From the age of seven, boys were influenced by men. A trusted male slave was given the responsibility of being the boy's constant companion. He accompanied the boy to and from school, and he stayed at school to observe the boy while he studied. The slave carried the boy's school supplies and protected him from harm. One of his main responsibilities was to teach the boy good manners. How different this was from encouraging a boy to steal as was done in Sparta!

What boys studied. Education in Athens was not controlled by the government as in Sparta. The purpose of Athenian education was to develop the abilities of each boy and make him a good citizen. Athenian boys studied reading, writing, speech, arithmetic, music, dancing, and gymnastics. Their main textbooks were the works of the Greek poets, especially Homer's *Iliad* and *Odyssey*. They read these books, memorized passages from them, and practiced their speech by reciting portions of them. For most boys, school ended at age fourteen. Only wealthy families could afford to send their sons for further education. Poorer boys found a job. At sixteen, those who could attend school went to a government-run gymnasium where they were trained to become citizen-soldiers. In addition to learning the art of war, they held discussions to improve their reasoning and speaking abilities.

The Athenian boys' oath. At the age of eighteen, Athenian boys became citizens of Athens. They made this pledge in a solemn ceremony:

> *We will never bring disgrace to this our city by any act of dishonesty or cowardice. We will fight for the ideals and sacred things of the city, both alone and with our companions. We will revere and obey the city's laws. We will try unceasingly to quicken the sense of civic duty in others. In every way we will strive to pass on the city to our sons greater and better than it was when our fathers passed it on to us.*

What girls learned. Greek girls did not go to school. The Greeks believed that all a girl needed to learn could be learned at home. This included cooking, making clothes, and caring for children. Some girls from wealthy homes also learned music, dancing, and poetry.

Wars

At one time in Greek history, Athens and Sparta put aside their differences and united against the threat of an invasion by the Persians. Although the Persian Empire was much larger than the land of Greece, the outnumbered Greeks fought hard and eventually won the Greco-Persian Wars.

Later, however, Athens and Sparta went to war with each other. All of the city-states in Greece had sided either with Athens or Sparta. In the end, Sparta and her allies defeated Athens and hers. However, less than a year later, the cities of Greece threw off the Spartan yoke and regained their independence.

Comprehension Check 10C

1. What was the first powerful city-state in ancient Greece?
2. What was the only occupation of citizens in that city-state?
3. Which city-state was the greatest cultural center in ancient Greece?
4. After age seven, boys from that city-state were influenced by ___?___.
5. At what age did Spartan young men become citizens? Athenian young men?

10.8 Philip of Macedonia

Macedonian Kings

Macedonia was a small country just north of Greece. Unlike Greece, Macedonia was ruled by powerful kings. The Greeks had no respect for the Macedonians, considering them an uncivilized people. They called them and anyone else who did not speak Greek, *barbarians.* Even so, the Macedonian kings claimed to have Greek ancestors, and they admired Greek culture. Although Macedonia was small and unimportant to the Greeks, it was to have a king who would become one of the greatest generals in all history—**Alexander the Great.**

The Father of Alexander the Great

Philip II, the father of Alexander, became king of Macedonia in 359 B.C. He desired to rule all of Greece, something that no man, not even a Greek, had accomplished. Philip had a few advantages that helped him. Macedonia had gold mines that helped pay for a well-equipped army of full-time soldiers. Philip's army was also trained to fight as a **phalanx** [fā′lăngks], a large group of foot soldiers who were armed with shields and with spears that were fourteen feet long. These highly trained soldiers moved together as if they were one giant soldier with one great spear and shield. This type of army was very effective in sweeping enemies out of its path. Usually, the phalanx was a 256-man square that fought alone. Sometimes, many phalanxes moved together, in which case the soldiers numbered several thousand.

Philip had many bold plans. After he conquered Greece, he planned to go to the Middle East and conquer the Persian Empire. This would be an enormous job. By 338 B.C., Philip had conquered most of Greece. He did not make heavy demands upon Greeks, hoping to persuade them to join him in his conquest of the Persian Empire. However, he did not have a chance to complete his plans. In 336 B.C., he was assassinated. His son Alexander, only twenty years old, became king in his place.

10.9 Alexander the Great: Conqueror of the World

King Alexander of Macedonia

From the beginning, Alexander proved himself a strong and capable leader. He was able to put an end to any spirit of rebellion in Greek cities. He united them in the **League of Corinth** and became its president. Next, he turned his attention to his father's plans—conquering Persia. No better description of Alexander's daring drive on the battlefield can be found than what Daniel wrote in his prophecy about Alexander (Dan. 8:5–7, 21). Alexander, the king of Greece, charged like a goat with a single, powerful horn—he was like a raging animal, shattering and trampling everything in its way.

Alexander the Great accepts the surrender of a conquered king.

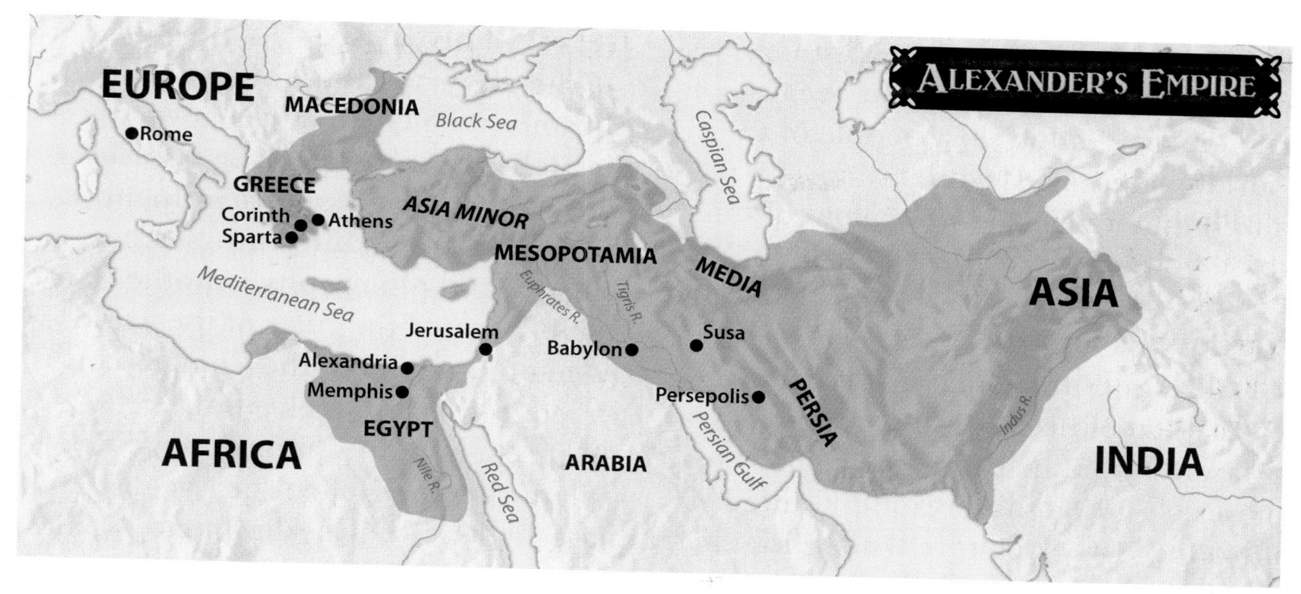

King Alexander of Asia

At this time in history, Persia ruled the Middle East. King Alexander began his invasion of the Middle East in 334 B.C. In a series of brilliantly fought battles, he swept eastward, conquering as he went.

The conquest of Egypt. Because the Egyptians hated their cruel Persian rulers, they welcomed Alexander. In fact, they claimed him as one of their gods. Alexander built many new cities in lands he had conquered, naming sixteen of these cities **Alexandria,** after himself. The Alexandria built in Egypt became the most important city in the world for that time period. It became a center for trade and was most famous for its great library that, with time, held a famous collection of over 700,000 ancient scrolls. Many Jews lived in Alexandria, and some of them translated the Old Testament into Greek. Alexandria and all the other cities Alexander built in lands he conquered helped to spread Greek culture throughout the ancient world.

The conquest of Persia. From Egypt, Alexander turned his army toward Persia. Babylon surrendered. Darius III, the King of Persia, ran away. Later, the important Persian cities of Susa [so͞o′sə: Shushan] and Persepolis [pər·sĕp′ə·lĭs] were captured. From both of these cities, Alexander's men carried away vast amounts of gold and silver. It took twenty thousand mules and five thousand camels to carry away the great treasures from Persepolis alone. Over 100 years before, the Persians had burned the great public buildings in Athens. For revenge, Alexander burned Persepolis with its palace and beautiful buildings. The people living there were either killed or sold into slavery. The Persian Empire had been defeated.

Alexander became the king of Asia, his conquered lands reaching all the way to India. He had not lost a single battle. The world has since given him the title **Alexander the Great** because of his military genius. Few people of the world, including Alexander himself, realized that it was God who allowed him to be powerful in battle.

Ruling His Empire

Alexander the Great made Babylon the capital of his large, new empire. From Babylon, he began to organize his empire. Although Alexander wanted to introduce Greek culture throughout his empire, he permitted many people to keep their local customs. When he conquered Jerusalem, he allowed the Jews to continue their religious practices.

Alexander the Great was very proud. He often became drunk and gave harsh orders. During the war against Persia, a close friend named Clitus [clē′təs] saved his life. After the war, in a drunken rage, Alexander lost his temper and killed this very friend who had saved his life. This deed cost him the respect of many Greek soldiers.

The book of Daniel had prophesied a short life for Alexander. On June 13, 323 B.C., Alexander the Great, only thirty-three years old, died of a high fever after a long time of drinking with his men.

Daniel had also prophesied that Alexander's empire would be divided into four smaller kingdoms. When Alexander died, he left an infant son, but this child died. No heir to his throne was left. Quarrels broke out among four of Alexander's top generals, and his empire was divided among the four of them.

The Hellenistic Age

The 200 years after the death of Alexander the Great were known as the Hellenistic Age. During the Hellenistic Age, Greek culture influenced the world's art, architecture, science, religion, and philosophy. Another land, **Rome,** became the ruler of the world during this time, but the Romans continued to spread Greek culture.

Throughout the empire, new cities built during the Hellenistic Age displayed a definite Greek influence. Cities in Egypt housed their gods in temples of Greek design, and Greek columns began to appear on new buildings.

The influence of Greek culture on art could be seen as far away as India. Statues influenced by Greek design were placed in temples as well as in streets. Sculptures of people became very realistic, and wealthy men had marble statues made of themselves. The demand for statues became so great that factories were built to produce them.

During the Hellenistic Age and even afterward, Greek became the most important language of the world. People all over the known world could understand Greek. The alphabets of all the major European languages (including English) were based on the Greek alphabet. Some Greek words, such as *music, poetry, democracy, atom, philosophy,* and *biology,* have become a part of the English language. God used the spread of Greek culture to prepare the way for the writing of the New Testament in the Greek language.

CHAPTER 10 CHECKUP

A Know these locations.

1. Balkan peninsula
2. Aegean Sea
3. Ionian Sea
4. Gulf of Corinth
5. Crete

B Define each term.

1. bard
2. philosopher
3. city-state
4. democracy
5. phalanx

C Identify the place from its description.

1. the body of water that cuts Greece almost in half
2. the three seas surrounding Greece
3. the peninsula Greece is located on
4. the largest Greek island
5. the city-state where the Olympics began in 776 B.C.
6. the country Alexander the Great came from
7. the empire Alexander the Great was determined to conquer

D Who am I?

1. the blind bard who wrote the *Iliad* and the *Odyssey*
2. the writer of the famous fables
3. the philosopher concerned with the question, "What is the best way to live?"
4. the most famous scientist of ancient Greece
5. the father of Alexander
6. the Greek god honored by the Olympics

E Describe each of these public places.

1. acropolis
2. agora
3. theater
4. gymnasium
5. stadium

F Sparta or Athens?

1. greatest cultural center in Greece
2. developed the idea of democracy
3. boys trained to be good citizens
4. boys trained to be loyal soldiers
5. boys became citizens at 18

(cont.)

6. philosophers and foreigners not welcome here
7. first city-state to become powerful
8. most men here could not read or write
9. all work was done by the helots
10. the most famous city-state

G Answer each question.

1. How far east did Alexander's empire extend?
2. Which book of the Bible prophesied Alexander's powerful reign and short life?
3. How many cities did Alexander name after himself? Which one was the most important in its day?
4. What do we call the 200-year period that began with the death of Alexander?
5. What became the most important language during this time period and why was it important?
6. What happened to Alexander's empire after his death?
7. What was the purpose of the Trojan horse? Who built it?

CHAPTER 11

ROME
Ruler of the Ancient World

During the time that Greece was ruling the world from the Balkan Peninsula, another great power was rising up on the Italian Peninsula—the city of **Rome.** Rome eventually conquered Greece and ruled most of the ancient world. The Romans were a practical-minded people with a sense of justice and a respect for law and order that they spread throughout their empire. In the providence of God, the Roman Empire helped to prepare the world for the coming of Jesus Christ, for Rome ruled the world when Jesus lived on earth.

11.1 The Land

The Italian or **Apennine Peninsula,** which is called **Italy** today, is shaped like a boot with a very high heel. This "boot" is west of Greece and extends into the Mediterranean Sea. Near the toe of the boot is the island of **Sicily** [sĭs′ə·lē]. Surrounding the boot are two arms of the Mediterranean Sea, the Tyrrhenian [tə·rē′nē·ən] Sea and the Adriatic Sea.

Mountains

To the north of Italy are the **Alps,** the largest mountain system in Europe. The Alps form a curving northern boundary of almost five hundred miles from west to east.

The **Apennines** is a great chain of mountains that runs down the length of Italy. They are not as high as the Alps and cover about two thirds of the Apennine Peninsula. To the west of the Apennines is a broad, fertile plain. The city of Rome was built on the rolling hills of this plain.

Rivers

There are two important rivers in Italy. The longest, the **Po River,** begins in the Alps and flows eastward, emptying into the Adriatic Sea. Almost all the rivers in northern Italy are branches of the Po. The fertile Po Valley con-

tains Italy's best farmland. The **Tiber** [tī′bər] **River** begins its course in central Italy in one of the Apennine Mountain ranges, and flows through Rome into the Tyrrhenian Sea.

11.2 The People

Italians, Latins, Etruscans, and Greeks

Around 1000 B.C., a group of people called the Itali settled on the Apennine Peninsula. Italy was named after them. Another group were the Latins, who settled near the Tiber River and built the city of Rome. The language used by the Romans was later called **Latin.** The Etruscans were a strong and powerful group who settled north of the Tiber River around 800 B.C. They built the first cities in Italy, some of which are still in existence today. By 800 B.C., the Greeks began building colonies in southern Italy and the nearby island of Sicily.

The "City of the Seven Hills"

About 17 miles east of the Tyrrhenian Sea on the Tiber River, there is a group of hills. Seven of these hills became important in the building of Rome. Rome was often called the "City of the Seven Hills."

How the Greeks Influenced Rome

The Greeks had built many colonies in southern Italy and on the nearby island of Sicily. In fact, Greece had built so many colonies in this area, that it became known as "Greater Greece." Greek culture strongly influenced the Romans as they built their Roman empire.

The Romans were much more practical than the Greeks who influenced them. While the Greeks had spent much time and money chiseling stone for buildings, the Romans built their cities with bricks that could be made quickly and cheaply. To give the appearance of stone, the Romans sometimes covered the brick walls of their important buildings with beautiful slabs of marble. The effect was just as beautiful as the Greek buildings, the cost was much less, and the buildings were similar in strength.

The Romans imitated the Greeks most in the area of the fine arts. Fine arts include such skills as music, painting, sculpture, and acting in the theater. The Romans also imitated the religion of the Greeks. They worshiped the same Greek gods, giving them Latin names, such as Jupiter, Mars, Mercury, Neptune, and Venus, and they made up new stories about them. Do you know why the names of these Roman gods are familiar to us today?

Comprehension Check 11A

1. On which peninsula is Rome located? What is it called today?
2. Name the two mountain ranges of Italy.
3. Name the two major rivers of Italy.
4. Which of the four groups that settled on the Apennine Peninsula built Rome?
5. Greek culture influenced the Romans most in the area of ___?___.

PEOPLE IN HISTORY

Romulus and Remus—A Legend about the Founding of Rome

A **legend** is a story that is passed down from person to person, year after year, until finally the story is written down. Legends are not usually true, but they are often interesting to read. The Romans made up legends concerning the building of their city. Many ancient people believed they were true. The most famous of these legends is the story of **Romulus** [rŏm′yə·ləs] and **Remus** [rē′məs].

According to the story, Romulus and Remus were twin infant brothers who were abandoned in a basket that was placed in the Tiber River by their uncle, the king. He did not want either of the twins to threaten his rule when they grew up. When their basket washed ashore, a wolf found them and cared for them. Later, a shepherd found the boys and raised them as his own sons.

After the boys were grown, they learned who they really were. They killed the wicked uncle and set out to build their own city. But they quarreled over where the city should be built. After Romulus began building the city, Remus jumped over the sacred ditch that surrounded the city. Such an act was considered very disrespectful, and for it Remus was killed. Romulus, then ruler of the new city, named it **"Roma"** for himself.

11.3 Life in Rome

Home Life

Clothing. All Romans wore a **tunic,** a short-sleeved garment that hung to or above the knees and was usually fastened with a belt. The **toga,** a long drape worn over the tunic, could be worn only by a Roman citizen. Most people wore **sandals.**

typical Roman dress

Education. The Roman children were taught much like the Greeks. For a while, their parents taught them. In wealthy homes, the children were often taught by a highly educated Greek slave. Higher education was usually for boys of wealthier families. Poorer families needed their sons to work. Among the school supplies were a wax tablet to write on, a stylus to write with, and books or scrolls to read.

Homes. Wealthy Roman homes were built around a central room called the **atrium** [ā′trē·əm]. An opening in the atrium's roof allowed rainwater to fall into a small, shallow pool below. The atrium was the main room of the house. In it stood an altar for worship of the family gods. There were rooms off each side

reconstruction of a Roman dining room

of the atrium for eating and sleeping. In the dining area, there were couches upon which the Romans reclined as they ate their meals.

Poorer Romans had one-room homes, and some Romans lived in apartments. The Romans were among the first people to build apartment houses, some of which were five stories high.

The Romans at Work

Rome's Mediterranean climate made it a good place for farming. The Romans grew grains, vegetables, and fruits, including many olive trees and vineyards. Some farmers raised flocks of sheep and goats on the hillsides. Other animals included hogs, poultry, donkeys, and mules.

The Romans were good farmers. They not only irrigated and fertilized their crops to provide water and food for the plants, but they rotated their crops to help save the land's fertility. **Crop rotation** is growing one kind of crop on a piece of ground for a while and then growing another kind of crop on that same ground.

As the Romans conquered other countries, they were able to use the goods made by these nations for their own use and for trade. These goods included pottery, linen, wool, silk, perfumes, silverplate, bronzeware, purple dye, parchment, and glassware.

Mining was very important to the Romans, although most mining was done outside of Italy. Marble was mined in northern Italy and Greece. Iron and silver were mined in Spain. Gold, copper, and tin were mined in other areas.

Roman Accomplishments

Roads, bridges, and tunnels. Have you ever heard the saying **"All roads lead to Rome"?** The Romans built a system of roads that connected the various kingdoms and countries within their empire to the empire's capital, Rome. At that time in history, nearly all roads of any importance did lead to Rome.

The Romans built bridges and tunnels to connect their highways over great distances. In this way, Rome could easily keep in touch with all parts of her empire. And if Roman soldiers were needed to stop an uprising, they could quickly get to the trouble spot by using the highways, bridges, and tunnels.

Roman road from the time of the empire

Aqueducts. Fresh, clean water is necessary for life. To transport water to areas that were not near a river or lake, the Romans built **aqueducts** [ăk′wĭ·dŭkts′]. An ancient aqueduct looked like a bridge. Along the top of this handmade stone "bridge" was a channel through which the water flowed. Sometimes the bottom level of the aqueduct served as a roadway while the top level carried water. The total length of all the Roman aqueducts was about 1,300 miles. Hundreds of thousands of gallons of water poured through their channels each day.

Concrete. Because the ancient Romans built their structures to last, they had to have building supplies that would provide lasting strength. To meet this need, the practical Romans invented concrete.

Government

The Roman Republic. From 509 B.C. to 27 B.C., Rome was a republic. The citizens of the Roman republic elected two **consuls.** These two consuls were rulers with equal power who each ruled for one year. There was also a **Senate,** whose members were the oldest and wisest men of Rome. Roman citizens were divided into two different classes: **patricians** [pə·trĭsh′ənz] and **plebeians** [plĭ·bē′ənz].

The Patricians. The patricians were born into wealthy, distinguished families. For many years, only patricians could hold high positions in the government or army.

The Plebeians. The plebeians were the common people—the farmers, peasants, and freed slaves. They could not hold public offices, but they were allowed to vote on laws. Slowly, over the centuries that the Roman Republic existed, the plebeians received more rights. By 200 B.C., they had most of the same rights that the patricians had.

During the period of the Roman Republic (509–27 B.C.), Rome became the mighty conqueror of the countries that surrounded the Mediterranean Sea.

ruins of a Roman aqueduct

Comprehension Check 11B

1. What is a legend?
2. Name the three main items of clothing worn by Romans.
3. What were a Roman student's main school supplies?
4. What does crop rotation mean to a farmer?
5. What did an aqueduct look like? What was its purpose?
6. Was a farmer a patrician or a plebeian?

11.4 How Rome Conquered the World

Rome Begins to Conquer

In 509 B.C., Rome overthrew the Etruscans, who had ruled over them for more than 100 years. The Latin tribes joined together with Rome to form the *Latin League.* The cities within this league helped each other fight their many enemies. The league worked fine for a while, but as Romans gradually grew stronger and stronger, the Latins began to fear them. By 338 B.C., the Romans had conquered the other Latins.

Fearing Rome, the Greek colonies in southern Italy asked the king of Greece for help in defeating Rome. The Greeks gave Rome several hard blows, but by 270 B.C., all the Greek cities in southern Italy belonged to Rome. This meant that almost all of the Apennine Peninsula now belonged to Rome.

Rome had been fighting its neighbors for over 200 years. The constant fighting was good training for Rome's soldiers, and it gave the Romans a "thirst" to keep on conquering. Perhaps it also gave the Romans a fear that someone would try to conquer them.

Rome Fights Carthage: The Punic Wars

Across the Mediterranean Sea from Italy was the great African city of **Carthage,** which the Phoenicians had founded as a trading post. By 300 B.C., Carthage had become a major power in the Mediterranean world. She had a powerful navy that allowed her to control parts of Spain and western Sicily, the island not far from Italy. Fearful of the power of Carthage and jealous of her wealth, Rome desired to conquer her.

The Romans were able to get an abandoned, oar-driven warship that was made in Carthage. Taking it to some shipbuilders, the Romans had 100 copies of the Carthaginian warship made in only 60 days. Although the Romans were not trained in naval warfare, they had the determination to beat Carthage. The Romans made a portable bridge that could be slammed into a Carthaginian ship from a Roman ship. Thus the Romans could board their enemies' ship and fight the way they knew best—hand to hand.

The war in which these naval battles took place lasted twenty-three years. It was the first of three wars that Rome fought with Carthage. These wars were called the Punic [pyōō′nĭk] Wars, after the Roman name for the Phoenicians. Rome won all of the wars, but not without a fierce struggle.

First Punic War. During the first war, Rome conquered the island of Sicily.

Second Punic War. During the second war, Carthage surrendered the Iberian Peninsula (modern Spain and Portugal) to Rome. Carthage was led by a great general named **Hannibal.** When Hannibal was nine years old, he had promised his father that he would conquer the Romans. When he grew up, he set out to do this. He knew that he would be defeated if he sailed directly to Rome. Instead, he decided to march over land to Rome. He sailed across the Mediterranean Sea to Spain. Through Spain and across **Gaul** (modern France) he marched with his army of about forty thousand men. Hundreds of mules and horses and thirty-seven war elephants carried the army's food and equipment. To get into Italy, Hannibal had to cross the steep, snow-covered Alps Mountains. Many men, horses, and elephants plunged to their death during the treacherous crossing, but at last the army arrived in Italy, where the Carthaginians won several battles before they were finally driven back to Africa by the Romans.

Third Punic War. During the third war, Rome completely destroyed the city of Carthage by burning it and sowing the land with salt. Salt made the land useless for growing plants for many years. Without crops to supply food, Carthage could not be rebuilt. Thus, she was no longer a threat to Rome. Rome was building an empire that now included the Apennine Peninsula, the Iberian Peninsula, and part of Africa.

Hannibal's war elephants

Rome Keeps Conquering

Macedonia and Greece. During the period of the Punic Wars, Rome also attacked other countries. Macedonia, the homeland of King Philip and Alexander the Great, had helped Carthage. To get even, Rome conquered Macedonia. At the same time, the city-states of Greece were quarreling among themselves. Rome also conquered them. By 146 B.C., 177 years after the death of Alexander the Great, the Balkan Peninsula was just another part of the Roman Empire. However, the culture of the Greeks continued to have a great influence on Rome.

Pergamum. The kingdom of Pergamum [pûr′gə·məm] was located in Asia Minor (modern Turkey). The king of Pergamum was friendly with Rome. In 133 B.C., Pergamum's king knew he was dying without any heir to his throne, and he asked Rome to take over his kingdom. Rome readily accepted. Pergamum was Rome's first **province** (land ruled by another country) in Asia. Now Rome's rule touched three continents—Europe, Africa, and Asia.

Syria and Mesopotamia. By 129 B.C., Rome had conquered Mesopotamia. In 64 B.C., Syria also became a Roman province. Palestine, which had been under Syrian rule, now had to obey Roman officials. This is how the Romans came to be the rulers of the Holy Land during the time of Christ.

The Rise of Julius Caesar

By 60 B.C., a Roman leader by the name of **Julius Caesar** [sē′zər] was on his way to becoming one of the greatest names in world history. In 59 B.C., he was elected as consul of Rome. At the end of his one-year term, Julius Caesar knew that he was well liked by the Roman people. Eager to gain fame and popularity, Caesar set out to conquer Gaul. It soon became clear that he had a natural ability to conquer. Indeed, he became one of the greatest military leaders in history.

Altogether, Caesar spent nine years in Gaul. He conquered Gaul, adding it to the territory that was soon to become the Roman Empire. He even crossed the English Channel to invade **Britain** twice. Later, Britain became the northwestern frontier of the Roman Empire.

Most Roman citizens were delighted to hear of Caesar's victories, but many government leaders were not happy at all. Pompey [pŏm′pē], a government leader, was very jealous of Caesar's popularity with the Roman citizens. In an effort to stop his fame, the Senate sent Caesar an order to disband his army and return to Rome. There may have even been a plot to kill Caesar on his way home. Leaving his army would leave him defenseless. Instead of obeying, Caesar led his army across the **Rubicon** [ro͞o′bĭ·kŏn′] **River** and into Italy. This was a direct act of disobedience to the government. Would the Roman citizens kill him for being a traitor or accept him as a hero? There was no turning back for Caesar. In fact, to this day, the term **"crossing the Rubicon"** means committing a deed that can never be reversed.

By crossing the Rubicon, Julius Caesar had begun a civil war among his own countrymen. As Caesar and his army approached, city after city in Italy opened its gates to him. Frightened by Caesar's military power, Pompey and most of the Senate fled Rome.

For five years, from 49 to 44 B.C., Julius Caesar controlled Rome and the lands that Rome conquered. With ease, Caesar became dictator for the rest of his life. (A **dictator** is a person who has absolute rule in his country's government, controlling all of its major decisions.) "Dictator" is not a very pleasant word to us, for most dictators rule their people selfishly and cruelly. However, Caesar worked to make his countrymen like him. Instead of killing or imprisoning his enemies, as past rulers had done,

Julius Caesar crossing the Rubicon

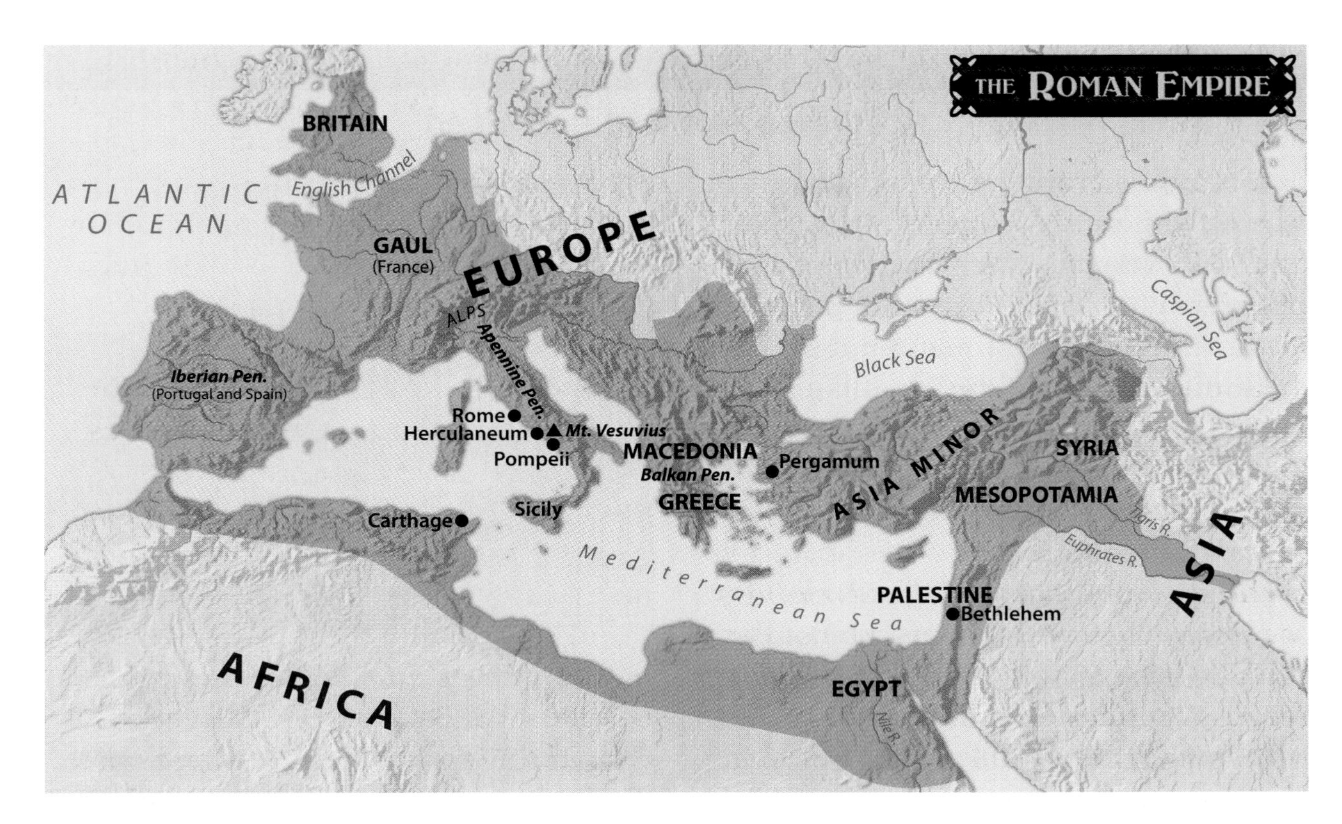

he pardoned them. He did his best to stop dishonesty. He improved the calendar. He worked to become a friend of the poor by providing jobs for them. He looked into his country's future by planning many projects that would benefit Rome. Among his plans were new public buildings, new roads, and new lands to be added to Rome's territory.

But Caesar hardly had time to begin work on his plans. There were still some jealous and selfish men in the Senate. This group of men plotted among themselves. On March 15, 44 B.C., they stabbed Julius Caesar to death. His murderers had hoped to become heroes. Instead, they had to flee Rome for their lives.

Mark Antony [ăn′tə•nē], Caesar's closest friend and assistant, seized power and began ruling in Caesar's place. Yet Julius Caesar had named his eighteen-year-old grandnephew, **Octavian** [ŏk•tā′vē•ən], as his heir. Both Octavian and Antony desired to rule. Would force and violence once again decide who would rule Rome?

Comprehension Check 11C

1. Why were the wars between Rome and Carthage called the Punic Wars?
2. Who was the Carthaginian general who used elephants in his weaponry?
3. What was Rome's first province in Asia?
4. What did Julius Caesar's "crossing the Rubicon" come to mean?

PLACES IN HISTORY

A Civilization Rediscovered

Sometime around noon on August 24, A.D. 79, without any warning, the top of Italy's Mt. Vesuvius was blown off in a violent explosion. Hot lava flowed down the northwest side of the mountain. On the southwest side of the mountain sat **Pompeii.** It was buried under volcanic stones, boiling water caused by the eruption, and ash. For three days the mountain and surrounding area were covered in flames, lightning, smoke, and clouds of poisonous gasses. About 2,000 of Pompeii's 20,000 residents were trapped in cellars or suffocated by the gas. For over 1,600 years, the city of Pompeii was to lie forgotten under hardened lava and ash.

ruins of Pompeii with Vesuvius in background

The city was rediscovered in 1748. Excavations have revealed much about life during the early period of the Roman Empire. The people of Pompeii were highly artistic. Their houses were filled with paintings, mosaics, and statues; even furnishings such as tables and chairs had intricately carved legs, tops, and sides. The citizens were interested in farming and fishing. The city was modern for its time, full of merchants, cobblers, bakers, and even surgeons. (A painting found in one of the houses depicts a surgery.)

One of the most remarkable discoveries is the writing on the walls. The people of Pompeii scratched messages and announcements on walls of their city. One person even wrote: "It is a wonder, O Wall, that thou has not yet crumbled into ruin under the weight of so much written nonsense." The writing is important because it gives us an accurate look into the everyday life of these people.

11.5 The Roman Empire (27 B.C.–A.D. 476)

Octavian and Mark Antony fought for many years over who would rule Rome. Mark Antony's ally was **Cleopatra,** the beautiful queen of Egypt. In 31 B.C., Octavian's and Mark Antony's navies met in battle, and Octavian won; Egypt became a Roman province. In 27 B.C., the period known as the Roman Republic ended, and the **Roman Empire** began. God's servant Daniel had prophesied that a powerful kingdom (empire)

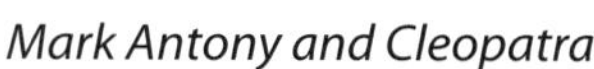

Mark Antony and Cleopatra

would come that would be as "strong as iron" (Dan. 2:40). That prophecy was fulfilled in the Roman Empire.

The Senate voted to give Octavian the name **Augustus,** which means "the exalted." After 27 B.C., Octavian was called **Augustus Caesar**, or Caesar Augustus. **Augustus Caesar** became the first emperor of the Roman Empire.

Augustus ruled for forty-one years, but his powerful influence continued to affect Rome for the next 200 years. The result of his wise rule was peace and prosperity, something that Romans had not known for 100 years. The 200 years of peace that followed the beginning of the Roman Empire is known as the **Pax Romana** (Roman Peace). Augustus expanded the Empire by adding new land to it. He organized a permanent army to protect the provinces belonging to the empire. He kept a navy in the Mediterranean Sea. To keep in contact with all parts of his huge empire, he built a system of well-paved roads reaching throughout the empire. Robbers and pirates were brought under control. Such improvements made travel much easier. As a result of the protection offered by the empire, trade and prosperity increased along with the growth of businesses. An efficient postal system was developed, providing even more communication. All of these improvements made possible the advance of the gospel in later years.

In an effort to tax the people more efficiently, Augustus attempted to find out the number of people living in each Roman province and the value of their property. This gathering of information is called a **census.** Taxes were based on the results of this census. One of Caesar Augustus' taxation decrees brought Mary and Joseph to Bethlehem where Christ the Lord was born (Luke 2:1–7).

The Roman Empire continued for about 480 years after the birth of Christ before falling to invaders from the north.

Roman coin bearing the image of Augustus Caesar

CHAPTER 11 CHECKUP

A Know these locations.

1. Apennine peninsula
2. Sicily
3. Alps
4. Apennines
5. Po
6. Tiber
7. Rome

B Define each term.

1. Latin
2. legend
3. tunic
4. toga
5. atrium
6. crop rotation
7. aqueducts
8. concrete
9. consuls
10. Senate
11. patricians
12. plebians

(cont.)

C Identify the term described by each clue.

1. land ruled by another country
2. a person who has absolute rule and controls all the country's major decisions
3. an official count of the people in a country

D Who am I?

1. legendary founders of Rome
2. Carthaginian general who nearly defeated Rome
3. dictator who was one of history's greatest generals
4. Julius Caesar's closest friend; wanted to rule after Caesar's death
5. Julius Caesar's grandnephew; chosen by Caesar as his heir
6. Mark Antony's beautiful Egyptian ally
7. Octavian's new name; "the exalted"

E Identify the place described in each clue.

1. island at the toe of Italy's boot
2. river that runs through Rome
3. powerful city in north Africa; Rome's rival
4. known today as "France"
5. Rome's first overseas province
6. city buried by Mt. Vesuvius's eruption in A.D. 79
7. island that became Rome's northwestern frontier

F Answer each question.

1. Finish: "City of the _?_ _?_."
2. Which people greatly influenced Roman culture?
3. Finish: "All roads _?_ _?_ _?_."
4. Name the series of wars fought between Rome and Carthage. How many were there? Who won all of them?
5. What was the result of each of these wars?
6. What did Hannibal use to transport food and equipment for his troops over the Alps?
7. Explain the expression "crossing the Rubicon."
8. Who was the first Roman emperor?
9. Who prophesied a powerful kingdom that would be "strong as iron"?
10. Name the 200-year period that followed the beginning of the Roman Empire. Describe the improvements made at this time that helped the spread of the gospel.

CHAPTER 12

CHRISTIANITY
The Greatest Force in History

12.1 The Greatest Event in History

When Jesus Came

The most important event in all history is the life, death, and resurrection of the Lord Jesus Christ. All through the ages that we call **"B.C."** (before Christ), God had been preparing the world for the time when His Son would come to earth and die for the sins of mankind. Now, after Caesar Augustus had been on the throne for thirty years, the time had arrived.

About half the people of the world were united peacefully under the Roman government. The roads that the Romans built throughout the empire would be used to speed the message of salvation. The Greek language, which was understood by most people in the eastern part of the empire, would be used to write the New Testament.

Many people realized by now that the old pagan gods were false. They were also looking for the truth about how to have eternal life and for a way to live the right kind of life here on earth.

The Earthly Ministry of Jesus Christ

When Jesus, the Son of God, came to earth, He did not come to the great city of Rome, but rather to the little Middle Eastern village of Bethlehem, not far from Jerusalem.

Jesus grew up in Nazareth, near the Sea of Galilee, and most of His earthly ministry took place among the Jews of Galilee. He preached for only three and a half years. He never wrote a book; He never conquered a kingdom; He never produced a work of art. He was sentenced to death and crucified when He was about thirty-three years old, but by Him all the nations of the earth have been blessed.

Every religious leader has died, or will die. Jesus died, too, giving up His life willingly for the sins of mankind. Unlike all the others, however, Jesus arose from the dead. He is alive now, at the right hand of God, ready to save all who put their trust in Him.

The Spread of the Gospel

Jesus taught truth not only for the Jews, but for all people everywhere. Before He went back to Heaven, He told His followers to tell the good news of salvation to those in Jerusalem, Judea, Samaria, and "unto the uttermost part of the earth" (Acts 1:8). The **Apostle Paul** was the first great missionary of the Christian church. Paul was born in Tarsus, a city of Asia Minor whose inhabitants had received the rights of Roman citizenship. He preached the gospel in many cities of Asia Minor and Greece, and he sailed as far west as Rome. Under his ministry, many became Christians. God used Paul and other apostles to write the books of the New Testament. Christians went all over the known world preaching the gospel and teaching the truths of the Bible.

12.2 Nero and the Persecution of the Christians

The Christians did not believe in the Roman gods and refused to join in the public ceremonies in which the emperor was worshiped as a god; therefore, they were disliked by the Roman rulers. But the Christians knew there was only one God, the Creator of Heaven and earth. Christians were very good citizens, for they knew that they were to obey those in authority over them. Because of their faith in Christ, however, they were cruelly persecuted.

The emperor **Nero,** the fifth emperor of the Roman Empire (A.D. 54–68), was an extremely evil man who had his own wife and his mother murdered. During his rule it became a crime to be a Christian. In July of A.D. 64, a great fire destroyed half the city of Rome. No proof was found of how the fire was started, but some people blamed Nero, and Nero blamed the Christians.

To punish them and put an end to Christianity, Nero began to persecute Christians. He punished them by tying them to poles, smearing their bodies with pitch, and then burning them as torches at night. For almost three hundred years, Christians were fiercely persecuted. Many brave men, women, and children lost their lives because of their faith in Christ.

The Colosseum

One of the Roman's favorite sports was to watch armed men called **gladiators** [glăd′ē· ā′tərz] fight and kill other men. This fighting was done in a huge outdoor arena called the **Colosseum,** which was built around A.D. 80. To vary the sport, called a circus, they sometimes imported wild beasts from Africa and turned them loose in the arena to fight men or other beasts. Eager, blood-

Nero blamed the Christians for the great fire in Rome.

gladiators fighting in the Colosseum

thirsty crowds gathered in the Roman Colosseum, which could hold over forty thousand spectators. Christians became the favorite victims to be thrown to the lions or the bears in the Colosseum.

The Spread of Christianity

By A.D. 200, there were Christians in every province of the Roman Empire. Many who were accused of being Christians were put to death; the only way to be pardoned was to deny Christ as Savior.

Polycarp and Blandina. In Asia Minor, an elderly Christian leader named **Polycarp** [pŏl′ē·kärp] was arrested and ordered to blaspheme the name of Christ. "I have served Him for eighty-six years," Polycarp replied, "How can I now blaspheme the name of Him who has saved me?" Polycarp was led to execution.

In Gaul (modern France), a slave girl named **Blandina** [blăn·dē′nə] became a Christian. The rulers tortured her horribly to compel her to change her faith, but she refused, saying, "I am a Christian." Finally they threw her to the bulls in the arena and then cut her throat.

Martyrs. These Christians who willingly gave up their lives rather than deny their Lord are called **martyrs** [mär′tərz]. The more the Christians suffered, the more people became Christians. This fact caused the great African Christian **Tertullian** [tər·tŭl′yən] to declare in A.D. 197, "The blood of the martyrs is the seed of the Church."

The Catacombs

Many Christians in Rome found refuge in vast underground passages and rooms called **catacombs,** which were used as cemeteries. The Christians could safely worship there because the Romans were afraid to enter a burial place. In niches [nĭch′ĕz] cut in the soft volcanic rock, the Christians buried their dead instead of burning the bodies, as was the custom of the Romans. On the walls, they drew pictures showing Christ as the Good Shepherd, and they painted pictures of scenes from the lives of the apostles and the events of the Old Testament.

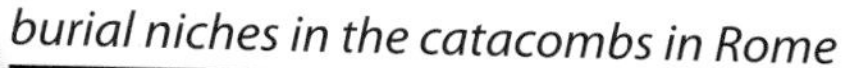
burial niches in the catacombs in Rome

Comprehension Check 12A

1. How is Jesus different from leaders of other religions?
2. Who was the first missionary of the Christian church?
3. Why did Roman leaders dislike Christians? Whom did Christians refuse to worship as God?
4. What emperor made it a crime to be a Christian?
5. What was the Romans' outdoor arena called?
6. What do we call a person who is killed for refusing to give up his faith?
7. Where did the Roman Christians find places to bury their dead?

CONCEPTS TO CONSIDER

Counting Time after Christ

The years after Jesus Christ often have the letters **A.D.** written with them. *A.D.* is Latin for *anno Domini,* "in the year of our Lord." A.D. 270 means "in the year of our Lord 270," or 270 years after the birth of Christ. The first hundred years after Christ are called the first century A.D. (A.D. 1–A.D. 100). The second hundred years (A.D. 101–A.D. 200) are the second century A.D. The twentieth hundred years after Christ (A.D. 1901–A.D. 2000) are the twentieth century A.D. In which century was the year 1620? 1492? 1890? In which century do you live?

12.3 The Rise of Constantine

In A.D. 306, **Constantine** became emperor. Constantine claimed that he saw a cross in the sky on which was written, "In this sign conquer." In a later dream, he said that God appeared to him and commanded him to carry a cross into battle for protection and victory. He claimed that he won all his victories because God was with him.

Constantine commanded that Christians should no longer be persecuted. He gave the people of his empire the freedom to worship any god they chose. The people no longer were required to think of their emperor as a god. At last, they could worship publicly without fear or worry. What a great relief this must have been to them! Later, however, Constantine paved the way for a new kind of persecution. He made it illegal *not* to be a Christian. This caused many people who were not truly Christians to claim that they were. The influence of non-Christian church members eventually weakened the spiritual power of the church and led to false teachings and practices.

Constantine

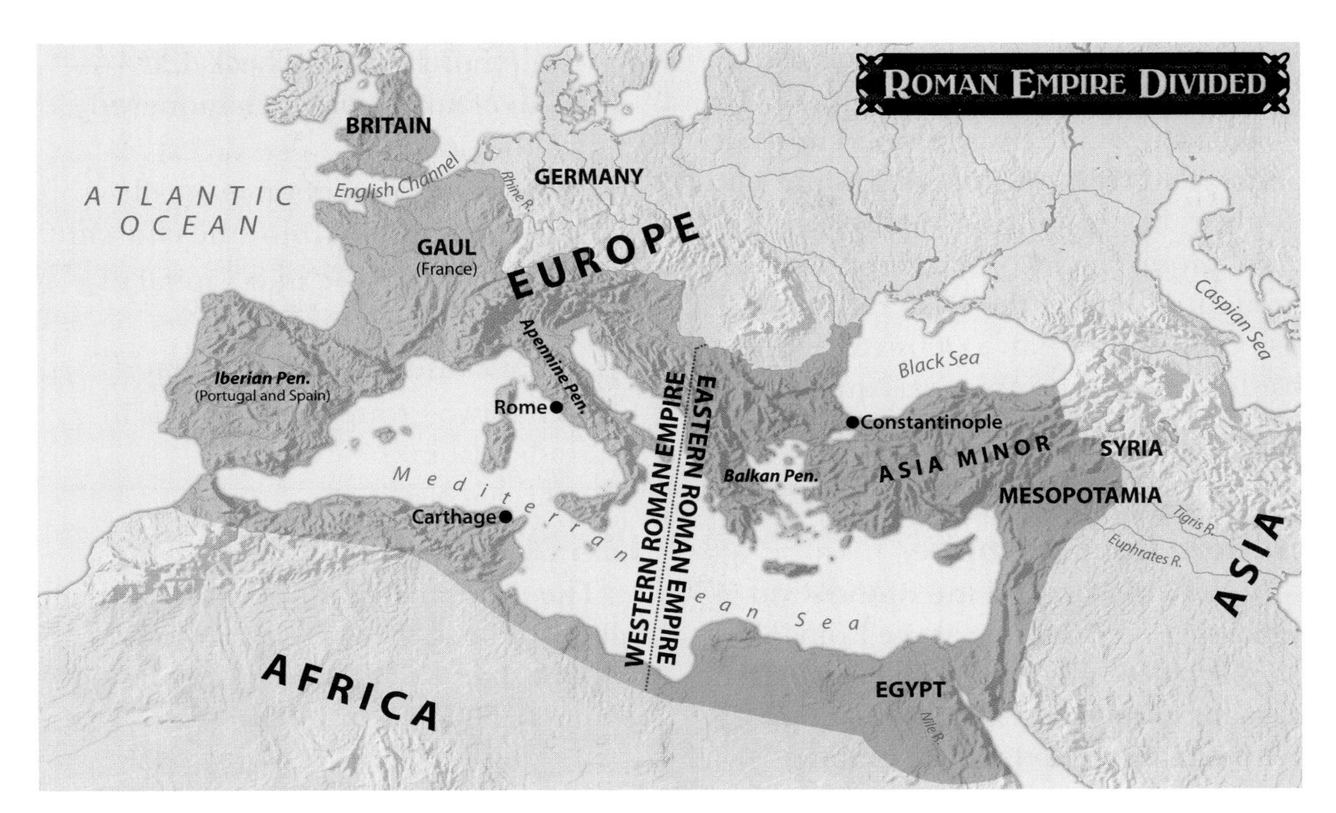

12.4 ✠ The Fall of Rome

A New Capital for the Roman Empire

While Constantine was still emperor, he decided to build a new capital city for the Roman Empire. He rebuilt the old city of **Byzantium** [bĭ·zăn′shē·əm] in Asia Minor and renamed it **Constantinople** [kŏn′stăn· tə·nō′pəl]. Constantinople was built to look like Rome. Today, it is called **Istanbul** (in modern Turkey).

Constantinople (now modern Istanbul)

A Troubled Empire

By this time in Roman history, the empire had begun to weaken. There was much selfishness among the people and the rulers. Slavery had caused the people to become lazy. The Romans lost their sense of justice and their respect for law and order. Many people were living in wickedness. A nation or empire can last only as long as its people have high standards of right and wrong. The Roman people lost their standards, and their great empire fell.

First the empire was divided into two parts. The Western Roman Empire had Rome as its capital, and the Eastern Roman Empire had Constantinople as its capital. Although the Eastern Empire lasted for more than 1,000 years, the Western Roman Empire was quickly destroyed, never to regain its strength.

The Germans Invade the Western Roman Empire

In Europe, beyond the Rhine River and along the frontiers of the Roman Empire, there was an area of land that the Romans called Germany. At that time, the Germans were made up of different tribes, each with its own name. The Romans called these people barbarians, for they had many cruel habits. They enjoyed alcoholic beverages, and they often went on drunken sprees, killing one another. Helpless people such as unwanted babies and old people were abandoned to die. The Germanic tribes sometimes sacrificed humans to their false gods.

In A.D. 410, a German tribe called the **Visigoths** [vĭz′ĭ·gŏths] captured and looted Rome, and then carried off their goods to Gaul where they settled for a while. In A.D. 455, a second German tribe called the **Vandals** invaded Rome. This tribe was so senselessly destructive that today we call anyone who destroys property without reason a *vandal.* In A.D. 476, the Germans got rid of the last Roman emperor and began to rule Rome themselves.

Comprehension Check 12B

1. Who claimed that he conquered by the cross?
2. What did Constantine make illegal? How did this hurt the church?
3. What became the new capital of the Roman Empire?
4. What caused the fall of Rome?
5. What two groups of Germans invaded Rome?

12.5 ✠ The Middle Ages

The thousand-year period after the fall of Rome is known as the **Middle Ages** or Dark Ages. The Middle Ages lasted from **A.D. 500 to A.D. 1500.**

Life in the Middle Ages

Peasants and lords. The warring barbarian tribes that took over the old Roman Empire murdered many people and destroyed the homes and fields of those who were left. The way of life changed drastically. For protection, the poor people, who were called **serfs** and **peasants,** promised to work for the landowners, who were called **lords.** (The wives of the lords were called **ladies.**) The peasants lived on the lord's land, which was called a **manor.**

The peasants promised to serve their lord as long as they lived, to do all the work that he asked of them, and to give him part of the crops that they grew or the goods that they made. In return, the peasants were lent a little piece of land, a small thatched-roof house with a dirt floor, and protection from outside enemies.

There were few schools for the common people. Even where schools were available, most children began at a very young age to work with their hands all day long, and thus they never learned to read. Life was difficult for the peasants, but they were able to keep their families alive.

serfs working the land

Castles and knights. The peasants' shelters were grouped together close to the lord's house, which was called a **manor house.** If they were attacked, the peasants could flee to the manor house for protection. The manor house was usually a castle made of stones and surrounded by high stone walls. Some castles were further protected by **moats** (deep ditches of water that surrounded the castle). A **drawbridge** would be let down over the moat to let friendly people enter the castle. When an enemy tried to attack, the drawbridge would be lifted. **Knights,** trained warriors kept by the lords, stood ready to ward off any enemies. The knights rode horses, and in the later Medieval period, they dressed in heavy, protective **armor.**

manor house

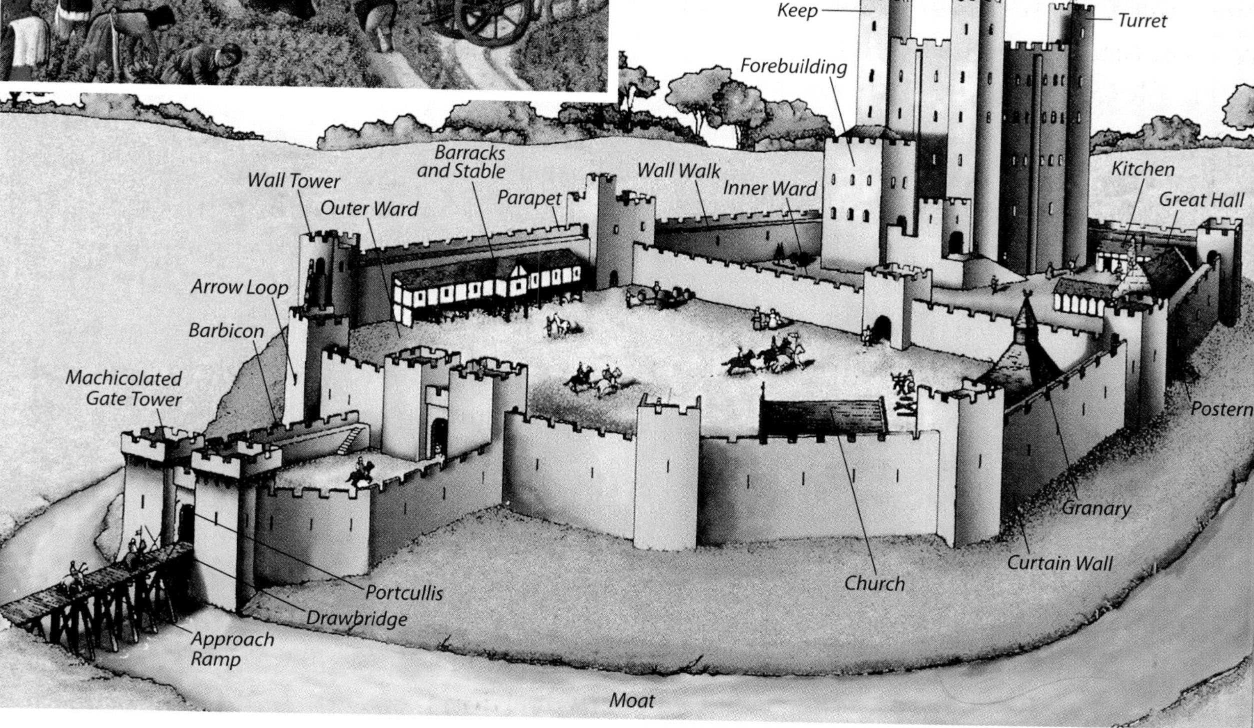

The Medieval Church

The Roman church. The church of the Middle Ages had become very different from the early church in the New Testament. In the time of Constantine, the church at Rome became very important and influential, so much so that churches in other parts of the Roman Empire looked to the church at Rome for spiritual leadership. Some church leaders taught that the church at Rome and its leaders had spiritual authority over all Christians.

Gradually, a vast church organization had developed with Rome as its headquarters and the bishop of the Roman church as the head (ruler) of the entire Christian church. It was known as the Catholic Church (*catholic* meaning "universal"), because it was the only organization of churches. The head of the church was called the **pope** (a Latin word meaning "father"). From Rome, the pope spiritually ruled the Christian churches of medieval Europe in much the same way that the Roman Empire had politically ruled the ancient Mediterranean world.

a large church, or cathedral, built during the Middle Ages

The revived Roman Empire. The Roman church was closely united with the political rulers of Europe. In A.D. 800, the pope crowned Charles the Great, or **Charlemagne** [shär′lə·mān′], as emperor of the Romans. The government used the Roman church to back up its political authority, and the Roman church often used the government to punish those who did not worship God the way the church wanted them to. After Charlemagne's son died, his empire fell apart. Later, in A.D. 962, the pope and a new emperor, **Otto the Great,** formed what they called the **Holy Roman Empire,** which lasted until 1806.

Two Catholic churches. In A.D. 869, the one Catholic church began to split. By A.D. 1054, there were two Catholic churches. The Roman Catholic Church kept its headquarters at Rome, and the **Eastern Orthodox Church** (also called the Greek Catholic Church) established its headquarters at Constantinople.

The Way to Eternal Life

The people of the Middle Ages did not know that the Bible teaches that a person is saved by faith in Christ alone because most of them could not read and only church leaders had access to Bibles. The Roman church taught that salvation was by and through the church. The people wanted eternal life so much that they did whatever the church leaders told them. They confessed their sins to **priests,** performed acts of **penance** to express their sorrow over their sin, and filled the church treasury with gold in an effort to secure their place in Heaven. Few ever heard about God's *free* gift of salvation by grace through faith in the finished work of Jesus Christ on the cross (Eph. 2:8, 9; Titus 3:5, 1 Pet. 1:18–19).

Monasteries

Church men who separated themselves from the world, promising to live a life of poverty and to never marry, were called **monks;** they were taught that this would make them more acceptable to God. Some monks chose to live all alone in a cave or hut; these secluded monks were called **hermits.** Others, called **friars** [frī′ərz], traveled around teaching people. However, most monks lived together in places called **monasteries** [mŏn′ə·stĕr′ēz]. Many women, called **nuns,** lived apart in their own monasteries, which were called **convents.** The monks and nuns contributed to medieval society by providing what little education and medical attention was available at that time.

Even though the Middle Ages (the Dark Ages) was filled with spiritual darkness and little intellectual progress, the monks did the world a great favor by keeping the Bible safe from the barbarian invaders. Because printing had not yet been invented, they wrote out many copies of the Scriptures by hand.

monks working in the fields

a French monastery from the Middle Ages

The Influence of Christianity

In spite of the wrong teachings of the Medieval church, Christianity eventually brought about many changes that made life more pleasant for all people in Europe. Sunday was established as a day of rest. Slaves were treated more kindly, and finally slavery was abolished. The gladiatorial shows were done away with. Human sacrifices and the killing of little babies came to an end. Strong family ties became very important. Women were treated better, and the poor and the sick were cared for.

The Crusades

Pilgrims go to Jerusalem. During the Middle Ages, people from all over Europe often made **pilgrimages** (long trips for religious purposes) to Jerusalem, where Christ had spent much of his earthly life and where He had died. They thought that they would receive special spiritual blessings for making these pilgrimages. For many years, the city of Jerusalem had been controlled by Arab Muslims who allowed the pilgrims to visit freely.

The Turks capture Jerusalem. In A.D. 1070, Jerusalem was captured by fierce **Turks** who had no respect or concern for Christians. The Turks mistreated the Christians, destroyed their churches, and put a stop to all pilgrimages. This greatly disturbed many Europeans. As the Turks gained power, the leader of the Eastern Empire became alarmed. He appealed to the pope for help.

Crusaders recapture Jerusalem. With cries from the leaders as well as the people, Pope Urban II called upon the people to fight for the church and gain back Jerusalem, the Holy City. Because these efforts were to be in the name of the cross, they were called **Crusades.** Many of the **crusaders** had true religious reasons, but many also went for selfish purposes. Few were prepared for the long journey, and still fewer for war. Some often stole to get food. There was arguing and distrust among the people. Many died before reaching the Holy Land. Eight different Crusades were attempted over the years. In A.D. 1099, a group of crusaders were able to drive the Turks out and gain control of Jerusalem. They kept control for parts of two hundred years.

Pope Urban II's urging led to the Crusades.

The Crusades bring changes. The crusaders were unable to gain permanent control of Jerusalem, but they did help make many changes in European life. They broke down the barriers between the rich and the poor and put an end to the feudal system, in which the rich owned the land and the poor supported them. As crusaders brought back goods from these distant countries and stories of great wealth in India and China, people became interested in trade and travel. The rugs, spices, paper, jewels, and customs of the East brought changes in the European way of life. The desire for Eastern goods eventually led to the search for new trade routes and the discovery of America.

Christian Heroes

Peter of Bruis. Some people during the Middle Ages did not believe all the teachings of the Roman church. One priest, **Peter of Bruis** [brōō·ē′], read the Bible and became a Christian. He preached the truth for twenty years in southern France until he was burned alive at the stake for not following the Roman religion. Peter of Bruis lived in the early 1100s. His followers were called **Petrobrusians** [pĕt′rō·brōō′zhənz].

Peter Waldo. In the late 1100s, another Christian hero, **Peter Waldo,** had the Bible translated into the language of the people who lived in the Alps. His followers, called the **Waldensians** [wŏl·dĕn′sĭ·ənz], spread the gospel to many parts of Europe. The Roman church called these people and others like them **heretics.** The church set up a special court called the **Inquisition** [ĭn′kwĭ·zĭsh′ən] that they used to find heretics and kill them if they would not renounce their faith and submit to the pope.

John Wycliffe. **John Wycliffe** [wĭk′lĭf], who lived in England in the 1300s, is called the **"Morning Star of the Reformation."** He spoke out against the power of the pope and said that the people had a right to read the Bible for themselves. He was the first man to translate the entire Bible into the English language. His followers, the **Lollards** [lŏl′ərdz], made handwritten copies of Wycliffe's translation of the Bible and traveled all over Europe preaching the gospel. So many people accepted the truth of the gospel that the church leaders took strong action against them. They said that anyone caught reading the Bible in English could have his land, goods, and even his life taken away from him. The Bible was so precious to these people that they read it anyway, and many faced terrible persecution.

John Wycliffe

John Huss. After Wycliffe died, a man in Bohemia [bō·hē′mē·ə: modern Czech (chĕk) Republic] named **John Huss** found Wycliffe's writings and became convinced that the Bible is the true authority for Christian beliefs. He preached that only God, not the priests, can forgive sin, and that salvation comes only through faith

John Huss was burned at the stake for his faith in Christ.

in Christ. The officials of the Roman church condemned Huss and had him burned at the stake. After John Huss's death, more and more people started following his teachings, despite persecution. By the 1500s, most of the people in Bohemia were followers of the Bible, and Bohemia became a model of a free country with Christian standards.

Comprehension Check 12C

1. What is another name for the Middle Ages? How long did it last?
2. Into what two churches was the Catholic church divided? Where were their headquarters?
3. The monks did the world a great favor by doing what two things with the Bible?
4. What were some changes that Christianity brought to Europe?
5. What were the trips to recapture Jerusalem called?
6. Name three Christian heroes of the Middle Ages.

12.6 The Invention of the Printing Press

Man with a dream. **Johann Gutenberg** [gōōt′′n·bûrg] lived in Germany in the 1400s. Gutenberg was a man with a dream. Many people in Germany were becoming interested in books at this time, but all books had to be written out by hand. Gutenberg wanted to make books available to more people. Most of all, he wanted to find a way to make the Bible available to the multitudes, because the more people read the Bible the more they became convinced that it is true and the only source for Christian belief. Gutenberg's wonderful dream led him to devise the most important invention in the history of the world: **the printing press.**

Movable type. Gutenberg's invention was called the **movable-type** printing press, because he made little individual metal letters (type) and moved them around to spell out words, sentences, and paragraphs. He arranged the letters in a wooden box, covered them with ink, and used a huge screw to press clean paper against them. Af-

Johann Gutenberg

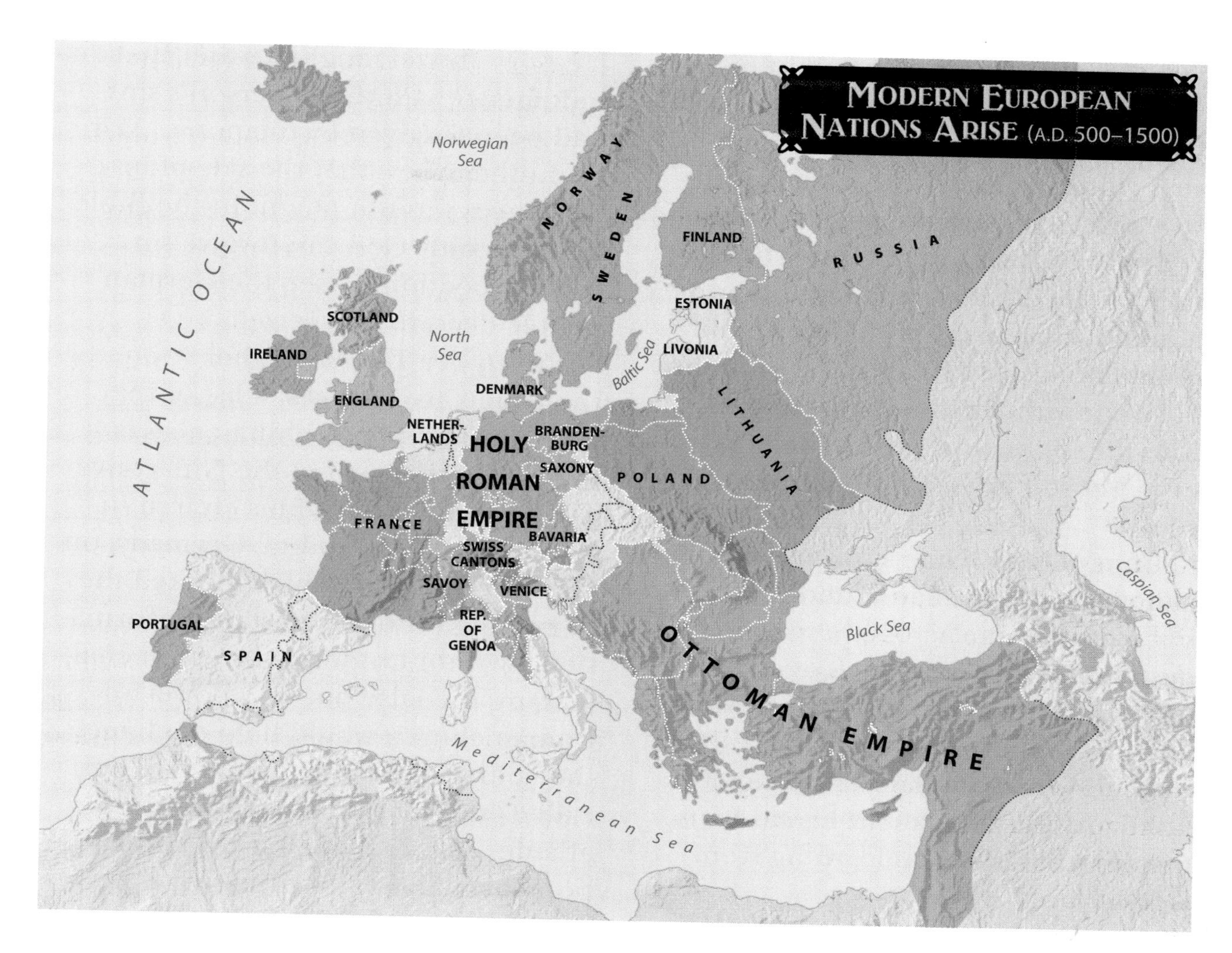

ter he had printed as many copies as he wanted of one page, he rearranged the type and printed another page. In this manner, the same letters were used over and over again, and books could be printed fairly cheaply.

The Gutenberg Bible. The first book that Gutenberg printed was a Bible, called the **Gutenberg Bible** in his honor. Soon, people all over Europe were printing Bibles and other books. Gutenberg's invention helped prepare the way for one of the most important events in history—the Protestant Reformation.

12.7 ✠ Martin Luther and the Protestant Reformation

A young boy in Germany. In 1483, just twenty-seven years after Gutenberg's Bible was printed, **Martin Luther** was born in Germany. He would do more than perhaps any other person to enable people all over the world to understand the truths of the Word of God. Martin's parents dedicated their son to God and saw that he received a good education. Young Martin Luther learned to read and write in both German and Latin.

A monk's life. When he went to the university, Martin Luther studied law.

He was very much interested in his soul's salvation. The church of his day taught many things about salvation that confused him. The church said that a person must do good works in order to be made fit for Heaven. Luther stopped studying law and became a monk. Surely this would make him good enough for Heaven, he thought. He went without food, prayed long into the night, and lived a life of poverty. Yet still he had no peace for his soul.

How to live. While studying the Bible as a monk in a Roman Catholic university, Luther came across these words—***the just shall live by faith*** (Rom. 1:17). Here, in the Bible, was the answer to Luther's longings. Not by works, but by faith, he came to Christ and knew that he was saved. Joyfully, he taught his students the new things he was learning from God's Word.

Tetzel and indulgences. In 1517, a friar named John **Tetzel** [tĕt′sĕl] traveled through Germany selling indulgences from the pope. **Indulgences** were certificates from the pope that excused a person from doing penance and shortened the required stay in **purgatory**. Roman Catholics believed purgatory to be a place of suffering where the souls of penitent sinners remained after death to be cleansed of sin and made ready for Heaven. Tetzel taught further that an indulgence said that a person's sins had been forgiven by the pope. Martin Luther knew that the sale of indulgences was not taught in the Bible and that only God can forgive sin. It disturbed him to see the German people deceived by Tetzel.

Ninety-five Theses. Luther wrote the **Ninety-five Theses,** a list of reasons why the sale of indulgences is wrong. Luther nailed the Ninety-five Theses to the door of his church in **Wittenberg** [wĭt′n·bûrg], **Germany,** on **October 31, 1517,** which marked the beginning of the **Protestant Reformation.** Martin Luther's bravery in challenging the false but very powerful Roman church would help to change the course of history. His action was called "the spark that set Europe aflame." By 1520 he was the most popular man in all Germany.

"Here I stand." The pope and the church leaders tried to get Luther

Luther nailing his Ninety-five Theses to the door of his church

to admit that what he had written was not true, but he would not. "Here I stand," he said. "I can do naught [nothing] else; so help me God." He had to hide from the religious leaders for a while. Then he returned to Wittenberg, where he translated the Bible into German, wrote hymns for the German people, and encouraged the German cities to set up schools so the children could be taught to read the Word of God and to be good citizens.

The Reformation spreads. Luther encouraged people in other lands to do the same for their countrymen, and soon people in England, Scotland, Switzerland, Norway, Denmark, Sweden, the Netherlands, and other countries began to follow the Bible rather than the pope. The Bible was translated into the languages of the people of these nations, and schools were started to teach the children reading, Bible, arithmetic, history, literature, grammar, and science. The truths of the Bible gave the world greater progress in freedom, good government, widespread education, science, literature, and the fine arts than mankind had ever known before.

CHAPTER 12 CHECKUP

A Define each term.

1. gladiator
2. Colosseum
3. martyrs
4. catacombs
5. serfs
6. lords
7. manor
8. moat
9. knight
10. pope
11. indulgences
12. purgatory
13. Ninety-five Theses

B Identify the term described by each clue.

1. church men who separated themselves from the world
2. the place where these men lived
3. monks who chose to live alone
4. monks who traveled and taught
5. women who lived apart in convents
6. long trips for religious purposes
7. eight different attempts to retake Jerusalem
8. people who refused to obey the Roman Catholic church
9. a special court set up to find and kill heretics
10. the most important invention in the history of the world

(cont.)

C Who am I?

1. first great missionary of the Christian church
2. emperor who made it a crime to be a Christian
3. elderly martyr who refused to blaspheme
4. slave girl martyred in Gaul
5. African Christian who said, "The blood of the martyrs is the seed of the Church."
6. emperor who made it a crime **not** to be a Christian
7. crowned emperor of the Romans by the pope
8. first Holy Roman Emperor

D Tell one important accomplishment of each person.

1. Peter of Bruis
2. Peter Waldo
3. John Wycliffe
4. John Huss
5. Johann Gutenberg
6. Martin Luther

E Answer each question.

1. What city did Constantine rebuild to be his new capital? What did he call it? What is it called today?
2. Why did Rome fall?
3. What two Germanic tribes invaded Rome?
4. What event marks the beginning of the Middle Ages? How long did the Middle Ages last?
5. What church was headquartered at Rome? At Constantinople?
6. What event led to the Crusades?
7. What changes occurred in European life because of the Crusades?
8. Who was the "Morning Star of the Reformation"? What were his followers called?
9. What was the first book printed by Gutenberg?
10. Where did Martin Luther nail his Ninety-five Theses to the church door? What event began because of this action?

F Think about these questions and answer them as clearly as possible.

1. What was the most important job of the monks in the monasteries?
2. What were the benefits of the Protestant Reformation?

CHAPTER 13

ENGLAND
and the British Isles

Europe, which is about the size of the United States, is the second smallest continent. (Australia is the smallest.) It lies between the Atlantic Ocean and the continent of Asia. To the south are the Mediterranean Sea and the continent of Africa, and to the north is the Arctic Ocean.

Sometimes Europe and Asia together are called **Eurasia.** Eurasia is the world's largest landmass. Europe makes up about 20 percent of Eurasia. The *Ural* [yo͝o′rəl] *Mountains,* the *Ural River,* the *Caspian Sea,* and the *Caucasus* [kô′kə·səs] *Mountains* form the boundaries between Europe and Asia. Locate all of these features on the map of Eastern Europe (p. 269).

Islands. Thousands of islands lie in the waters around Europe. The largest and most important is **Great Britain,** which is the eighth-largest island in the world. It is part of the **British Isles,** which include Great Britain, Ireland, and a number of much smaller islands. Other important islands in Europe are *Crete, Sicily, Sardinia* [sär·dĭn′ē·ə], *Corsica* [kôr′sĭ·kə], and *Iceland.* Locate all of these islands on the map (p. 224).

13.1 The British Isles

Land of influence. Great Britain is separated from mainland Europe by the **English Channel** and the **North Sea.** England, Scotland, and Wales are on the island of Great Britain. Four countries, England, Scotland, Wales, and Northern Ireland, are united and are called the **United Kingdom of Great Britain.** The southern part of Ireland is a separate country, called the **Republic of Ireland.**

The United Kingdom is only half the size of France. It could fit about 40 times into the land area of the United States and almost 70 times into Russia. Yet despite its size, this tiny kingdom has had a great influence on the entire world. At one time, it ruled one fourth of the earth's people and controlled one fourth of the earth's land.

The "Mother Country." Britain (especially England) is very important to Americans, because our language, many of our laws, our representative form of government, and our love of freedom are all part of our British heritage. England is called the "Mother Country" of the United States, Canada, Australia, and several other countries.

At the time that the British colonized America, the Bible had an important influence on almost everyone in England. This **biblical heritage** was the most important gift that the British colonists brought to America. British colonists and missionaries also took the Bible with them to Australia, New Zealand, and many parts of Africa and Asia. The Bible, as we shall see, was the secret of England's strength.

13.2 Great Events in English History

Early Days

Ancient history. At one time, Britain was the northwestern frontier of the Roman Empire. The Romans ruled the **Celts** [kĕlts], or Britons, who lived there, for about four hundred years. After the Roman soldiers left, Germanic tribes called Angles and Saxons defeated the Celts and founded the English nation. The country was named "Angleland," or *England,* after the Angles, and the language of the **Anglo-Saxons** eventually developed into the English language that we know today.

Middle Ages. During the Middle Ages, many important events took place in England. One early king, **Alfred the Great,** defeated the fierce Viking invaders called the Danes, and set England on the road to becoming a strong nation with just laws, a written history, and a powerful navy. But the Danes later conquered England, and Canute the Dane ruled England, Denmark, and Norway for a time. In 1066, **William the Conqueror,** from Normandy, France, invaded England, won the Battle of Hastings, and became king of England. His victory was called the **Norman Conquest.** For a hundred years French was the main language used in England, and many French words, such as *rule, royal,* and *sir,* became a part of the English language.

Alfred the Great

The Magna Carta. One of the most important events of the Middle Ages was the signing of the **Magna Carta** in 1215. The Magna Carta established the English tradition that the monarch is limited by the laws of the land. The Magna Carta defined the traditional rights of Englishmen and led the way to constitutional government, or rule by law. It also started England on its way to representative government, in which the people have an active role in the government. By 1295, England had its first official representative assembly, the **Parliament.**

The liberties and republican principles that the English established in the Magna Carta later became a part of the American system of government and of the governments of the free countries of Europe. Some clauses of the Constitution of the United States are very similar to parts of the Magna Carta. Two of these are, "No person shall be deprived of life, liberty, or property without due process of law," and "The accused shall enjoy the right to a speedy and public trial."

THE BRITISH ISLES

ATLANTIC OCEAN

Highlands

SCOTLAND

GREAT BRITAIN

Lowlands

Edinburgh

Glasgow

Uplands

UNITED KINGDOM

Londonderry

NORTHERN IRELAND

Belfast

PENNINE MOUNTAINS

Irish Sea

North Sea

IRELAND

Dublin

Shannon R.

Limerick

Cork

WALES

ENGLAND

Cardiff

London

White Cliffs of Dover

Thames R.

Chunnel

Strait of Dover

English Channel

FRANCE

The Bible in English. During the Middle Ages, the Roman Catholic Church had much control over the people of England. In 1382, **John Wycliffe,** seeing the great need for people to read the Bible for themselves, produced the first translation of the entire Bible into the English language. His followers, the **Lollards,** eagerly read the handwritten copies of the Wycliffe Bible despite terrible persecution. Gutenberg's printing press of the 1400s opened the way for even more people to read the Bible, and in 1525 **William Tyndale** produced the first **printed** version of the English New Testament. Ten years later, **Miles Coverdale** published the first printed version of the entire English Bible.

Comprehension Check 13A

1. What tiny kingdom once controlled one fourth of the earth?
2. What three countries are on the island of Great Britain?
3. What was the most important gift the British colonists brought to America?
4. Why was the Magna Carta important?
5. Who was the first person to translate the entire Bible into English?

The Beginning of Modern England

The English Reformation. The English Bible prepared the way for the English Reformation, which began during the reign of **King Henry VIII** (who ruled from 1509 to 1547). The English

King Henry VIII

William Tyndale with the first Bible printed in English

Reformation was very important to American history, for it meant that the colonists who went to Canada and the United States took a strong biblical heritage with them.

The age of exploration. In 1497, **John Cabot** became the first modern explorer of any nation to reach North America, and he claimed North America for England. This caused conflicts with Spain, which had sent many explorers to South America and the islands near North America.

John Cabot, in his ship the Matthew, *claimed North America for England.*

The Elizabethan Age

England rules the seas. **Queen Elizabeth I,** the daughter of Henry VIII, ruled England from 1558 to 1603. During her reign, England became a great sea power and began to settle the New World. Queen Elizabeth sent many explorers to the New World, including **Sir Francis Drake,** the first Englishman to sail around the world, and **Sir Walter Raleigh,** who founded "The Lost Colony" at Roanoke Island, North Carolina.

In 1588, Queen Elizabeth's fleets defeated the **Spanish Armada,** which was one of the greatest naval forces the world had ever seen. As the ships that had survived the fighting tried to escape, a terrible storm arose. Many of the fleeing ships were dashed to pieces on the rocky shore.

According to one story, when the Spanish king received news of the Armada's disaster, he calmly and simply said, "I sent my ships to fight against men and not against the winds and waves of God." The defeat of the Spanish Armada destroyed Spain's plans to rule the world and set England on the way to becoming the world's most powerful nation.

the defeat of the Spanish Armada

Age of greatness. The years that followed the defeat of the Spanish Armada were called the **Elizabethan Age.** This was one of the most noted periods in the history of the world. **William Shakespeare,** one of the greatest writers of all time, wrote many famous plays, including *Julius Caesar, Hamlet,* and *Romeo and Juliet,* during the Elizabethan Age.

William Shakespeare

Age of Bible reading. During the Elizabethan Age, there were not many Bibles in print yet, and many people could not read. The people were so hungry for the Word of God that an order went out for a large Bible to be set up in every church. People flocked to the churches to read the Scriptures for themselves. Men with good, strong voices were appointed to read aloud for the benefit of those who had no education. Later, smaller, less expensive Bibles became available; soon every home had its own Bible for the families to read daily. One great historian wrote, "England became a people of a book, and that book was the Bible."

How the Bible changed England. Because of the Bible, a great moral change came over the people of England. Greediness was replaced by kindness; laziness by industry; ignorance by a great desire to learn to read. The liberties of the English people, the prosperity of their businesses, the growth of education, and the justice that prevailed in the land were all the result of obedience to the Word of God.

The Age of the Puritans

Seventeenth-century England. The emphasis on the Bible during the Elizabethan Age brought in the next great period of English history, the seventeenth century, which is called the **Age of the Puritans.** As Englishmen studied the Bible, many of them began to feel that England's official church, the Church of England, was still too much like the Roman Catholic Church. They also realized that Christians should live holy lives and not act, dress, and think just like the world. Englishmen who felt this way were called **Puritans** because they wanted to purify the Church of England. Some wanted to separate entirely from the Church of England; they were called **Separatists.**

King James I. The king who ruled after Queen Elizabeth I was **King James I** (ruled 1603–1625). He tried to limit the power of Parliament and the traditional freedoms of Englishmen. He also tried to force the Puritans out of England. God used his persecutions of the Puritans and Separatists to begin a migration of Bible-believing Englishmen to America. In 1620, during the reign of King James, one group of Separatists sailed for the New World from England, and became known to the world as the **Pilgrims.**

God also used King James in another special way—to sponsor a new translation of the Bible into the English language. In **1611,** scholars completed the **King James** or **Authorized Version** of the Bible, the best-loved and most widely used English translation of God's Word ever produced.

King Charles I. **King Charles I** (ruled 1625–1649), the son of King James I, was even harder on Parliament, English liberties, and the Puritans than his father had been. During his reign, more than 25,000 Puritans left England for freedom of worship in America. Some of those who remained joined with other members of Parliament in trying to get King Charles to obey the principles of the Magna Carta. Soon a civil war broke out between the Cavaliers, who were loyal to the king's policies, and the Roundheads, who thought the king should obey the law of the land. The Roundheads, led by **Oliver Cromwell,** won the war. To the horror of many Englishmen, they also executed the king.

King James I

King Charles I

The Commonwealth. The Roundheads set up a new government called the Commonwealth, with Oliver Cromwell as leader. Cromwell ruled in many ways like a dictator, and yet he did give more religious freedom than had previously been allowed. His son became ruler after his death, but he was not a good leader. Soon England was a monarchy again with **King Charles II,** the son of Charles I, on the throne.

Literature of the Puritan Age. The Puritans of seventeenth-century England produced some of the most amazing works the world has ever known. Two Puritan writers are still widely read today. **John Milton,** a great poet, wrote *Paradise Lost,* which tells about Adam and Eve in the Garden of Eden. **John Bunyan,** a poor tinker (mender of pots and pans), wrote one of the most beloved books of all times, *Pilgrim's Progress.*

John Bunyan

Puritans and science. The Puritans lived during the time that Galileo was making his great discoveries about the heavens (in Italy), and they were some of the first in the world to support his work. They started England's first scientific society, an organization to study the new sciences and conduct experiments. Great English scientists during the seventeenth century included the following:

1. **Sir Isaac Newton,** who discovered the law of gravity,
2. **Francis Bacon,** who devised the scientific method,
3. **William Gilbert,** who wrote the first English science book,
4. **William Harvey,** who discovered the circulation of blood in the body,
5. **Robert Boyle,** the "Father of Modern Chemistry,"
6. **Edmund Halley,** the astronomer who predicted Halley's Comet, and
7. **Robert Hooke,** the first man to see a living cell.

Some of these great scientists were Puritans, and all of them had a great respect for the Bible. The Bible gave them the understanding they needed to look for the laws that God established for the world that He created, and science gave them one way to help others as the Bible commands. Sir Isaac Newton, who was possibly the greatest scientist of all time, spent much of his time studying the Bible.

William Harvey demonstrating his theory of the circulation of the blood

Comprehension Check 13B

1. Who was the first modern explorer to reach North America? For whom did he claim the land?
2. Who was the great English play writer during the Elizabethan Age?
3. What group wanted to leave the Church of England?
4. What is the best-loved and most widely used English translation of the Bible?
5. Who led the Roundheads to defeat the king?
6. Who wrote *Pilgrim's Progress*?
7. What great scientist discovered the law of gravity?

The Restoration

Loss of righteousness. King Charles II's coming to the throne was called the Restoration, for now the crown was restored to its rightful heir. King Charles II was known for his love of pleasure. He encouraged the English people to disregard biblical standards. Soon England lost the righteousness, respect, and excellence that it had known under the Puritans. Few lasting works of literature were produced during this time. One book from this time is still popular today, however—Daniel Defoe's *Robinson Crusoe.*

The plague [plāg]. The reign of Charles II was marked by religious persecution and two calamities. The first calamity was the **plague,** a disease that started in the East and spread rapidly over Europe. It raged everywhere, but nowhere worse than in London. Whole families died within a few days. Some people were able to flee to the country and find healthier conditions, but the poor had to stay in the city to die of either the plague or starvation. Many people of the time said that the plague was a punishment for the wickedness into which England had fallen. Across the doors of the plague-stricken houses, the people wrote, "God have mercy on us."

The great fire of London. In 1666, the second great calamity came. A **great fire** broke out in London. For three days the flames raged uncontrollably until much of the city was burned to the ground. Thousands of people lost their homes. As they looked back on it, many people decided that the fire was a blessing in disguise, for it cleared the air of the plague germs and prepared the way for rebuilding London in a new and better way. After the fire, the great architect, **Sir Christopher Wren,** designed thirty-five new churches and rebuilt London's famous St. Paul's Cathedral.

the great fire of London, 1666

New rulers. The next king, James II, was disliked by the English people. Many feared he would bring back the tyranny experienced under James I and Charles I. In 1688, the English offered the crown to **William and Mary of Orange,** James's son-in-law and daughter, from Holland. The **English Bill of Rights** was written and agreed on, and England became a **constitutional monarchy.** After the death of King William, **Queen Anne** came to the throne.

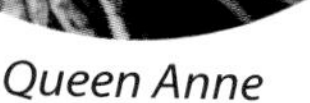

Queen Anne

John Wesley

The Wesleyan Revival

England had forgotten the Bible during the Restoration period, and by 1702, when Queen Anne began her reign, the land was known for its poverty, drunkenness, and crime. The people were slaves to their own evil desires. Even many of the ministers were preaching that God does not care how we live on earth or what becomes of us. God does care, however, and He had not forgotten England. In His mercy, He sent a great revival to the land during the eighteenth century. Two men whom God used to bring about this revival were George Whitefield and John Wesley.

George Whitefield. **George Whitefield** was perhaps the most powerful voice in England. He began preaching when he was only twenty-three and immediately became England's most famous preacher. He preached the truth of the Scriptures tirelessly for thirty-four years in almost every town in England, Scotland, and Wales. He went to Ireland twice, and seven times he sailed across the Atlantic Ocean to hold huge outdoor meetings in America. For many years, George Whitefield was the best-known man in the American colonies, and he did much to turn the colonists back to God. His great, booming voice could be heard by 30,000 people at a time, according to the estimates of Benjamin Franklin, who was one of his friends in America. The eighteen thousand sermons that George Whitefield preached in his lifetime were a powerful force in turning the people in both Great Britain and America back to God.

John Wesley. The other great English revivalist, **John Wesley,** is one of the most famous men in English history. John Wesley was born into a large family in England in 1703. He, his brother Charles (who became a hymnwriter), and the other Wesley children owed much of their early training to their mother, Susanna. She taught them to read, to be obedient, and to respect the Word of God.

For sixty-five years, John Wesley rode horseback across the plains, hills, and valleys of England, preaching the gospel wherever he went. Thousands responded to the message of salvation through faith in Christ, and their lives were transformed. England became a changed country. Once again, the English were "a people of a book, and that book was the Bible." The fruits of the great **Wesleyan Revival,** as it is called, lasted through the rest of the eighteenth century and most of the nineteenth century, which was the century of England's greatest power and influence on the world.

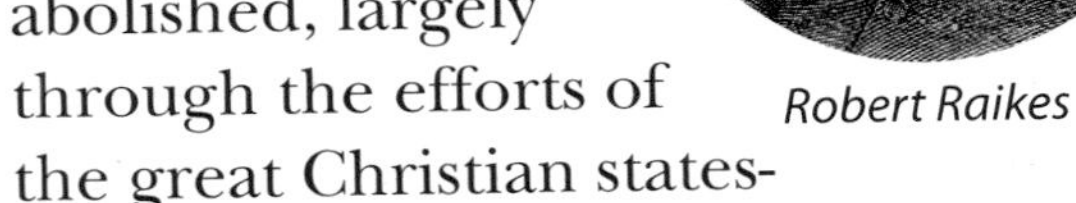
Robert Raikes

Changes in England. During the years that followed the Wesleyan Revival, many changes took place in England. The slave trade was abolished, largely through the efforts of the great Christian statesman William Wilberforce. Sunday schools were started for the poor children of the land by a newspaper publisher, **Robert Raikes** [rāks], the "Father of the Sunday School Movement." At that time in England, children had to work long hours in factories six days a week. Only the rich children had a chance to go to school. Robert Raikes gathered up the poor children of his city on Sundays, their only day off, and taught them the Bible, manners, right living, reading, writing, and arithmetic. His Sunday school lasted from early in the morning until late in the afternoon. Soon, there were similar Sunday schools throughout England, Ireland, Scotland, and Wales. Later, when laws were passed against child labor, two different Christian groups started weekday schools for the children, and the Sunday schools became more like what we know today. For many years in England, the regular schools were supported by churches and Christian individuals, and English children continued to receive training about the Bible and character along with the other subjects. Children trained in this manner grew up to be the kind of people who could help England to remain a good, strong country.

Exploration and missions. In 1792, modern missions began in England with the work of **William Carey.** Many nations were exploring new parts of the world during William Carey's boyhood. One famous English explorer was Captain **James Cook,** who explored New Zealand, Australia, New Guinea, the coast of Antarctica, and many islands before he was finally killed by natives in Hawaii. As young William Carey read Captain Cook's account of his voyages, he was struck by the fact that people in many parts of the world had never seen a Bible and had never heard the gospel message. Carey struggled to get an education and determined that he would do what he could to spread the gospel to "the uttermost part of the earth." In 1793, he sailed for India, where he translated the Bible into many of the Indian languages. William Carey is known as the "Father of Modern Missions." His motto was, "Attempt great things for God; expect great things from God." Many Christians from England and other countries followed his example, and the Age of Missions began. Some famous missionaries from England were J. Hudson Taylor, Henry Martyn, Wilfred Grenfell, and John Williams.

Comprehension Check 13C

1. What two calamities took place in the seventeenth century?
2. What famous architect helped to rebuild London after the Great Fire?
3. Under whose rule was the English Bill of Rights written?
4. What two men brought revival to England in the 1700s?
5. Who started Sunday schools in England?
6. Who was the first great English missionary?

The Rise of Industry

A new way of doing work. The **Age of Industry** began in England at the time of the Wesleyan Revival. Before the Age of Industry, there were two ways to do work: by using animals or by using one's own muscles. The Age of Industry introduced machines constructed on scientific principles to do work. The use of machines brought such a change to the world that the period was called the Industrial Revolution. (*Revolution* means "change.")

Changes in agriculture. The change began on the farms. As many farmers began to pay serious attention to the Bible, they began to see that *all* the work that we do is a service to God and should be done heartily (Col. 3:23). This understanding brought about the **Protestant work ethic,** the biblical teaching that God expects all men to work and that all work is a noble duty to be performed toward God. People began looking for ways to get jobs done faster and to make better use of their land. They learned to rotate their crops and to increase milk and meat production in scientific ways. New tools were invented for plowing, planting, and reaping. With new, efficient farming methods, many farm workers were freed to work at other jobs.

The textile industry. For many years the production of textiles (cloth) had been important in England, but it had always been done with slow-moving spinning wheels and hand-operated looms. Inventive Englishmen went to work to create machines that would bring about faster and more efficient production. The flying shuttle, the spinning jenny, and the

one of Watt's steam engines at work at a coal mine

power loom all helped to speed up the process and give jobs to many people. After **James Watt** of Scotland had perfected the **steam engine,** the textile factories had all the power they needed, and production increased greatly.

Other changes. Englishmen now went to work solving other problems. They found an inexpensive way to change iron into steel and better and safer ways to work their coal mines. They dug canals, built better ships, laid railroads, and before long were making use of such American inventions as the steamship and the telegraph. Cities grew along with the factories, and many new cities sprang up in England. England began to increase its trade with other countries to get more **raw materials** to refine in the factories. (Raw materials are natural resources that can be used for producing other goods. Some raw materials are cotton, which can be turned into cloth; iron, which can be changed to steel; clay, which can be used for making china; and milk, which can be turned into cheese.)

The Four Georges and William

After Queen Anne's reign, England was ruled by four different kings named George. During the time of **King George II,** England fought the **French and Indian War** in America and won possession of Canada. During the reign of **King George III,** England lost the thirteen New World colonies in America's **War for Independence.** After George IV died, his brother William IV came to the throne. He was the uncle of **Queen Victoria,** who ruled England for almost sixty-four years.

The Victorian Age

Childhood resolution. When Victoria was just a girl, she realized that she would probably be the next queen of England. Her uncles had ruled poorly because they were disobedient to God's moral laws. Princess Victoria determined that she would not follow their example. **"I will be good,"** she resolved when she was eleven years old. When she was just eighteen, she became queen. All through her long life she kept her childhood resolve, and England reaped the blessings of having a righteous ruler. The Bible says, *"When the righteous are in authority, the people rejoice: but when the wicked beareth rule, the people mourn"* (Prov. 29:2) and *"Righteousness exalteth a nation: but sin is a reproach to any people"* (Prov. 14:34). Queen Victoria was so beloved by her subjects that British people ever since have looked back to her reign with

King George III

Queen Victoria

respect and pride. The years of her rule are called the **Victorian Age** in her honor.

The British Empire. During the reign of Queen Victoria, England ruled the largest empire in history. "The sun never sets on the British Empire," people said, and they were right. Because England had control of various countries around the globe, at any given time at least one country was on the side of the earth experiencing daylight. Millions of people around the world—one quarter of the earth's population at that time—were under the rule of Queen Victoria. God used her empire to keep peace and order in the world through the establishment of wise laws and through the work of the many missionaries who went out from Britain to the far corners of the empire. The empire gave Britain wealth and power, and Britain shared with the countries it ruled its biblical heritage and its tradition of representative government. India, Pakistan, Australia, New Zealand, Canada, Jamaica, Egypt, Sudan, Nigeria, Rhodesia (modern Zimbabwe), and South Africa were just some of the lands included in the vast British Empire. British industry prospered so much at this time that Britain was called the "Workshop of the World."

Victorian literature. Many excellent books were written during the Victorian Age. Robert **Browning** and Alfred, Lord **Tennyson** were two famous poets. Charles **Dickens** wrote many short stories and novels that are still enjoyed today, including *A Christmas Carol* and *David Copperfield.* Rudyard **Kipling** wrote stories set in the many interesting colonies of the British Empire, including the children's classic, *The Jungle Book.*

Michael Faraday

Victorian scientists. The Victorian Age was a time of great scientific discoveries and inventions. Two of the most respected Victorian scientists were Michael **Faraday** and Lord **Kelvin.** Both men were Christians who had a high regard for the Bible. They did much to help the English people understand the principles of science.

Victorian benevolence. *Benevolence* means doing kind deeds for others. The Victorian Age was a time of great benevolence. Missionaries who went to the British colonies taught the people to read and gave them Bibles and other books in their own language. At home, many people thought of ways to help those who were less fortunate than they. **George Müller** [myōō′lər], a man of great faith and prayer, started orphanages in which he housed and fed thousands of homeless children. He depended on God alone to send in the money to keep the orphanages going. **William Booth** started the Salvation Army to help people in the slums of London lead transformed lives by the power of Christ. **Florence Nightingale** started the modern nursing profession and opened the first school for nurses in England. Many Christian groups built hospitals in England and throughout the empire in order to care for the sick.

Florence Nightingale

Queen Victoria giving a Bible to an African chief as the secret of England's greatness

The secret of England's greatness. Once, a great chief from one of the African colonies went to London to see Queen Victoria. "What is the secret of your country's greatness?" he asked. The queen did not take him to the Tower of London and show him the glittering crown jewels. She did not speak to him of the brilliant politicians who debated in Parliament. She did not even point to England's long heritage of freedom. Instead, she gave the chief a Bible. "Here is the secret of England's greatness," said the queen, and the English people agreed. About the same time, a prince of India recognized this truth. "Where did the English-speaking people get all their intelligence, and energy, and cleverness, and power?" he asked. "It is their Bible that gives it to them. And now they bring it to us and say, 'This is what raised us. Take it and raise yourselves.' "

Comprehension Check 13D

1. How did methods of doing work change during the Industrial Revolution?
2. What is the Protestant work ethic?
3. Who perfected the steam engine?
4. What queen ruled England well because of a decision made when she was young?
5. Who started an orphanage in England?
6. What great benevolent group was started by William Booth? By Florence Nightingale?

England's Decline

During the twentieth century England lost its great empire, much of its wealth, and its position as a world leader. There were many causes for this decline.

Modernism. England's problems began in the late nineteenth century when many of her church ministers began to deny the truth of the Bible. The false ideas that the Bible does not mean what it says and that men must use their reason alone to find truth are called **modernism** or **liberalism.** Religious modernism was the result of a humanist movement in France during the 1700s called the Enlightenment. The wicked ideas of the Enlightenment and modernism spread throughout Europe during the nineteenth century. Modernism has caused great harm to every nation that has been affected by it.

Evolution. Another false teaching that arose during the nineteenth century was **Charles Darwin's** theory of evolution. Many people who doubted the Bible began to accept Darwin's <u>false idea that man has descended from the animals</u>. Such a belief took away man's dignity as a creature made in the image of God, and it caused people to stop being concerned about their soul's salvation. It also caused a decline in science, for scientists began to accept an untested idea as truth, an attitude that goes against the scientific method.

Charles Darwin

The World Wars. Through the centuries, England's island location had protected it from attack by foreign nations. With the invention of submarines and airplanes in the twentieth century, however, this protection was gone. Although Britain fought bravely for the Allies in both wars and won, damage to the land was great. Enemy submarines sank English ships during World War I. During World War II, **Sir Winston Churchill** was the prime minister or leader of the British government. He led the British troops to victory, but the loss of lives and property was terrible. For eight months, enemy planes dropped bombs over London almost every night. Children were sent away to the countryside to live with family members and even strangers until the danger passed. The courage of the British people and Churchill's inspiring speeches during this time of continual attacks helped to win the war for the Allies. About 360,000 British people died during World War II, and great sections of London and other cities were destroyed.

Winston Churchill

air war over Britain during World War II

Welfare state. In the twentieth century, the English government began to take over responsibilities that had always been handled by individuals, churches, and families before. Because the people lost their respect for the Bible, they also lost much of their self-respect. England became a **welfare state.** Because the government gave the people so many things that they had not worked to earn, many people became irresponsible. Some even lost the traditional British respect for law and order. They gave away much of their hard-earned liberty in order to be taken care of by the government, and the government became very poor under the burden of caring for so many people "from the cradle to the grave."

Restoring England's Greatness

In Queen Victoria's footsteps. By the middle of the twentieth century, the political power in England had shifted from the kings and queens to the prime minister. When **Margaret Thatcher** became prime minister in 1979, Queen Elizabeth II was on the throne. Prime Minister Thatcher worked hard to restore the Christian heritage of Great Britain by promoting family values and the private ownership of property. Mrs. Thatcher was the most influential British Prime Minister since Winston Churchill, and held that position longer than any other British leader in the twentieth century. Her fearless stand for Christian morality and free enterprise helped to make Great Britain a better place to live.

Margaret Thatcher

Return to the Protestant work ethic. Margaret Thatcher bravely faced the problems of the welfare state by insisting that able-bodied people work for their living rather than accept government handouts. By turning government-controlled businesses back to individuals, she encouraged thrift and wise management, which meant that many people who had been on welfare could have jobs.

Freeing the nation from debt. For the first time in decades, employers could keep more of their profits. This enabled them to expand their businesses and to hire more workers. People who had once been on welfare could now have jobs to support themselves and their families. Great Britain, which had been hopelessly in debt as a social welfare state, began to regain some of her prosperity as the people returned to the Protestant work ethic.

As brave as Churchill. Margaret Thatcher faced a foreign crisis when Argentina invaded the British colony of the **Falkland Islands** in 1982. Although her critics grudgingly admitted that her economic policies were working, many wondered if she could handle a military crisis.

Margaret Thatcher appealed to the patriotism of the British. Several thousand citizens of the Falklands, mostly sheepherders from Scotland, were now under the military rule of an Argentine dictator.

The Falklands War. After a series of naval, air, and ground battles, the Argentine forces were defeated. Many citizens of Argentina saw the foolishness of this war and eventually demanded an end to their military dictatorship. Although some British men had given their lives in the conflict, freedom had been restored to the Falklands. Moreover, a refreshing tide of patriotism rolled across the British Isles.

Conflicts with Iraq. England sent troops to aid the United States in removing Iraq from Kuwait in 1991 and in freeing the Iraqi people from the dictatorship of Saddam Hussein in 2003. Political ties between the United Kingdom and the United States remain strong.

13.3 England

The Land

England, the largest country in the United Kingdom, takes up the greater part of the island of Great Britain. A low mountain range, the **Pennine** [pĕn′īn′] Chain, runs down the center of northern England and is often called the "backbone of England." England's Lake District, west of the mountains, is noted for its scenic hills, beautiful waterfalls, and long, narrow lakes. Many famous poets have lived there, and it is a favorite spot for vacationers. Most of the people of England live in the gently rolling plains of the lowlands, which extend over most of the country.

London, England's capital and the capital of the United Kingdom, is one of the largest and most important cities in the world. It is located on England's principal river, the **Thames** [tĕmz]. Near the narrowest part of the English Channel is the Strait of Dover. Dover is famous for its great white cliffs, which are made of chalk. If the weather is clear, a person can stand in Calais [kă′lā′], France, and look across the Strait at the **white cliffs of Dover.**

England's Lake District

The Chunnel is a 31-mile-long tunnel that runs beneath the English Channel linking Great Britain and France. Work began on the Chunnel in 1987. In 1994, the first high-speed train raced through the tunnel cutting travel time between London, England, and Paris, France, from 7 hours to less than 3 hours.

Chunnel

The English People

Character. The English people are known for their dry sense of humor, politeness, shyness with strangers, patriotism, love of freedom, and respect for tradition.

Work. England is a highly industrialized nation; only about 5 percent of the people are farmers. The others mine coal; work in steel plants; help manufacture ships, planes, or automobiles; or work in the offices, shops, or banks of the large cities. Some help produce England's famous bone china or sterling silver.

Customs. The people of England dress much like Americans and Canadians; they especially like warm woolens, tweeds, and conservative colors. Some of their favorite foods are roast beef, cabbage, steak and kidney pie, Yorkshire pudding, and fish and chips (fried potato wedges). Tea is the favorite hot drink. At four o'clock every afternoon many Englishmen pause for a cup of tea and a snack.

Language. The people of England speak English with a different accent than the people in the United States, and they use some words differently. *Petrol* is gasoline, a *wireless* is a radio, a *lift* is an elevator, a *lorry* is a truck, a *bonnet* is the hood of a car, a *biscuit* is a cookie, and a *sweet shop* is a place where candy and ice cream are sold.

Love of sports. The English are known for their love of sports and the outdoors. Soccer (called *football* in England), cricket (a game that is a combination of bowling, tennis, baseball, and horseshoes), and rugby (similar to American football) are favorite team sports. The English also enjoy lawn bowling, horse racing, polo, and fox hunting. If you are a sports fan, you might want to check an encyclopedia to see how some of the English sports are played.

a game of cricket

Comprehension Check 13E

1. What are modernism and liberalism?
2. What man started the idea of evolution?
3. Who led the British troops in World War II?
4. What is a welfare state? Why is it damaging to a country?
5. Which British leader served longest as prime minister in the twentieth century?
6. What is England's capital? On what river is it located?

farmland in Northern Ireland

peat bog with stacks of cut peat

13.4 Ireland, Scotland, and Wales

Ireland

The "Emerald Isle." The island of Ireland, which is separated from Great Britain by the Irish Sea, has a cool marine west coast climate and receives a great deal of rain. Ireland is so green that it is often called the "Emerald Isle." It is shaped somewhat like a bowl, with a central plain surrounded by low mountains along the coasts. Ireland's principal river, the **Shannon River,** winds across most of the plain. It is the longest river in the British Isles.

Peat bogs. Some areas of the lowlands are very swampy. Plants decay in these areas, forming **peat bogs,** which cover one sixth of Ireland. Peat, the partly decayed plant matter found in the bogs, is a thick, spongy mat of dead plants. It is valuable as a fuel and is Ireland's most important natural resource.

People. The Irish people are known for their friendliness, storytelling ability, and love of poetry. About one third of them are farmers, and many are poor. Their most famous dish is Irish stew, which is made of potatoes, onions, and mutton (sheep). Potatoes are the most important food crop.

A shrinking population. In the 1850s, a disease spread among the potato plants and caused a great famine in Ireland. During the **potato famine,** thousands of Irish people starved to death. Another million and a half emigrated (moved) to other countries, especially to Canada and the United States. Today there are four times as many people of Irish descent in the United States as in Ireland, and they have played an important role in United States history. During the past century, many other people have moved away from Ireland to find better jobs, making Ireland one of the only countries in the world that has fewer people today than it had a hundred years ago. Thousands of people still leave Ireland every year, but the government is encouraging new industries to come in to provide much-needed work.

The Republic of Ireland. In 1949, the Republic of Ireland gained complete independence from Great Britain. Although Northern Ireland chose to remain a part of the United Kingdom, the Republic of Ireland still claims the land there. Ninety-five percent of the people in the Republic of Ireland are Roman Catholics. **Dublin** is the capital and largest city, and Cork is the second largest city. Another leading city is Limerick. The country has two official languages, English and **Gaelic** [gā′lĭk], which is the language of the ancient Celts from whom many of the Irish descended. **Eire** [âr′ə] is the Gaelic name for the Republic of Ireland.

Northern Ireland. Although Northern Ireland is not on the island of Great Britain, it is part of the United Kingdom. Sometimes called Ulster, Northern Ireland is known for its production of fine linen. **Belfast** is the capital and largest city. Another well-known city is Londonderry. Most of the people of Northern Ireland are Protestants of Scottish descent. **Amy Carmichael** (1867–1951) was a well-known missionary from Northern Ireland who worked with children and women in India.

Scotland

The Scottish Highlands. Scotland, which covers the northern third of Great Britain, is also part of the United Kingdom. It is a high, rugged land. The northern part of Scotland, the Scottish Highlands, is mostly uninhabited moor (treeless highlands), where coarse grasses and low shrubs called heather grow. Fjords (called *firths* in Scotland) cut into the land from the sea in many places. Many lakes (called *lochs* in Scotland) dot the land. The people who live in the Highlands are mostly shepherds and fishermen.

Loch Tummel in central Scotland

Scottish Attire

The Scottish Highlanders (those who live in the mountainous regions of Scotland) are very famous for their unique style of traditional dress. It is characterized by **tartan,** the name for their plaid cloth patterns. Today, the Highlanders wear their tartans only for ceremonial occasions. The dress consists of a ***kilt,*** or pleated skirt that comes to the knees, and a ***plaid,*** a long piece of tartan like a blanket worn over the left shoulder and fastened with a brooch. The Highlander may also wear a *sporran* (a pouch) hanging in front of his waist, a *doublet* (a jacket), and a *bonnet* (a cap). His stockings may also be made of tartan, and his *brogues* (shoes) are low-cut slip-ons with a buckle.

a Scottish bagpiper

The Central Lowlands. The Central Lowlands south of the highlands are where the majority of the people live. Most of them farm the fertile, gently rolling plains, mine the rich deposits of coal, or work in industrial plants. Scotland's two largest cities, **Glasgow** [glăs′kō] and **Edinburgh** [ĕd′'n·bûr′ə], are located in the Central Lowlands. Edinburgh, Scotland's capital, is one of Europe's most beautiful cities. Glasgow is the largest city in Scotland and is noted for its shipyards.

The Southern Uplands. The Cheviot [chĕv′ē·ət] Hills in the Southern Uplands form the border between Scotland and England. Many sheep graze there. Scotland is especially famous for **bagpipes.**

Famous people. One of the best-known men of Scotland was the Protestant reformer **John Knox.** Knox stood so firmly and bravely for the truth of the

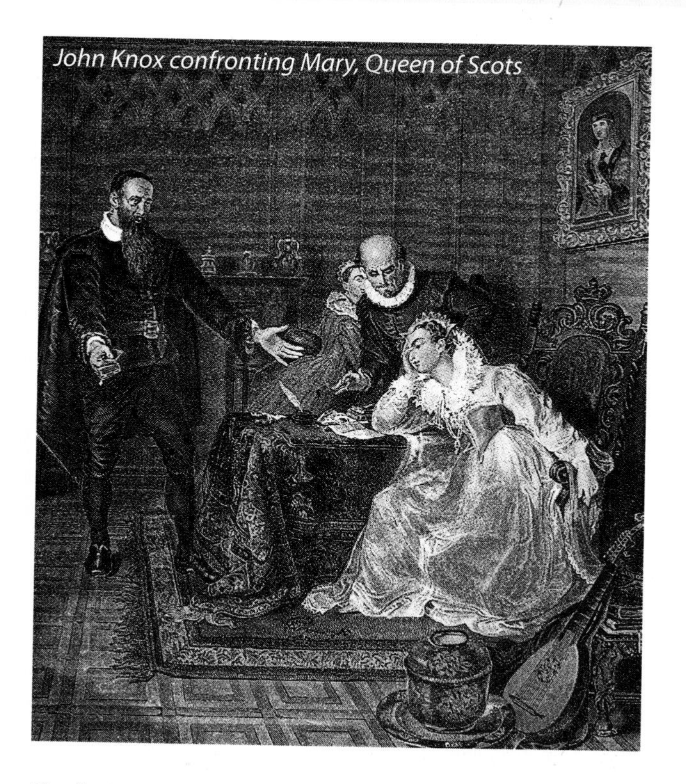
John Knox confronting Mary, Queen of Scots

Scriptures that the queen of the land, **Mary, Queen of Scots,** who did not want Protestants in Scotland, could not prevail against him. On one occasion, Queen Mary cried out, "I fear John Knox's prayers more than an army of ten thousand men!" John Knox, who was a follower of John Calvin, helped to establish the Scottish Presbyterian Church, and for many years people called Scotland "that Bible-loving land." Many famous missionaries went out from Scotland, including Robert Moffat, David Livingstone, and Mary Slessor, who went to Africa; and John G. Paton, who went to the islands of the Pacific Ocean. Some famous Scottish writers were **Robert Burns, Sir Walter Scott,** and **Robert Louis Stevenson. James Watt** was famous for perfecting the steam engine.

Wales

Wales, the smallest country on the island of Great Britain, is west of England. It, too, is part of the United Kingdom. **Cardiff** is its capital and largest city. Wales is a land of low mountains and deep, green valleys. The country has two official languages, English and **Welsh.**

Wales is especially noted for the great religious revivals that broke out there in the nineteenth century and at the beginning of the twentieth century. The last Welsh revival, in 1904–1905, reached people all over Wales and then spread around the world.

Thoughts of the love of Christ filled the Welsh people with song, and they became famous for their singing; many beautiful hymns have come from Wales. Perhaps you are familiar with one of the most famous Welsh tunes, "All Through the Night." In Welsh, its title is, "Ar Hyd y Nos." One of the most important industries in Wales is coal mining, and some of the most famous singers of Wales have been the hymn-singing Welsh coal miners.

farmland in Wales

CHAPTER 13 CHECKUP

A Know the countries and capitals of the British Isles and their locations. (See Continent Study 3, p. 324.)

B Know these locations.

1. Great Britain
2. English Channel
3. North Sea
4. Thames River
5. United Kingdom
6. Pennine Mountains

C Define each term.

1. Celts
2. Anglo-Saxons
3. Parliament
4. Lollards
5. Puritans
6. Separatists
7. Cavaliers
8. Roundheads
9. Industrial Revolution
10. Protestant Work Ethic
11. raw material
12. modernism
13. evolution
14. welfare state

D Tell the most important fact about each person.

1. Alfred the Great
2. William the Conqueror
3. John Wycliffe
4. William Tyndale
5. Miles Coverdale
6. John Cabot
7. Sir Francis Drake
8. Sir Walter Raleigh
9. William Shakespeare
10. John Milton
11. John Bunyan
12. Sir Christopher Wren
13. George Whitefield
14. John Wesley
15. Robert Raikes
16. William Carey
17. James Cook
18. James Watt
19. George Müller
20. William Booth
21. Florence Nightingale

E Who am I?

1. During my reign the Spanish Armada was defeated and the English became a people of "the Book."
2. authorized a new translation of the Bible in 1611
3. defeated the king in the Civil War; ruled during the Commonwealth
4. executed by the Roundheads
5. wrote the first English science book
6. discovered circulation of the blood

(cont.)

7. "Father of Modern Chemistry"
8. England's first constitutional monarchs
9. king during the French and Indian War
10. king during America's War for Independence
11. queen who said as a child, "I will be good."
12. made the idea of evolution popular
13. led Great Britain to victory in World War II
14. returned Great Britain to the Protestant Work Ethic
15. Mary, Queen of Scots feared my prayers more than she feared an army.
16. missionary from Northern Ireland to India

F Answer each question.

1. What is the world's largest landmass?
2. What mountain ranges and bodies of water separate Europe from Asia?
3. Which island is the eighth largest in the world?
4. Which country in the British Isles is *not* a part of the United Kingdom?
5. England is called the "__?__ Country" of the United States.
6. What was the most important gift that British settlers brought to America?
7. What document granted Englishmen certain rights and started England on its way to representative government? What year was this document signed?
8. What great English scientist discovered the law of gravity?
9. What two calamities occurred during the reign of Charles II?

G Identify the location described by each clue.

1. the mountain range known as the "backbone of England"
2. the largest country in the United Kingdom
3. the underwater tunnel that links Great Britain and France
4. the country known as the Emerald Isle
5. the longest river in the British Isles
6. the country known for its peat bogs and potato famine
7. the country known for its bagpipes, tartan, and lochs

Other Countries of WESTERN EUROPE

West of Asia, beyond the Ural Mountains and the Caspian Sea, the continent of **Europe** reaches out like a great peninsula to the Atlantic Ocean. History reminds us of the importance of Europe as the birthplace of western civilization—from Rome and the Christian martyrs of the Colosseum, to England and the Magna Carta, to Germany and the Protestant Reformation. The laws and forms of government found in the modern Western world began among the early European civilizations of Greece and Rome. Traditional standards of right and wrong held in the West actually come from Israel. However, the moral values of Judaism and Christianity took root and flourished in Europe rather than Asia, partly because Islam blocked the spread of Christianity eastward.

Today, the influence of Western civilization can be seen in Africa, Asia, Australia, and the Americas because European powers such as Great Britain, Spain, and France had established colonies there. Although Europe's colonial days have passed, the continent continues to influence the world through its economic and political dealings with other countries. Modern-day Europe has developed some of the most advanced and prosperous nations in the world.

14.1 Two Europes

For almost half of the twentieth century, Europe was divided into **Communist Eastern Europe** and **free Western Europe.** However, in the late 1980s and early 1990s, the Soviet empire began to crumble and Communism seemed to lose its hold on the countries of Eastern Europe. Those Eastern European countries, which are struggling to become free and strong, will be discussed in Chapter 15.

Victoria Station in Mumbai (Bombay) reflects the past influence of the British in India.

WESTERN EUROPE
ICELAND
Reykjavik
Arctic Circle (66°)
LAPLAND
Norwegian Sea
ATLANTIC OCEAN
FINLAND
NORWAY
SWEDEN
Helsinki
Oslo
Stockholm
ESTONIA
LATVIA
LITHUANIA
Baltic Sea
UNITED KINGDOM
North Sea
DENMARK
Copenhagen
IRELAND
RUSSIA
NORTHERN EUROPEAN PLAIN
BELARUS
NETHERLANDS
Hamburg
Strait of Dover
Amsterdam
Elba R.
The Hague
Rotterdam
Berlin
POLAND
English Channel
Brussels
BELGIUM
Rhine R.
Leipzig
GERMANY
Seine R.
Paris
LUXEMBOURG
CZECH REPUBLIC
UKRAINE
Danube R.
BLACK FOREST
SLOVAKIA
Bay of Biscay
FRANCE
JURA MTS.
Munich
Zürich
Vienna
SWITZERLAND
Salzburg
Bern
LIECHTENSTEIN
AUSTRIA
Geneva
HUNGARY
Lyon
Matterhorn
Mont Blanc
ALPS
SLOVENIA
ROMANIA
Milan
Venice
Rhone R.
Turin
CROATIA
Oporto
Toulouse
Genoa
Po R.
Douro R.
PYRENEES
Nice
SAN MARINO
BOSNIA-HERZEGOVINIA
Danube R.
PORTUGAL
ANDORRA
Marseille
Pisa
Florence
SERBIA
MONACO
APENNINES
Lisbon
Madrid
Elba
Adriatic Sea
MONTE-NEGRO
KOSOVO
BULGARIA
Tagus R.
Corsica
VATICAN CITY
SPAIN
Rome
ITALY
Valencia
MACEDONIA
Naples
Mt. Vesuvius
Seville
Sardinia
Pompeii
ALBANIA
GIBRALTAR
GREECE
Aegean Sea
Strait of Gibraltar
Mediterranean Sea
Gulf of Corinth
Sicily
Mt. Etna
Ionian Sea
Athens
Corinth Canal
AFRICA
MALTA

Many countries in Western Europe—such as France, Italy, Portugal, Ireland, Germany, Austria, and Switzerland—are **republics,** where the people elect their leaders. Others—such as Spain, Norway, the United Kingdom, Sweden, and Denmark—are **constitutional monarchies** with a king, queen, prince, or princess for a leader, and other important leaders who are elected by the people. In a constitutional monarchy, all leaders are required to obey the laws of the land.

Western Europe's most populous countries are Germany, the United Kingdom, France, Italy, Spain, the Netherlands, Greece, Belgium, Portugal, Sweden, Austria, and Switzerland.

WONDERS OF WORLD GEOGRAPHY

Peninsulas

Five peninsulas reach out from the continent of Europe. They are the **Balkan Peninsula,** the **Apennine Peninsula,** the **Iberian Peninsula, Jutland,** and the **Scandinavian Peninsula.**

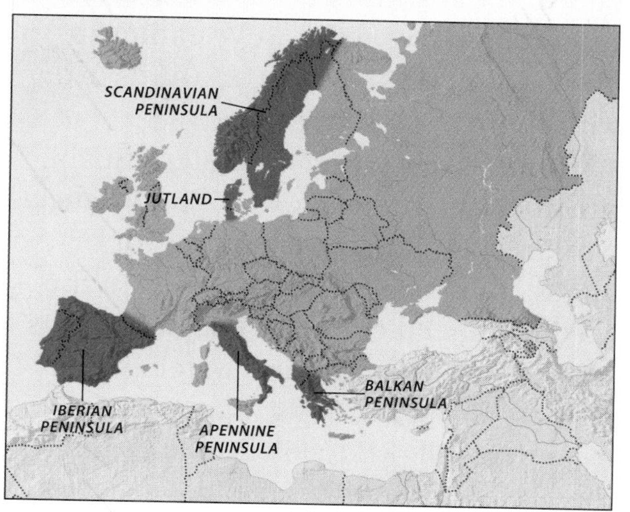

14.2 Mediterranean Europe

European countries that lie along the Mediterranean are often grouped together as Mediterranean Europe. Except in their mountainous regions, each of these countries experience a Mediterranean climate. Locate Spain and Portugal, Italy, and Greece on p. 224 and the map below. What is special about these countries besides their position on the Mediterranean?

Spain: Home of the Ancient Armada

Spain, which shares the Iberian Peninsula with Portugal, is the largest country in southern Europe and the third largest country in all of Europe. It is surrounded by Portugal, the Atlantic Ocean, the **Bay of Biscay,** France, and the Mediterranean Sea. The narrow Strait of Gibraltar separates southern Spain from Africa by about eight miles. Spain's capital city, **Madrid** [mə·drĭd′], is located almost exactly in the center of the country.

An "island." Spain's geography caused it to be like an island cut off from the rest of the world. The **Pyrenees** [pĭr′ə·nēz′] Mountains form a great bar-

Madrid

rier between the Iberian Peninsula and the rest of Europe, because the mountains have few passes. On all other sides, Spain is surrounded by water. Spain has 1,500 miles of coastline but few natural harbors. Spain is Europe's third-highest country (after Switzerland and Austria).

"The Tidelands." South of the city of **Seville** [sə·vĭl′] is a huge swamp known as "The Tidelands" that covers fourteen hundred square miles. In winter, most of the area is covered by water. In the spring, the water begins to evaporate, and the swamp becomes mostly a grassy meadow. Rice is raised in the shallow waters that remain. In the hot summer, "The Tidelands" receives almost no rainfall. The ground hardens and dries, and the area becomes a place to raise bulls for the bullfighting arenas.

Meseta. Spain is mainly a high, broad, arid plateau called the *Meseta* [mə·sā′tä: Spanish for "plateau"]. The Meseta is crossed by a series of mountain ranges and river valleys. The rivers through the Meseta are in deep valleys, or gorges. Few towns have grown up on the plateau because the summers are very hot, the winters very cold, and the rainfall sparse. Though the plateau's soil is fertile, there is no practical way to irrigate the land. However, where there is enough water, crops that have a short growing season thrive.

Temperate climate. All of Spain lies in the temperate zone. The inland is dry and sunny; summer and winter droughts are common. The islands and coastal plains have mild, rainy winters and hot, dry summers. The northern mountains have mild, wet weather in all seasons. Atlantic Ocean winds bring with them a steady drizzle.

ancient olive tree

orange grove in Spain

Oranges and olives. In eastern Spain, much citrus fruit is grown. The **Valencia** [və·lĕn′shē·ə] region is famous for oranges. Olive trees also grow well in the Mediterranean climate. The deep roots of the olive trees can find water even in times of drought. Some Spanish olive trees that still produce olives are more than one thousand years old.

Agriculture and industry. Because of poor soil, a largely dry climate, and poor farming methods, agriculture is the weakest part of Spain's economy. Although most of Spain's land is used for crops or pastureland, the harvest is too small to feed the Spaniards, and so Spain must import much of its food. Spain's chief agricultural products are grains, olives, wine grapes, oranges and lemons, wool (mainly from sheep), corn, and cork.

Spain is a leading fishing country. It is one of the world's leading producers of ships. It also manufactures automobiles, cement, shoes, and clothing.

The people. The people of Spain speak Spanish, although pronunciation differs slightly from place to place. Most Spaniards are Roman Catholic, but many do not attend services.

Spaniards enjoy spending much of their free time outdoors. Folk singing and dancing are favorite activities. Soccer and bullfighting are the favorite sports. **Matadors** [măt′ə•dôrz: bullfighters] who are skillful often become famous. Spain's Mediterranean coast is a favorite vacation spot of many Europeans.

matador at a bullfight

donkey being used to work the land in Spain

Village life. In areas of rough terrain, some of Spain's farm villages are very poor. Village women fetch water from wells and do laundry in irrigation ditches. Water is so scarce in some areas that men carry it in jugs and sell it door to door. Work animals—mostly oxen and donkeys because they are less expensive than horses—are still used to till the land.

Famous Spaniards. Well-known men of Spain include the painter El Greco [ĕl grĕk′ō] and the writer Miguel de **Cervantes** [mē•gĕl′ dā′ sər•văn′tēz], who wrote the humorous book, *Don Quixote* [dŏn kē•hō′tē]. Familiar explorers from Spain include **Cortés** and **De Soto.**

Past glory. Spain's past glory can be seen in its magnificent art and architecture. The Prato Museum in Madrid has one of the world's finest art collections. The main cathedral in Seville is Europe's second largest church (the largest is St. Peter's in Rome, Italy). About 1,400 castles and palaces still stand in Spain.

Exploration. Spain was a leader in exploring the New World. The Spanish crown claimed much foreign land. In the sixteenth century, gold from Spanish colonies in America helped to make Spain Europe's wealthiest nation. The sixteenth century was Spain's Golden Age.

When England destroyed Spain's fleet, the Spanish Armada, in 1588, Spain also began to sink. The country grew constantly weaker and gradually lost colonies and influence.

Spain's government. Between 1939 and 1975, General Francisco **Franco** [frăng′kō] ruled Spain as a dictator. When he died, Spain became a constitutional monarchy with **Juan Carlos** [hwän′ kär′ləs] as the king. Modern Spain is not as isolated as she was in the past. Spain joined NATO in 1982 and the European Union in 1986.

The Rock of Gibraltar. The British dependency of Gibraltar is a small peninsula in southern Spain. On Gibraltar's southern tip is a mountain called the **Rock of Gibraltar.** The mountain juts out into the narrow Strait of Gibraltar. The Rock of Gibraltar and a similar mountain in northern Africa are together called the **Pillars of Hercules.**

Rock of Gibraltar

PEOPLE IN HISTORY

Famous Explorers for Spain

1492 **Columbus,** an Italian hired by Spain, sailed on his first voyage and claimed the New World for Spain.

1513 **Balboa** discovered the Pacific Ocean. He claimed the land bordering it for Spain.

1513 **De Leòn** made the first Spanish landing on the mainland of North America.

1521 **Cortés** conquered Mexico for Spain.

1536 **Mendoza** founded Buenos Aires [bwā′nəs âr′ēz], Argentina, for Spain.

1541 **De Soto** discovered the Mississippi River.

1565 **Menéndez** founded St. Augustine, Florida, for Spain.

Comprehension Check 14A

1. Name three constitutional monarchies in Western Europe.
2. Name the five peninsulas reaching out from Europe. On which peninsula is Spain located?
3. What is Spain's capital city?
4. What mountains divide Spain from the rest of Europe?
5. What do the Spanish call their high, arid plateau?
6. Name three famous Spanish explorers.

Portugal: Home of Explorers

Little land. Small Portugal is the westernmost country of mainland Europe. It is bounded on the north and east by Spain and on the south and west by the Atlantic Ocean. The little, rectangular country covers most of the west coast of the Iberian Peninsula.

Much highland. Most of Portugal is hilly, and the northern and southern ends are quite mountainous. Because of the mountainous terrain, only about ⅖ of Portugal's land is suitable for agriculture.

Forests. Thick forests cover Portugal's hills. These forests yield one of Portugal's main sources of wealth: cork. A special type of oak tree called the cork oak grows all over Portugal. The bark of this tree is cut off about every 10 years and corks are cut from it. Cork oak is hardy and can grow on hillsides where other vegetation cannot thrive. Large groves of pine trees also grow in Portugal, as well as some nutbearing trees, such as the almond, chestnut, and walnut.

a cork oak forest with bark being harvested

Rivers and cities. The Douro River flows through the richest part of Portugal and provides an excellent waterway to **Oporto** [ō·pôr′tō], a very important Portuguese seaport. The **Tagus** [tā′gəs], the longest river of the Iberian Peninsula, cuts through mountains and divides Portugal in half (*Tagus* means "to cut"). Its mouth forms a wide bay at **Lisbon** [lĭz′bən], Portugal's capital and largest city. This bay is the finest harbor on the Iberian Peninsula and one of the best in the world.

Temperate climate. Because of Portugal's location on the Atlantic coast, the country enjoys a marine west coast climate. Both summers and winters are mild. The southern part of Portugal is particularly suited to vineyards, and grape growing is one of Portugal's major industries. Wheat is the leading grain grown in Portugal, but the country also must import wheat to meet its needs.

Portuguese workers. The people of Portugal speak Portuguese, which is very similar to Spanish. Their main religion is Roman Catholicism. Most of the Portuguese today are farmers, forest workers, or fishermen. They are also noted for their skill in lacemaking and pottery.

Although Portugal is one of the poorest nations in Europe, Portuguese fishermen often find their occupation to be profitable. The seas off Portugal's coasts are teeming with fish, including great schools of tuna and sardines. The Portuguese also use their seafaring skills to fish for cod off Africa's west coast. Fish, an important part of the Portuguese diet, is often eaten at each meal. Portugal also exports vast quantities of fish.

Rich in history. The Portuguese people take pride in the fact that once they were among the most powerful nations on earth and rulers of a vast empire. In the 1400s and 1500s, Portugal played an important part in the great exploration of the New World.

The Age of Discovery. In 1385, John I became king of Portugal. His reign marked the start of Portugal's greatest days of glory. King John had a son who was an avid sailor and explorer. He was called **Prince Henry the Navigator.** Prince Henry urged Portuguese explorers to sail into uncharted waters and establish new trade routes. He even offered rewards to navigators who discovered new lands. Thus, Portugal led the way in the great age of exploration.

PORTUGUESE EXPLORERS

A Portuguese school for geographers and sailors trained many famous explorers. Portugal's Ferdinand **Magellan** [mə·jĕl′ən], the first man to sail around the world, studied there. Portuguese explorers discovered islands that were added to the Portuguese empire. In 1488, **Bartolomeu Dias** [dē′əs] sailed all the way to the Cape of Good Hope at the

Portuguese fishermen with their catch

Prince Henry the Navigator

tip of Africa. Many Europeans had said such an accomplishment was impossible.

Further goals reached. Dias's success encouraged others to sail even farther. In 1498, **Vasco da Gama** became the first European to sail to India by going around Africa. Now Portugal had a path to the fabulous wealth of the mysterious Orient, and her own wealth and power grew. In 1500, **Pedro Cabral's** [kə·brälz′] discovery of Brazil marked the beginning of Portugal's empire in the New World.

Declining power. In the 1500s, Portugal's power began to decline, and by 1580, Portugal had come under Spanish domination. Sixty years later Portugal regained its independence, but it was never again as powerful as it had once been.

Portugal's government. Portugal is now a republic with a president, a prime minister, and a Parliament. The people elect their president, who stays in office for five years. The prime minister works as a helper to the president. The Socialist and Communist Parties, who want the government to control the economy, are very powerful in Portugal.

Comprehension Check 14B

1. What is the only country that borders Portugal?
2. What river cuts Portugal in half?
3. What is Portugal's capital?
4. What famous seaman encouraged Portuguese exploration?
5. What Portuguese explorer was the first to find a water route for trade to India?

Italy: Home of the Renaissance

Bordered on the north by France, Switzerland, Austria, and Slovenia [slō·vē′nē·ə], the Italian "boot" is as much a part of the Mediterranean scenery today as it was in ancient times. The Alps and the Apennines still stand, and the **Po River** still waters northern Italy. Rome remains a city of worldwide importance. However, many changes have taken place on the Apennine Peninsula since the time that Rome ruled the world.

The Italian Renaissance

Near the end of the Middle Ages, great works of art and music were produced in Italy. Because it seemed as if the land were waking up from medieval darkness, this period, which lasted from A.D. 1300 to 1600, was called the **Italian Renaissance** [rĕn′ĭ·säns′], or "rebirth." Three of the most important Renaissance Italians were artists: **Leonardo da Vinci** [lā·ō·när′dō dä vēn′chē], **Michelangelo** [mī′kəl·ăn′jə·lō], and **Raphael** [răf′ē·əl].

Leonardo da Vinci (1452–1519) was truly a remarkable man. He was not only a master painter but also an architect, sculptor, inventor, and engineer who was centuries ahead of his time. On pages in his notebooks, he wrote out plans for a flying machine (airplane), a parachute, tanks, and a movable bridge. He made scientific drawings of the human body showing bones, muscles, and tendons. Such accurate drawings had never been known before. To read his notebooks, one has to use a mirror, for he was left-handed and found it easier to write backward, from right to left. Two of Leonardo's most famous paintings are ***Mona Lisa,*** the woman with the mysterious smile, and ***The Last Supper,*** which shows Christ and His disciples in the Upper Room.

Another great artist of the Renaissance was **Raphael** (1483–1520), who completed several hundred paintings even though he lived for only 37 years. One of his famous paintings is called the ***Sistine*** [sĭs′tēn] ***Madonna.*** Raphael was also an architect [är′kĭ•tĕkt′: a designer of buildings and bridges]. He directed the building of St. Peter's church in Rome.

Many people consider **Michelangelo** (1475–1564) to be the greatest artist of the Renaissance. His paintings of the Creation, Adam and Eve, and the Flood are some of the greatest art the world has ever seen. For two years, Michelangelo lay on his back on top of high scaffolds (raised platforms) to paint these scenes on the ceiling of Rome's **Sistine Chapel.** Two of his most famous works of sculpture are his statues of the biblical leaders **David** and **Moses.**

Italian People

Italians are noted for their expressiveness, liveliness, and love of fine art and music. Their delicious foods, including pastas (dishes using spaghetti, macaroni, and noodles) and spumoni [spo͞o•mō′nē: an ice cream made with cherries and nuts], have become favorites of people around the world today.

Explorers. Many Italians have been important to world history. In the late 1200s, **Marco Polo** became the first European to travel all the way across Asia. His lively accounts of his journeys caused many Europeans to become interested in finding out about the rest of the world. **Christopher Columbus,** the discoverer of America, was born in Genoa [jĕn′ō•ə], Italy, in 1451. He later moved to Portugal, however, and made his discoveries in the name of Spain. **John Cabot** (1450–1498) was also an Italian, but his discovery of North America was made in the name of England. The

sketch of a military tank, by da Vinci

Mona Lisa *by da Vinci*

Michelangelo's David

first man to realize that the New World was truly a new world and not just a part of Asia was the Italian seaman **Amerigo Vespucci** [ä·mā·rē′gō vĕs·po͞o′chē: 1454–1512], for whom America was named.

Vespucci

Mussolini

A great scientist. One of the founders of modern science, **Galileo** [găl′ə·lē′ō: 1564–1642], was from Italy. Galileo was one of the first men to view the heavens through a telescope and to show that the earth revolves around the sun. His discoveries and writings led to many other great scientific discoveries in England and other parts of Europe.

Musicians. Many famous composers (writers of music) and musical performers have come from Italy. The most important musical form in Italy is the opera, a sad or funny story that is acted out and sung on stage. Two famous Italian opera writers were **Verdi** [vâr′dē: 1813–1901] and **Puccini** [po͞o·chē′nē: 1858–1924].

Changes in Government

Divided and conquered. After the fall of the Roman empire in 476, Italy was divided into a collection of small, weak states that were often invaded and conquered by foreign powers. Barbaric tribes, the popes, the Holy Roman Empire, France, Spain, and Austria are just some of the peoples who ruled all or part of Italy at one time or another.

In 1861, Italy finally became a united kingdom under King Victor Emmanuel II. After World War I, however, the Italians came under the dictatorship of **Benito Mussolini** [bə·nē′tō mo͞o′sə·lē′nē], the leader of the **Fascist** [făsh′ĭst] political movement. (**Fascism** is a form of government that lets people keep their private property but takes away their freedoms.) Mussolini ruled first as premier [prĭ·mĭr′] and then as dictator from 1922 until Italy was defeated by the Allies in World War II (1943).

The Italian Republic. Since 1946, Italy has been a republic, with a president, a premier, and a Parliament. The members of Parliament are elected by the people, and Parliament elects a president. The president appoints the premier, who runs national affairs and is the most important man in Italian government. Italy has many political parties. Sometimes as many as fifteen parties run candidates for Parliament. The Communist party is stronger in Italy than in any other country of Western Europe.

Geographical Regions

The Po Valley. In northern Italy, between the Alps and the Apennines, is a broad valley drained by the Po River. The Po Valley is Italy's industrial center and its most important agricultural region.

Most of Italy has a Mediterranean climate, which means that crops must be irrigated in the summer. The Po Valley, however, has a **humid continental climate,** much like that of the Southern United States. The warm, rainy summers and cool, rainy winters combined with the fertile soil make the valley an excellent place for growing rice, corn, wheat, and many other products. The leading cities of the Po Valley are *Milan* [mĭ·lăn′], *Genoa,* and *Turin* [to͝or′ĭn].

Western coastal plain. There is also much good farmland on the coastal plains and highlands of central Italy. Olives and grains grow well in central Italy's Mediterranean climate, and it is also a good area for raising livestock. *Rome, Florence,* and *Naples* [nā′pəlz] are the most important cities in that region.

Mountains. The Italian Alps are not as high as the Swiss Alps, and many good roads and tunnels pass through them. Water from the swift streams that flow down the mountains provides hydroelectric power for the industries in the nearby Po Valley. Easily available electric power is one thing that makes the Po Valley Italy's main manufacturing center. The Alps and the Apennines are both used for grazing and forestry.

Islands. Sicily and Sardinia are the two large islands that form a part of Italy. On the map (p. 224), it looks as though the toe of Italy's boot is about to kick Sicily. This island is mostly a rugged plateau, and it has Europe's highest active volcano, **Mt. Etna.** Sardinia, which is very mountainous, is used for raising livestock, especially sheep.

Mt. Etna

Cities

Rome. Rome, Italy's capital and largest city, is located on the western coastal plain. Today, Rome extends far beyond the seven hills on which the city was originally built. Travelers from all over the world visit Rome to see the ruins of its ancient glory, to view the great works of art that were produced during the Italian Renaissance, and to study music and art, for which Italy is still noted.

St. Peter's Basilica, Vatican City

Many Catholics from around the world make pilgrimages to Rome to see the pope and the magnificent buildings of the **Vatican** [văt′ĭ·kən] **City,** an independent state within the city of Rome that is world headquarters for the Roman Catholic Church. **St. Peter's Basilica** [bə·sĭl′ĭ·kə] in Rome is the world's largest Catholic church building.

Florence. Florence, which is north of Rome on the Arno [är′nō] River, was the birthplace of the Italian Renaissance. It is one of the world's most famous centers of art. Tourists in Florence can see many of the works of Michelangelo, Leonardo da Vinci, and other great Renaissance artists who lived and worked there. West of Florence is the little town of **Pisa** [pē′zə], which is famous for its **Leaning Tower.**

Naples. Naples, Italy's third largest city and an important manufacturing center, lies about one hundred miles south of Rome. It is one of Italy's most musical cities and is also well known for its pastas. Naples is believed to be the birthplace of pizza, a favorite food in many countries. Famous tourist attractions near Naples are **Mt. Vesuvius,** mainland Europe's only active volcano, and the ruins of **Pompeii** [pŏm·pā′] and other ancient Roman cities.

Mt. Vesuvius

Cities of the Po Valley. Since the A.D. 100s, **Milan,** Italy's second largest city, has been an important center of trade because of its location near a pass through the Alps. Today it is a leading manufacturing and banking center of Italy. Music lovers from all over the world visit Milan to hear performances in **La Scala** [lä skä′lə], one of Europe's most famous opera houses. **Genoa,** the birthplace of Christopher Columbus, is Italy's largest port and the second largest port on the Mediterranean Sea. (Marseille [mär·sā′], France, is the largest.) Genoa is also an important industrial center. **Turin** is located near the source of the Po River and is surrounded by mountains. Its beautiful surroundings make it a favorite tourist site. Turin is a leading manufacturing center. Because it specializes in the manufacture of automobiles and motorscooters, it has been called the "Detroit of Italy."

Leaning Tower of Pisa

Venice. Venice, which is located near the mouth of the Po River, is one of Italy's loveliest cities. It is built on 118 small islands in the Adriatic Sea that are connected by 400 bridges and a system of canals. Instead of cars, the people use motor boats and **gondolas** [gŏn′dl·əz] for transportation within the city.

gondola along a canal in Venice

Comprehension Check 14C

1. What two mountain ranges are located in Italy?
2. Name two great Italian artists and one of their great works of art.
3. Who became the Fascist dictator of Italy after World War I?
4. What two islands are part of Italy?
5. What is the capital of Italy?
6. What is the headquarters for the Roman Catholic Church called?
7. What city is known for its canals and bridges?

Greece: Home of Early European Civilizations

Greece—the land of Homer, Aesop, Plato, and Alexander the Great—was the home of the earliest European civilizations. Located west of Asia Minor (modern Turkey), in the southeastern corner of Europe, modern Greece consists of the southern Balkan Peninsula and more than 2,000 islands, mostly in the Aegean and Ionian seas. **Crete,** the largest Greek island, lies south of the mainland in the Mediterranean Sea. Over 70 percent of the mainland is covered with mountains. Southern Greece consists of an islandlike peninsula that is separated from the mainland by the Gulf of Corinth and the Corinth Canal. Locate Greece, Crete, the Aegean and Ionian seas, and the Gulf of Corinth on the map (p. 224).

History. The first Europeans settled on the islands and mainland of Greece shortly after the dispersion from Ba-

farmland in Crete

bel. Over the centuries, the ancient Greeks developed an advanced civilization of independent city-states. The greatest of these, Athens and Sparta, acquired colonies throughout the Mediterranean and waged war against the Persian Empire and each other. The Greek city-states were finally united under Philip II of Macedonia. His son, Alexander the Great, went on to conquer North Africa and parts of Asia, spreading Greek culture from Egypt to India.

Shortly after Alexander's death, his empire crumbled, and Rome picked up the pieces. The Greek language served as the common tongue of the Roman Empire, and Greek culture continued to influence the Mediterranean world for centuries. The New Testament was written in the common Greek of the people. After the Roman Empire split between east and west, Greece became a possession of the Byzantines, who introduced the religion of Eastern Orthodoxy, later called Greek Orthodoxy. The last empire to dominate the Greeks, the Ottoman Empire, ruled the country until 1830 when Greece won its independence.

Modern Greece is a democratic republic with an elected parliament. The majority of the people are native Greeks, and the rest are immigrants, mainly from western Asia.

Resources and industries. Although agriculture still employs approximately ¼ of the people, more and more of the Greek population is moving to the cities. Nearly ⅓ of the nation's people live in crowded **Athens,** the capital city. In spite of their rugged, rocky land, Greek farmers manage to grow wheat, garden vegetables, olives, citrus fruits, and nuts. Many of these crops are exported along with textiles, chemicals, and electronics. Greece has one of the largest commercial fleets in the world and a well-established tourism industry encouraged by its many historic sites.

modern Greek market

14.3 Central Europe

The Central European countries of **France, Andorra** [ăn·dôr′ə], **Monaco, Switzerland, Liechtenstein** [lĭk′tən·stīn], **Austria,** and **Germany** are characterized by snowcapped mountain peaks, lush river basins, and dense broadleaf forests. This region holds the most breathtaking scenery in the world. Can you find all of these Central European countries on the map (p. 224)?

Every Central European country (except tiny Andorra) contains at least a portion of the **Alps,** the mountain range that is Central Europe's most prominent feature. The Pyrenees, a smaller range, form the border between France and Spain. Europe's most important inland waterway, the **Rhine River,** flows through Germany and along the borders of France and Switzerland.

Westerly winds warmed by the water of the Atlantic Gulf Stream cross much of Central Europe, bringing the regular

the Rhine River

WONDERS OF WORLD GEOGRAPHY

Mountains

The most famous mountains in Europe are the **Alps,** which form the largest mountain system in Europe. They are about the same height as North America's Rocky Mountains. **Mont Blanc** [mônt blăngk], in France, is the highest mountain in the Alps. The **Matterhorn,** which is on the border of Switzerland and Italy, is a favorite place for daring mountain climbers from all over the world.

The Alps are Europe's watershed, or continental divide. A **divide** is a stretch of high land that separates river basins. Many of Europe's rivers have their source high in the Alps. From the Alps they flow in all different directions. The Rhine River and the Rhône River begin at almost the same place, but the Rhine flows north and empties into the North Sea, and the Rhône flows south to the Mediterranean. Other rivers flow from the Alps into the Black Sea and the Adriatic Sea.

Smaller mountain chains in Europe are the **Pyrenees,** which form the neck of the Iberian Peninsula, the **Apennines,** which cover much of Italy (the Apennine Peninsula), and the **Caucasus** Mountains. **Mt. Elbrus,** in the Caucasus chain, is Europe's highest peak. Two famous active volcanoes are **Mt. Vesuvius** [vĭ·so͞o′vē·əs], in the Apennines, and **Mt. Etna,** in Sicily. Both are in modern Italy. Locate these mountains and mountain chains on the map.

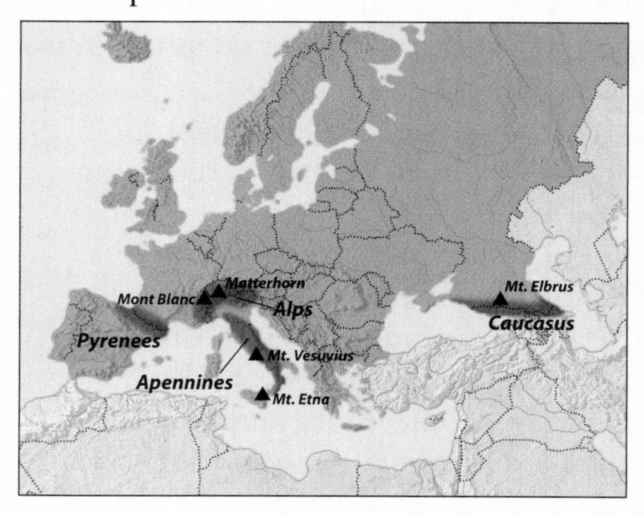

rainfall and mild temperatures associated with a marine west coast climate. Farther inland, particularly in the higher elevations, the climate is humid continental, with warm, sunny summers and harsh, snowy winters.

Comprehension Check 14D

1. What is the largest Greek island called?
2. Name Greece's capital city.
3. Give one important fact about the Rhine River.
4. Name the largest mountain range in Europe. What is the highest mountain in that range?
5. What is a divide?
6. What two active volcanoes are located in Italy?

France: Land of Revolution

Location. France is the largest country in Central Europe. It lies to the west of Germany, between the Bay of Biscay and the Mediterranean Sea. It is separated from Spain by the Pyrenees Mountains and from England by the English Channel.

Mont Blanc

Land forms. France's highest peak, **Mont Blanc,** is located in the French Alps. West of the mountains are highlands and plateaus. Western and northern France are covered by flat or rolling plains.

People and Events

France is noted for its famous painters, cooks, sculptors, scientists, and fashion designers. The French people love beauty, and they enjoy trying to think of new ways to do things. Unfortunately, many times in history their desire to change things and to find a better life has only brought them more hardships.

French explorers made important discoveries in North America, and for many years France controlled most of Canada. At one time, France had colonies in many parts of the world, and there are places in Africa, Asia, the Americas, and the Pacific islands where the French language is still spoken today.

Famous men and women. A French explorer, **Jacques Cartier** [zhäk kăr•tyā′: 1491–1557], was the discoverer of the

Jacques Cartier

Madame Marie Curie

St. Lawrence River in the New World. **Louis Pasteur** [lo͞o′ē păs·tûr′: 1822–1895], a French scientist, taught the world the importance of protecting the body against harmful germs. **Madame Marie Curie** [kyo͝or′ē: 1867–1934], a Polish-born scientist who did her work in France, is known for discovering radium. **Joan of Arc** (1412–1431) was a young peasant girl who lived during the Middle Ages. She helped the French defeat the English in an important battle, but then she was burned at the stake by the English. Queen **Marie Antoinette** [än′twä′nĕt′: 1755–1793] was beheaded during the French Revolution.

John Calvin and the Reformation. During the Protestant Reformation, some French people turned to the truth of the Bible. Their leader, **John Calvin** (1509–1564), was one of the famous Frenchmen in history. The Roman church drove him out of France, and he became an influential Protestant leader in nearby Geneva [jə·nē′və], Switzerland. The Protestants in France were later known as **Huguenots** [hyo͞o′gə·nŏts′]. In Holland, those who followed Calvin's teachings were known as the Reformed Church, and in Scotland they were called Presbyterians [prĕz′bĭ·tĭr′ē·ənz].

The Huguenots. The French Huguenots underwent terrible persecution for their faith. In just three days in 1572, perhaps as many as 100,000 of them were massacred. Those who survived were later driven out of the country. About half a million Huguenots fled to other European countries, and Huguenots were among the first Protestants to settle in America. The American hero **Paul Revere** was from a French Huguenot family.

The Enlightenment. Not long after the Huguenots were forced to flee, a number of French philosophers began to challenge established authority in France by attacking the government and religion. These philosophers called their movement the **"Enlightenment,"** although it was really a new "Dark Age" for France. Some French thinkers, such as **Voltaire** [vōl·târ′] and **Rousseau** [ro͞o·sō′], insisted that man must apply human reason or understanding to all areas of life (humanism). If man could not

Rousseau

understand it, it must not be true. Such thinking became the foundation for attacks against the Bible and Christianity. The authority of God and His Word came under great attack. In time, this rebellion against established authority led to the French Revolution.

The French Revolution. In 1789, the people of France revolted against their government. The French Revolution filled the land with bloodshed. The people tried to set up a new government that did away with everything that reminded them of their old rulers and of Christianity. They made a new calendar that abolished (did away with) Sundays, Easter, and Christmas. The weeks would be ten days long rather than seven, they said, and no longer would people figure centuries in relationship to the birth of Christ. They closed the churches and decreed (officially stated) that there is no life after death. All of these attempts at changing truth failed miserably, of course. Soon, the French were worshiping men and reason as their gods. Before long, France came under the power of one of history's most ruthless dictators, **Napoleon Bonaparte** [nə·pō′lē·ən bō′nə·pärt′: 1769–1821].

Napoleon Bonaparte. When Napoleon was only thirty years old, he drove out the existing government and became the ruler of France. Five years later, in 1804, he crowned himself emperor of France and set out to conquer the world. The Napoleonic Wars kept much of Europe busy trying to defend their lands against Napoleon and the French. Napoleon was finally defeated and sent to the island of Elba and then to the island of St. Helena [hĕl′ə·nə] as an exile. His followers had destroyed the governments of many European countries, and it took Europe and France many years to recover from the wars. France went through more changes and bloodshed before it became a stable country again.

The 20th century. In more recent years, France fought alongside Great Britain and the United States in World War I and World War II. After World War II, the French war hero **General Charles de Gaulle** [də gōl′] set up a democratic government called the Fifth Republic. (It was fifth because four other attempts at republican government had failed in France.) In 1981, France elected a socialist as its president. A **socialist** is a person who believes that a country's businesses and industries should be taken away from individual

Napoleon Bonaparte

owners and put under the control of the government. Several Communists were given important jobs in this government.

More recently, the government has responded to the people's request for more private ownership of business and property. France continues to have more family-owned farms than any other country in Europe.

Geography

Rivers. The Rhine River forms part of the border between France and Germany. Some other rivers are the **Rhône** River, which flows into the Mediterranean Sea, and the **Seine** [sān] River, which flows into the English Channel. Many of the rivers are connected by canals and are widely used for transportation and shipping.

Climate. Most of France has a mild marine west coast climate. The Mediterranean climate of the southeast makes that area ideal for growing grapes, for which France is famous.

Natural resources. More than 90 percent of France is fertile and good for farming. **Iron ore,** the most important mineral in France, has made the northwest a major steel-producing area. There are many forests in the highlands and mountains, and new forests are being planted.

Cities. **Paris,** France's capital and largest city, is located on the banks of the Seine River. It is one of the world's great cities. People from all over the world enjoy visiting the **Eiffel** [ī′fəl] **Tower** and the **Notre Dame** [nō′trə däm] **Cathedral,** eating in Paris's world-famous restaurants and sidewalk cafes, and visiting the art galleries. The **Louvre** [lo͞ov′rə] in Paris is the largest art museum in the world. Other French cities are *Marseille, Lyon* [lē·ōn′], *Toulouse* [to͞o·lo͞oz′], and *Nice* [nēs].

Comprehension Check 14E

1. What famous French scientist discovered radium?
2. Who led the Reformation in France?
3. What were Calvin's followers in France called?
4. What powerful French leader set out to conquer the world?
5. What is the capital of France?
6. What is the largest art museum in the world?

Notre Dame Cathedral

Louvre

Switzerland: Mountain Republic

Switzerland, the most mountainous country in Europe, is also one of Europe's oldest republics. It is known for its heritage of freedom and peace, its leadership in the Protestant Reformation, and its highly skilled workers. Cheese, chocolate, wood carvings, watches, and music boxes are well-known Swiss products. **Bern** [bûrn], the capital of Switzerland, is also the country's manufacturing center.

Switzerland has long been a **neutral** nation, a nation that has a policy against fighting in wars. Because of this, many people from all over the world put their money in Swiss banks, where they feel it is safe. Switzerland has three official languages: **German, French,** and **Italian.**

People and Events

Independence. Switzerland gained its independence from the Holy Roman Empire in 1499. According to a Swiss legend, **William Tell** was the great hero of Swiss liberty.

William Tell, great hero of Swiss liberty

Reformation. The Protestant Reformation did more than perhaps anything else to help Switzerland remain a free and prospering nation. **Ulrich Zwingli** [o͝ol′rĭk tsvĭng′lē: 1484–1531] and **John Calvin,** two prominent Reformation leaders, preached and taught in Switzerland. Zwingli, a native Swiss who introduced Reformation truths to Switzerland, had his headquarters at **Zurich** [zo͝or′ĭk], the country's largest city. When John Calvin was driven from France, he went to **Geneva,** where he set up a training school for Protestant scholars. Geneva became a model of a city run by Christian principles, and it was the international center of Protestantism. A group of Protestants called Swiss Brethren or Anabaptists [ăn′ə·băp′tĭsts] were also centered in Switzerland.

Engineers. Skillful Swiss engineers have constructed roads, bridges, and tunnels throughout the mountainous areas to simplify travel for tourists and citizens. The first automobile tunnel through the Alps and one of the longest railway tunnels in the world are both in Switzerland.

Dairy farmers. Most farmland in Switzerland is used for hay for the dairy cattle. In the summertime, the men and older boys have taken the cattle to pastures high in the mountains. The women and other children stay below to plant gardens and raise grass for hay. In the fall, the men come back down, and the cattle have hay to eat all through the cold winter. Milk from the cattle is used for butter and for the famous Swiss cheeses and milk chocolates that are sent all over the world.

Famous people. Switzerland's most famous authors wrote children's books. *Heidi,* by **Johanna Spyri** [shpē′rē], tells what life was like for a boy and girl living in the Alps. *The Swiss Family Robinson,* by **Rev. Johann Wyss** [vēs], is an exciting adventure tale about a Swiss pastor and his family who are marooned on a deserted tropical island.

Jean Henri Dunant [zhän än′rē′ do͞o′nän′] of Geneva was a very wealthy banker from a Christian home who devoted his entire fortune to helping others. He was responsible for the founding of the **International Red Cross.** The Red Cross flag, a red cross on a white background, is very similar to the Swiss flag. In 1901, Dunant became one of the first people to be awarded the Nobel [nō·bĕl′] Peace Prize.

Jean Henri Dunant

Geography

Switzerland is a **landlocked** country, a country that has no seacoast. It is completely surrounded by France, Italy, Austria, and Germany.

Rivers. The Swiss people have found a way to transport goods to and from the sea, however. They float them down the Rhine River on barges to ocean vessels in the North Sea. This enables them to carry on world trade. Switzerland's snow-fed rivers, which include the Rhine River and the Rhône River, are the country's most important natural resources. Dams built on the rivers store water for the production of electricity, which is the power source for all the Swiss homes and industries.

Landforms. The spectacular **Swiss Alps** cover the southern 60 percent of Switzerland. **The Matterhorn,** a majestic peak that experienced mountain climbers love to challenge, is part of the border between Switzerland and Italy. In the north, the **Jura** [jo͝or′ə] **Mountains** cover another 10 percent of the land. Between the two mountain ranges is a plateau area, where most of the people live. The plateau extends from **Lake Geneva** to **Lake Constance,** the largest of many long, narrow lakes nestled between the mountains of Switzerland.

Climate. Altitude (distance above sea level) is the most important factor in Switzerland's climate. Much of the

the Matterhorn

nation has a highland or alpine climate, which means that it is cold and snowy in the winter and cool and rainy in the summer. Many of the mountain peaks are covered with snow all year. In the valleys, the weather is warmer (sometimes hot). The plateau is cold and often foggy in the winter and warm and sunny in the summer.

Austria: Land of Culture and Beauty

Mountains, music, castles, the capital city of **Vienna** [vē·ĕn′ə], and the beautiful Danube River are all characteristics of Austria, a landlocked highland country next to Switzerland.

History. Native Austrians are a mix of the earlier Celtic, Roman, Germanic, and Slavic peoples who settled in the area. Most of them speak a softly pronounced German. In the past, Austria was very powerful as the center of a large empire. After World War I, Austria was reduced to its present size. During World War II, it was seized by Germany and not given up until the war was over.

Culture. Vienna, located on the "Blue Danube," is known as a great cultural center for its beautiful medieval architecture and Germanic art, literature, and music. The people of Vienna take pride in living in the city where great composers such as Mozart, Haydn, Schubert [shōō′bərt], and Strauss [strous] wrote and performed their music.

Resources and industries. Austria is one of the world's chief sources of graphite, the "lead" used in pencils. It is also known for its delicate Austrian crystal glassware. Only a small percentage of the land is devoted to agriculture, yet farmers meet most of their country's food demands and are able to export dairy products. Tourism, in both the skiing areas of the Alps and in cities such as Vienna and **Salzburg** [sôlz′bûrg], is also a main part of the country's economy.

Austrian homes

Comprehension Check 14F

1. What is the capital of Switzerland?
2. What is a neutral nation?
3. What Swiss brought the Reformation to Switzerland?
4. For what is Jean Henri Dunant known?
5. What type of land covers most of Switzerland? What is the name of this area?
6. What famous musical center is the capital of Austria?

Germany: Land of the Reformation

Early Events

Middle Ages and Reformation. **Germany** is a large country in the center of Europe. It became important during the Middle Ages as a part of the Holy Roman Empire, which was ruled by people from Germany and Austria. Because Martin Luther began the Protestant Reformation in Germany in 1517, it is often called the "Land of the Reformation." After the Reformation, Germany was a leader in education, music, and Bible study. The people and their leaders eventually left the truth of the Scriptures, however, and much of the good done by the Reformation was lost in Germany.

The rise of Prussia. Between 1618 and 1648, there was terrible fighting between Protestant and Catholic forces in Germany. This fighting, known as the Thirty Years' War, left Germany a very poor land with no central government. The land of **Prussia** to the east of Germany gained power and took control of much of Germany. Later, a famous king of Prussia, **Frederick the Great** (1712–1786), made Prussia a world power. In 1871, Germany became an empire with Wilhelm I of Prussia as the first **kaiser** [kī′zər: emperor].

Frederick the Great

The World Wars

World War I. Kaiser Wilhelm I and his grandson Kaiser Wilhelm II pushed so hard to add new lands to the German Empire that other European countries grew alarmed. This rush to expand their empire, combined with the chaos and humanist ideas of the Enlightenment and the French Revolution, caused conditions in Europe to become more and more tense. Finally, in 1914, World War I broke out. Europe was divided into two groups. The **Allies,** which included Great Britain, Russia, France, Japan, and eventually the United States, were fighting against the aggression of the **Central Powers**—Germany and its partners. Soon countries from every part of the world were fighting in the great and terrible World War I.

Germany and the Central Powers lost the war, and much of the territory that Germany had conquered was taken away. She was also required to pay for the damages that the war had caused. Germany was a torn and broken country.

Hitler. In the 1930s the **National Socialist Party** [or Nazis: nät′sēz], headed by **Adolf Hitler,** became powerful in Germany. Hitler's promises to make the German people rich and powerful again made him a popular man. When he became chancellor (a high official), he overthrew the new constitution that the German people had set up. He said that Germans had the right to conquer and rule the world.

Adolf Hitler

The National Socialists. Hitler allowed only one political party in Germany—the Nazis. The people were told that the government was more important than the people and that some people were inferior to others. The German people were so eager to regain their position in the world that they gave up their freedom and blindly followed one of the cruelest dictators the world has ever known, Adolf Hitler.

World War II. Hitler's desire to conquer led to **World War II,** which eventually brought most of the world into battle. Battles were fought on three continents: Africa, Asia, and Europe. Germany joined with Japan and Italy to fight the rest of the world; these three countries were called the **Axis.** The countries fighting against them were called the **Allies**—Great Britain, the Soviet Union, China, and the United States.

The Allies finally won the war in 1945, but not without much bloodshed and destruction. Germany was again a

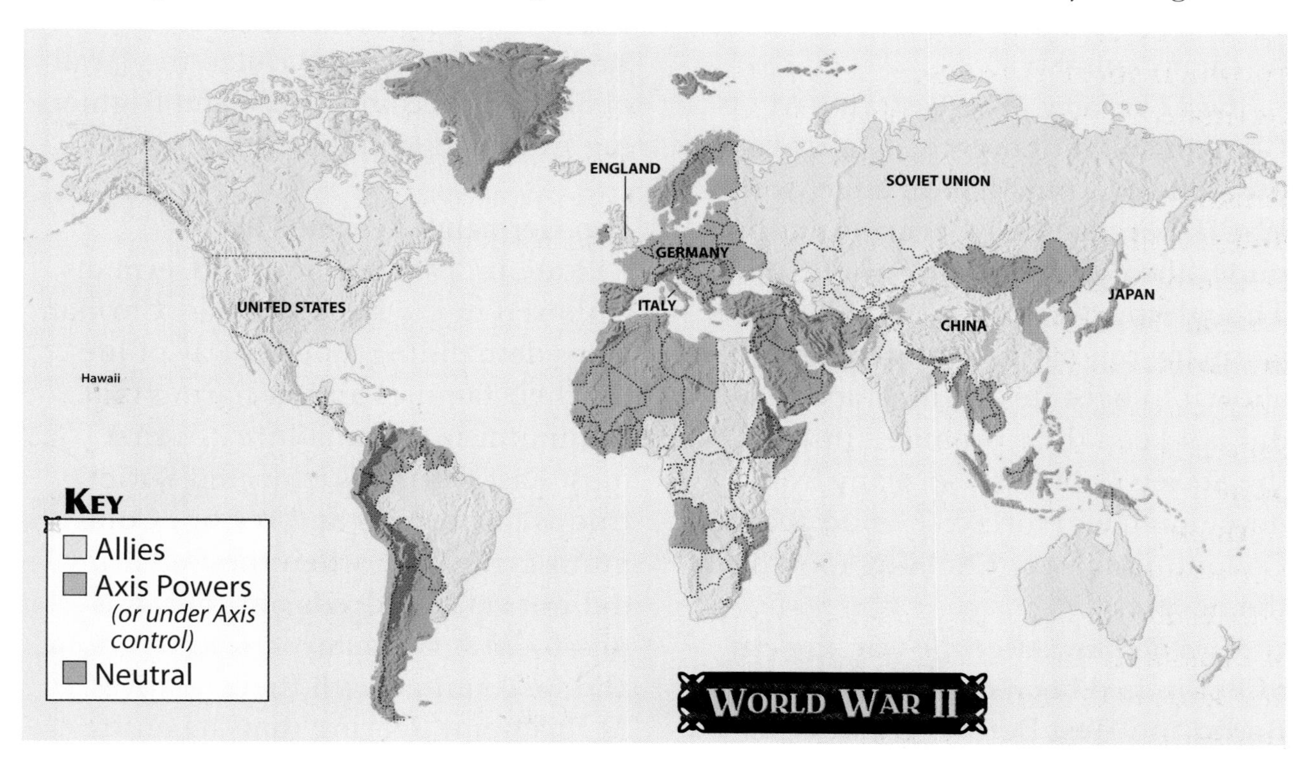

torn land, as was much of Europe. The Germans under Hitler had even killed many of their own people, including six million Jews.

A Divided Germany

West Germany. After World War II, the United States, Great Britain, and France took over the government of the western part of Germany for a time until it could recover from the damages of the war. These countries helped **West Germany** to rebuild its cities, homes, industries, and farms and to become self-governing. Then they withdrew, and West Germany became a thriving industrial nation. The West Germans established a constitutional democracy. This means that it is governed by laws and that the people elect leaders to represent them in government. They chose the city of **Bonn** to be their capital.

East Germany. The eastern part of Germany did not become a prosperous, self-governing nation after World War II, because **East Germany** was put under the control of the Soviet Union. Though the Soviets agreed to help East Germany rebuild its resources and to allow it to become a democracy, they did not keep their promise. Instead, the Soviets kept East Germany from developing and forced them to accept Communism by withholding food from the people.

Two Berlins. After the war, the city of Berlin had been divided into **East Berlin** and **West Berlin.** West Berlin

Berlin Wall

became a part of free West Germany, and East Berlin was given to the Soviet Union. East Berlin became the capital of East Germany. Because great numbers of East Germans tried to escape Communism by fleeing to West Berlin, the Communists built a wall between the two sections of the city in 1961. The **Berlin Wall,** which was called the "Wall of Shame," became a dark and frightening symbol of Communism.

Two Germanys Become One

Late in 1989, millions of Germans gathered in the streets of East German cities demanding a better way of life for their families and declaring that Communism was a failure. At first, most East Germans expected Soviet troops to storm in and restore Communist rule. But when the Red army did not act, hundreds of thousands fled to West Germany to find freedom and be reunited with their relatives. At this point, fearing that the entire

Wonders of World Geography

Rivers

Many rivers flow through Europe and empty into the seas. Ships can sail up these rivers to bring goods to inland cities. This is just one of the reasons Europe has been an important center of world commerce (trade) for many centuries. The rivers provide **transportation** routes, water for **irrigation,** and, today, power to generate **electricity.**

Europe's longest river is the **Volga** [vŏl′gə]. The **Danube** is Europe's second longest river, and the **Rhine** is Europe's most important inland waterway. Other important European rivers are the *Dnieper* [nē′pər], the *Oder,* the *Seine,* and the *Po.* Locate all of these rivers on the map below. ⁂

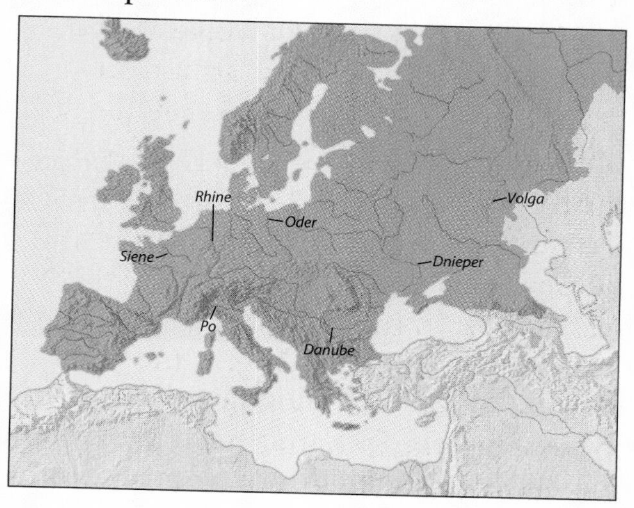

population would leave East Germany, the Soviet Union announced that they would tear down the "Wall of Shame" and allow East Germany to join the West German Federated Republic. In return, the West Germans would give large amounts of money and technology to the Soviet Union. East German soldiers, freed from their Communist masters in Moscow, were among the first to tear cement blocks out of the Berlin Wall early in 1990. Although the Communists had planned to regain control after allowing a small window of freedom, the united Germany is still enjoying its freedom.

Geography

Cities and rivers. Germany's largest cities are **Berlin,** the capital of united Germany, *Hamburg, Leipzig* [līp′sĭg], and *Munich* [myo͞o′nĭk]. The beautiful Rhine, Europe's most important inland waterway, cuts deeply into the surrounding land, and along its high banks stand many of the old stone castles of the Middle Ages. The Rhine River has become a symbol of Germany. Other famous rivers are the *Oder,* the *Elbe* [ĕl′bə], and the *Danube.*

Land regions. The northern part of Germany is a broad, fertile plain whose rivers empty into the North Sea and the Baltic Sea. In the south, the land is higher. Two famous southern regions are the Black Forest and the Bavarian [bə·vâr′ē·ən] Alps.

The **Black Forest** is famous for its heavy growth of fir and spruce trees and as the imaginary home of Hansel and

the Black Forest

Gretel, Little Red Riding Hood, Snow White, and other characters in the Grimm fairy tales collected by two German brothers, Jacob and Wilhelm Grimm.

The **Bavarian Alps** are a part of the Alps Mountains. They are well known for their beautiful scenery. During the summer, farmers take their sheep, goats, and cattle high up into the mountains to graze until fall. The people also grow hay for the wintertime in the plains down below.

Climate. The northwestern part of Germany has a marine west coast climate. The winters are mild and the summers are cool. Farther away from the sea, the climate is humid continental, with hotter summers and colder winters.

The German People

Character. The German people are famous for their hard work, thriftiness, intelligence, and respect for authority. Many of the world's great musicians and scientists have come from Germany.

Musicians. German musicians include Johann Sebastian **Bach** [yō′hän sə·băs′chən bäk: 1685–1750], the "Father of Modern Music," who wrote beautiful music for the Protestant churches; George Frederick **Handel** (1685–1759), famous for *The Messiah,* which is about the life of our Lord Jesus; and Ludwig van **Beethoven** [lŭd′wĭg vän bā′tō′vən], who wrote beautiful music even after he lost his hearing.

Scientists. Perhaps the most famous German scientists were Johannes **Kepler** (1571–1630), who described how the planets orbit around the sun, and Albert **Einstein** (1879–1955), a German Jew who was one of the greatest scientific geniuses the world has ever known. (Einstein became an American citizen in 1934.) Many other German scientists have made important discoveries in chemistry, medicine, and physics.

Industry. The hard work, thriftiness, and scientific ability of the German people have made Germany one of the leaders in world industry. Germany is noted for its manufacture of automobiles, chemicals, clothing, cameras, and electrical equipment.

Bach

Einstein

Comprehension Check 14G

1. Why is Germany called the Land of the Reformation?
2. Who started the growth of the German Empire?
3. Who became a powerful leader in Germany after World War I?
4. What was his political party called?
5. What happened to Germany after World War II?
6. What city was divided after the war?
7. What is Europe's most important inland waterway?
8. Who was the German who became one of the greatest scientific geniuses in the world?

14.4 ⌘ The Low Countries

The Netherlands, Belgium [bĕl′jəm], and Luxembourg [lŭk′səm·bûrg] occupy some of the lowest land in Europe. Much of this flat land lies just above the North Sea, and some is below sea level, kept from flooding by man-made dikes. Most of the region enjoys a marine west coast climate. Rainfall is frequent year round, and autumn often brings long periods of fog and mist. Locate each of the Low Countries on the map (p. 224).

klompen

The Netherlands: Land Below Sea Level

Tulips, windmills, and wooden shoes are familiar symbols of **The Netherlands,** the country that is often called Holland. The Netherlands, a small kingdom on the North Sea, is bordered by Germany and Belgium. The people of the Netherlands are known as ***Hollanders*** or ***Dutch.***

How the Dutch Made Holland

The word *nether* means "low." Much of the Netherlands lies below sea level; some of it once lay *under* the sea. The Netherlands is a small country; as it grew and prospered more land was needed. Sometimes in the past when a country needed more land it declared

tulip fields alongside a canal in Holland

Dutch windmill on a dike

war on its neighbors and seized their land. The Dutch people thought of a better way. They *made* land on low-lying swamps, lakes, and bays.

First, the Hollanders built **dikes,** which are damlike barriers made of earth and stone. Then they pumped out the water behind the dikes, using **windmills** as the power source. (Electric motors do the job of windmills today.) A system of canals is used to carry water to the sea and to irrigate the land. By draining the land, the Dutch nearly doubled the amount of farmland in the Netherlands. This is how the old saying, "God made the world, but the Dutch made Holland," originated.

People and Events

The people of the Netherlands are noted for their neatness and hard work. The Netherlands is one of the most densely populated countries in the world, and yet it does not appear to be crowded. This is because the Dutch believe that cleanliness is next to godliness. "If everyone sweeps his own doorstep," they say, "the whole world is clean." The Dutch take pride in doing their part to keep the country pleasant and livable. Perhaps you know the story of the little Dutch boy who put his finger in a hole in the dike to hold back the sea. Near the city of Haarlem the Dutch have built a statue in honor of the boy in this story, because he symbolizes the feeling that the Hollanders have for their country.

Great artists. After the Protestant Reformation, Holland produced some of the greatest artists the world has ever known. Many simple Dutch homes displayed the works of such great Dutch masters as **Rembrandt** [rĕm′brănt′: 1606–1669] and **Vermeer** [vər·mâr′: 1632–1675]. Rembrandt, whom some have called the greatest painter of all times, specialized in Bible scenes, portraits (pictures of individuals), and warm scenes from everyday life. Other great Dutch masters have included Rubens [ro͞o′bənz: 1577–1640] and Van Gogh [văn gō′: 1853–1890].

The Lacemaker, by Vermeer

"Father of Dutch Liberties." For many years, Holland was under the rule of Spain. The people lived in great fear of the dreaded **Spanish Inquisition,** which tortured people to try to force them to follow the pope. The Dutch longed to have a free and independent nation. In the 1580s, the Dutch nobleman **William the Silent,** the Prince of Orange, defended his country against attacks from the Spanish ruler Philip II and led the Netherlands to independence. He was called the "Father of His Country" and the "Father of Dutch Liberties." Throughout the century that followed (the seventeenth century), the Netherlands was a leading sea power and the center of world trade. It had colonies throughout the world. The seventeenth century was called the "Golden Age of the Netherlands."

Land of refuge. Before and after its independence, Holland was a land of safety for people from many nations who were persecuted for their religious beliefs. It was one of the first nations in the world to offer religious liberty. Religious liberty brought both spiritual and physical blessings to Holland, for the skilled craftsmen and industrious merchants who went there for religious freedom helped to bring about Holland's Golden Age. One church group from England, the **Pilgrims,** found refuge in Leyden [lī′dn], Holland, for several years before they sailed to America and founded **Plymouth Colony.**

The Dutch in the New World. In the early 1600s, the English navigator **Henry Hudson** sailed to the New World for the Netherlands and discovered Delaware Bay and the Hudson River. The Dutch came to the area that Hudson claimed for the Netherlands and founded the colony of **New Netherland,** which the English later captured and renamed **New York.** The Dutch also established **New Amsterdam,** which now is called **New York City.**

Cities

Amsterdam, the largest city and official capital of the Netherlands, is kept from sinking into the water by millions of piles (huge wooden beams) driven deep into the mud. Like Venice, Italy, it has many bridges and canals. The government buildings are at **The Hague** [hāg]. **Rotterdam** is the major port for shipping on Europe's important Rhine River.

Agriculture and Industry

The flat, fertile lands below sea level that have been reclaimed from the sea

houses in Amsterdam

are Holland's best farmlands. Every spring, field upon field of colorful tulips, daffodils, and hyacinths [hī′ə·sĭnths] burst into bloom in the lowlands. These flowers are raised for their bulbs, which are shipped to all parts of the world. Fruits, grains, and vegetables are also grown. Dutch farms are small, but fertilizers and modern farm machinery help farmers make the best of the land that they have.

Dutch farmers sometimes wear wooden shoes called *klompen* [klämp′ən] when they are out in the damp fields. When they go inside, they leave the shoes on the doorstep and change to leather shoes. At one time, *klompen* were worn by almost everyone in Holland because they protect feet from dampness better than leather shoes do. (See picture, p. 251.)

From the port at Rotterdam, the Netherlands is able to import raw materials and export meat products, dairy products (butter, cheese, milk, and eggs), cut flowers, and a variety of manufactured goods.

A Classic Book about Holland

Hans Brinker, or the Silver Skates, an exciting children's classic by the American author Mary Mapes Dodge, has been called "one of the best books about Holland ever written."

Belgium and Luxembourg

Directly south of the Netherlands lie the smaller countries of **Belgium** and **Luxembourg.** The Belgian countryside is a mixture of forests, grasslands, pastures, and low mountains. Luxembourg's southern region, called the Gutland [go͞ot′lănd: "goodland"], is much more fertile than the plateau region in the north.

At one time, **Belgium** was a part of the Netherlands. Belgium is famous for its handmade Brussels **lace,** named for **Brussels,** the national capital. It is also famous for artists who lived in an area called **Flanders.** Many battles have been fought in Belgium by armies of other nations because of its location between Germany and France.

The **capital** of tiny **Luxembourg,** also named Luxembourg, is a major center of European banking and finance.

Belgian woman making lace

Comprehension Check 14H

1. Why do people say the Dutch made Holland?
2. What were windmills used for?
3. What great Dutch artist specialized in Bible scenes?
4. Who is the "Father of Dutch Liberties"? Why?
5. What is the official capital of Holland? However, the government buildings are located where?
6. Brussels, Belgium, is famous for what type of material?

14.5 Scandinavia: Land of the Vikings

Peoples and Events

Vikings. During the Middle Ages, fierce warriors called **Vikings** lived on the Scandinavian Peninsula and Jutland. The Vikings, who traditionally were tall people with blond hair and blue eyes, were skilled craftsmen and daring seamen. They raided many European nations, and they explored and settled Greenland and Iceland. They even landed in North America about 500 years before Columbus, but they started no lasting colonies there.

The Scandinavians. The adventurous Vikings were ancestors of the people who live in Norway, Sweden, Denmark, and Iceland today. Their language was the basis for the Scandinavian languages. **Norway, Sweden,** and **Denmark** (and sometimes **Finland** and **Iceland**) are called the **Scandinavian** countries. Find these five countries on the map (p. 224). Because they are situated so far to the north, most of these countries are less populated than other European countries.

Reformation. The ideas of the Protestant Reformation were brought to Scandinavia by Scandinavian students who studied in the German universities. Within a few years, all the Scandinavian countries had adopted Lutheranism, and most of the people belonged to the Lutheran church. Many of the Lutheran churches in the United States were started by Scandinavians who immigrated to America in the 1800s.

fierce Viking raiders

Welfare states. Today, the countries of Scandinavia are welfare states. This means that the government takes the responsibility of caring for the people "from the cradle to the grave." Jobs, medical care, child care, and other services are provided by the government. This form of **socialism** has caused many problems in Scandinavia. It has put the countries deeply in debt and forced the people to pay heavy taxes. More importantly, it has encouraged some industrious people to become less responsible. Because they can get everything they need from the government, there is less reason for individuals to take the initiative (responsibility) to provide for themselves and their families.

Bodies of water

Peninsulas make Europe's coastline very uneven and very long (over one and a half times as long as the distance around the equator). Many large seas and gulfs fill in the spaces between and around the peninsulas, giving Europe an abundance of good harbors for shipping. The largest bodies of water surrounding Europe are the **Atlantic Ocean,** the **Mediterranean Sea,** and the **Norwegian Sea.** Other important bodies of water are the **Black Sea,** the **Aegean Sea,** the **Adriatic** [ā′drē·at′ĭk] **Sea,** the **Bay of Biscay,** the **North Sea,** and the **Baltic Sea.**

An interesting inland lake is the **Caspian Sea,** which is the world's largest lake. It is called a sea because it contains salt water, but a lake because it is landlocked. The northern shore of the Caspian Sea is Europe's lowest point.

Locate these bodies of water on the map below. Find the **Strait of Gibraltar** on the map. It is a narrow stretch of water that connects the Mediterranean Sea with the Atlantic Ocean and separates the Iberian Peninsula from Africa.

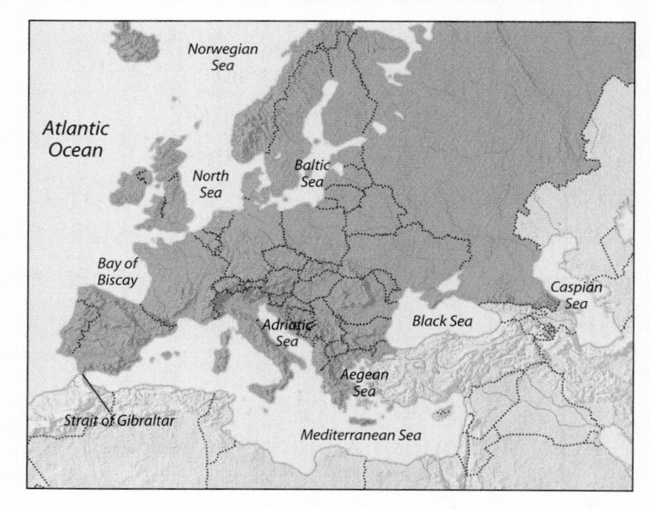

Norway: Land of the Midnight Sun

Midnight sun. **Norway** extends farther north than any other European country, with its northernmost regions lying above the Arctic Circle. Norway is called the **"Land of the Midnight Sun"** because the area above the Arctic Circle has sunshine twenty-four hours a day from mid-May through July. For ten weeks in the winter, the sun is not seen at all in this area.

Rugged land. Norway has one of the most jagged coasts in the world. The coast is penetrated by many **fjords,** which are long, narrow inlets of the sea

a fjord in Norway

with high, rocky banks. They are often as deep as mountains are high. The fjords provide sheltered coves and fine harbors for fishing boats and merchant ships. High plateaus and mountains cover much of the interior.

Economy. Manufacturing, forestry, and fishing (especially for salmon) are Norway's most important industries. The swift mountain rivers, which are used to produce electricity, are the most important natural resource. Because there is little good farming land, most of the food has to be imported.

Climate. Norway has a milder climate than most regions so far north, because warm currents from the Atlantic Ocean keep the coastal areas from getting too cold.

Capital and government. About half of Norway's people live in or near **Oslo** [ŏz′lō], the capital city. Most of the others live in smaller cities along the coast. Norway is a constitutional monarchy. The prime minister is the most important leader, and the king is in charge of ceremonies.

Sweden: Largest Scandinavian Country

Capital and government. **Sweden,** which lies to the east of Norway, is the largest Scandinavian country. Its capital and largest city, **Stockholm** [stŏk′hōm], is called the "Venice of the North" because of the water channels that run through the city. Like Norway, Sweden is a constitutional monarchy.

Land areas. Sweden is not mountainous like Norway, except along the Norwegian border. A vast area in the north is covered with pine and spruce forests, providing resources for the important lumbering industry. Some of the richest iron ore deposits in the world are found there. Most of the people live in the fertile plains of the south where most of the country's food is grown. Lakes cover about one tenth of Sweden's area.

Climate. Southern Sweden has warm summers and mild winters. In the north, summers are cool and winters are very cold. Sweden is covered with snow from two to six months of the year.

Stockholm, the "Venice of the North"

Industry. Important industries of Sweden are mining, forestry, shipbuilding, fishing, and the production of paper pulp and high-quality steel.

Comprehension Check 14I

1. What is the world's largest lake?
2. What fierce warriors were the ancestors of modern-day Scandinavians?
3. What are the three Scandinavian countries? What other countries are often included?
4. What is called the "Land of the Midnight Sun"? Why?
5. What is the largest Scandinavian country?
6. What is the capital of Sweden?
7. By what other name is this city sometimes called?

Denmark: Home of Hans Christian Andersen

Former power. Little **Denmark,** on the Jutland Peninsula, was once the most powerful state in northern Europe. It controlled Norway, Sweden, Finland, Iceland, and Greenland for many years. Before that, Denmark's king, **Canute the Dane,** had succeeded in taking over England for a while. Today, Denmark is a constitutional monarchy with a king or queen, a prime minister, and a parliament. **Copenhagen** [kō′ pən·hā′ gən] is the capital and largest city.

Canute the Dane

People. The people of Denmark, who are called **Danes,** are closely related to the Norwegians and Swedes. Most of them live on one hundred islands near Jutland. The most famous Danish writer was **Hans Christian Andersen** (1805–1875), whose fairy tales, including "The Ugly Duckling" and "The Snow Queen," are known to children in many parts of the world.

Agriculture and industry. Denmark is a part of the Northern European Plain. The land is very fertile, and most of it can be used for farming. The most familiar Danish exports are ham, silverware, and finely crafted furniture.

The world's largest island. **Greenland,** the world's largest island, belongs to Denmark, even though it is thousands of miles away. Only the coastal areas of Greenland are green; the rest is covered by thick glaciers [glā′shərz], or large masses of ice.

Copenhagen

Iceland: Land of Fire and Ice

The republic of Iceland is perhaps one of the most unusual countries in the world. It lies on an island in the Atlantic Ocean just south of the Arctic Circle, and was settled by Norwegians in A.D. 870. Although most of Iceland is a high plateau, the majority of the people live on the lowlands along the coast. The lowlands have a mild climate that is warmed by ocean currents, but there are many glaciers on the plateau. Volcanoes, hot springs, and steaming geysers [gī′sərz] found alongside the glaciers cause Iceland to be called the **"Land of Fire and Ice."** Most of the houses in **Reykjavik** [rā′kyə·vēk′], the capital, are heated by hot water piped from nearby hot springs.

Finland: Scenic Forest Land

Many of **Finland's** people are of Russian origin rather than descendants of the Vikings. Their land lies between the Scandinavian Peninsula and Russia. After being a Swedish territory for centuries, Finland was forced to sign agreements with Russia. However, taking advantage of the 1917 Russian Revolution, the Finns declared their independence. They made the largest city, **Helsinki** [hĕl′sĭng′kē], their capital. Finland is a low, scenic land covered with thick forests and dotted with thousands of lakes. Forestry and the production of forest products provide most of the country's economy.

The European Tundra

The far northern parts of Norway, Sweden, Finland, and Russia, and the interior of Iceland are **tundra** regions. (In the Western Hemisphere, the far north of Alaska and Canada are tundra areas.) Locate the tundra regions on the climate map (p. 339). Most of the tundra is north of the Arctic Circle, in the **Frigid Zone.** Check the temperature map (p. 340) to find the average July temperature of the tundra.

Marshes and permafrost. The word *tundra* is Russian for "marshy plain." (A **marsh** is an area of low, wet, soft land. It is also called a **swamp** or a **bog.**) The tundra is marshy only in summer, however; the rest of the year it is frozen solid. Even in the summer, the ground is frozen about three feet below the surface. This permanently frozen ground is called **permafrost.**

Winters are long and bitterly cold on the tundra, but the short, cool summers have many hours of sunshine, causing the ice and snow to

geyser in Iceland

melt. Then the tundra is dotted by many lakes, ponds, and marshes, where mosses, lichens [lī′kənz], and some low shrubs grow. Flowers, such as poppies and bluebells, blanket the land with color. No trees grow, however. The tundra is above the **timber line** (a point on a mountain or in polar regions beyond which trees cannot grow because of the cold).

The main animals that live on the tundra are reindeer, musk oxen, wolves, Arctic foxes, hares, and mouselike creatures called lemmings. They all have thick fur that helps them conserve body heat. Insects, especially mosquitoes, are abundant in the summer. Ducks, falcons, geese, loons, ravens, sandpipers, and snowbirds can also be seen during the summer.

The most familiar people of the tundra are the **Inuit** [ĭn′yo͞o·ĭt: formerly called Eskimos], who live in villages in Greenland, Siberia (the northern part of Russia), Alaska, and Canada. They are excellent hunters and fishermen, and much of their livelihood comes from the sea animals, especially the seal. During winter hunting trips, they sometimes live in **igloos,** which are temporary shelters made of snow blocks.

The **Lapps,** who are native to northern **Norway, Sweden,** and **Finland,** depend mostly upon fishing for their livelihood. Many of them also have small farms, and some of them herd reindeer. The area where they live is called **Lapland.** Other groups of Arctic people, especially those in the northern parts of Russia, lead nomadic lives. They wander around herding reindeer, which provide their main source of food and income.

Lapp woman in traditional dress

Inuit building a temporary igloo

Timberlines are found on mountains and in polar regions.

Comprehension Check 14J

1. On what peninsula is Denmark located?
2. What is Denmark's capital?
3. What large island belongs to Denmark?
4. Why is Iceland called the "Land of Fire and Ice"?
5. What is the capital of Iceland?
6. What does tundra mean? Do trees grow in the tundra?
7. Name two groups of people who live in tundra areas.

14.6 Languages of Europe

Three language groups. When the Roman Empire broke up, European people sought to form separate nations with their own languages and governments. There are three main language groups in Europe today, and all three are members of the same large Indo-European language family. They are the **Romance** languages, the **Germanic** languages, and the **Slavic** [slä′vik] languages.

Romance Languages

Latin was the official language of the Roman Empire. It is no longer a spoken language, but many present-day languages have come from it. They are called **Romance** languages because they originated near Rome. Italian, Spanish, Portuguese, and French are four important Romance languages. They all had their origins in **southern** Europe.

Italian, which is spoken in Italy, is the Romance language that is most like the Latin language. Many musicians throughout the world study Italian, for it is the language of music.

Spanish, of course, is the language of Spain. It is also spoken in much of Central and South America, for at one time Spain controlled most of South America and parts of North America. The parts of the Western Hemisphere south of the United States (Mexico, Central America, the West Indies, and South America) are called **Latin America** because the Latin-based languages, especially Spanish, Portuguese, and French, are spoken there. Spanish, the most widely spoken language in Latin America, is not spoken in quite the same way in the New World as it is in the Old World.

Portuguese is the language of Spain's neighbor, Portugal. Most of the Portuguese-speaking people live in Brazil, the largest country of South America. This is because the large country of Brazil (about the size of the United States) was once a colony of little Portugal.

French, the language of France, is called an international language. Diplomats often learn either French or English, because these two languages can be understood in almost any part of the world. French is spoken in parts of Africa and Asia that once belonged to France; in Guiana [gē·ăn′ə], South America; on the island of Haiti [hā′tē]; and in parts of Canada.

Germanic Languages

The Germanic languages were named for the Germanic tribes that invaded the Roman Empire. Most of the people in northern Europe speak Germanic languages, and they have spread their languages and cultures around the world. The **Germanic** languages are **German, Dutch, Icelandic** [īs·lăn′dĭk], **Swedish, Danish, Norwegian,** and **English.** Do you know which Germanic language is spoken most?

German is spoken in Germany, Austria, and parts of the nearby countries. **Dutch,** which is similar to German, is spoken in the Netherlands (Holland) and in other places that once were Dutch possessions. The descendants of the Dutch people who colonized South Africa many years ago speak a form of Dutch called *Afrikaans* [ăf′rĭ·käns′]. **Icelandic, Swedish, Danish,** and **Norwegian** are called **Scandinavian** languages. Icelandic is almost the same as the language of the Viking ancestors of the Scandinavian people. Swedish and Norwegian are spoken in some Lutheran churches in America even today.

English is quite different from the other Germanic languages because many English words have come from French or Latin. Some of the first people in England were Germanic tribes, and their language formed the basis of English grammar. During the time of the Roman Empire, Latin was introduced into the island, and it was the language of scholars and churchmen for many centuries. Examples of English words from Latin are *butter, cheese, pepper, pound, inch, mile, candle, priest,* and the names of the months.

In 1066, England came under the rule of a French duke, **William the Conqueror;** thus many French words became a part of English. Some English words from French are *rule, royal, fashion, dainty,* and *sir.*

As the British people spread to all parts of the world, words from many other languages also became a part of English. This diversity makes English one of the richest languages in the world and also one of the most difficult languages for foreign people to learn. Some of the places where English is spoken today are Great Britain, Canada, the United States, Australia, and New Zealand. English, along with French, is an international language.

Slavic Languages

Most of the people of Eastern Europe speak **Russian,** which was the official language of the former Soviet Union. The Russian alphabet has 33 letters, and it looks very different from our own Roman alphabet. Some other Slavic languages are **Polish, Ukrainian** [yo͞o· krā′nē·ən], and **Bulgarian** [bŭl·gâr′ē·ən].

Other European Languages

Modern **Greek** is a form of the ancient Greek language, upon which all the European alphabets are based. Greek is not a member of one of the three main European languages. There are other very ancient European languages that also have not been mixed with other languages.

Concepts to Consider

How Do They Say It?

Here is how people who speak some of the Romance languages say some very important words and phrases. You might enjoy learning the words from one of these lists. Perhaps you or your parents speak one of these languages. If so, give your classmates some words to learn.

English	Italian	Spanish	Portuguese	French
hello	**ciao** (chou)	**buenos dias** (bwā′nōs dē′äs)	**alô** (ə·lō′)	**bonjour** (bōn′zho͞or′)
yes	**si** (sē)	**si** (sē)	**sim** (sēm)	**oui** (wē)
Mother	**madre** (mä′drā)	**madre** (mä′drā)	**mãe** (mā)	**mère** (mâr)
Father	**padre** (pä′drā)	**padre** (pä′drā)	**pai** (pī)	**pere** (pâr)
boy	**ragazzo** (rä·gät′sō)	**muchacho** (mo͞o·chä′chō)	**rapaz** (rə·päz′)	**garçon** (gär·sôn′)
girl	**ragazza** (rä·gät′sä)	**muchacha** (mo͞o·chä′chä)	**moça** (mō′sə)	**jeune fille** (zhûn′ fē′y’)
How are you?	**come sta?** (kō′mə stä)	**¿Como está usted?** (kō′mō ĕs·tä′ o͞o·stĕd′)	**Como está?** (kō′mo͞o ĭsh′tä)	**Comment allez vous?** (kô′môn·täl′ā vo͞o′)
thank you	**grazie** (gräts′yə)	**gracias** (gräs′yäs)	**obrigado** (ō′brē·gä′do͞o)	**merci** (mĕr′sē′)
God is love.	**Dio e amore.** (dē′ō ā ä·mō′rā)	**Dios es amor.** (dē′ōs ĕs ä·mōr′)	**Deus é amor.** (dā·əs ā ə·mōr′)	**Dieu est amour.** (dē′yə ĕ ə·mo͞or′)

Counting to Ten in German, Dutch, and Norwegian

Here is how to count from one to ten in some Germanic languages. If you know someone who speaks a Germanic language (other than English), perhaps he will teach you some more words.

English	German	Dutch	Norwegian
one	**eins** (īnz)	**een** (ūn)	**en** (ĭn), **et** (ĭt)
two	**zwei** (zvī)	**twee** (twā)	**to** (to͞o)
three	**drei** (drī)	**drie** (drē)	**tre** (trī)
four	**vier** (fēr)	**vier** (vēr)	**fire** (fēr)
five	**fünf** (fūnf)	**vijf** (vīf)	**fem** (fĭm)
six	**sechs** (zēks)	**zes** (zās)	**seks** (sĭks)
seven	**sieben** (zē′bən)	**zeven** (zā′vən)	**syv** (sēv)
eight	**acht** (äkt)	**acht** (ăkt)	**atte** (ōt′ə)
nine	**neun** (noin)	**negen** (nē′gən)	**ní** (nē)
ten	**zehn** (tsān)	**tien** (tēn)	**ti** (tē)

Three European Alphabets

Here are some letters from the three major European alphabets. The Roman alphabet, which we use, and the Russian alphabet were both derived from the Greek alphabet. Most European languages use the Roman alphabet.

Roman	Greek	Russian
A a	Α α (alpha)	А а
B b	Β β (beta)	Б б
D d	Δ δ (delta)	Д д
E e	Ε ε (epsilon)	Э э
F f, Ph	Φ φ (phi)	Ф ф

CHAPTER 14 CHECKUP

A Know the countries and capitals of Western Europe and their locations. (See Continent Study 3, p. 324.)

B Know these locations.

1. Bay of Biscay
2. Pyrenees
3. Rock of Gibraltar
4. Alps
5. Mont Blanc
6. the Matterhorn
7. Mt. Elbrus
8. Rhine River
9. Volga River
10. Danube River

C Name the **five** peninsulas of Europe and list the countries found on each.

D Define each term.

1. matadors
2. Renaissance
3. divide
4. Huguenots
5. socialist
6. neutral
7. landlocked
8. National Socialist Party
9. fjord
10. tundra
11. permafrost
12. timberline

E Identify each term from the clue.

1. the huge swamp south of Seville, Spain
2. formed by the Rock of Gibraltar and a similar mountain in northern Africa
3. a special kind of oak; its bark is harvested about every 10 years
4. a form of government that allows private property but takes away people's freedoms
5. a French movement that rebelled against authority and promoted humanism
6. a dam-like barrier made of earth and stone
7. wooden shoes worn by Dutch farmers
8. a temporary shelter made of ice blocks

F Tell the most important accomplishment of each person.

1. Cortés
2. Magellan
3. Marco Polo
4. Jacques Cartier
5. Louis Pasteur
6. John Calvin
7. J. S. Bach
8. Handel
9. Beethoven

G Who am I?

1. Spain's most famous writer
2. the first European to sail to India by going around Africa
3. famous for painting the *Mona Lisa* and *The Last Supper*
4. famous for painting the ceiling of the Sistine Chapel and for sculpting *David* and *Moses*
5. Italian who was one of the founders of modern science
6. Italy's fascist dictator during World War II
7. known for the discovery of radium
8. a young French peasant girl who helped win a great victory
9. ruthless French dictator who tried to conquer the world
10. World War II hero who later became president of France's Fifth Republic
11. legendary hero of Swiss independence
12. founded the International Red Cross
13. the leader of the Nazis
14. perhaps the greatest scientific genius of the twentieth century
15. the "Father of Dutch Liberties"

H Identify the country

1. windmills, tulips, the Hague
2. matadors, the Meseta, oranges, olives
3. gondolas, Leaning Tower of Pisa, Renaissance
4. the Eiffel Tower, Notre Dame, the Louvre
5. cheese, chocolates, watches, music boxes
6. "Land of the Midnight Sun"
7. "Land of Fire and Ice"
8. Bavarian Alps, Black Forest

I Answer each question.

1. What is Europe's highest active volcano? Mainland Europe's only active volcano?
2. What two large islands are located off the coast of Italy?
3. What is the name of the independent state located within the city of Rome? What church is headquartered here?
4. Name two famous Italian composers.
5. Name two famous Dutch painters.

(cont.)

6. What group of people from England lived for a time in the Netherlands before coming to the New World?
7. Who were the fierce warriors living in Scandinavia during the Middle Ages?
8. Which country extends farther north than any other Western European country?
9. Which is the largest Scandinavian country?
10. What is the world's largest island? What Scandinavian country owns it?
11. What is Europe's most mountainous country?
12. Which country is one of Europe's oldest republics?
13. During World War I, who led Germany? What alliance did Germany belong to? What were the countries fighting against Germany called?
14. During World War II, who led Germany? What alliance did Germany belong to? What were the countries fighting against Germany called?
15. Which German city was divided after World War II?
16. What are Europe's three main language groups?
17. What are the two international languages?
18. What do we call the part of the New World where Spanish and Portuguese are spoken?
19. What language is not a part of the three main language groups?
20. What language which is no longer spoken formed the basis for the Romance languages?

J Use the clue to identify each location.

1. Europe's largest mountain range
2. the highest peak in Europe
3. the highest peak in the Alps
4. the mountain peak expert climbers like to challenge
5. Europe's most important inland waterway

CHAPTER 15

Countries of EASTERN EUROPE

15.1 Eastern Europe

The largest country in Eastern Europe is **Russia,** the world's largest nation. Only a portion of Russia lies in Eastern Europe, however; the rest of the nation extends across northern Asia.

Communism is a system of government that says there is no God and allows people no freedom. It first took control of an entire nation when it took root in Russia in the early 1900s. As the Communists invaded Eastern European nations, Communism began to spread. The empire that the Communists built in Eastern Europe was called the **Soviet Union.** Later, Communism also spread to many other parts of the world.

Communism ruled over the people of Eastern Europe for over 70 years, taking away their homes, businesses, churches, and freedoms. The people became so poor and so weary of Communism that they rose up against it. Many of the countries of Eastern Europe are now struggling to become free and strong. Find the Eastern European countries on the map (p. 269) as you read about them in this chapter. Notice the size of Russia on the Eastern Hemisphere map (pp. 312–313).

15.2 Russia under the Czars

Russia's beginnings. Like most Europeans, the Russian people are descendants of Noah's son Japheth. During the ninth century A.D., a Viking tribe known as the **Rus** invaded the area that is now European Russia. The area became known

as the Land of the Rus, or "Russia," after the Viking tribe. In A.D. 988, **Vladimir the Saint** introduced the Russians to a form of Christianity called Eastern Orthodoxy. The city of **Kiev** [kē′ĕf] became the political and religious center of Russia.

About 1240, the **Mongols** conquered Russia and controlled it for nearly 250 years. During this time the religious center of Russia moved from Kiev to Moscow. The prince of Moscow began to use the Russian church as a tool to gain more and more power. In 1380, a Russian army defeated Mongolian troops. By 1480, **Ivan** [ī′vən] **III,** prince of Moscow, became the first true national leader of a united Russia.

The first Czar. Ivan IV took the title of **czar,** which means "emperor." Known as **Ivan the Terrible,** this czar passed laws tying the peasant farmers to the land. This created a new class of people in Russia—serfs, who were little more than slaves. Thus, when Western Europe was moving out of the Middle Ages and the system of serfs, lords, and manors was fading away, Russia was just beginning to follow the same system. Some later famous czars were **Peter the Great, Catherine the Great,** and **Alexander I.**

Vision for an empire. Many of the czars wanted to make Russia into a huge empire by expanding Russian territory in all directions. Around 1637, the Russians moved into Siberia. Between 1805 and 1812, Russia started colonies in the New World (Alaska and Northern California). During the reign of **Czar Nicholas I** (1825–1855), Russia added many countries to its empire. Nicholas crushed a revolt of the Russian people against the government and also crushed efforts by eastern European countries to break away from Russia's empire. The power of the central government kept growing stronger. The Russian secret police were organized at this time to control the press, the universities, and every part of Russian life. From 1854 to 1856, Russia fought and lost the **Crimean** [krī·mē′ən] **War** against England, France, Turkey, and Sardinia. From 1850 to 1900, the Russian empire continued to expand further into eastern Europe and into central and east Asia.

Napoleon's defeat by the Russian winter. In 1812, the French emperor **Napoleon** marched into Russia with an army of 600,000 men. He occupied Moscow, but loyal Russians burned the city, leaving the French soldiers with no food. Discouraged, Napoleon ordered his army to withdraw. French soldiers, not used to the bitterly cold Russian winters, died by the thousands from hunger and cold.

Ivan the Terrible

Catherine the Great

Czar Nicholas I

EASTERN EUROPE
(Asian)
RUSSIA
Arctic Circle (66°)
URAL MOUNTAINS
Norwegian Sea
(European)
RUSSIA
FINLAND
NORWAY
SWEDEN
NORTHERN EUROPEAN PLAIN
ESTONIA
Volga R.
Moscow
Ural R.
LATVIA
Baltic Sea
DENMARK
LITHUANIA
RUSSIA
Gdansk
Minsk
Dneiper R.
BELARUS
KAZAKHSTA
Elbe R.
Warsaw
GERMANY
POLAND
Kiev
Volga R.
Prague
CZECH REPUBLIC
UKRAINE
Caspian Se
SLOVAKIA
Bratislava
Danube R.
Budapest
MOLDOVA
AUSTRIA
HUNGARY
Tisza R.
SLOVENIA
ROMANIA
CAUCASUS MOUNTAINS
CROATIA
Mt. Elbrus
GEORGIA
BOSNIA-HERZEGOVINA
Bucharest
Danube R.
Black Sea
AZERBAI
SERBIA
ARMENIA
Adriatic Sea
MONTE-NEGRO
KOSOVO
BULGARIA
Sofia
ITALY
BOSPORUS
MACEDONIA
IRAN
Tiranë
TURKEY
ALBANIA
TURKEY
Aegean Sea
DARDANELLES
Mediterranean Sea
GREECE
SYRIA
IRAQ

Serfs' "freedom." In 1861, Alexander II set the serfs free. Because the serfs had no place to go, the government bought land and gave it to them. The serfs had to pay the government back for the land. Actually, the serfs were still serfs, but their master was now the czar.

The last czar. In 1881, Alexander II was assassinated. Alexander III was determined to crush whoever dared speak out against the government. Alexander III's son Nicholas II (1894–1917) wanted to preserve the past.

Nicholas II, the last czar, attempted some reforms to help the people, but political unrest and spiritual darkness brought terror and revolution to the land.

15.3 ✠ How Communism Began

While events were building to the breaking point in Russia, the idea of **Marxism (Communism)** took hold. **Karl Marx** (1818–1883), a German Jew who had been exposed to Christianity but rejected it, wanted the working class to control the government, and he wanted Christianity and the upper middle classes to be abolished.

Marx

Marx was opposed to the **free enterprise system,** or **capitalism.** (Capitalism is the American way of running businesses and handling money that has helped make our United States such a great world leader.) He did not believe that people should be allowed to own factories and businesses. All property should be taken away from the people and put in the hands of the government. That way, Marx thought, no one would make any more money than anyone else, and everyone would be "equal." If your father owned a gas station or a clothing store, would you want someone to take it away from him and give it to the government?

To make Karl Marx's idea work in a country, a leader would have to use cruel tactics against those people who resisted having their possessions stolen from them. This is what happened in Russia and later in many other countries of the world where Communists took over. Countries that follow Karl Marx's ideas are called Communist countries.

Comprehension Check 15A

1. What is the largest nation in the world?
2. What was the Communist empire in Eastern Europe called?
3. Who became the first leader of the united Russia?
4. What is a czar? Who was the first czar of Russia?
5. What French emperor tried unsuccessfully to defeat Russia?
6. Whom did Alexander II set free? Were they really free?
7. What idea of government and economics did Karl Marx begin?

15.4 ✠ Birth of the Soviet Union

The Russian Revolution. In 1917, the Russian people overthrew the czar's government and set up their own temporary government. Their government was much like a Western representative democracy with individual liberty. They agreed to establish a permanent government later.

Bolsheviks in power. However, some people started listening to the Russian followers of Marx, who were called Communists or **Bolsheviks** [bōl′shə·vĭks]. Their leader was Vladimir (Nikolai) **Lenin** [vlăd′ə·mîr′ nyĭk·ə·lī′ lĕn′ĭn]. Lenin said that in order to have a successful Communist government, it is necessary to kill entire classes and groups of people. On November 6, 1917, the Bolsheviks overthrew the government that the people had set up. Lenin became the leader of the first Communist state in history. The Bolsheviks ended the only hope Russia had ever had for a truly representative government.

Lenin

Lenin's tyranny. The Russian people resisted Lenin's Communism, but Lenin forced his power upon them:

1. The government took control of all land.
2. The government took control of all banks and major industries.
3. Workers were forced to join government-controlled trade unions and were not allowed to go on strike for improved conditions.
4. Food and goods were distributed by the government as the government saw fit. All private trade was stopped.
5. All church lands were taken by the government, and churches were either closed or put under the control of the government.

Civil War. In 1918–1920, Russia was torn by civil war. Those who opposed the Communists were called **White Russians;** those who favored Communism were called **Red Russians.** In the end, the Red Russians won the war.

Capitalism. By 1921, Communism brought about the complete collapse of the Russian economy. To keep the Russian people from starving to death, Lenin put the country's economy on a system that included some ideas from capitalism. Some private business was once again allowed. Still, the Communists would not admit to the failure of their ideas nor would they give up their vicious control of the people.

Smothered freedom. Being led by Lenin the Communist was worse than being led by a czar. Lenin took away all Russian freedoms, including freedom of speech, freedom of the press, and freedom of religion. "Enemies of the state" were put into prison or executed. Human life had no value.

Communists took over education and taught that capitalism and Christianity are evil. Artists, writers, and musicians were forced to work for the government. They had no freedom to create the kind of works that they thought were good—only what could be used as propaganda for the Communist Party. (**Propaganda** is usually using deceptive means to try to convince people of something.)

Struggle for power. After Lenin died in 1924, two Russian leaders, **Leon Trotsky** [trŏt′skē] and **Joseph Stalin** [stä′lĭn], struggled for power. Stalin overthrew Trotsky in 1927 and had him exiled (sent away) from Russia. In 1940, Communist agents, under the direction of Stalin, found Trotsky in Mexico and murdered him.

Stalin

Brutal Stalin. Stalin, one of the most brutal rulers of all time, ruled from 1927 to 1953. Anyone who opposed him was killed, and millions of Russians lost their lives because they disagreed with his Communist government.

Stalin ordered small private farms to band together into collective farms, and he ordered farmers to give their crops to the government. Farmers who protested were either killed or sent to prison camps.

The remaining farmers destroyed or hid their grain. Stalin ordered the army to seize all the food they could find and keep it from anyone who opposed Communism. Severe famine resulted, and millions of Russians starved to death.

Great Purge. Stalin took serious measures to make sure he would stay in power. He ordered heavy industries, run by the government, to be built up. In the mid-1930s, he had people who were the slightest threat to his authority either thrown out of the Communist Party or killed. His reign of terror is called **the Great Purge.**

Third International. In 1919, before Lenin's death, the Russian Communists had organized the Third International, a group dedicated to causing a worldwide revolution in order to make the whole world a Communist state. Since 1919, Communists have overthrown many governments and forced their control upon the people. In 1959, Fidel Castro pretended that he was bringing democracy to Cuba. Instead, he brought the island under Communist control. Many countries in South and Central America, Africa, Eastern Europe, and Asia have been or are still controlled by the Communists. Communists have boasted that they will one day control the United States. **Nikita Khrushchev** [kro͞osh′chĕf], who ruled the Russian people from 1953 to 1964, shouted to America, "We will bury you."

Khrushchev

Government. In countries that are under the control of Communism, the Communist Party controls all areas of the nation's life. The Communist Party leaders are cruel dictators who tell their people that they are free but allow them no freedom at all.

Communist terrorism. For many years, the Soviet government was active in terrorism toward other countries. It provided other countries with money and weapons to use against countries that the Soviet Union wanted to force into Communism. The Soviet government supported many training camps for terrorists in the Middle East. Many experts said that most major terrorist groups in the world could not last long without help from the Soviet Union. Leaders in Moscow said that they did not support terrorism but tried to help countries to be free. History has proved that they were not telling the truth.

15.5 Changes in the Soviet Union

By the mid-1980s, the leaders of the Soviet Union admitted that their nation was in deep trouble. The Soviet Empire was spending so much money to support a large army and overthrow peaceful governments throughout the world that the government was hopelessly in debt. For many years, the people of the Soviet Union had lived under the strict control of the government. They had been told where to work and where to live, and had not been allowed to own their own property or make their own choices. As a result, many had lost the desire to work, and many had turned to alcohol in their frustration. Other Russians had begun to secretly attend underground churches where preachers taught the gospel.

No food to buy. Although the Communist Party tried to hide its problems, Russian families became worried when they went to the store and could not get enough food for their children. For years the Communist Party had promised them more food, better housing, and medical care. These promises had not been kept. In Moscow, the most advanced of all Russian cities, families still lived in poorly built, overcrowded apartments where several families often had to share one unsanitary bathroom. Because medical care was poor or unavailable, the children of the average Russian citizen had to wait hours and even days to see an overworked doctor in a shabby public hospital. Many babies died for lack of proper care, and even more were killed by abortion. In spite of these hardships, the privileged officials of the Communist Party were treated to the very best food, housing, and medical care the country could provide (still below the standards of the free world).

Although these problems had existed since the time of the Communist Revolution in 1917, the people were now facing extreme difficulties. When the government tried to get the farmers to produce more food, many of the farmers refused to cooperate. Like their grandfathers before them, whom Stalin had brutally murdered, they wanted to own their own land.

Disaster in Afghanistan. In the past, the Soviet army had marched in and crushed independence movements. But by the mid-1980s, the Communist bosses of the Soviet Union were not sure they could trust their own soldiers. The Communists had always been careful to give the families of soldiers extra food and better housing. In this way, they had hoped to buy their soldiers' loyalty. But when the Communists invaded Afghanistan [ăf·găn′ĭ·stăn′: see map p. 67] in 1979, the people of that little Asian country fought hard against the Soviets. Many Soviet soldiers were killed and wounded, and many more became convinced that they should return to the Soviet Union because the Afghans did not want Communism. For the first time in Communist Russia's history, the Red Army began to question Communism.

A step backward. The Communist bosses became nervous when the people began to ask why the families of Communist Party officials were better fed, clothed, and housed, and why they got to see the best doctors when they were ill. A Communist official named **Mikhail Gorbachev** [mĭk·hīl′ gôr′bə·chôf′] suggested a new plan of action to satisfy the people *and* make Communism stronger.

Mikhail Gorbachev

Perestroika and Glasnost. Gorbachev had been head of the Secret Police (KGB), which spied on and tortured those who disagree with Communism and sent them to slave labor camps. The Secret Police had been Lenin's idea. Now Gorbachev took another of Lenin's ideas—allow some free enterprise to keep the people from starving. This policy was soon called **Perestroika** [pĕr′ĭ·stroi′kə], a Russian word for "restructuring" of business. Gorbachev also suggested a policy of **Glasnost** [gläs′nəst], which means "openness," or seeking peace with the free nations of the world.

Comprehension Check 15B

1. What were the Russian followers of Marx's beliefs called?
2. Who was the leader of the first Communist state?
3. What is "propaganda"?
4. After Lenin's death, what two men struggled for power? Who won?
5. During the invasion of what country did the Red Army first begin to question Communism?
6. Which Soviet leader began the programs of Perestroika and Glasnost?

15.6 ✠ Changes in Eastern Europe

Crushed under the Communist boot. In the 1950s and 1960s, Soviet troops and tanks had brutally put down attempts of Eastern European countries to reestablish freedom. The brave patriots of East Berlin were crushed under the boot of the Soviet army in 1953. In 1956, the beautiful city of Budapest, Hungary, had many of its downtown buildings destroyed by Russian tanks when young freedom fighters, many of them teenage boys, tried to fight the Communists, using unregistered rifles and other weapons. The people of Prague [präg], Czechoslovakia [chĕk′ə·slə·vä′kē·ə], sought freedom in the spring of 1968, only to be threatened by Soviet tanks prowling their streets. By the mid-1980s, the complete failure of Communism and the desire for freedom caused the people of this region to rise up again against the Soviet Empire.

A brave Pole challenges the Soviets. The people of Poland had suffered much because of food shortages and bad living conditions under Communism. A shipyard worker named **Lech Walesa** [lĕk wä·lĕn′sə] organized many workers into a group called **Solidarity** to call for free elections and restore Polish freedom. The whole world watched, especially other enslaved people of Eastern Europe. Would the Soviets arrest Lech Walesa and destroy Solidarity?

Walesa

Budapest, Hungary, after Communists destroyed many buildings in 1956

SPOTLIGHT ON HISTORY

The Worldwide Spread of Communism

Communism under the Soviet Union ruled most of Asia and much of Europe. It also had a tremendous amount of influence in Africa and Latin America. Even today, Communism has a great deal of influence and control in countries all around the world. Cuba, which is just ninety miles from the United States, was overthrown by Communists in 1959. Communists are now trying to take over other countries in Central America, South America, Africa, and Asia. The Communists say they want peace and the rule of the people, but their actions show that they really want a worldwide Communist dictatorship. ✠

The Russian people vs. the Communist Party. Poland produced many valuable goods for the Communist world. Now the Polish people threatened to shut down all Polish factories and farms. After threatening Poland with an invasion and beating Poles who supported Solidarity, the Communist bosses in the Soviet Union tried to buy Polish loyalty by shipping in food and giving them financial aid. Shoppers in Moscow noticed that sausages disappeared from the grocery shelves. Because the Communists were sending Russia's food to Poland, people in Warsaw, the capital of Poland, were eating better than the people in the Russian capital! The Russian people began to complain that they were being denied food in order to keep Poland in line.

More Communist lies. The Communist Party had pushed the people too far. Communist business practices had resulted in shortages of food, housing, and goods. For years the resources of Eastern Europe had been used to run much of the Soviet Empire, but now Communism had ruined that region as well.

At this point, the Communists received a promise from the United States and the free nations of Western Europe. If the Soviet Empire promised not to invade Poland, the nations of the free world would give Poland food, money, computers, and other technology. The Communist Party decided that they would allow some freedom in Eastern Europe and the Soviet Union. This would keep Communism from collapsing by convincing the people that the system really worked.

Events happened rapidly from 1989 to 1990. Czechoslovakia and Hungary were allowed to have more independence, providing that the free world would rebuild their economies. The cruel Communist dictator of Romania was overthrown. The **Baltic Republics** of Lithuania, Latvia, and Estonia asked for their independence from the Soviet Empire. They were refused, but the people of these little countries were very brave and still hoped to achieve their freedom.

Finally, in 1990, the Communists promised to let the East Germans rejoin the free republic of West Germany. The West Germans promised to rebuild East Germany and give huge amounts of money and technology to the Soviet Union, two commodities the Communists have always wanted and can now receive by promises to be peace-loving followers of free enterprise.

Under Communist rule, many Russian churches were closed down and others were put under strict Communist control.

15.7 Life in the Soviet Union

Atheism. Communists are **atheists** (people who believe there is no God). The Communists destroyed many churches in Russia and made some churches into tools of the Communist Party. They killed many church leaders who refused to become Communists. They put Christian parents in jail for teaching the Bible to their children. In spite of great persecution, there were still many Christians in the Soviet Union who stood for the gospel of Christ. Those Christians who lived for years in persecution under Communist rule are some of the greatest heroes of modern times.

Few freedoms. The freedoms of Russians were severely limited by their Communist government. Few were allowed to travel outside the country. Russian citizens even had to have the government's permission just to move from one apartment to another. Because of a great housing shortage brought about by the Communist system, families often had to wait several years for an apartment of their own. Many times, two families had to live together in one small room. Shopping for simple needs was a difficult, time-consuming task. Meat was in short supply and expensive, and many times fresh vegetables, milk, eggs, and other needed items were not available.

Government control. The Soviet government owned and planned businesses and set prices for almost all goods that were sold. Most Russians living in rural

Concepts to Consider

Russians in the Soviet Union Worked Longer to Buy Things

Products	Amount of Time Worked
1 cotton shirt	U.S.—1 hr. U.S.S.R.—15 hrs.
1 man's suit	U.S.—23 hrs. U.S.S.R.—175 hrs.
1 tube of toothpaste	U.S.—20 min. U.S.S.R.—5 hrs.
1 bicycle (small)	U.S.—17 hrs. U.S.S.R.—75 hrs.
1 dozen eggs	U.S.—17 min. U.S.S.R.—2 ½ hrs.
1 woman's dress	U.S.—4 ½ hrs. U.S.S.R.—75 hrs.

This chart shows how long a person in the Soviet Union and a person in America had to work in the early 1980s to earn enough money to buy similar goods. How long did it take an American to buy a small bicycle? A Russian? How much longer did the Russian have to work? If your dad had to work an hour to buy one shirt, how many shirts could he buy in 15 hours? In the Soviet Union, even after people had earned enough money to buy the things they needed, those things were often not available. Many times Russians had to stand in long lines or be put on long waiting lists to get the necessities of life. The American free enterprise system of doing business brings much more prosperity to a country than does Communism.

(farm) areas worked on huge collective farms. Many women were forced to do heavy physical labor, such as digging ditches and repairing streets. Most children were kept in government nurseries and kindergartens all day long until they were seven years old so that they could be trained to think the way the Communists wanted them to think.

In an attempt to make the Soviet Union look good to the rest of the world, Russian education stressed science and mathematics. The books in Russian libraries were chosen by the government, and the schools could teach only what the government wanted the children to learn. All schools taught Communism as the best form of government and society, and the children were told that capitalism is very evil. Children's after-school clubs included Communist teaching, also.

The Communist government controlled all sports, music, writing, and art in the Soviet Union. The government paid for the training of talented young people, not because the government was interested in helping those people develop their talents, but rather because the government wanted to use their talents for propaganda purposes. Soviet propaganda involved taking advantage of people in order to make the Soviet Union and Communism look attractive in the eyes of the world. The Communists used propaganda so much that thinking people found it hard to believe anything that the Communist governments said. No wonder so many gifted Russian writers, artists, musicians, and athletes escaped from the Soviet Union to find freedom in the United States and other Free World countries! They realized that the Communist dream was more like a nightmare.

Comprehension Check 15C

1. What Polish worker organized a group to work for the restoration of Poland's freedoms?
2. What was the group that he organized called?
3. What "religion" do Communists follow?
4. What were the children in the Soviet Union taught?

15.8 The Soviet Union and the United Nations

After World War II, the United Nations was organized to promote peace among all the nations of the world. It has not only failed to promote peace, but it has been used by the former Soviet Union and other Communist governments to help promote Communism in the world. Since the charter of the UN was signed, over seventy-five wars have been fought around the world, many of them started by Communist terrorist groups. Over one billion people have been enslaved to Communism, and more than forty million people have been executed by Communists.

Each member nation of the UN is supposed to share in the expenses of the United Nations, but many do not do their part. The United States is by far the largest contributor to the United Nations. When countries have needed protection, most of the soldiers have been Americans.

Since the United States gives the United Nations so much financial support and does most of the fighting that is needed when member countries are in trouble, you would think that the United States would have a great deal to say in how the United Nations is run. This is not true. More than half the UN member nations have a population smaller than that of New York City, and yet their vote counts just as much as the vote of the United States. Many American citizens feel that the United Nations, which has its headquarters in New York City, has been a propaganda base for Communist activities.

UN headquarters in New York City

15.9 The Fall of the Soviet Empire

In August 1991, a startling event occurred in the Soviet Union. Fearing that Gorbachev's policy of Perestroika would lead to the downfall of Communism, a group of Communist leaders and military men arrested Mikhail Gorbachev and attempted to take control of the nation. Observers outside the Soviet Union were not sure what had actually happened. Some even believed that Gorbachev had staged his own downfall in order to return to a stricter Communist control.

Boris Yeltsin. News camera crews from the United States and Western Europe were allowed to film what was going on in the two major Russian cities, St. Petersburg and Moscow, where thousands of ordinary citizens rallied in the open air and demanded the return of the reform government. In Moscow, **Boris Yeltsin** [yĕlt′sĭn], the newly elected president of the Russian Republic, had surrounded himself with armed guards while thousands of Moscow citizens stood outside his headquarters and refused to move when tanks sent by the Communist leaders and military men rolled into the city.

Yeltsin

The entire world watched by satellite television as soldiers and tanks approached the offices of the Russian parliament, where Yeltsin awaited them.

The troops moved in at night, but after killing three people in the streets, the young men of the Russian army put down their guns. They decided not to fire against their countrymen and joined the citizens in supporting Yeltsin. As suddenly as it had started, the military threat seemed to melt away; Boris Yeltsin emerged as the hero of the hour, and Mikhail Gorbachev was released. But something had changed. Yeltsin was now the most powerful man in Russia.

Russia quits the Soviet Union. Boris Yeltsin declared the Republic of Russia to be an independent nation and took over all Communist Party property in Russia. He proclaimed a democratic, free-market system of government and even allowed religious freedom, giving the Eastern Orthodox Church preferred treatment over other churches. Soon other Soviet republics began to declare their independence as well.

The death of the Soviet Union. By January 1992, the Communist flag of the Soviet Union no longer flew over Communist headquarters in Moscow. It had been pulled down and replaced by the tri-color red, blue, and white flag of the Russian Republic. All of the former member states of the Soviet Union had declared their independence—the Soviet Union had ceased to exist as a nation.

flag of the Russian Republic

The Commonwealth of Independent States. Most of the independent republics agreed to join together in a loose organization called the **Commonwealth of Independent States.** Ukraine and Kazakhstan [kə·zäk′stän′] became the two largest independent nations outside of Russia in the Commonwealth. Other new republics included Belarus and Moldova in Europe, and Georgia, Armenia, Azerbaijan [ăz′ər·bī·jän′], Turkmenistan [tûrk′mĕn·ĭ·stăn′], Uzbekistan [o͞oz·bĕk′ĭ·stăn′], Tajikistan [tä·jĭk′ĭ·stăn′], and Kyrgyzstan [kĭr·gĭ·stän′] in Asia (see map of Asia, p. 67). Christians in the United States and Europe rushed to get the gospel to the new nations and to help the churches, which had been persecuted for many years, to reach more people for Christ.

Caution! Communists at work. Boris Yeltsin served as president of Russia from 1991–1999. Yeltsin was succeeded by Vladimir Putin. Under Putin's leadership many of the new freedoms were reversed. Dimitri Medvedev became president in 2008 in what was considered another undemocratic election. Despite all of the apparent changes in the old Soviet Union, most areas of the government are still controlled by dedicated Communists. They are doing all in their power to encourage unrest in order to regain control. The gospel is the only hope for the people of the former Soviet Union.

In other parts of the world, Communism is still at work. Communist China still holds much power over its people, while Communists in other countries continue to promote their ideas and look for opportunities to overthrow existing governments.

Comprehension Check 15D

1. What organization was formed after World War II to promote world peace?
2. What country pays most to help in world peace through the United Nations system?
3. Who has the greatest voting power in the United Nations?
4. When the Soviet Union collapsed, who emerged as the most powerful man in Russia?
5. Is it true that there is no further threat from Communism now that the Soviet Union has collapsed?

15.10 Modern Countries of Eastern Europe

Russia

European Russia. About three fourths of the Russian people live in the part of Russia that lies in Europe. Most of the industry and much of the richest soil are in this part of the country. The **Ural Mountains,** which stretch from north to south for 2,500 miles, form a barrier between European Russia and Asiatic Russia, but the mountains are not a great hindrance to transportation and trade. The Northern European Plain dominates European Russia, covering the area from the Baltic Sea to the Ural Mountains. The **Volga,** Europe's longest river, and the Dnieper are among the many rivers that water this fertile plain. In the south, the Caucasus Mountains, which include **Mount Elbrus,** Europe's highest peak, separate European Russia from Asia.

Asiatic Russia. Just east of the Urals lies the **West Siberian Plain** (see map of Asia, p. 82), the largest level region in the world. This plain of over one million square miles blends into the Central Siberian Plateau. The plateau's southern mountains contain **Lake Baikal** (see map, p. 82), the world's deepest freshwater lake. Tundra covers the extreme north of the land. Mountains rise in the south and east, to the west are plains and marshes, and to the southwest is desert.

Lake Baikal

the cold bleakness of vast Siberia

Cold Siberia. In the extreme north of Asian Russia lies **Siberia,** a land of short summers and long, cold winters (–90 °F in some places). Siberian rivers are frozen as much as nine months out of each year. Until the late 16th century, only nomads and hunter-gatherers roamed the land. Later, it became a place of exile for criminals and religious and political prisoners. Although the completion of the Trans-Siberian Railroad helped populate the region, millions of square miles remain largely uninhabited. Siberia is famous for its precious metals, natural gas, and petroleum. It is also known for some of its mammals, including the Siberian husky and the **Siberian tiger,** the largest living cat in the world.

a Siberian tiger

The people. The majority of the people in Russia are descendants of eastern Slavs and the Viking Rus who invaded the area and gave Russia its name. Some large minorities are the Turks, Ukrainians, and Mongolians. The official language is Russian, but the various minorities speak many languages.

Before the Communists took over, Russia had many world-famous writers and musicians, including the writers **Tolstoy** [tōl′stoi], **Dostoevsky** [dŏs′tə·yĕf′skē], and **Chekhov** [chĕk′ôf], and composer **Tchaikovsky** [chī·kôf′skē]. The control of Communists over all areas of life led many talented Russians to flee their homeland for freedom in the West. Some, including the writer Alexander **Solzhenitsyn** [sōl′zhə·nēt′sĭn], were forced into exile for their stand against the evils of Communism.

In spite of Russia's vast size, most of the people live in cities and towns, and the majority of them live in the European portion of the country. **Moscow,** the capital of Russia, is Eastern Europe's largest city.

Shipping trade. Because much of Russia's coastal waters remain frozen during the year, the country has few ports. To reach the Mediterranean Sea from the Black Sea, Russian ships must pass through the **Bosporus** [bŏs′pər·əs] and the **Dardanelles** [där′dn·ĕlz′],

modern Moscow

two narrow straits that are controlled by Turkey. Many disagreements have arisen between Russia and Turkey over the control of this trade route.

Forests and creatures. Forests cover about one third of the country's land. In the forests are deer, elk, lynx, brown bears, beavers, rabbits, and squirrels.

Animals in the tundra include ermine, Arctic foxes, reindeer, hares, and lemmings. Huge flocks of waterfowl spend the summer along the Arctic coast. In the eastern steppes, graceful antelope can be seen. In the deserts and mountains, hyenas, leopards, and tigers roam.

Many kinds of fish are caught off the country's coast. Fish from the Caspian Sea provide a famous Russian dish, black **caviar** [kăv′ē·är′: salted fish (especially sturgeon) eggs].

Resources and industries. Russia is blessed with abundant mineral resources, vast forests, and plenty of fertile land. Communism, however, kept the people from realizing their economic potential. With the fall of the Soviet Union, the Russian economy began to turn slowly toward free enterprise capitalism. It began when ownership of many enterprises was returned to the people. However, years of Communist inefficiency made the transition difficult, and the government kept their control over the larger industries. Today, Russia must import large quantities of food from neighboring Ukraine, Lithuania, and other countries to feed its large population. At the end of the 20th century, Russia's economy remained weak and unstable.

Comprehension Check 15E

1. What is Europe's longest river? Its highest peak?
2. What is the world's deepest freshwater lake?
3. What is the huge frozen section of Russia called?
4. What is the capital of Russia?
5. What straits, owned by Turkey, have been a cause for much contention between Turkey and Russia?
6. What famous Russian food is made of fish eggs?

The Baltic States

Because of their location on the Baltic Sea, the nations of **Estonia, Latvia,** and **Lithuania** are often called the Baltic States. This region is a combination of low plains and hills that are covered with deposits of stones and debris left

black caviar

Estonians in traditional costume

by ancient glaciers. Many rivers and lakes are scattered throughout the area. The Baltic Sea helps to moderate the climate, which ranges from marine west coast to humid continental.

In spite of years of Communist domination by the Soviet Union, the Baltic States have maintained their own cultural identities as can be seen by their distinctive music festivals and folk art. One major reason that the Soviet Union desired to control these countries was their abundant resources. Forests cover much of the land, and crops and livestock do well in the temperate climate. The Soviets depended on Lithuania in particular to help meet Russia's demand for food.

Belarus and Ukraine

The modern countries of **Belarus** and **Ukraine,** the second-largest European country (after Russia), lie south of the Baltics and west of Russia. Both countries consist of hills, uplands, and plains, including part of the Northern European Plain.

Before these nations declared their independence from the Soviet Union in 1991, the people of this area were ruled by nations such as Nazi Germany and Russia. The Belarusians and Ukrainians are descendants of Slavic settlers, and they speak languages related to Russian.

fertile farmland in the Ukraine

Kiev, Ukraine's capital, was one of the original settlements of the Rus. By the eleventh century, it had become the region's greatest cultural center. The city is famous for its traditional folk music, theater, and literature. **Minsk,** the capital of Belarus, contains impressive centers for ballet, opera, and theater. It is also the headquarters of the Commonwealth of Independent States.

Excellent farmland and pastures have allowed Belarus and Ukraine to become major agricultural producers. Ukraine has some of the most fertile farmland in the world. Today, farmers produce large quantities of grains, potatoes, sugar beets, and livestock.

Poland

Poland, a large country located mainly on the Northern European Plain, is covered with fields, forests, and small lakes. Although foreign conquerors divided Poland several times in the 1700s until it no longer existed as a country, the Poles never

Gdansk, Poland

Warsaw, Poland

lost their identity as a people. Poland became a country again after World War I. World War II, however, brought Nazi storm troopers and concentration camps, including the infamous camp at Auschwitz [oush′vĭts′]. After the war, Poland came under the tyranny of the Soviet Union. But Polish workers under the leadership of Lech Walesa and his Solidarity labor union rose up against the Communist oppressors. Today, **Warsaw** is the capital of the Polish republic, and the people have free elections and a popularly elected president. Many of Poland's present leaders, however, are Communists.

Poland's economy still suffers from the effects of Communism, but the nation is beginning to move toward free enterprise. Major industries include the production of chemicals, steel, and household appliances. Around the city of Gdansk [gə·dänsk′], shipbuilding has been a large source of income. The rich soil of the plains produces large quantities of food, mainly potatoes and sugar beets.

Comprehension Check 15F

1. Name the three Baltic States.
2. What is the second-largest European country? Its capital?
3. What city is the capital of Belarus as well as the headquarters for the Commonwealth of Independent States?
4. What is the capital of the Polish republic?

The Czech Republic and Slovakia

After being linked as **Czechoslovakia** for much of the twentieth century, the **Czech Republic** and **Slovakia** established themselves as independent nations in 1993. The Czech Republic retained **Prague,** the former capital of Czechoslovakia, as its capital. Slovakia took **Bratislava** as its capital. Both countries are landlocked. Important rivers of the area are the Elbe and the Danube.

More than a century before the Protestant Reformation began in Germany, the preaching and writing of John Huss was used to bring reformation to the

Czechs and Slovaks of Bohemia, as the area was then called. Though by the 1500s most Bohemians were members of Hussite churches, Bohemia came under the control of Catholic Austria. After World War I, the Czechs and Slovaks, no longer under the control of Austria, remained together as Czechoslovakia. Although the union was often forced and sometimes shaky, the two peoples stayed together until the collapse of the Soviet Union, when Slovakian leaders declared independence.

The Czech Republic's economy is based largely on industry; its major products include textiles, steel, and glass. Slovakia is more of a farming country growing large quantities of cereals, potatoes, and fruit, and raising livestock. Both countries are still working to counter the effects of Communism on their economies.

Hungary

Hungary's most distinctive features are its plains. The climate is dryer than in other parts of the continent, but the mighty Danube and Tisza rivers flow the entire length of the country, making the plains fertile.

Before World War I, many nationalities and cultural groups lived inside Austria-Hungary's borders. After the war, the country was partitioned among the surrounding nations, leaving the region where the native Hungarians lived to Hungary. Later, Soviet-backed Communists overran the country. In 1956, the Hungarians rebelled against the Soviets and demanded freedom, but they were so brutally crushed by Communist troops that opposition to the Soviets was not heard again in Hungary for over 40 years.

The Hungarian-speaking Magyars still form the majority of the population. The capital, **Budapest,** is the cultural and educational heart of the nation. It is made up of Buda and Pest, separated by the Danube River.

Hungary has always been one of the most economically successful countries in Eastern Europe. The Hungarians produce much of their food and are able to export many agricultural products. They are also involved in mining and manufacturing.

modern Budapest, looking from Buda across the Danube River to the Parliament Building in Pest

farmland in Hungary

Romania

Romanians are the only people of the Balkan States that speak a Romance language. Although they were part of Communist-dominated Eastern Europe, the people of this nation are culturally similar to those of the West. In fact, the capital, **Bucharest,** has been called "the Paris of the Balkans" because of its culture and architecture.

Romania has beautiful scenery, including a coastline on the Black Sea. The Danube River runs through the country for about 900 miles. Romania has also been home to one of the largest settlements of **Gypsies** in Europe. Over the centuries, these traditionally nomadic people have spread from India to the Middle East, Europe, the Americas, and even Australia. Gypsies have often chosen to live separate in their own communities, even choosing their own king.

Romania has all the resources of its more successful Hungarian neighbor, but its economy struggled due to the Communist policies enforced by former dictator Nicole Ceausecu and other leaders. Today, both economic and social progress is being made.

countryside in Romania

Bulgaria

Because of the southern climate and the rich soil of the plains, the country of **Bulgaria** is known as the "garden of Eastern Europe." It was named for the Bulgars, a Turkish people who settled among the Slavs of the region. Most Bulgarians today live in cities and towns, including the capital, **Sofia.**

Bulgarians have a variety of resources, but their economy is poor due to years of Communism. Many crops grow on the plains; mining and fishing are important industries; and tourism, especially along the Black Sea, is a source for much-needed cash.

Former Yugoslavian Republics

Yugoslavia was a federation of six states from 1945 until 1991. Under the strong Communist leadership of **Marshal Tito** [tē′tō], the country appeared unified. However, there were many tensions among the peoples. Many language and religious barriers separated the groups. As a result, the country broke up in the early 1990s with fighting and bloodshed. The new nations that would emerge from Yugoslavia's breakup include Slovenia, Croatia, Macedonia, Montenegro, Serbia, Bosnia-Herzegovina, and Kosovo.

Tito

Agriculture, especially the growing of grains and cereals, is an important part of the economy of these nations. In addition to wheat, corn, and rice, the southern countries grow large crops of olives, melons, grapes, and citrus fruits. Mining is done in some areas. Other industries include metal refining, food processing, and the production of textiles.

Albania

Because of the rugged mountains that occupy 70 percent of **Albania,** most of the people live in rural areas along the coast of the Adriatic Sea. Though the mountains limit the space available for agriculture, they supply most of the minerals, ores, and fuels that are a mainstay of Albania's otherwise struggling economy.

For years, a hard-core Communist government kept the Albanians in virtual isolation from the rest of the world and banned religious groups and practices. Albania's government was the last of the Eastern European governments to succumb to public demand for change, and only recently did **Tiranë,** the capital city, open its doors to the West.

village in Kosovo

Albania's rugged, mountainous terrain

CHAPTER 15 CHECKUP

A Know the countries and capitals of Eastern Europe and their locations. (See Continent Study 3, p. 324.)

B Define each term.

1. Communism
2. Soviet Union
3. Marxism
4. capitalism
5. free enterprise
6. Third International
7. Perestroika
8. Glasnost
9. atheism
10. caviar
11. propaganda

C Tell the most important fact about each person.

1. Vladimir the Saint
2. Ivan III
3. Ivan IV
4. Nicholas II
5. Karl Marx

D Who am I?

1. founder of the first Communist state
2. When Lenin died, I took control of the Soviet Union; I am known for the Great Purge.
3. overthrown by Stalin and exiled from Russia
4. Communist leader who shouted to America, "We will bury you."
5. tried to maintain Communist power by introducing Perestroika and Glasnost
6. worked to restore Polish freedom by founding Solidarity
7. won the release of Gorbachev and became the most powerful man in Russia
8. strong Communist ruler of Yugoslavia

E Use the clues to identify each place

1. largest country in the world
2. second largest country in Europe
3. the largest level region in the world
4. the world's deepest freshwater lake
5. the cold region in the extreme north of Asian Russia
6. the **two** straits that control access to the Black Sea
7. the "garden of Europe"
8. Europe's highest peak

F Answer each question.

1. What dictator tried to conquer Russia but was instead conquered by the Russian winter?
2. What was the name given to the Russian followers of Marx?
3. What is the name of the organization founded after World War II to promote world peace?
4. What is the name given to the nomadic people of Eastern Europe?

G Write a paragraph describing what Lenin did to gain total control of the Soviet Union.

UNIT 4

AUSTRALIA, OCEANIA, & ANTARCTICA

CHAPTER 16

"THE LAND DOWN UNDER" & Beyond

In the early days of ocean travel, sailors had not ventured much beyond the equator. The southern areas of the Pacific Ocean had never been mapped out and no one knew for sure what lands, if any, existed there. However, people believed that there must be an unknown land below the equator to balance the lands of the Northern Hemisphere. The idea of this unknown land continued through the years until the early 1600s when seamen anchored off the west coast of Australia. Then in the 1700s, **Captain James Cook,** the famous English sea captain who was the greatest explorer of his time, landed on Australia's east coast. Cook sailed on to discover many islands across the Pacific and became the first man known to sail below the Antarctic Circle.

Captain James Cook

Australia, Antarctica, and the islands of the Pacific Ocean are well known today, but they continue to fascinate people with their unusual animals, dramatic landscapes, and unique cultures.

Australia, Oceania, & Antarctica

- Giant rock structures called *tors* tower over the red sands on Australia's desert floor. The most impressive tor is Uluru Rock (formerly called Ayers Rock), a large single rock that measures over 1,000 feet high and 6 miles around.
- Some of the thousands of islands in Oceania are the tops of active and inactive volcanoes; others are coral reefs.
- The ice covering Antarctica is two miles thick in some places.
- Antarctica is one of the few places in the world where you can find penguins, and it is the home of five different kinds—the Emperor, the King, the Adélie, the Chinstrap, and the Gentoo.

16.1 ✠ Australia: The "Island Continent"

The continent of **Australia** has been of interest to people for many years. It is the home of some of the world's most unusual animals along with a variety of landscapes and colorful culture. Today it is also a thriving center of agriculture, mining, industry, and trade.

AUSTRALIA

Timor Sea
Arafura Sea
Coral Sea
INDIAN OCEAN
PACIFIC OCEAN
INDIAN OCEAN
Tasman Sea

Darwin
NORTHERN TERRITORY
QUEENSLAND
GREAT SANDY DESERT
Tropic of Capricorn
23°
WESTERN PLATEAU
WESTERN AUSTRALIA
Uluru Rock
GREAT ARTESIAN BASIN
Central Lowlands
Great Dividing Range
Great Eastern Highlands
Great Barrier Reef
Australian Dog Fence
Brisbane
SOUTH AUSTRALIA
GREAT VICTORIA DESERT
Darling R.
Murray R.
NEW SOUTH WALES
Perth
Adelaide
Sydney
Canberra
AUSTRALIAN CAPITAL TERRITORY
VICTORIA
Mt. Kosciusko
Melbourne
TASMANIA
Hobart

Land and Climate

Size. Australia is the only continent in the world that is made up of just one nation. As a continent, it is the world's smallest. As a nation, it is the sixth largest in land area and is about the same size as the United States. Australia is three times as large as Greenland, the world's largest island. (It looks smaller than Greenland on the world map, p. 314, because the map is a flattened-out globe and cannot show the true size of all areas at once. Use a world globe to compare Australia and Greenland in size.) Because it is small for a continent, and because it is completely surrounded by water, Australia is often called the "Island Continent."

Location. Australia is located in the southern part of the Eastern Hemisphere. It is the only continent besides Antarctica that is entirely below the equator, and thus it is sometimes referred to as the **"Land Down Under."** The Tropic of Capricorn runs through the middle of the continent.

On the map of Australia (p. 292), locate the Indian Ocean and its branches, the Timor [tē′môr] Sea and the Arafura [ä′rə·fo͞o′rə] Sea that surround Australia to the north and west. Find two branches of the Pacific Ocean, the Coral Sea and the Tasman [tăz′mən] Sea that surround Australia to the east and south. The island of **Tasmania,** a part of Australia, is 150 miles south of the mainland.

Great Barrier Reef. Off the northeast coast of the continent lies the **Great Barrier Reef,** the longest coral reef in the world. A **reef** is a line or ridge of rock, coral, or sand lying at or near the surface of the water.

Eastern Highlands. Australia has three major land regions—the **Eastern Highlands,** the **Central Lowlands,** and the **Western Plateau.** Many of the country's people live in the **Eastern Highlands,** a narrow strip of land that stretches along the entire east coast. The **Great Dividing Range** follows the eastern coastline. High in the mountains of the southeast, heavy snows fall during the winter. The Snowy Mountains, one of the divide's many ranges, contain Australia's highest peak, **Mount Kosciusko** [kŏz′ĭ·ŭs′kō]. This series of high mountains is often called the Australian Alps.

The Great Dividing Range got its name because it is a divide. Some rivers flow east from the Great Dividing Range toward the Pacific Ocean, and others flow west toward the Central Lowlands.

Central Lowlands. The Central Lowlands lie west of the Great Dividing Range. Because large parts of the Central Lowlands do not receive enough rain for farming and ranching, few people live there. In the river basins, however, there are some excellent grazing areas.

The **Murray** [mûr′ē] **River,** Australia's longest river flowing year-round, flows westward from its source in the southern part of the Great Dividing Range until it is joined by the **Darling River,** which is the longest and only other important river in Australia.

Murray River

Australia's outback

The Murray-Darling Basin has the best agricultural land in the Central Lowlands suitable for raising **sheep, cattle,** and **wheat.** North of the Murray-Darling Basin lies the **Great Artesian** [är·tē′zhən] **Basin,** the largest artesian basin in the world. (An **artesian basin** is an area of underground water.)

Western Plateau. The vast area west of the Central Lowlands is called the Western Plateau. This region covers well over half the continent. It rises about 1,200 feet above sea level and is mostly flat, though a few low mountains rise above it. The rivers and lakes are usually dry, except after a heavy rain. Less than ten inches of rain fall each year. With the exception of the southwest coast, the Western Plateau is arid and almost empty. Two huge deserts are located there, the **Great Sandy Desert** and the **Great Victoria Desert.** The Central Lowlands and Western Plateau are often referred to as Australia's **"outback."**

Opposite seasons. Since Australia is in the Southern Hemisphere, its seasons are just the opposite of those in Europe, Asia, and North America. Christmas comes in the summer, which lasts from December to February. Winter extends from June to August. Check the temperature map (p. 340) to see what the average temperature is in the summer month of January. What is the average temperature of most of Australia in the winter month of July?

Comprehension Check 16A

1. How many nations are on the continent of Australia?
2. Because it is entirely below the equator, Australia is sometimes called _?_.
3. What Australian island lies south of the mainland?
4. The longest coral reef in the world, called _?_, lies just off the northeast coast of Australia.
5. What Australian mountain range follows the east coast and acts as a divide?
6. Name Australia's two main rivers.
7. What season does Australia have in July? In January?

WONDERS OF WORLD GEOGRAPHY

Great Barrier Reef

The beautiful **Great Barrier Reef** is a 1,250-mile chain of some 2,500 coral ridges and small sandy islands. The reefs are not rocks, but are made up of living creatures called *polyps,* and sometimes called coral polyps. These creatures are soft and fleshy, and are coated with an exoskeleton. They attach themselves to hard places in the reefs (usually the skeletons of other polyps). After attachment, they divide, forming other polyps. When they die, their hard skeletons, too, become part of the reefs.

Coral polyps are not the only inhabitants of the Great Barrier Reef. The clear, tropical waters that the polyps thrive in are home to many beautiful and strange creatures. There are red and blue starfish; sea urchins with waving tentacles that snare food; fish with venomous spines; the evil-looking, ferocious moray eel, and highly decorated fish with colors such as red, blue, brown, and yellow, and patterns such as polka dots and stripes. Some varieties of fish can change their colors and patterns to confuse predators and prey. You will also find sponges, which are actually animals who live attached to rocks. They filter their food from water that passes through their bodies.

The living coral polyps off the shore of the reefs make the area a very interesting place for skin divers; however, it can be a very dangerous place because of huge sharks and poisonous sea snakes.

The Great Barrier Reef is an undersea "garden" of beautiful colors and strange plants and animals. It is a testimony to the brilliance of God's creation. ⌘

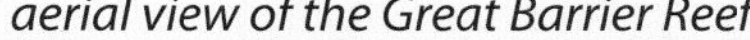

aerial view of the Great Barrier Reef

Plants and Animals

Trees. Most of the Australian trees are evergreens, trees that do not lose their leaves in the winter. Some of them, such as the **eucalyptus** [yo͞o′kə·lĭp′təs] **tree,** shed their bark throughout the year. In Australia, the eucalyptus is known as a **gum tree.** It is native to Australia and has been grown in few other places of the world besides Florida and California. As Australia's most important tree, it is useful for its **oil, gum,** and **timber.** The tree grows rapidly and may reach a height of three hundred feet. Another valuable tree, the **acacia** [ə·kā′shə], has a dark wood that is used for making fine furniture.

Bushes and flowers. In the dry areas, a valuable plant called the **saltbush shrub** grows. Sheep thrive on the leaves of the saltbush, which are covered with a dark, salty substance. In times of drought, the sheep can survive with nothing but this plant as food. Many other scrubby bushes grow in the outback, and a surprising number of wildflowers bloom there. Many of the hottest desert areas are covered with sand dunes, where few plants can grow.

Marsupials. Most of the native animals of Australia differ greatly from those in other parts of the world. Two thirds of the mammals of the country are **marsupials** [mär·sū′pē·əlz], mammals that have pouches for carrying their young. Some marsupials are the size of mice. Others are huge, such as the **great kangaroo,** which can be seven feet tall. The powerful back legs and strong tail of the kangaroo enable it to jump twenty-five feet in one bound. Another marsupial, the **koala** [kō·ä′lə], looks like a teddy bear. Koalas never drink water, and they feed on nothing but eucalyptus leaves. Other marsupials are the **wallaby** [wŏl′ə·bē], which is like a small kangaroo, and the **wombat,** a thickset animal about three feet long that lives in underground burrows. Wombats make good pets.

Platypus. Perhaps the strangest animal of Australia is the **duck-billed platypus** [plăt′ĭ·pəs]. It is a warm-blooded mammal that lays eggs and has webbed feet and a bill like a duck. It has soft brown fur and may often be seen in ponds and streams, feeding on insects and worms in the water.

wombat

wallaby

duck-billed platypus

Echidna. The echidna [ĭ•kĭd′nə], or **spiny anteater,** has a body covered with coarse hair and sharp spines. It has no teeth, but it uses its long, sticky tongue to catch ants and other insects. It lays a single egg and hatches it in its pouch. (Because it lays eggs, it is not grouped with the marsupials even though it has a pouch.)

Birds. A large running bird of Australia, the **emu** [ē′myo͞o], resembles the African ostrich. The plumage of the emu is long and hairlike. Like the ostrich, the emu cannot fly, but it is a very swift runner. The **kookaburra** [ko͝ok′ə•bûr′ə] is a famous Australian bird noted for its harsh call that sounds like laughter.

History

Early history. Before the arrival of European explorers and colonists, the **Aborigines** [ăb′ə•rĭj′ə•nēz], or native inhabitants of Australia, led nomadic lives. Women and children gathered fruits and berries, and men hunted with spears and **boomerangs,** pieces of wood carved in such a way that when thrown, they can wound or kill an animal as much as 500 feet away. (Today, some boomerangs used for sport or to kill small game are designed to return close to where they were thrown.) Most tribes lived along rivers and coasts, but often moved from water hole to water hole. Their homes were caves or small shelters built from tree branches, bark, and grass. Some Aborigines continue to live as they have for centuries, but others have become cowboys or sheepherders.

European settlement. Explorers from Europe began sailing to Australia around A.D. 1600. Abel Tasman led many of the Dutch explorations of western and southern Australia. The Dutch soon lost interest in what they saw as a dry and barren land. Before leaving the area, however, Tasman discovered a large island south of the mainland. Today that island is called Tasmania.

In 1770, Captain James Cook claimed a large tract of land on the fertile east coast of the continent for Great Britain. For many years, England used Australia as a prison colony. Most of the first British settlers to Australia were people who

Aborigine carrying a non-return hunting boomerang

had been in British jails for political reasons or for being too poor to pay their debts. In 1788, these people established a settlement at **Sydney.** Pioneers who were not prisoners came later. Christian groups in England and Scotland sent Christian leaders to establish strong churches on the continent, and missionaries took the gospel to the Aborigines.

Comprehension Check 16B

1. What are Australia's two most important trees and how are they used?
2. What unusual group of animals are native to Australia? Give some examples.
3. Who were the first people to live in Australia?
4. What unusual weapon did they use for hunting?
5. Who discovered and claimed Australia for England?

Government

Commonwealth member. Australia is a member of the Commonwealth of Nations, an association that includes Great Britain and about fifty-two nations that were once British colonies. The Commonwealth nations and their territories cover about one fourth of the earth's land surface and have about a fourth of the world's population. The king or queen of England is the symbolic head of the Commonwealth nations, but each has its own government. Some of the members are Australia, Canada, Jamaica, New Zealand, Ghana, and India.

States and territories. Australia is divided into six states and two mainland territories. Locate each state and its capital city on the map (p. 292). Each capital city is located on or very near the seacoast, for that is where living conditions are best in Australia.

Locate the Northern Territory and Australian Capital Territory on the map. **Canberra** [kăn′bər·ə], Australia's capital, is in Australian Capital Territory.

Republican government. Australia has a republican form of government. This means that the people take part in the government. The governor general, who is appointed by the British monarch, is the symbolic leader. The Prime Minister and the members of Parliament are the active leaders. Every Australian who is eighteen or older is required to vote in elections.

Cities

More than half of Australia's people live in the six state capitals. Each capital is a **seaport** (a town that has a port or

Sydney Harbor

harbor where ocean ships may anchor safely) or is very near a seaport, and each is an **industrial center** (a place where much manufacturing is done). **Sydney,** where the first British settlers came, is the largest city, and **Melbourne** is second largest. Australian cities are very similar to cities in the United States. Many Australian customs, however, are British. Australians drive on the left side of the road, drink hot tea, and enjoy such British sports as cricket and rugby. They are similar to the English, Canadians, and Americans in food, dress, work, and recreation.

Country Life

Away from the cities are many huge ranches, or **stations.** Ranch life is similar to life on the large farms of the Western United States. Some stations in the outback are so huge that the ranchers seldom see other people. Travel is done by airplane, and two-way radios are used for communication. Children on the outback stations often study by correspondence courses because they are so far away from the country's schools. Sometimes they receive their lessons over two-way radios.

The Australian Dog Fence is one of the most unusual sights in the country. It is a 6-foot-tall fence that is over 3,000 miles long. Its purpose is to keep **dingoes,** or wild dogs, away from Australia's millions of sheep. This structure needs constant supervision and repair because of fence-ripping kangaroos and pesky emus that run along the wiring looking for openings until they decide to crash through.

Language. English is the official language. However, Australians speak English with a different accent than that spoken in England, Canada, or the United States. Some of their words are also unique to Australia. For instance, a *jackaroo* is a ranch worker, a *mate* is a close friend, and a *yakka* [yăk′ə] is a hard worker. Australian ranches are called *stations,* and meadows are called *paddocks.*

large sheep station

a jackaroo

a dingo

Industry and Resources

Agriculture. During the early years of settlement, agriculture was the most important occupation in Australia. Today, wool and wheat are two of the most important agricultural products.

Australia is the world's leading wool producer. *Woolybacks* (sheep) were introduced to Australia by the European settlers who found the Australian climate especially suitable for raising sheep. Today, sheep outnumber the people by more than six to one and provide Australia with some of its greatest wealth—wool. Australia is famous especially for the fine wool of the **Merino** sheep, which originally came from Spain.

Very little of the land in Australia is able to be farmed, and there are only two major crops—wheat and sugar cane. However, in spite of the small area available for growing wheat, Australia is one of the leading wheat exporters in the world.

Mineral wealth. Australia is rich in natural resources, especially mineral resources such as coal, iron ore, and gold. After gold was discovered in 1851, mining and industry began to be more important than agriculture to the country's economy. Australia is one of the six largest gold-mining countries in the world. Even so, coal and iron ore are more important than gold to Australia's economy.

Manufacturing. Australia's mineral resources provide it with valuable fuels and raw materials for the manufacturing industry. Australia is one of the most highly industrialized nations in the world.

Comprehension Check 16C

1. What are the divisions of Australia called?
2. What is Australia's national capital?
3. What is a seaport? An industrial center?
4. What are Australian ranches called?
5. What are dingoes?
6. Australia is the world's leading producer of __?__.

16.2 Oceania: Islands of the Pacific

Oceania

Location and size. North and east of Australia, scattered throughout the wide Pacific Ocean, lie between 20,000 and 30,000 islands. These Pacific islands are known collectively as **Oceania.** The islands vary in size from rock piles to thousands of square miles. Some are uninhabited, and others are crowded with people.

Polynesia. The islands of Oceania are divided into three main groups—**Polynesia** [pŏl′ə·nē′zhə], **Melanesia** [mĕl′ə·nē′zhə], and **Micronesia** [mī′krō·nē′zhə]. *Polynesia,* which means "many islands," is the largest group. The Polynesians are the tallest and fairest of the Pa-

Polynesian boy climbing a coconut tree

cific Islanders. Their islands, including **New Zealand, Hawaii,** and **American Samoa,** are spread over a large area, mostly in the Western Hemisphere. Despite the large area covered, Polynesian culture is remarkably uniform from one island to the next. The cultures of New Zealand and Hawaii are unique because they have been greatly influenced by Europe and North America.

Melanesia. The island group with the largest population is *Melanesia,* which means "black islands." It is inhabited by short, dark-skinned Melanesians, most of whom live in **Papua New Guinea.**

Micronesia. Many of the "small islands" of *Micronesia* have less than one square mile of land. The Micronesians have a height and skin tone between that of the Polynesians and Melanesians. The **Northern Marianas** and **Guam,** both American Territories, are included in this group of islands.

On the map (p. 302), locate as many of these Pacific Islands as you can. Did you find the Northern Marianas, Guam, American Samoa, and Hawaii?

Climate. Although the high, mountainous areas of the larger islands receive occasional snowfalls, most of the islands are covered with tropical rain forests and enjoy a warm, moist

Most of the islands of Oceania are covered with rain forests and enjoy a warm, moist climate.

typical South Pacific scenery

Micronesian children

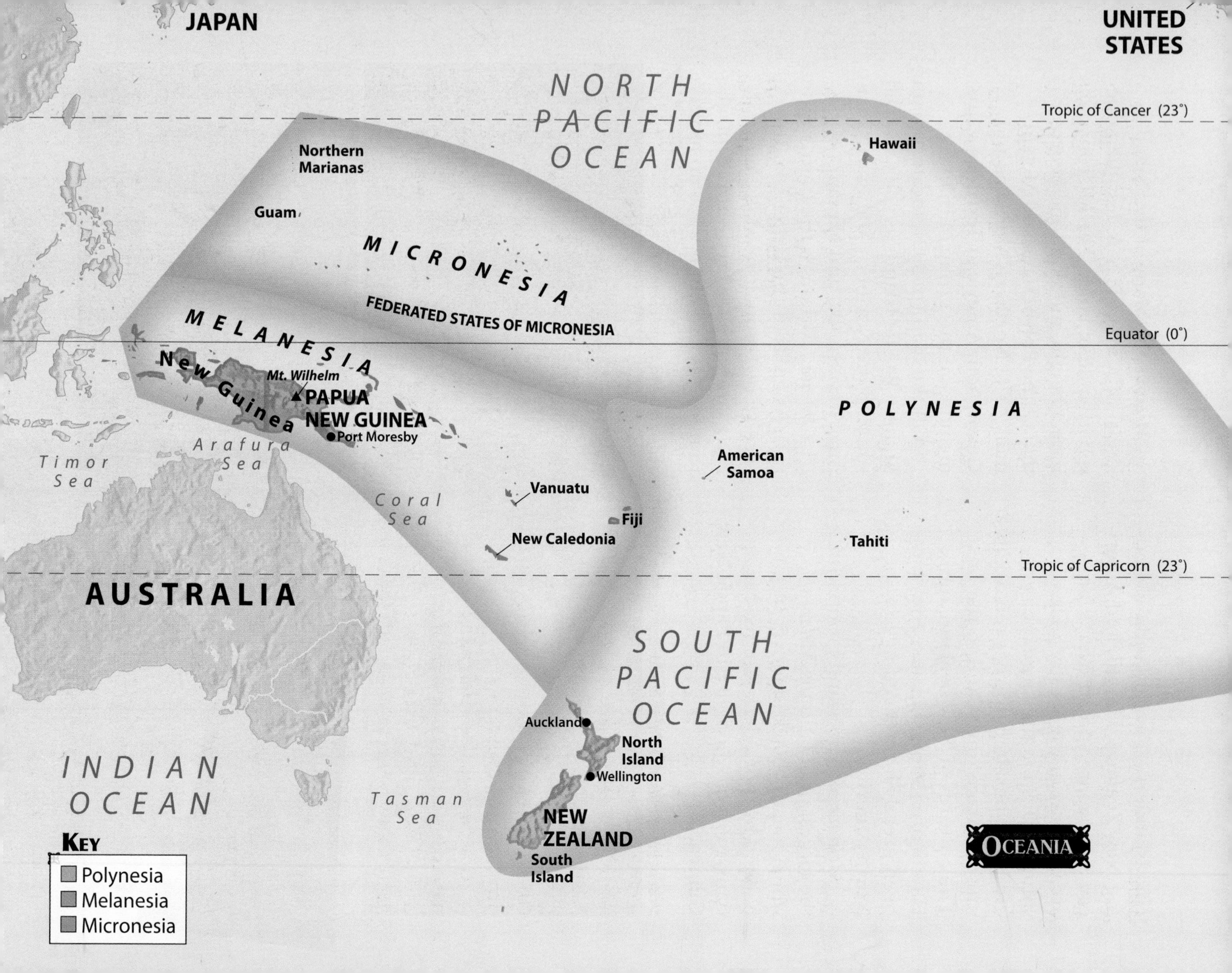

OCEANIA

JAPAN

UNITED STATES

NORTH PACIFIC OCEAN

Tropic of Cancer (23°)

Northern Marianas

Guam

Hawaii

MICRONESIA

FEDERATED STATES OF MICRONESIA

Equator (0°)

MELANESIA

New Guinea

Mt. Wilhelm

PAPUA NEW GUINEA

Port Moresby

POLYNESIA

Arafura Sea

Timor Sea

American Samoa

Vanuatu

Coral Sea

Fiji

New Caledonia

Tahiti

Tropic of Capricorn (23°)

AUSTRALIA

SOUTH PACIFIC OCEAN

Auckland

North Island

Wellington

INDIAN OCEAN

Tasman Sea

NEW ZEALAND

South Island

Key

- Polynesia
- Melanesia
- Micronesia

climate. Seasons are marked by changes in rainfall rather than changes in temperature. The amount of rainfall varies from area to area, but most places see annual wet and dry seasons. Some islands average only a few inches of rain, while monsoons bring other islands up to 300 inches in one year. Much of Oceania is subject to typhoons, storms that sweep over entire islands, often destroying everything in their paths.

Resources and industries. Many of the Pacific islanders raise their own food and make their own shelters and clothing. Fishing is an important occupation, and there is some farming. The **coconut tree** is an important source of food and timber for the islanders. Other crops include sugar cane, bananas, coffee, cocoa, and palm oil. A few islands, including New Guinea, New Caledonia, and Fiji [fē′jē], have mining industries.

Government. By 1900, all of the inhabited islands were controlled by countries of Europe, Australia, and North America who used the islands for colonies and military bases. Today, many of the islands, such as the Federated States of Micronesia, Fiji, New Zealand, and Papua New Guinea, are independent again. Others, such as American Samoa, the Northern Marianas, Guam, and Tahiti, remain dependencies or commonwealths.

New Zealand

New Zealand is made up of two main islands, North Island and South Island. The capital, **Wellington,** and the largest city, **Auckland** [ôk′lənd], are located on North Island where most of the people live.

Wellington

New Zealand countryside

People in History

John G. Paton: Missionary to the Pacific Islands

Perhaps the most famous missionary to the Pacific Islands was John G. Paton of Scotland. For 49 years, from 1858 until 1907, he lived in the New Hebrides islands (modern Vanuatu). Because some of the islanders were cannibals, his life was often in danger. But he worked diligently to learn the languages and customs of the islanders and to gain their friendship so he could teach them the way of salvation. God miraculously delivered him from death on several occasions and allowed him to continue his ministry of preaching, medical work, and teaching. Under his ministry, the entire population of the island of Aniwa [än′ē·wä] burned their idols, turned from their cannibalism, and came to Christ. The island's ruler, Chief Namakei [näm′ə·kī], learned to read so he could read the Bible in his own language and teach it to his people.

John G. Paton helped the islanders to build a church, gave them a hymnbook in their own language, and started two orphanages. His visits to churches in Australia, Scotland, and England inspired many other Christians to become missionaries. ⌘

The first people to settle in New Zealand were the **Maoris** [mou′rēz], a people famous for their skill in sailing and navigation. After Captain Cook claimed New Zealand for England in the 1700s, British whalers settled there, and missionaries came to bring the gospel to the Maoris. Later, more British settled on the islands.

New Zealand has much rich pastureland. Sheep, dairy cattle, and beef cattle supply important agricultural products such as wool, meat, butter, and cheese, the country's main industries and leading exports.

Papua New Guinea

Just to the north of Australia lies the island of New Guinea. The eastern half of the island, along with about 600 smaller islands off its shores, is called **Papua** [pä′po͞o·ä′] **New Guinea** [gĭ′nē]. The capital is **Port Moresby.**

The main island is crossed by rugged mountain peaks, including **Mt. Wilhelm,** the highest island peak in the

Port Moresby

jungle village in Papua New Guinea

world. Crocodiles thrive in the swamps along the coast and on the plains, and the thick rain forests that cover steep mountainsides receive over 300 inches of rain in a year.

Papua New Guinea has more languages spoken than any other country in the world. Although English is the official language, over 700 individual languages are spoken on the island.

Until recent years, the dense jungles isolated some of the world's most primitive people. Missionaries began work on the coasts as early as the 1850s, but were barred from the fierce natives of the island's interior until after World War II. Over the years, many natives have trusted Christ, and several villages have turned their battlefields into mission stations.

Many islanders make their living on small farms growing yams, bananas, and sweet potatoes. People along the coasts supplement their diet with fish. Natives in the highlands hunt birds, wallaby, tree kangaroo, and wild boar for food.

Comprehension Check 16D

1. Name the three main groups of islands located within Oceania.
2. What is the capital of New Zealand?
3. Who were the first people to settle New Zealand?
4. Who was the famous missionary to the Pacific Islands?
5. Which island country has the most languages spoken of any country in the world?

16.3 Antarctica: The Coldest Continent

At the Bottom of the World

The continent of **Antarctica** is "at the bottom of the world." As you can see by looking at the world map (pp. 314–315), it is in both the Eastern and Western Hemispheres. Because a map is a flattened-out globe, the world map cannot show what Antarctica really looks like. If you peel an orange carefully and try to flatten out the peel, you will find that it stretches and tears. This illustrates why it is very difficult to show the round world exactly on a flat surface. On the world map, Greenland looks much larger than it actually is, and Antarctica cannot be shown in its true shape.

Map study. To see what Antarctica really looks like, study the map of Ant-

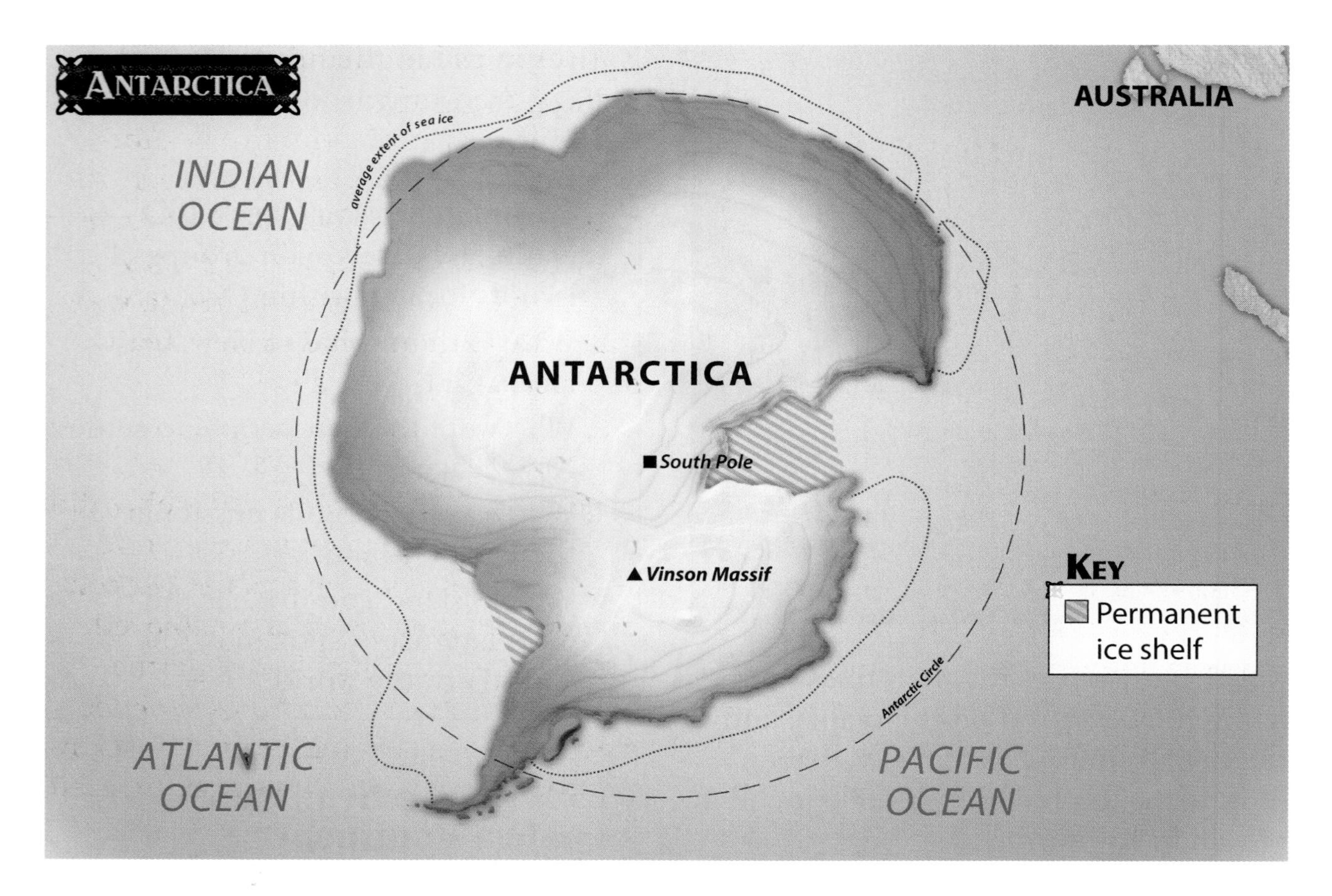

arctica above. Find the Antarctic Circle. How much of Antarctica is not inside the Circle? Find the South Pole. What direction did you have to go to get to the South Pole? (If you are not sure, locate the South Pole on a globe.) To go from the South Pole to any other place on earth, what direction would you have to go? What three oceans surround the South Pole?

Landforms. Antarctica is frozen at all times. (The average annual temperature is –11 °F.) Beneath the snow are mountains, some with an altitude of more than 14,000 feet. The tallest peak, **Vinson Massif** [vĭn′ sən mă·sēf′], has an altitude of 16,864 feet. The South Pole is on a plateau 10,000 feet high. Glaciers move down the mountains inch by inch and push icebergs into the oceans.

Life. Hardy mosses and lichens cover the hillsides in the summer. No trees or shrubs can grow in Antarctica.

icebergs breaking away from Antarctica

seals on an ice floe

Living on the clumps of mosses and lichens and swimming in little ponds made by melted snow are tiny spiders, insects, and microscopic animals. The largest land animal on the continent is an insect less than one tenth of an inch long!

In the waters surrounding Antarctica there are thousands of whales and millions of seals. The seals rest on the ice islands, but they depend on the sea for food and shelter. Penguins, squat birds that cannot fly, spend some of their time on the islands to the north of Antarctica. God designed them with a compact body shape and layers of fat that protect them from the cold. The largest penguin, the emperor, weighs up to one hundred pounds. Every summer, a sea bird called the **Arctic tern** flies 11,000 miles from the Arctic to Antarctica.

Arctic tern

It is often called the migration champion of the world.

The only people who live on Antarctica are scientists and explorers although many tourists now visit each year. Special clothing and specially constructed dwellings designed to withstand the extreme cold protect both scientists and visitors alike.

Discovery and Exploration

For many years, maps and globes did not show Antarctica, because no one knew that it existed. It was the last continent to be discovered and explored. Though it is not suitable as a permanent home for man, this most isolated place on earth is being studied by scientists for possible ways that it can be used for man's benefit.

Antarctic explorers. People from many nations played parts in finding the icy continent and exploring its possibilities. In the 1770s, **Captain James Cook** of England became the first man to sail around the Antarctic Circle, but he did not know that there was a continent there. In 1840, **Charles Wilkes,** a United States naval officer, became the first person to insist that Antarctica actually was a continent. In 1911, **Roald Amundsen** [rō′äl ä′mənd·sən], a famous Norwegian explorer, became the first

Roald Amundsen

man to reach the South Pole. Rear Admiral **Richard Byrd** of the United States Navy was the most famous Antarctic explorer. He was the first man to fly over the *North* Pole, and he led many important explorations of Antarctica by airplane and supervised the mapping of much of Antarctica between 1929 and 1957. He wrote several books about his explorations. Other explorers came from the former Soviet Union, France, Norway, Australia, and Ireland. Exploration of the continent was dangerous. One party of five, led by English naval captain **Robert Scott,** perished in 1912 on their way back from the South Pole because of extremely bad weather and lack of food.

Richard Byrd

Scientific research. In 1961, Antarctica was set aside as a preserve for scientific research. Several countries have sent scientists there to study the continent's effects on the world's weather and to find out if it has natural resources that can be valuable to man. One of the stations where the scientists live is fueled by a nuclear energy plant and the stations are all linked to the rest of the world by airplanes and radios.

This bleak land, like the rest of the earth, bears silent testimony to the fact that *the earth is the Lord's, and the fulness thereof; the world, and they that dwell therein.* —Psa. 24:1

McMurdo Sound research station

ANIMALS AROUND THE WORLD

Penguins in Antarctica

In the coldest places on earth lives the penguin. The largest species, the Emperor penguin, lives his entire life on the frozen continent of Antarctica and in its waters.

The Emperor penguin can grow 3–4 feet tall and weigh 50–100 pounds. When winter approaches and ice begins to form, the Emperor penguin leaves the ocean and finds a place

to start a family. The female will lay her egg and her mate will care for it, balancing it on his feet, and keeping it warm by covering it with a special flap of skin from his belly. The female leaves to find food, traveling 80 miles or more before she can dive into the water and eat. No matter how far she travels, she will always come back when the egg is ready to hatch. When the chick emerges, she feeds him with krill she has saved in a small sack, called a *crop,* in her throat.

It takes a few months for the chick to grow his adult feathers. While he is waiting for his waterproof feathers, he meets the other chicks in the penguin *rookery.* The chicks huddle together for warmth, while their parents take turns going for food.

By the time the chick's adult feathers have grown, it is the beginning of summer—time for him to go to the ocean and catch his own food. No one has to teach him how to swim, for God gave him that knowledge before he was even hatched. While swimming, he eats and plays, keeping a watchful eye for leopard seals, who love to eat penguins.

All during the summer, the penguin lives in the water. When winter comes again, it will be time to travel across the forming ice to the place where he was born, time to find his own mate, time to begin his life as an adult. In a hostile, cold world where very little can survive, the penguin has been specially designed by God to thrive.

CHAPTER 16 CHECKUP

A Write the most important fact about each place.

1. Tasmania
2. Great Barrier Reef
3. Great Dividing Range
4. Mt. Kosciusko
5. Murray River
6. Darling River
7. Great Artesian Basin
8. outback
9. Sydney
10. Oceania
11. Polynesia
12. Melanesia
13. Micronesia
14. Papua New Guinea
15. Mt. Wilhelm
16. Vinson Massif

B Answer each question.

1. What is the smallest continent?
2. Why is Australia called the "Land Down Under"? "The Island Continent"?

(cont.)

3. During which season do Australians celebrate Christmas?
4. What name is given to mammals whose young develop in pouches?
5. Australia is the world's leading producer of ___?___.
6. The migration champion of the world is the ___?___.

C Define each term.

1. Aborigines
2. boomerang
3. seaport
4. industrial center
5. stations
6. dingoes
7. Maoris

D Tell the most important accomplishment of each person.

1. John G. Paton
2. Captain James Cook
3. Charles Wilkes
4. Roald Amundsen
5. Richard Byrd

E Know the countries and capitals. (See Continent Study 4, p. 325.)

GEOGRAPHY HANDBOOK

Atlas Index

Continent Studies Index

Geography Facts Index

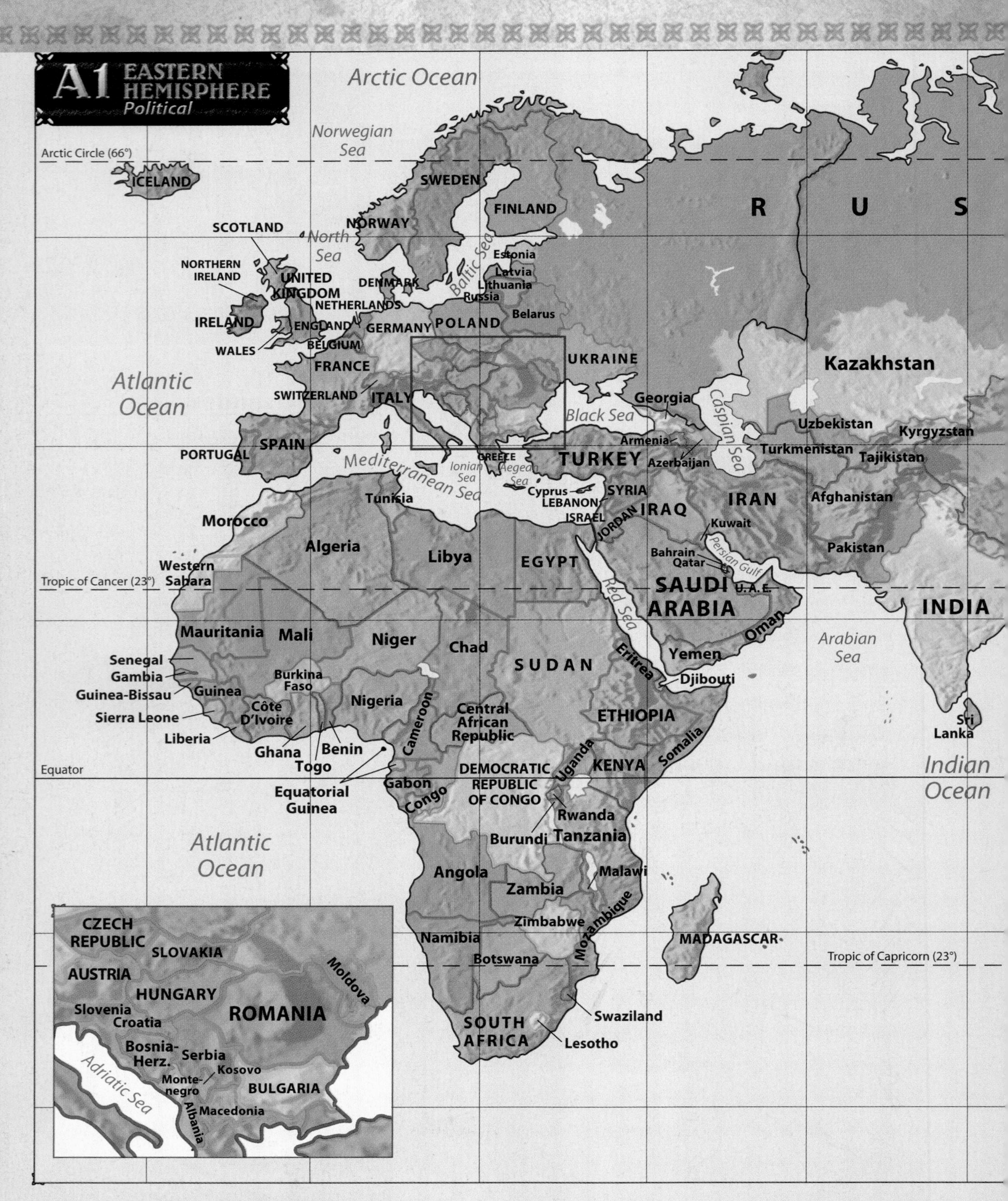

A1 EASTERN HEMISPHERE
Political
Arctic Ocean
Norwegian Sea
Arctic Circle (66°)
ICELAND
SWEDEN
FINLAND
R U S
NORWAY
SCOTLAND
North Sea
NORTHERN IRELAND
UNITED KINGDOM
DENMARK
Baltic Sea
Estonia
Latvia
Lithuania
Russia
NETHERLANDS
IRELAND
ENGLAND
GERMANY
POLAND
Belarus
WALES
BELGIUM
FRANCE
UKRAINE
Kazakhstan
Atlantic Ocean
SWITZERLAND
ITALY
Georgia
Caspian Sea
Black Sea
Uzbekistan
Kyrgyzstan
Armenia
SPAIN
PORTUGAL
GREECE
TURKEY
Azerbaijan
Turkmenistan
Tajikistan
Mediterranean Sea
Ionian Sea
Aegean Sea
Cyprus
LEBANON
SYRIA
IRAQ
IRAN
Afghanistan
Tunisia
ISRAEL
JORDAN
Kuwait
Morocco
Algeria
Libya
EGYPT
Bahrain
Qatar
Persian Gulf
Pakistan
Western Sahara
Tropic of Cancer (23°)
Red Sea
SAUDI ARABIA
U.A.E.
INDIA
Mauritania
Mali
Niger
Chad
SUDAN
Eritrea
Yemen
Oman
Arabian Sea
Senegal
Gambia
Guinea-Bissau
Guinea
Burkina Faso
Djibouti
Sierra Leone
Côte D'Ivoire
Nigeria
Cameroon
Central African Republic
ETHIOPIA
Sri Lanka
Liberia
Ghana
Benin
Togo
Somalia
Equator
Uganda
KENYA
DEMOCRATIC REPUBLIC OF CONGO
Indian Ocean
Gabon
Congo
Equatorial Guinea
Rwanda
Burundi
Tanzania
Atlantic Ocean
Angola
Malawi
Zambia
Zimbabwe
Mozambique
Namibia
MADAGASCAR
Botswana
Tropic of Capricorn (23°)
Swaziland
SOUTH AFRICA
Lesotho
CZECH REPUBLIC
SLOVAKIA
AUSTRIA
Moldova
HUNGARY
Slovenia
Croatia
ROMANIA
Bosnia-Herz.
Serbia
Adriatic Sea
Kosovo
Montenegro
BULGARIA
Albania
Macedonia

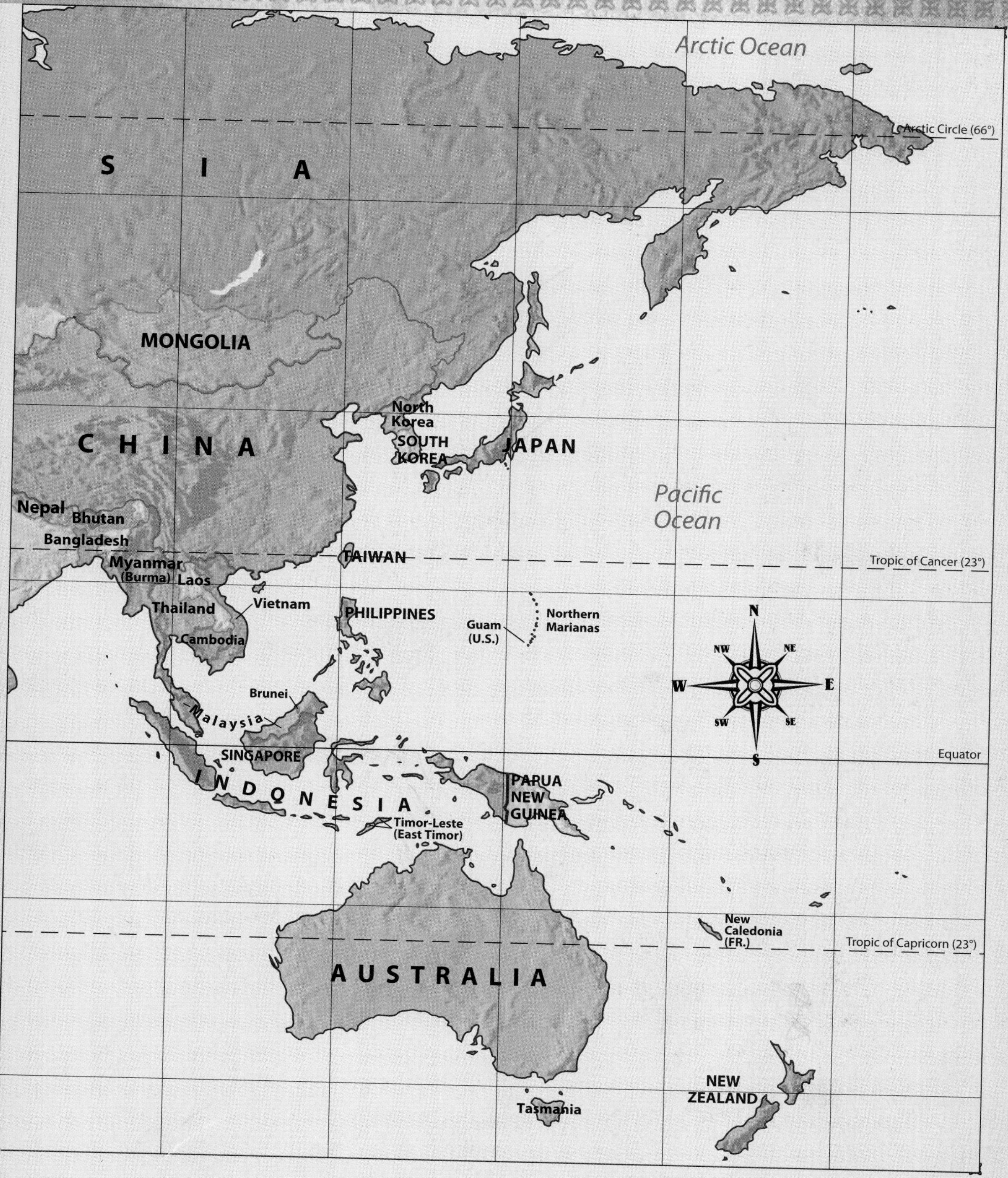

Arctic Ocean

Arctic Circle (66°)

S I A

MONGOLIA

North Korea

SOUTH KOREA

JAPAN

C H I N A

Pacific Ocean

Nepal

Bhutan

Bangladesh

Myanmar (Burma)

Laos

TAIWAN

Tropic of Cancer (23°)

Thailand

Vietnam

PHILIPPINES

Guam (U.S.)

Northern Marianas

Cambodia

N

NW

NE

W

E

SW

SE

S

Brunei

Malaysia

SINGAPORE

Equator

I N D O N E S I A

PAPUA NEW GUINEA

Timor-Leste (East Timor)

New Caledonia (FR.)

Tropic of Capricorn (23°)

A U S T R A L I A

NEW ZEALAND

Tasmania

A2 WORLD Physical
Western Hemisphere
Greenland
NORTH AMERICA
SOUTH AMERICA
Atlantic Ocean
Pacific Ocean
Arctic Circle (66°)
Tropic of Cancer (23°)
Equator (0°)
Tropic of Capricorn (23°)
Antarctic Circle (66°)
Prime Meridian
Frigid Zone
Temperate Zone
Torrid Zone
Temperate Zone
Frigid Zone
N
NE
E
SE
S
SW
W
NW
A N
Rockies
Matterhorn
Mont Blanc
Alps
Atlas
Andes
Rivers
1 Mississippi
2 Missouri
3 Amazon
4 Thames
5 Rhine
6 Danube
7 Volga
8 Nile
9 Congo
10 Euphrates
11 Tigris
12 Indus
13 Huang He
14 Yangtze
Seas
15 Caribbean
16 Norwegian
17 North
18 Baltic
19 Mediterranean
20 Aegean
21 Black
22 Caspian
23 Red
24 Arabian

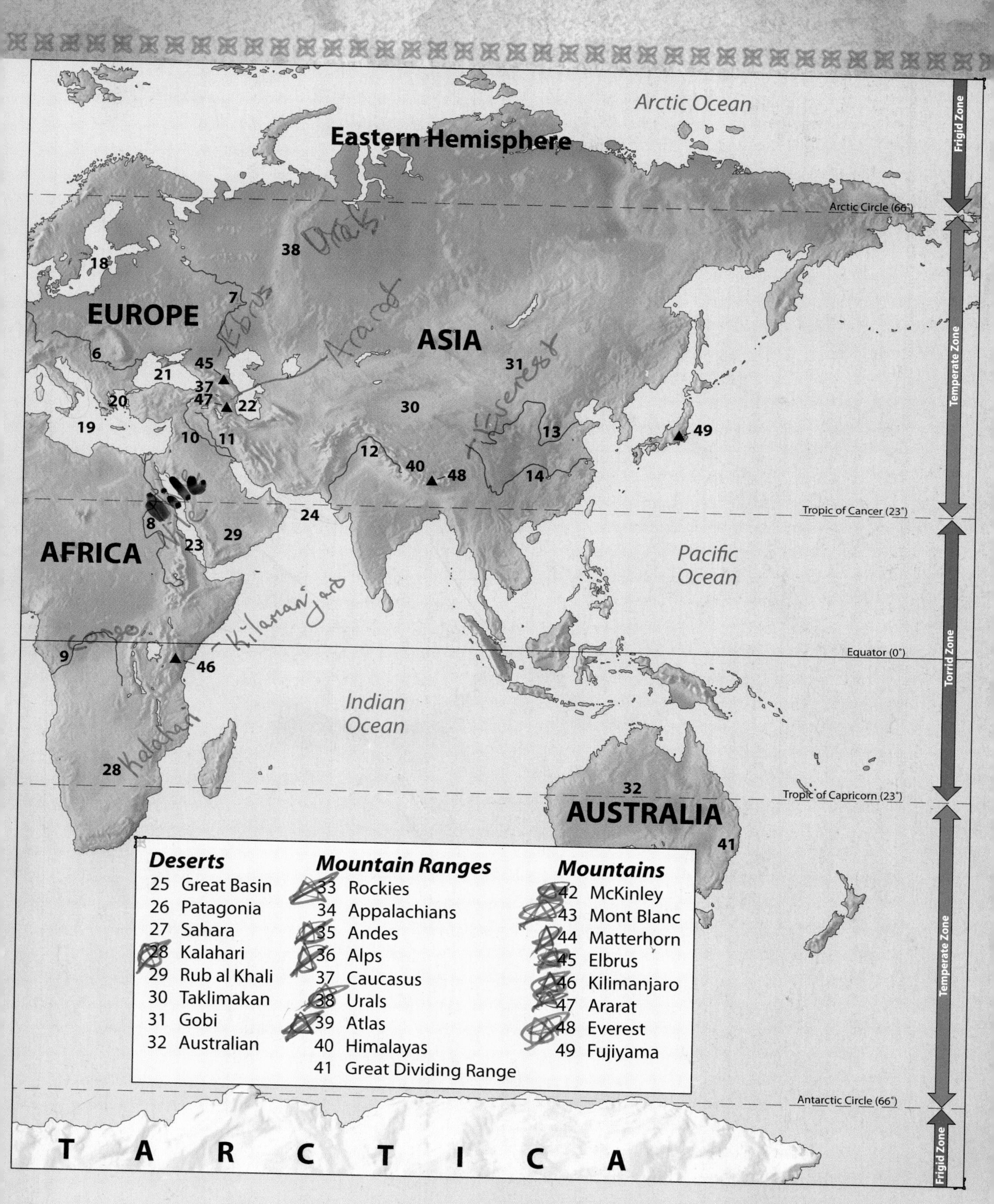

Eastern Hemisphere
Arctic Ocean
Arctic Circle (66°)
Tropic of Cancer (23°)
Equator (0°)
Tropic of Capricorn (23°)
Antarctic Circle (66°)
Frigid Zone
Temperate Zone
Torrid Zone
Temperate Zone
Frigid Zone
EUROPE
ASIA
AFRICA
AUSTRALIA
ANTARCTICA
Pacific Ocean
Indian Ocean
6
7
8
9
10
11
12
13
14
18
19
20
21
22
23
24
28
29
30
31
32
37
38
40
41
45
46
47
48
49
Deserts
25 Great Basin
26 Patagonia
27 Sahara
28 Kalahari
29 Rub al Khali
30 Taklimakan
31 Gobi
32 Australian
Mountain Ranges
33 Rockies
34 Appalachians
35 Andes
36 Alps
37 Caucasus
38 Urals
39 Atlas
40 Himalayas
41 Great Dividing Range
Mountains
42 McKinley
43 Mont Blanc
44 Matterhorn
45 Elbrus
46 Kilimanjaro
47 Ararat
48 Everest
49 Fujiyama

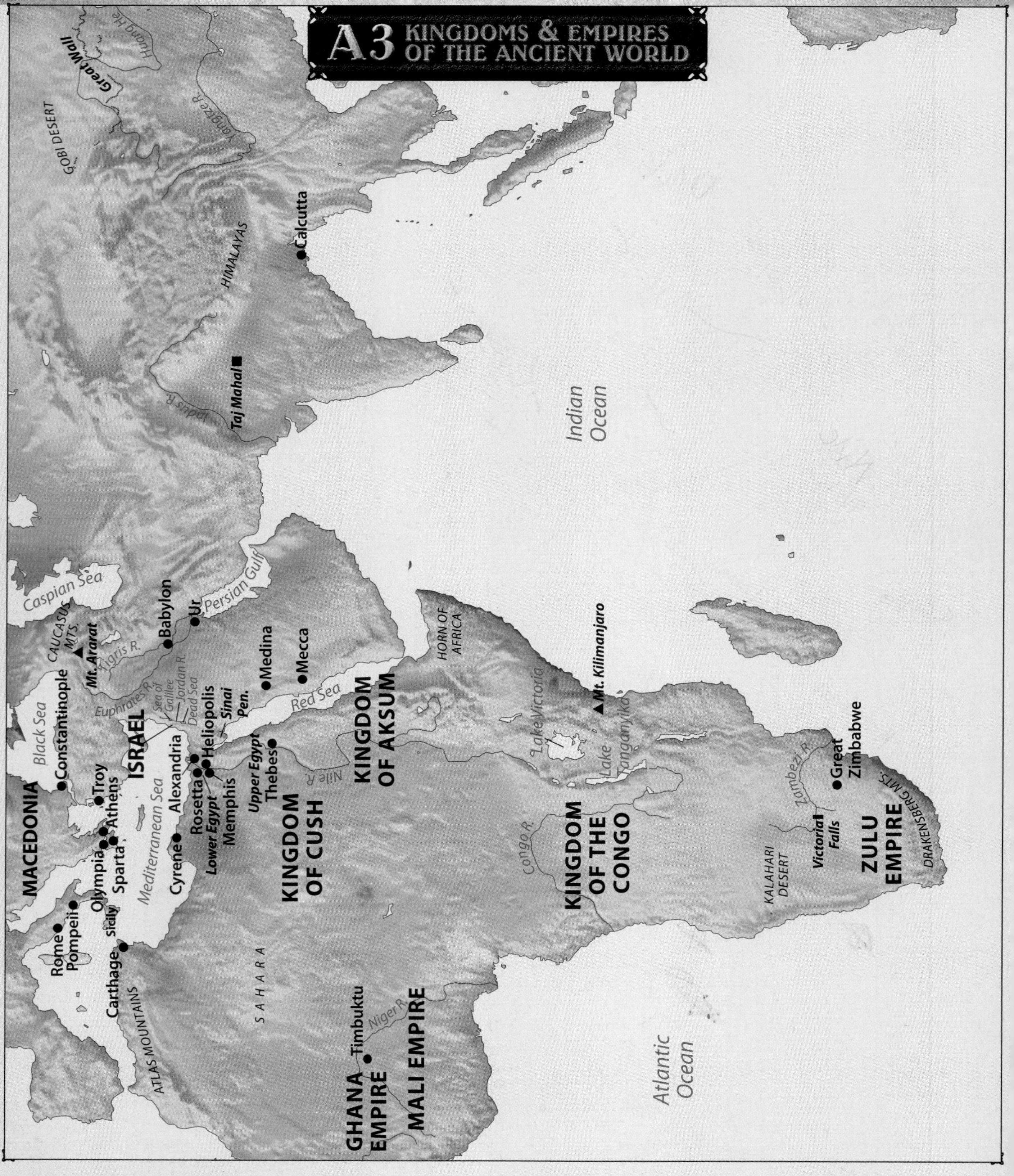

A3 KINGDOMS & EMPIRES OF THE ANCIENT WORLD

MACEDONIA
Black Sea
Caspian Sea
Rome
Pompeii
Constantinople
CAUCASUS MTS.
Mt. Ararat
GOBI DESERT
Great Wall
Huang He
Olympia
Troy
Carthage
Sicily
Sparta
Athens
ATLAS MOUNTAINS
ISRAEL
Euphrates R.
Tigris R.
Mediterranean Sea
Sea of Galilee
Jordan R.
Dead Sea
Babylon
Ur
Cyrene
Alexandria
Rosetta
Lower Egypt
Heliopolis
Memphis
Sinai Pen.
Persian Gulf
Indus R.
Taj Mahal
HIMALAYAS
Yangtze R.
SAHARA
Upper Egypt
Thebes
Medina
Mecca
Calcutta
KINGDOM OF CUSH
Nile R.
Red Sea
GHANA EMPIRE
Timbuktu
Niger R.
KINGDOM OF AKSUM
MALI EMPIRE
HORN OF AFRICA
Congo R.
Lake Victoria
KINGDOM OF THE CONGO
Mt. Kilimanjaro
Lake Tanganyika
Indian Ocean
Atlantic Ocean
KALAHARI DESERT
Zambezi R.
Victoria Falls
Great Zimbabwe
ZULU EMPIRE
DRAKENSBERG MTS.

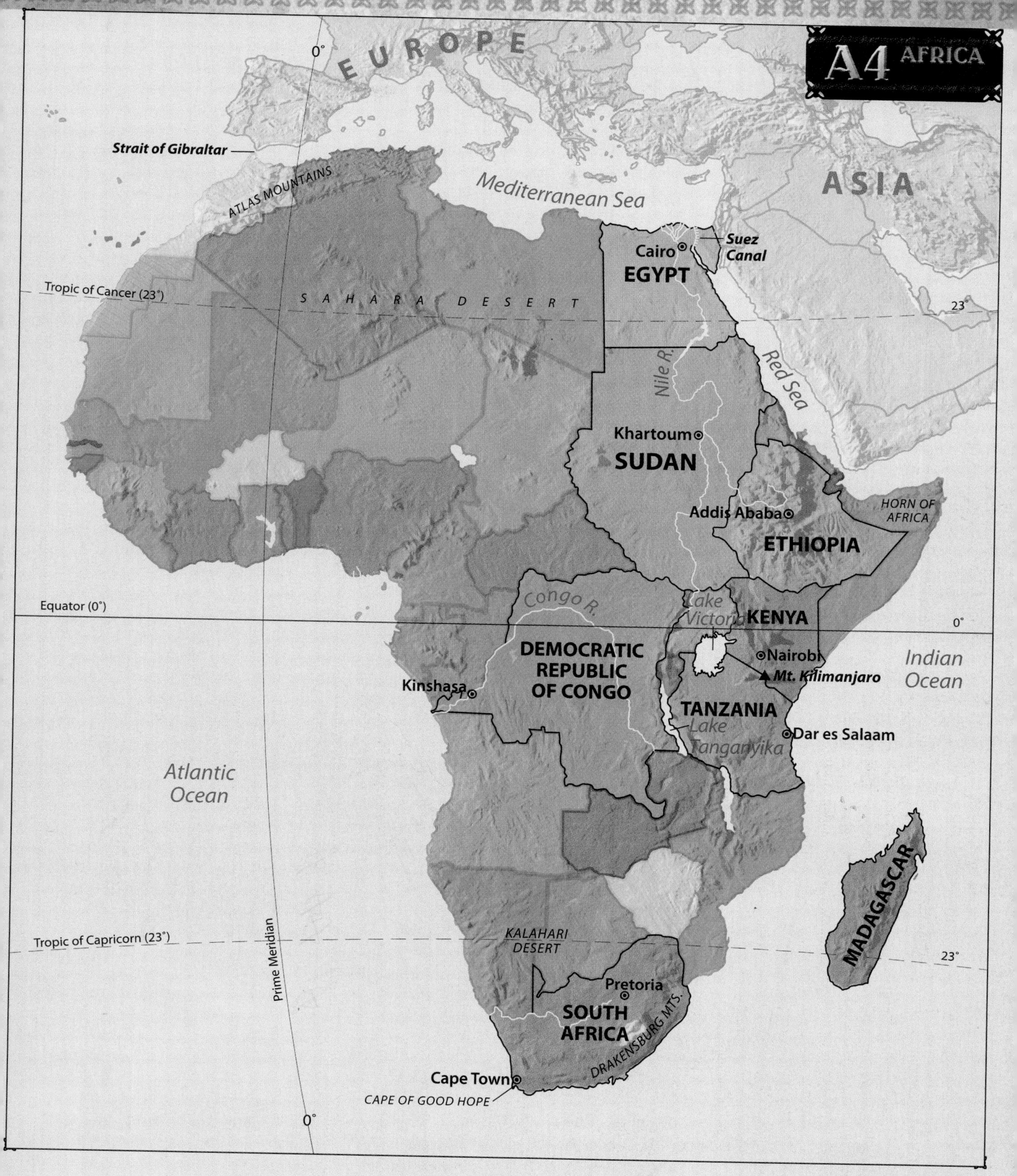

A4 AFRICA

EUROPE
ASIA
0°
Strait of Gibraltar
ATLAS MOUNTAINS
Mediterranean Sea
Cairo
EGYPT
Suez Canal
Tropic of Cancer (23°)
SAHARA DESERT
23°
Nile R.
Red Sea
Khartoum
SUDAN
Addis Ababa
ETHIOPIA
HORN OF AFRICA
Equator (0°)
Congo R.
Lake Victoria
KENYA
0°
DEMOCRATIC REPUBLIC OF CONGO
Nairobi
Mt. Kilimanjaro
Indian Ocean
Kinshasa
TANZANIA
Lake Tanganyika
Dar es Salaam
Atlantic Ocean
MADAGASCAR
KALAHARI DESERT
Tropic of Capricorn (23°)
23°
Prime Meridian
Pretoria
SOUTH AFRICA
DRAKENSBURG MTS.
Cape Town
CAPE OF GOOD HOPE
0°

A5 LANDFORMS & BODIES OF WATER

volcano

plateau

oasis

canyon

desert

river mouth

plain

gulf

sound

islands

sea

peninsula

peak / summit
mountain
mountain range
valley
source
lake
tributary / branch
hill
river
rapids
upstream
waterfall
downstream
delta
harbor
strait
canal
channel
bay

A6 UNITED STATES
CANADA
WASHINGTON
Olympia
MONTANA
Helena
Missouri River
NORTH DAKOTA
Bismarck
OREGON
Salem
IDAHO
Boise
SOUTH DAKOTA
Pierre
WYOMING
Cheyenne
NEBRASKA
Lincoln
Sacramento
Carson City
NEVADA
Salt Lake City
UTAH
Denver
COLORADO
CALIFORNIA
Topeka
KANSAS
ARIZONA
Phoenix
Santa Fe
NEW MEXICO
OKLAHOMA
Oklahoma City
Pacific Ocean
TEXAS
Austin
HAWAII
Honolulu
ALASKA
Juneau
MEXICO

CANADA

Great Lakes

MINNESOTA
St. Paul
WISCONSIN
Madison
MICHIGAN
Lansing
IOWA
Des Moines
ILLINOIS
Springfield
INDIANA
Indianapolis
OHIO
Columbus
MISSOURI
Jefferson City
KENTUCKY
Frankfort
TENNESSEE
Nashville
ARKANSAS
Little Rock
LOUISIANA
Baton Rouge
MISSISSIPPI
Jackson
ALABAMA
Montgomery
GEORGIA
Atlanta
FLORIDA
Tallahassee
SOUTH CAROLINA
Columbia
NORTH CAROLINA
Raleigh
VIRGINIA
Richmond
WEST VIRGINIA
Charleston
Washington, D.C.
MARYLAND
Annapolis
DELAWARE
Dover
NEW JERSEY
Trenton
PENNSYLVANIA
Harrisburg
NEW YORK
Albany
CONNECTICUT
Hartford
RHODE ISLAND
Providence
MASSACHUSETTS
Boston
VERMONT
Montpelier
NEW HAMPSHIRE
Concord
MAINE
Augusta
Mississippi River
Atlantic Ocean
N
NE
E
SE
S
SW
W
NW

ASIA

10 Most Populous Countries

RANK	COUNTRY	CONTINENT	POPULATION (2007)
1	China	Asia	1.3 billion
2	India	Asia	1.1 billion
3	United States	North America	301 million
4	Indonesia	Asia	235 million
5	Brazil	South America	190 million
6	Pakistan	Asia	165 million
7	Bangladesh	Asia	150 million
8	Russia	Europe and Asia	141 million
9	Nigeria	Africa	135 million
10	Japan	Asia	127 million

PRACTICE locating the following landforms and bodies of water on the world map, pp. 314–315.

Seas
Black Sea
Caspian Sea
Red Sea
Arabian Sea

Rivers
Tigris River
Euphrates River
Indus River
Huang He
Yangtze River

Mountain Ranges
Urals
Caucasus
Himalayas

Mountains
Ararat
Everest
Fujiyama

Deserts
Rub al Khali
Gobi Desert

LEARN these Asian countries and their capitals. ***PRACTICE*** locating each country on the maps of Asia, pp. 49, 67, and 82.

The Middle East
Israel—Jerusalem
Lebanon—Beirut
Syria—Damascus
Jordan—Amman
Iraq—Baghdad
Saudi Arabia—Riyadh
Turkey—Ankara
Iran—Tehran

Southern Asia
India—New Delhi

The Far East
China—Beijing
Taiwan—Taipei
South Korea—Seoul
Japan—Tokyo
Thailand—Bangkok
Singapore—Singapore
Philippines—Manila

MASTER these fascinating facts. Turn the book upside down for the answers.

1. The largest continent
2. The continent with the most people
3. The world's largest lake
4. The world's highest mountain system
5. The highest mountain in the world
6. The altitude of Mt. Everest
7. The most mountainous continent
8. The mountain ranges that form boundaries between Europe and Asia
9. The world's coldest desert (outside of Antarctica)
10. The largest country in the world
11. The country with the most people

(1) Asia (2) Asia (3) Caspian Sea (4) Himalayas (5) Mt. Everest (6) 29,035 ft. (7) Asia (8) Urals/Caucasus (9) Gobi (10) Russia (11) China

CONTINENT STUDY 2 AFRICA

PRACTICE locating the following landforms and bodies of water on the world map, pp. 314–315.

Rivers
Nile River
Congo River

Deserts
Sahara
Kalahari

Mountain Range
Atlas

Mountain
Kilimanjaro

Sea
Red Sea

LEARN these African countries and their capitals. ***PRACTICE*** locating each country on the map of Africa, p. 317.

Northern Africa
Egypt—Cairo
Sudan—Khartoum

Tropical Africa
Democratic Republic of Congo—Kinshasa
Ethiopia—Addis Ababa

Tropical Africa *(cont.)*
Kenya—Nairobi
Tanzania—Dar es Salaam

Southern Africa
South Africa—Cape Town, Pretoria

MASTER these fascinating facts. Turn the book upside down for the answers.

1. The second largest continent
2. The world's longest river
3. The world's largest desert
4. Africa's highest mountain

(1) Africa (2) Nile River (3) Sahara Desert (4) Mt. Kilimanjaro

Mt. Kilimanjaro

Sahara Desert

CONTINENT STUDY 3 EUROPE

MASTER these fascinating facts. Turn the book upside down for the answers.

1. The largest country in the world
2. The only continent with no large desert
3. The world's largest lake
4. Europe's most important inland waterway
5. Europe's largest mountain system
6. The highest mountain in the Alps
7. The highest spot in Europe

(1) Russia (2) Europe (3) Caspian Sea (4) Rhine River (5) Alps (6) Mont Blanc (7) Mt. Elbrus

LEARN these European countries and their capitals. ***PRACTICE*** locating each country on the maps of Europe, pp. 201, 224, and 269.

British Isles
England—London
Wales—Cardiff
Scotland—Edinburgh
Northern Ireland—Belfast
Ireland—Dublin

Western Europe
Portugal—Lisbon
Spain—Madrid
France—Paris
Italy—Rome
Greece—Athens
Switzerland—Bern
Austria—Vienna
Germany—Berlin
Belgium—Brussels

Western Europe *(cont.)*
the Netherlands—Amsterdam
Denmark—Copenhagen
Norway—Oslo
Sweden—Stockholm
Finland—Helsinki
Iceland—Reykjavik

Eastern Europe
Russia—Moscow
Ukraine—Kiev
Poland—Warsaw
Czech Republic—Prague
Slovakia—Bratislava
Hungary—Budapest
Romania—Bucharest
Bulgaria—Sofia

PRACTICE locating the following landforms and bodies of water on the world map, pp. 314–315.

Rivers
Thames River
Rhine River
Danube River
Volga River

Seas
Norwegian Sea
North Sea
Baltic Sea
Black Sea
Caspian Sea

Seas *(cont.)*
Mediterranean Sea
Aegean Sea

Mountain Ranges
Alps
Caucasus
Urals

Mountains
Matterhorn
Mont Blanc
Elbrus

castle on the Rhine River

CONTINENT STUDY 4 AUSTRALIA, OCEANIA, & ANTARCTICA

MASTER these fascinating facts. Turn the book upside down for the answers.

1. The world's smallest continent
2. The only continent with no permanent inhabitants

(1) Australia (2) Antarctica

iceberg in Antarctica

LEARN these countries and capitals.

Australia—Canberra
New Zealand—Wellington
Papua New Guinea—Port Moresby

Gorgonian sea fans and coral, Australia

PRACTICE locating these landforms and bodies of water on the world map, pp. 314–315.

Mountain Range

Great Dividing Range

Desert

Australian *(Great Victoria and Great Sandy)*

PRACTICE locating these countries, islands, and continents on the map, p. 302.

Australia
New Zealand
Papua New Guinea
Antarctica

Milford Sound, New Zealand

Geography Facts 1

The Circle of the Earth

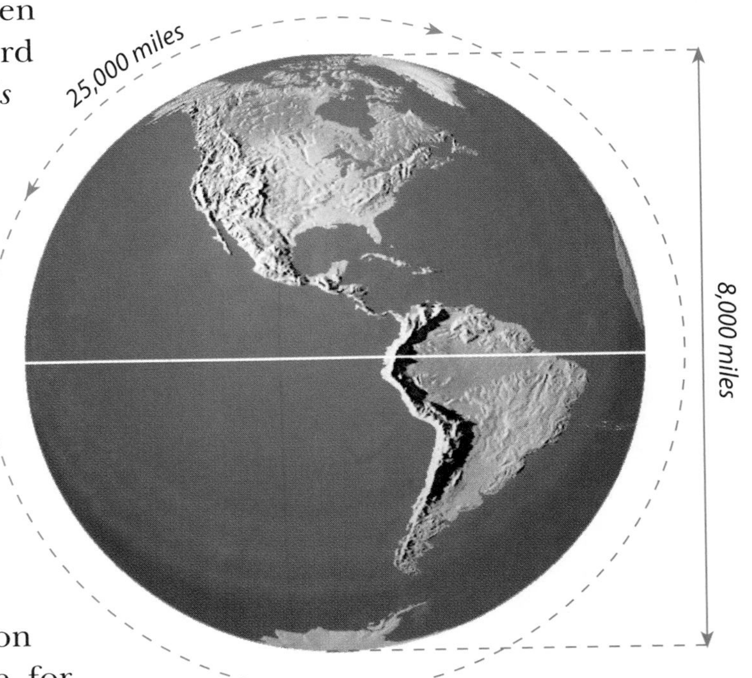

The description of the earth given in the Bible is our first written record of the geography of the earth. *"It is he that sitteth upon the circle of the earth"* (Isaiah 40:22). *"He stretcheth out the north over the empty place, and hangeth the earth upon nothing"* (Job 26:7).

When you look at a picture of the earth taken from a satellite, you can quickly see that the earth is round, or in the shape of a ball. A round ball is called a *sphere.*

The earth is a huge sphere of land and water, with air around it on all sides. (It is not a perfect sphere, for it is slightly flattened at the North Pole and the South Pole.) Most of the land is rock, but the surface of the land is covered in most places by a fine layer of gravel, sand, or soil. Even the bottom of the ocean is mostly rock. Most of the plants that we depend on for food grow in the layer of soil above the rock. In some places, the bare rock comes to the surface. Nearly all deep mines are in firm rock, and in these mines are found most of the coal and oil, and the iron ore, copper, gold, and other minerals useful to man.

The **diameter** of the earth, or the distance from side to side through the center, is nearly 8,000 miles (13,000 kilometers). The **circumference,** or the greatest distance around the earth, is about 25,000 miles (40,000 kilometers).

The Earth's Oceans and Seas

More than 70 percent of the surface of the earth is covered with water. The oceans, which are the largest bodies of water, are all connected, forming one vast body of water which we often call "the sea." The rain waters that fall to the earth and the winds that blow over the earth giving us our weather come from the sea.

Three of the oceans surround the frozen South Pole continent of Antarctica. They are the **Pacific Ocean,** the **Atlantic Ocean,** and the **Indian Ocean.** Near the North Pole, the Pacific Ocean and the Atlantic Ocean merge into the **Arctic Ocean.** ***PRACTICE*** locating the four oceans on the world map (pp. 314–315).

The **Pacific** is the world's largest ocean. It is much larger than all of earth's land put together. It covers more than one third of the earth's surface and is twice as large as any other ocean. In many places, it is 10,000 miles wide. A large number of islands rise above the surface of the Pacific Ocean.

The **Atlantic** is half the size of the Pacific and about 3,000 miles wide. It has been very important to history because it separates the American continents from Europe and Africa.

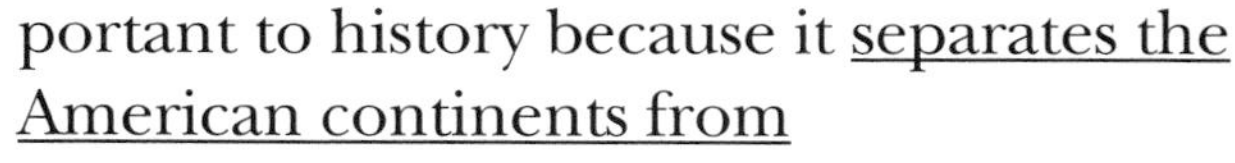

The broad arm of the sea between Africa and Australia is called the **Indian Ocean.** It is about one third the size of the Pacific Ocean. The Indian Ocean is the world's warmest ocean.

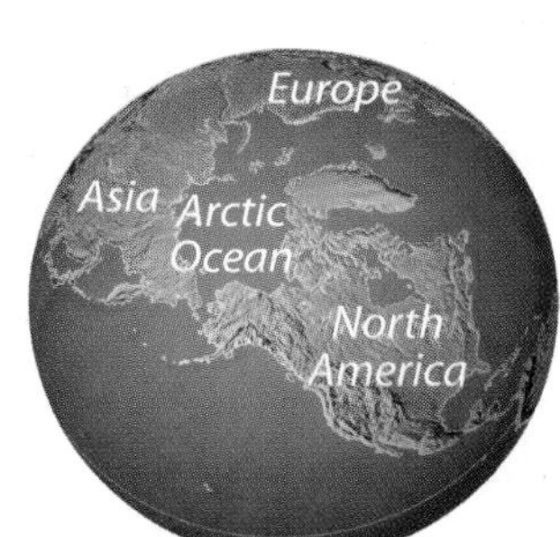

The smallest and coldest ocean, the **Arctic,** surrounds the North Pole. Most of it is frozen all year long.

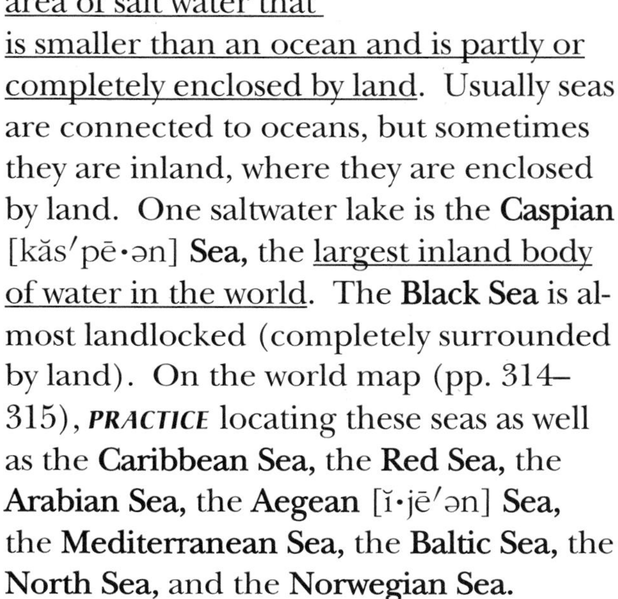

A **sea** is a large area of salt water that is smaller than an ocean and is partly or completely enclosed by land. Usually seas are connected to oceans, but sometimes they are inland, where they are enclosed by land. One saltwater lake is the **Caspian** [kăs′pē·ən] **Sea,** the largest inland body of water in the world. The **Black Sea** is almost landlocked (completely surrounded by land). On the world map (pp. 314–315), ***PRACTICE*** locating these seas as well as the **Caribbean Sea,** the **Red Sea,** the **Arabian Sea,** the **Aegean** [ĭ·jē′ən] **Sea,** the **Mediterranean Sea,** the **Baltic Sea,** the **North Sea,** and the **Norwegian Sea.**

GEOGRAPHY FACTS 3

The Seven Continents

Rising out of the earth's oceans are the **continents**—the seven largest areas of land. They are **North America, South America, Africa, Europe, Asia, Australia,** and **Antarctica.** ***PRACTICE*** locating them on the world map (pp. 314–315).

Asia is the largest continent and has the greatest population (number of people). Because Asia is connected by land to Europe, the two continents together are often referred to as **Eurasia** [yo͞o•rā′zhə].

Africa is the second largest continent and has the second greatest population. Africa was once connected to Asia by a narrow strip of land called the isthmus of Suez. (An **isthmus** is a narrow strip of land that connects two larger bodies of land.) The Suez Canal now cuts through this isthmus, making a waterway between Africa and Asia. (A **canal** is a narrow, man-made channel of water that joins other bodies of water. It is used for navigation or irrigation.)

North America and **South America** are next in size after Africa. They are separated from Europe, Asia, and Africa by the Atlantic Ocean and the Pacific Ocean. North and South America were once connected by the **isthmus of Panama,** but the Panama Canal now separates them.

At the "bottom of the world" is the frozen continent of **Antarctica.** It is the only continent where no people live, except for some explorers and scientists who live there temporarily.

Even though **Europe** is next to the smallest continent in size, it has been very important in world history.

Australia, the smallest continent, is the only continent that is also a country. It is the world's sixth largest country.

(arranged largest to smallest in area)

Continent	Asia	Africa	North America	South America	Antarctica	Europe	Australia and Oceania
Area	17,140,000 square miles	11,700,000 square miles	9,400,000 square miles	6,900,000 square miles	5,400,000 square miles	4,000,000 square miles	3,300,000 square miles
Population*	4,001,623,990	934,499,752	522,807,432	379,919,602	—	729,871,042	33,552,994

*2007 estimates

The Earth's Hemispheres

A **globe** is a map of the world in the shape of a sphere. A globe lets you easily see the shape of the earth. If you have a world globe at home, bring it to class for discussion. As you look at a globe, you can see only half of the sphere at one time. Half a sphere is called a **hemisphere.**

The earth can be divided into hemispheres at the **equator,** the imaginary line that runs halfway between the **North Pole** and the **South Pole.** All the area between the equator and the North Pole is the **Northern Hemisphere,** or the northern half of the earth. The **Southern Hemisphere** is the southern half of the earth, between the equator and the South Pole.

Another way to divide the earth into hemispheres is to divide it between east and west. The **Eastern Hemisphere** has more land,

and the **Western Hemisphere** has more water.

The Eastern Hemisphere has four continents—Europe, Asia, Africa, and Australia. The Western Hemisphere has two continents, North America and South America. The seventh continent, Antarctica, is at the southern tip of both hemispheres, all around the South Pole.

Six sevenths of the world's people live in the Eastern Hemisphere today. World history began in the Eastern Hemisphere, and all the inhabitants of the Western Hemisphere are descendants of people from the Eastern Hemisphere. This is why the Eastern Hemisphere is often called the **Old World** and the Western Hemisphere the **New World.** Even the Indians of North and South America are descendants of people who originally came from the Eastern Hemisphere.

Latitude and Longitude

Geographers (people who study the surface of the earth) have divided the globe with imaginary lines of latitude and longitude.

The **parallels of latitude** run east and west around the globe. The **equator** is the line of latitude that divides the Northern Hemisphere from the Southern Hemisphere halfway between the North Pole and the South Pole. The other latitude lines measure the distance north or south of the equator.

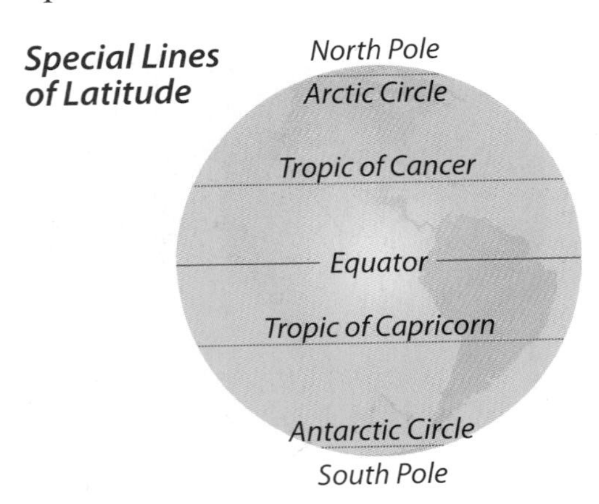

The **Arctic Circle** and the **Tropic of Cancer** are important lines of latitude in the Northern Hemisphere. The **Antarctic Circle** and the **Tropic of Capricorn** are important lines of latitude in the Southern Hemisphere.

The **lines of longitude** run north and south and come together at the North Pole and the South Pole. The lines of longitude are also called *meridians.* The **prime meridian** runs through the western parts of Europe and Africa. Its starting point goes through **Greenwich** [grĕn′ĭch], **England.** The meridians are used to measure distance east or west of the prime meridian.

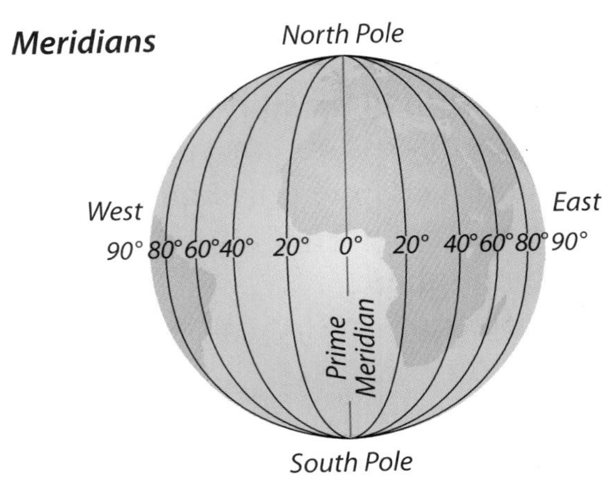

The Western Hemisphere includes the lands west of the prime meridian, and the Eastern Hemisphere includes the lands east of the prime meridian. (As you can see from the globe, the prime meridian does not divide the hemispheres exactly.)

When the lines of latitude and the lines of longitude are shown together on a map, they form a grid of squares. By using the numbers on the grid we can pinpoint any location on earth.

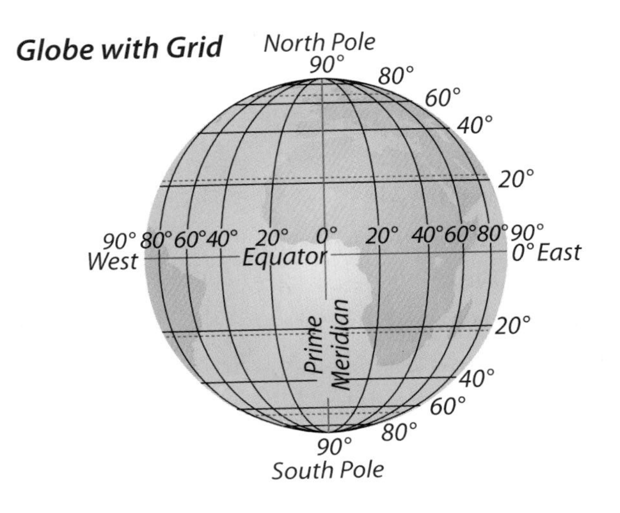

GEOGRAPHY FACTS 6

Bodies of Water

A part of a body of water smaller than a sea that reaches into the land, generally with a wide opening, is called a **bay.** A **gulf** is a part of an ocean or sea that reaches into the land. Bays and gulfs often make useful harbors. A **harbor** is a sheltered place where ships may anchor safely.

A **strait** is a narrow body of water connecting two larger bodies of water. A **channel** is similar to a strait but usually wider. The deepest part of a river or harbor is also called a channel. A man-made channel is called a **canal.** Canals are used for navigation or irrigation. A **sound** is usually wider than either a strait or a channel. Sometimes a sound separates an island from the mainland.

A **lake** is a large body of water surrounded by land. Lakes are fed by rivers or smaller streams that flow into them.

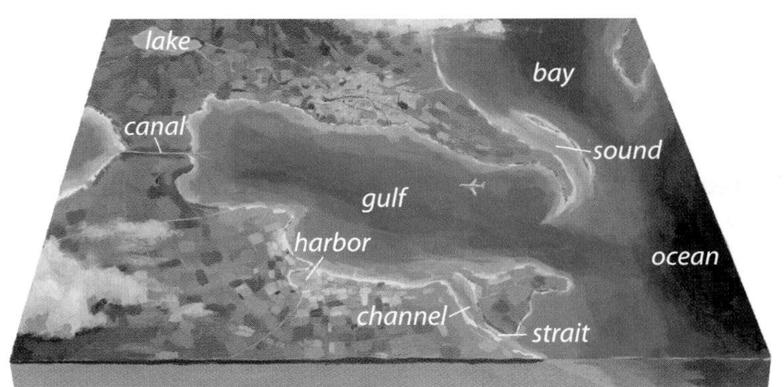

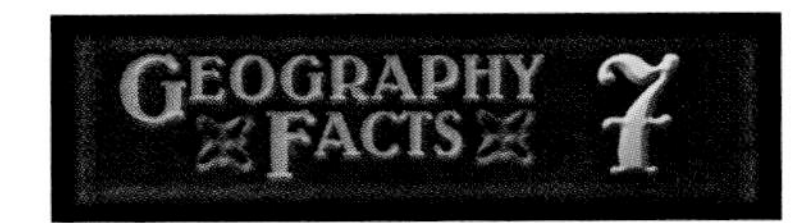

Rivers

A **river** is a large stream of fresh water flowing over the land. The beginning of a river is called its **source.** A **tributary** or **branch** is a river or creek that flows into a larger river. The **mouth** of a river is the place where the river flows into a larger body of water, such as a lake, bay, or ocean. Sometimes a river leaves soil at its mouth. The land thus deposited at the mouth of a river is called a **delta.**

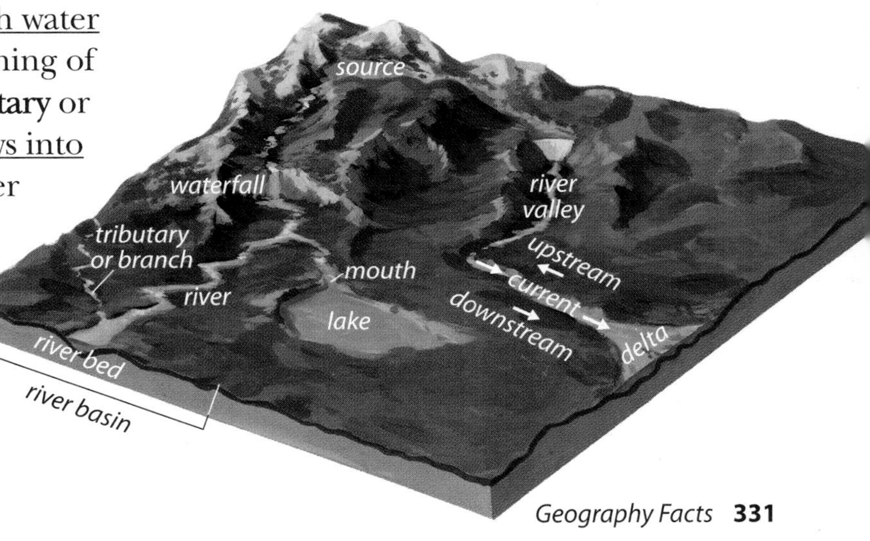

The direction in which a river flows is **downstream.** The direction from which it flows is **upstream.** If you go upstream, you have to struggle against the **current,** which is the movement of a stream of water. A part of a river where the current is swift is called a **rapids.** Sometimes the water tumbles over a cliff to form a **waterfall.**

Rivers are very important for irrigation, transportation, and energy. In modern times, dams and hydroelectric plants have been built on many rivers to provide electricity for homes and industries.

The low land through which a river flows is called a river valley. All the land drained by a river and its branches is called a **river basin.** The bottom of a river over which the water flows is called the **riverbed.**

LOCATE the following rivers on the world map, pp. 314–315.

GREAT RIVERS OF THE WORLD

NAME	LOCATION	FACTS TO REMEMBER
Nile	Africa	Longest river in the world Center of ancient Egyptian civilization
Amazon	South America	Second longest river in the world Largest river in the volume of water it carries
Congo	Africa	Second largest river in the volume of water it carries
Yangtze [yăng′sē′] *(or Chang Jiang)*	Asia	Third longest river in the world Longest and most important river in China
Huang He [hwäng′ hə′] *(formerly Hwang Ho or Yellow River)*	Asia	Center of ancient Chinese civilization
Tigris [tī′grĭs] and **Euphrates** [yo͞o·frā′tēz]	Asia	Center of the earth's earliest civilization, in Mesopotamia
Indus [ĭn′dəs]	Asia	Center of an ancient civilization in India
Volga [vŏl′gə]	Europe (Russia)	Longest river in Europe
Danube [dăn′yo͞ob]	Europe	Second longest river in Europe
Rhine	Europe	Europe's most important inland waterway
Mississippi	North America	Largest river in North America
Missouri	North America	Longest river in North America

Landforms

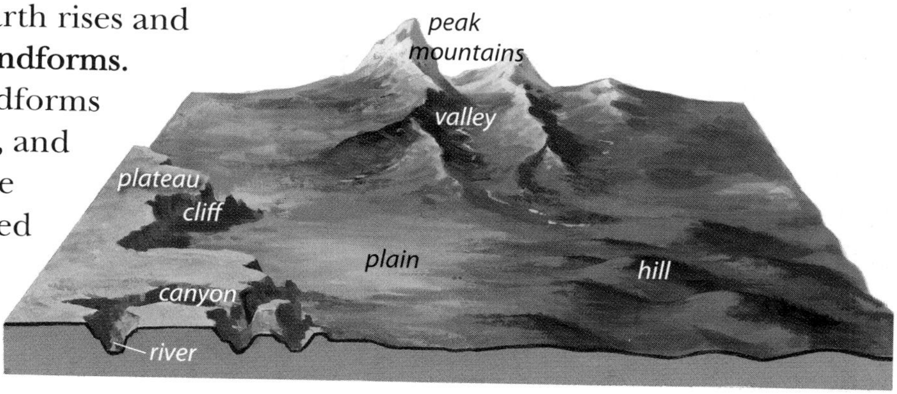

The surface of the earth rises and falls in features called **landforms.** The most important landforms are **plains, plateaus, hills,** and **mountains** which give the land an uneven and varied surface. It may surprise you to learn that the floor of the ocean is just as uneven as the land. It is covered with high mountains and very deep valleys. At its deepest part, the Pacific Ocean is almost seven miles deep. Mt. Everest, the earth's highest mountain, could be buried in it.

Plains and plateaus. A **plain** is a flat or level area of land. Most of the people in the world live on plains, for flat land is ideal for farming, and it is easier to build cities on plains than in highlands.

A **plateau** is a highland plain. Plateaus usually stand high above the surrounding country at least on one side and have flat, level tops. Plateaus often receive little rainfall, and so they are not good places to raise crops, though some people graze animals on them. They often have **canyons** (deep, narrow valleys with steep sides) and river valleys cutting through them. Few people live in most plateau areas.

Hills and mountains. Hills and mountains are similar to each other, but mountains rise higher above the surrounding land. The low land between hills or mountains is called a **valley.** Hilly or mountainous land is harder to farm than plains. About one fifth of the earth's land surface is covered with mountains. Very few people live in mountainous areas. Those who do usually make a living by mining, herding, or lumbering. Swift streams that begin in the mountains are often used to generate electric power.

The landform model above shows a cut-away section of land. How are hills different from plateaus? How are plains and plateaus different? What is the difference between a mountain and a hill?

GEOGRAPHY FACTS 9

Mountains and Mountain Ranges

About one fifth of the earth's land surface is covered with mountains. **Asia,** the most mountainous continent, has the highest mountain system in the world, the **Himalayas** [hĭm′ə· lā′əz]. The **Alps,** which are the largest mountain system in Europe, are famous for their rugged, snowcapped peaks.

The height of a mountain is not measured by its distance above the land around it, but by its distance above **sea level** (the level of the sea waters). The height above sea level is called **altitude** *or* **elevation.**

A long row of mountains is called a **mountain range.** The pointed top of a mountain is its **peak,** and the highest peak of a mountain is its **summit.**

A **volcano** is a mountain with openings in the earth's crust through which lava or steam escapes. A volcano is **active** when erupting, **dormant** during a long period of inactivity, or **extinct** when all activity has finally ceased.

PRACTICE locating the following mountains and mountain ranges on the map on pp. 314–315.

Mountain Ranges of the World

NAME	LOCATION
Rocky Mountains	Western North America
Appalachians	Eastern United States
Andes	South America
Atlas Mountains	Northwest Africa
Alps	Europe
Urals	Russia
Himalayas	Asia
Great Dividing Range	Australia

SOME FAMOUS MOUNTAINS			
NAME	ELEVATION	LOCATION	FACTS TO REMEMBER
Mt. Everest	29,035 feet	Himalayas	World's highest peak
Mt. McKinley *(also called Denali)*	20,320 feet	Alaska	North America's highest peak
Mt. Kilimanjaro [kĭl′ə·mən·jär′ō]	19,330 feet	Tanzania, Africa	Africa's highest mountain
Mt. Elbrus [ĕl·bro͞os′]	18,510 feet	European Russia	Europe's highest peak
Mt. Ararat	16,804 feet	Turkey	Landing place of Noah's Ark
Mont Blanc [mônt′ blăngk′]	15,771 feet	France	Alps' highest peak
Matterhorn	14,692 feet	Swiss-Italian Alps	Often climbed by daring mountaineers
Mt. Fuji	12,388 feet	Japan	Held as sacred and visited annually by many Japanese

The World's Great Deserts

A **desert** is a land too dry or too cold to grow many plants. Most deserts receive less than ten inches of rainfall per year. Almost one fifth of the earth's land surface is covered by desert. Every continent but Europe has at least one large desert. (Even Antarctica is mostly desert, though it is a cold desert rather than a hot desert.) The world's largest desert is the **Sahara,** in northern Africa. Find the desert areas on the climate map, p. 339.

In the torrid zone, the deserts are very hot and very dry. They have the highest temperatures on earth and the lowest precipitation (rainfall). At noon the temperature can be 110 °F or higher. At night it can be a cold 25 °F.

The plants and animals of the desert have been designed by God to conserve water so they can live in dry regions. Cactuses and desert shrubs can store water, and they lose little water by evaporation. Hardy desert **grasses** can withstand the extreme heat and dryness. The most famous animal of the desert is the camel, or dromedary [drŏm′ĭ· dĕr′ē], a one-humped camel. The camel stores fat in its hump when food and water are plentiful. When food and water are scarce, it lives off the fat in the hump, which can supply it with both food and water. In this way, it can go for a week or more without water and for ten days without food. Desert people use camels as their chief source of transportation. Camels have been called the "ships of the desert."

Few people live in the deserts, because the living conditions are almost impossible. Desert people usually live near an **oasis** [ō·ā′sĭs], <u>a desert area made fertile by the presence of water, usually from springs or wells</u>. The Nile Valley is the world's largest oasis. Many people of the desert live wandering lives, traveling on camels in **caravans,** or groups. They herd their goats, sheep, and camels with them from oasis to oasis. The best-known desert people are the wandering Arabs, or Bedouins, of the Sahara Desert. Another wandering desert tribe are the **bushmen** who live in Africa's Kalahari Desert.

Far inland, the temperate zone has some deserts that are similar in many ways to the tropical deserts. The plants and animals are very much the same. The subtropical deserts are much colder in the cold season, however, and they may be covered with snow. The **Gobi Desert** in Asia is the world's coldest desert outside of Antarctica.

PRACTICE locating the following deserts on the world map (pp. 314–315).

GREAT DESERTS OF THE WORLD

(Listed in order from largest to smallest.)

NAME	LOCATION
Sahara [sə·hâr′ə]	Africa
Gobi [gō′bē]	Asia
Patagonia [păt′ə·gō′nē·ə]	South America
Rub al Khali [ro͝ob′ ăl kä′lē]	Asia
Kalahari [kä′le·här′ē]	Africa
Australian	Australia
Taklimakan [tä′klə·mə·kän′]	Asia
Great Basin (North American)	North America

Yardan land formation, Gobi Desert

Climate Zones of the Earth

If you know the latitude of any region on earth, you can have a fairly good idea of what kind of climate it might have. The **climate** of a region is its weather conditions over a period of many years. These conditions include **temperature** (how hot or cold an area is) and **precipitation** (how much rain, snow, sleet, etc., it receives). Climate is not the same as weather. **Weather** can change from day to day, but the climate of an area is the same for many years.

Three things help determine the climate of a region: its **latitude,** its **distance from an ocean,** and its **altitude.** Latitude is the most important factor.

Climate helps to determine the kind of clothing people wear, the kind of food they are able to grow, the kind of homes they need, and their mode of transportation. It also determines the plant and animal life that will be native to an area.

Torrid Zone. The region between the Tropic of Cancer and the Tropic of Capricorn receives the most sun all year and is called the **torrid zone,** the **Tropics,** or the low latitude climates. *Torrid* means "scorching."

Frigid Zones. Between the Arctic Circle and the North Pole and between the Antarctic Circle and the South Pole are the **frigid zones,** or the high latitude climates. *Frigid* means "extremely cold." The frigid zones are cold all year.

Temperate Zones. The torrid zone and the frigid zones are areas of extremes; one is extremely hot all year and the other is extremely cold all year. You can probably understand why most of the earth's people live in between these two zones, in the **temperate zone,** or the middle latitude climates. *Temperate* means "neither very hot nor very cold." There are two temperate zones, one between the Tropic of Cancer and the Arctic Circle, and the other between the Tropic of Capricorn and the Antarctic Circle. The temperate climates are also called the **climates of seasonal change.** (A **season** is a part of a year in which the weather conditions are somewhat alike.) Most of Europe, Asia, and North America are in the North Temperate Zone. What continents have some land in the South Temperate Zone?

Many different types of climates are found within these climate zones. Study the chart on p. 338 to see the characteristics of each climate. Then check the climate map on p. 339 to see what climate your area of the world has.

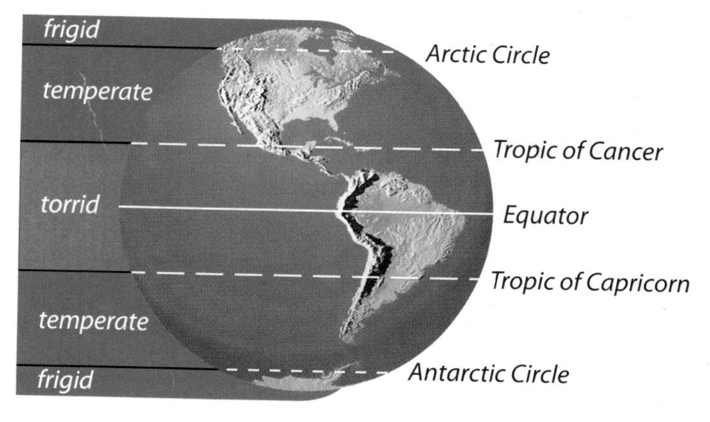

CLIMATE ZONES

POLAR CLIMATES
(always cold)
Frigid

Icecap: Frozen all year.

Tundra: Extremely cold. A few months above freezing, but never warm. Some small plants grow, but no trees.

CONTINENTAL
(seasonal extremes)
Temperate

Subpolar: Very cold winters, cool summers. Cone-bearing trees (conifers) grow in vast forests, often called *taigas.*

Humid Continental: Cold winters, warm to hot summers. Rainfall decreases toward interior of continent. Vegetation can be trees or prairies. Found in middle latitudes, on continents of Northern Hemisphere.

MILD
Temperate

Marine West Coast: Mild winters, cool summers. Rainfall all year. Trees grow well. Usually found on western coasts of continents.

Humid Subtropics: Mild winters and hot, moist summers. Trees grow well. Usually on eastern sides of continents, near tropics.

Mediterranean: Mild winters with some rain and hot, dry summers. Scattered, small trees, woody shrubs, and some grasses grow. Found on western sides of continents.

TROPICAL CLIMATES
(always hot)
Torrid

Savanna: Warm to hot all year. Dry in winter. Tall, tough grasses and some trees grow. Found between tropical forests and desert regions.

Rain forest: Always hot and humid, with thick forests, vines. Found at or near the Equator.

DRY CLIMATES
(always dry)
Torrid, Temperate

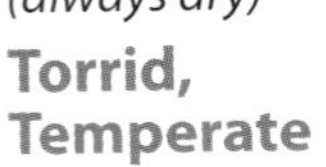

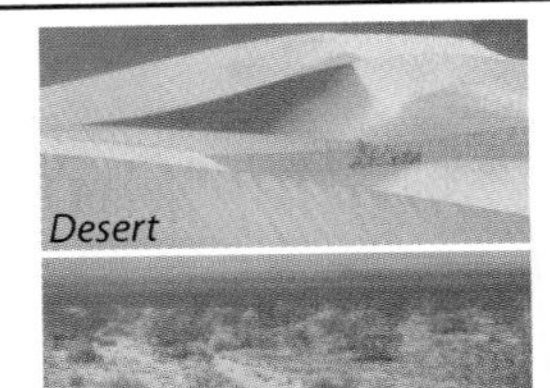

Desert: Very little or almost no rainfall. Tropical deserts are hot all year. Middle-latitude deserts have colder winters. Cacti, shrubs, and sparse grasses grow.

Steppe: Little rainfall. In tropical regions, temperatures always warm. In middle latitudes, winters are cold. Mostly short grasses grow with no trees.

HIGHLAND CLIMATES
(climate caused by elevation)

Highlands: Mountain regions of high elevation. Temperatures get colder as elevation increases. At higher elevations trees cannot grow, and only tundra plants can live. Highest elevations are ice covered.

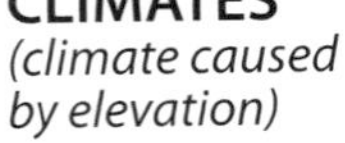

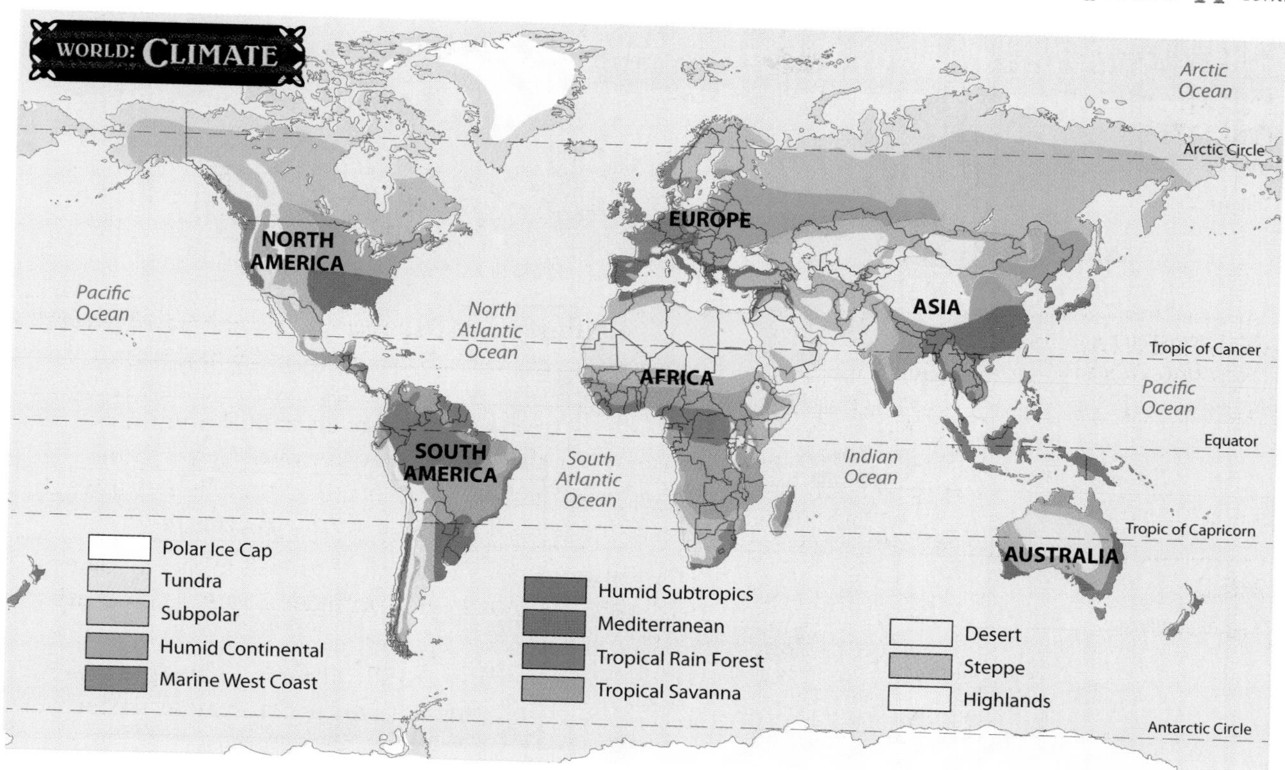
WORLD: CLIMATE
Arctic Ocean
Arctic Circle
EUROPE
NORTH AMERICA
ASIA
Pacific Ocean
North Atlantic Ocean
Tropic of Cancer
AFRICA
Pacific Ocean
Equator
SOUTH AMERICA
South Atlantic Ocean
Indian Ocean
Tropic of Capricorn
AUSTRALIA
Polar Ice Cap
Tundra
Subpolar
Humid Continental
Marine West Coast
Humid Subtropics
Mediterranean
Tropical Rain Forest
Tropical Savanna
Desert
Steppe
Highlands
Antarctic Circle

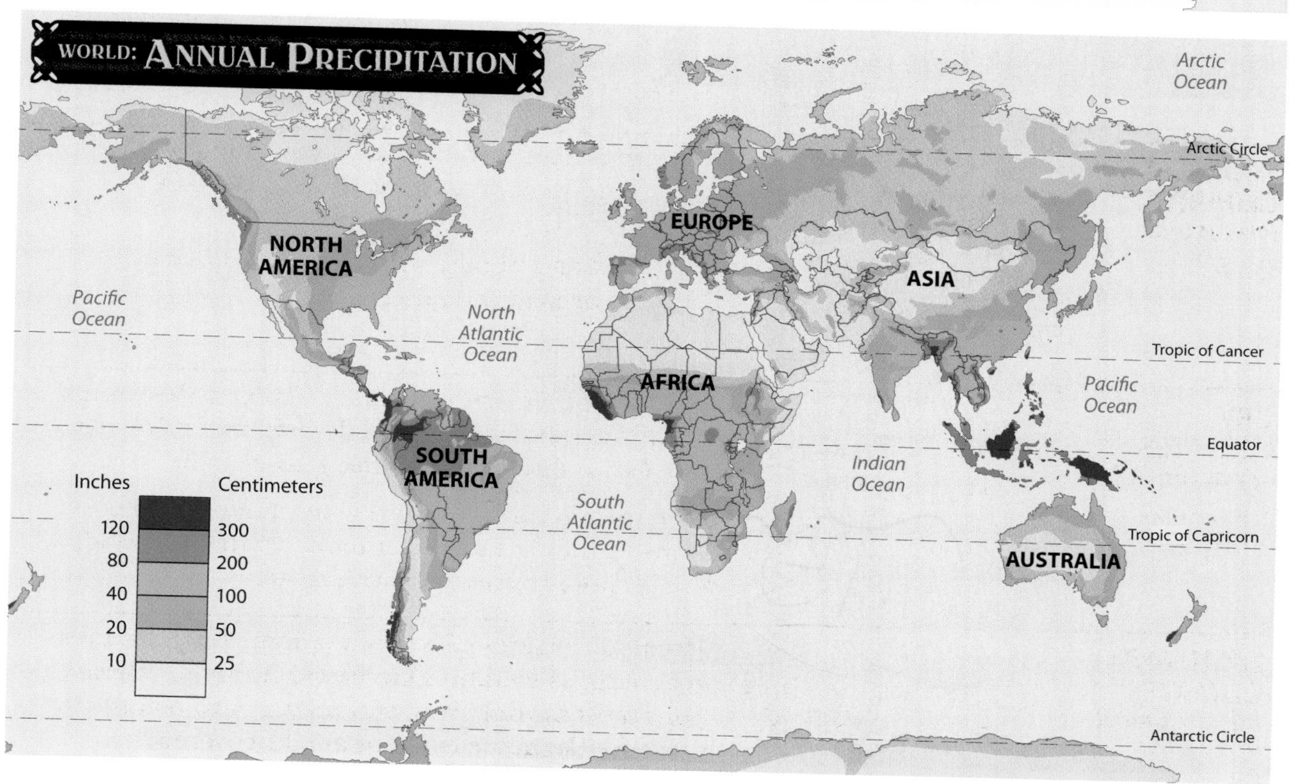
WORLD: ANNUAL PRECIPITATION
Arctic Ocean
Arctic Circle
EUROPE
NORTH AMERICA
ASIA
Pacific Ocean
North Atlantic Ocean
Tropic of Cancer
AFRICA
Pacific Ocean
Equator
SOUTH AMERICA
Indian Ocean
Inches
Centimeters
120
300
80
200
40
100
20
50
10
25
South Atlantic Ocean
Tropic of Capricorn
AUSTRALIA
Antarctic Circle

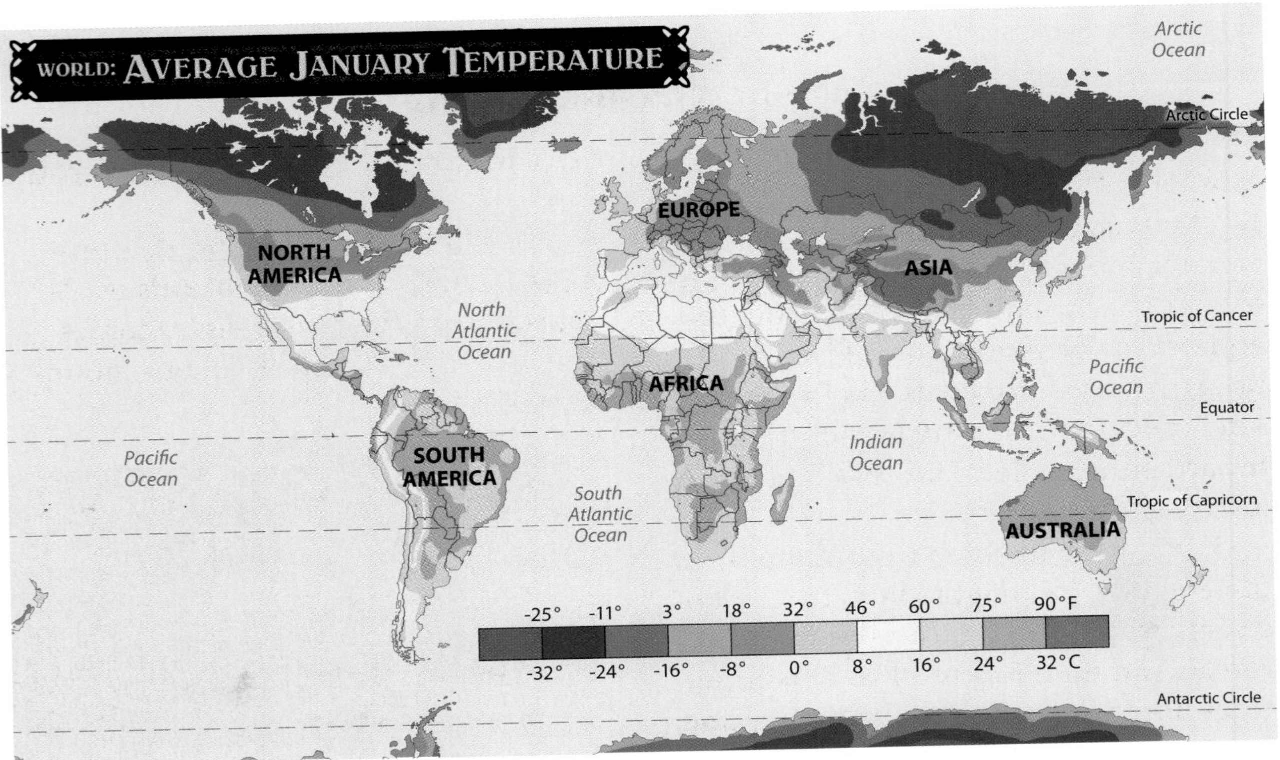
WORLD: AVERAGE JANUARY TEMPERATURE
Arctic Ocean
Arctic Circle
EUROPE
NORTH AMERICA
ASIA
North Atlantic Ocean
Tropic of Cancer
Pacific Ocean
AFRICA
Equator
Pacific Ocean
SOUTH AMERICA
Indian Ocean
South Atlantic Ocean
Tropic of Capricorn
AUSTRALIA
-25° -11° 3° 18° 32° 46° 60° 75° 90°F
-32° -24° -16° -8° 0° 8° 16° 24° 32°C
Antarctic Circle

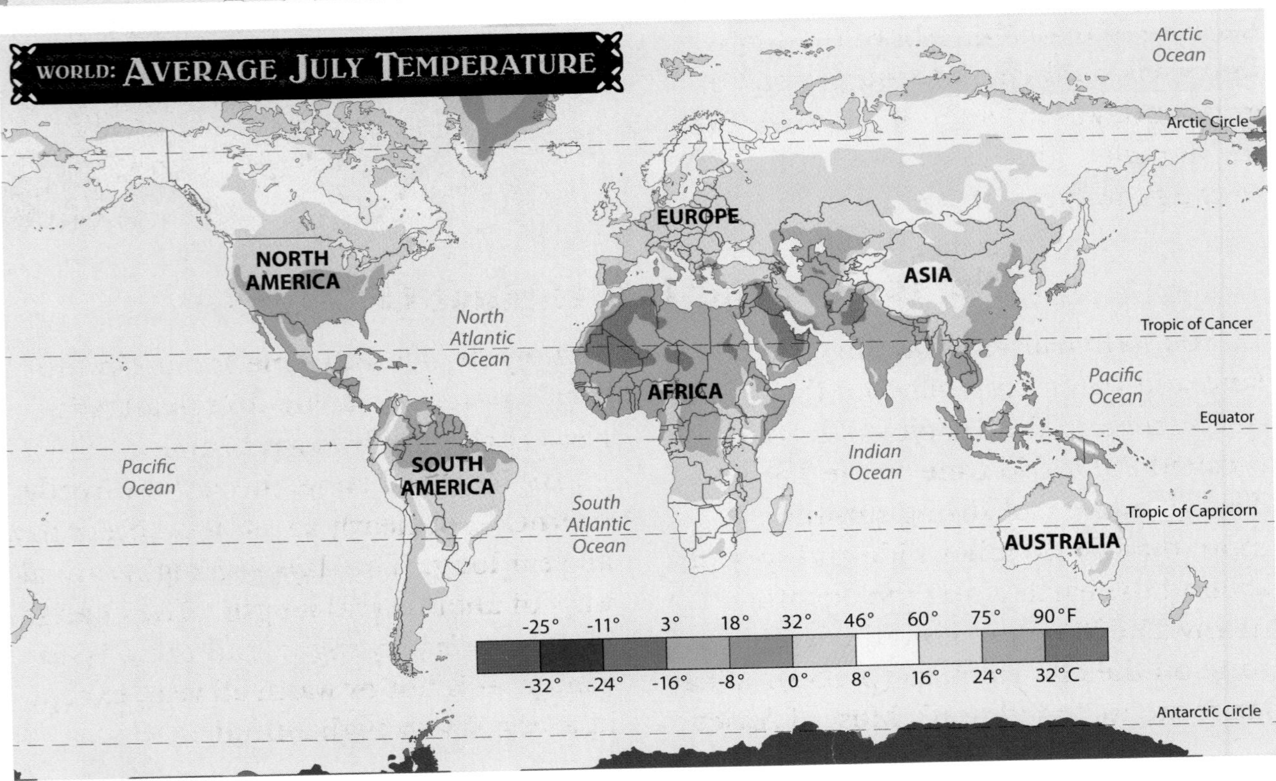
WORLD: AVERAGE JULY TEMPERATURE
Arctic Ocean
Arctic Circle
EUROPE
NORTH AMERICA
ASIA
North Atlantic Ocean
Tropic of Cancer
AFRICA
Pacific Ocean
Equator
Pacific Ocean
SOUTH AMERICA
Indian Ocean
South Atlantic Ocean
Tropic of Capricorn
AUSTRALIA
-25° -11° 3° 18° 32° 46° 60° 75° 90°F
-32° -24° -16° -8° 0° 8° 16° 24° 32°C
Antarctic Circle

Mountains and Climate

High in the mountains, the air is thinner and colder than the air below. By climbing a high mountain near the equator, a person may feel the same changes in climate as in going from the equator to the North Pole. Five miles up in the air is as cold as it is five **thousand** miles along the surface of the earth toward either pole. This is how **altitude** affects climate.

If you were to climb a mountain near the equator, you might climb from a hot, steamy tropical rain forest to broadleaf forests and then forests of cone-bearing trees until you arrived at the **timber line,** a point beyond which trees cannot grow because of the cold. Above the timber line you would climb through a steep grassland, which might be used for grazing animals. Finally, you would come to the **snow line.** Above the snow line, there is snow on the mountains all year long.

The climate in high mountainous areas is often called a **highlands** or alpine climate. The word *alpine* comes from the Alps, the most famous mountains of Europe.

The Torrid Zone: Low Latitude Climates

You have learned that the wide belt of land and water lying between the Tropic of Cancer and the Tropic of Capricorn is called the **torrid zone** or the **Tropics.** This great zone of strong sunshine is more than 3,000 miles wide and spreads around the earth along the equator nearly 25,000 miles. Find the torrid zone on the climate map (p. 339). What lands are included in it? Most of Africa and much of South America are in the torrid zone. India and Southeast Asia also reach into the torrid zone.

In the torrid zone, the sun is directly overhead, or nearly so, at noon every day, all year long. The days and nights are always of about equal length. The change of seasons is very slight, and there is no winter. It is hot or warm all year, except in areas of very high altitude.

Tropical Rain Forests

Near the equator in Africa, Asia, Central America, South America, and the islands of the Pacific are lush, green rain forests. Check the climate map (p. 339) to find where the tropical rain forests are. Which continents have no tropical forests? Why is this true for Antarctica?

The temperature is **always hot** in the rain forests, usually about 80 °F. Heavy rains fall almost every day of the year, making the air very **humid.** The trees are tall, broad-leaf evergreens, and heavy vines grow up many of them. The trees form a **canopy** [kăn′ə·pē: covering] high up in the air, making the forest floor a dark place where few shrubs or grasses can grow. Brightly colored flowers grow on trees and vines. Many trees yield sweet-tasting fruits, and there is always some kind of fruit growing, no matter what time of year it is. *More kinds of trees grow in the tropical rain forests than anywhere else on earth.*

Countless parrots and other birds of beautiful colors live in these forests, and insects are abundant. There are more species of amphibians [ăm·fĭb′ĭ·ənz], birds, insects, mammals, and reptiles in rain forests than anywhere else in the world. Monkeys, sloths, bats, frogs, lizards, and snakes feed up in the trees. On the forest floors are anteaters with tongues nearly two feet long, tigers, leopards, lions, and gorillas.

Until very modern times, few people lived in the rain forests. Those who did live there led very simple lives and had few needs. They were often inactive rather than industrious because of the hot, humid weather and because food came easily to them and they had few responsibilities. A **temporary hut** made of grasses or palm leaves was often all the shelter they needed, and they did not need many clothes for warmth. Since they could find fresh fruits and animals for meat in the jungle all year long, they did not need to develop ways of storing and preserving food; they had little need for trade. For **transportation,** they either made simple river boats or walked. They often lived in tribes, led by a chief who had all power. Some tribes in the rain forests cleared a small patch of land by chopping down trees and burning the brush. They grew crops there until the good soil was used up, and then they moved on to another place. Some tribes in the rain forests still live in primitive ways, but there are also large, modern cities in the rain forests today.

Tropical Savannas

Tropical savannas are vast areas of grasslands that are often located above and below rain forests. Locate them on the climate map (p. 339). A **savanna** is a plain covered with thick grass. The savannas have two very distinct seasons—the **dry season,** when little or no rain falls and the temperature often rises to 100 °F; and the **wet season,** when rain falls in abundance and the rivers become raging torrents. A savanna is characterized by **hot, dry summers** and **hot, rainy winters.**

Tall, tough grass is the main vegetation (plant life) of the savannas. A few trees grow in scattered areas. Closer to the rain forests, the vegetation becomes more abundant.

The savannas of Africa are especially noted for the huge animals that roam through the sea of grass, often grazing in large herds. Elephants, giraffes, zebras, rhinoceroses, hippopotamuses, gnus [n͞o͞oz], antelopes, and fierce African buffaloes live there. In some areas many of these animals have been killed by hunters, but the Africans have set up large parks to protect them. Crocodiles sun themselves along the muddy banks of the streams. Huge termite mounds dot the landscape. Snakes and lizards abound, and swiftly running ostriches can often be seen.

The people of the savannas often live in tribes, and many of them are excellent hunters as well as farmers. They grow corn, wheat, pumpkins, peas, beans, and sweet potatoes. In Africa, they also grow cotton and peanuts. Many of them raise cattle for milk. They trade regularly with other tribes. In the modern cities, there are factories for processing farm products and harbors for shipping and trade.

African savanna

Document Memorization

Documents are an important part of the history of our United States. Memorizing these historical documents will help you understand why America has become such a great nation. As you learn each document, you will get a glimpse of the thoughts and ideas of our Founding Fathers and of other patriotic Americans throughout history. You will also learn our fifty states and capitals and the names of our Presidents.

The American's Creed *(4 weeks)*

I believe in the United States of America as a government of the people, by the people, for the people, whose just powers are derived from the consent of the governed; a democracy in a republic; a sovereign Nation of many sovereign States; a perfect Union, one and inseparable; established upon those principles of freedom, equality, justice, and humanity for which American patriots sacrificed their lives and fortunes.

I therefore believe it is my duty to my country to love it, to support its Constitution, to obey its laws, to respect its flag, and to defend it against all enemies.

—William Tyler Page

from The Declaration of Independence *(6 weeks)*

In Congress, July 4, 1776

When, in the course of human events, it becomes necessary for one people to dissolve the political bands which have connected them with another, and to assume, among the powers of the earth, the separate and equal station to which the laws of nature and of nature's God entitle them, a decent respect to the opinions of mankind requires that they should declare the causes which impel them to the separation.

We hold these truths to be self-evident:—That all men are created equal; that they are endowed by their Creator with certain unalienable rights; that among these are life, liberty, and the pursuit of happiness. That, to secure these rights, governments are instituted among men, deriving their just powers from the consent of the governed; that, whenever any form of government becomes destructive of these ends, it is the right of the people to alter or to abolish it, and to institute new government, laying its foundation on such principles, and organising its powers in such form, as to them shall seem most likely to effect their safety and happiness. Prudence, indeed, will dictate that governments long established should not be changed for light and transient causes; and, accordingly, all experience hath shown that mankind are more disposed to suffer, while evils are sufferable, than to right themselves by abolishing the forms to which they are accustomed. But, when a long train of abuses and usurpations, pursuing invariably the same object, evinces a design to reduce them under absolute despotism, it is their right, it is their duty, to throw off such government, and to provide new guards for their future security. . . .

Preamble to the Constitution (2 weeks)

We the people of the United States, in order to form a more perfect Union, establish justice, insure domestic tranquillity, provide for the common defense, promote the general welfare, and secure the blessings of liberty to ourselves and our posterity, do ordain and establish this Constitution for the United States of America.

First Amendment to the Constitution (2 weeks)

Congress shall make no law respecting an establishment of religion, or prohibiting the free exercise thereof; or abridging the freedom of speech, or of the press; or the right of the people peaceably to assemble, and to petition the government for a redress of grievances.

The Rights of Americans (2 weeks)

1. **The right to** worship God in one's own way.
2. **The right to** free speech and press.
3. **The right to** petition for grievances—in fair and honest judgment.
4. **The right to** privacy in our homes.
5. **The right to** own private property.
6. **The right to** own, keep, and bear arms.
7. **The right to** move about freely at home or abroad.
8. **The right to** habeas corpus—without excessive bail.
9. **The right to** trial by jury—innocent until proven guilty.
10. **The right to** free elections and personal secret ballots.
11. **The right to** the service of government as a protector and referee.
12. **The right to** freedom from arbitrary government regulation and control.
13. **The right to** work in callings and localities of our choice.
14. **The right to** bargain for goods and services in a free market.
15. **The right to** contract about our affairs.
16. **The right to** go into business, compete, and make a profit.

Lincoln's Gettysburg Address *(6 weeks)*

Fourscore and seven years ago our fathers brought forth upon this continent a new nation, conceived in liberty, and dedicated to the proposition that all men are created equal.

Now we are engaged in a great civil war, testing whether that nation, or any nation so conceived and so dedicated, can long endure. We are met on a great battlefield of that war. We have come to dedicate a portion of that field as a final resting place for those who here gave their lives that that nation might live. It is altogether fitting and proper that we should do this.

But, in a larger sense, we cannot dedicate—we cannot consecrate—we cannot hallow—this ground. The brave men, living and dead, who struggled here, have consecrated it far above our poor power to add or detract. The world will little note nor long remember what we say here, but it can never forget what they did here. It is for us, the living, rather, to be dedicated here to the unfinished work which they who fought here have thus far so nobly advanced. It is rather for us to be here dedicated to the task remaining before us—that from these honored dead we take increased devotion to that cause for which they gave the last full measure of devotion; that we here highly resolve that these dead shall not have died in vain; that this nation, under God, shall have a new birth of freedom; and that government of the people, by the people, for the people, shall not perish from the earth.

States and Capitals (6 weeks)

(Memorize States and Capitals)

State	Capital	Abbreviations*	Date of Admission	Order of Admission	Popular Name†
Alabama	Montgomery	Ala., AL	1819	22	Heart of Dixie
Alaska	Juneau	Alaska, AK	1959	49	Last Frontier
Arizona	Phoenix	Ariz., AZ	1912	48	Grand Canyon State
Arkansas	Little Rock	Ark., AR	1836	25	Natural State
California	Sacramento	Calif., CA	1850	31	Golden State
Colorado	Denver	Colo., CO	1876	38	Centennial State
Connecticut	Hartford	Conn., CT	1788	5	Constitution State
Delaware	Dover	Del., DE	1787	1	First State
Florida	Tallahassee	Fla., FL	1845	27	Sunshine State
Georgia	Atlanta	Ga., GA	1788	4	Empire State of the South
Hawaii	Honolulu	Hawaii, HI	1959	50	Aloha State
Idaho	Boise	Idaho, ID	1890	43	Gem State
Illinois	Springfield	Ill., IL	1818	21	Prairie State
Indiana	Indianapolis	Ind., IN	1816	19	Hoosier State
Iowa	Des Moines	Iowa, IA	1846	29	Hawkeye State
Kansas	Topeka	Kans., KS	1861	34	Sunflower State
Kentucky	Frankfort	Ky., KY	1792	15	Bluegrass State
Louisiana	Baton Rouge	La., LA	1812	18	Pelican State
Maine	Augusta	Maine, ME	1820	23	Pine Tree State
Maryland	Annapolis	Md., MD	1788	7	Old Line State
Massachusetts	Boston	Mass., MA	1788	6	Bay State
Michigan	Lansing	Mich., MI	1837	26	Great Lakes State
Minnesota	St. Paul	Minn., MN	1858	32	North Star State
Mississippi	Jackson	Miss., MS	1817	20	Magnolia State
Missouri	Jefferson City	Mo., MO	1821	24	Show Me State

*The standard abbreviation is given first. The second abbreviation should be used with ZIP code.

†Popular names taken from *The World Almanac and Book of Facts 2008.*

State	Capital	Abbreviations*	Date of Admission	Order of Admission	Popular Name†
Montana	Helena	Mont., MT	1889	41	Treasure State
Nebraska	Lincoln	Nebr., NE	1867	37	Cornhusker State
Nevada	Carson City	Nev., NV	1864	36	Sagebrush State
New Hampshire	Concord	N.H., NH	1788	9	Granite State
New Jersey	Trenton	N.J., NJ	1787	3	Garden State
New Mexico	Santa Fe	N.Mex., NM	1912	47	Land of Enchantment
New York	Albany	N.Y., NY	1788	11	Empire State
North Carolina	Raleigh	N.C., NC	1789	12	Tar Heel State
North Dakota	Bismarck	N.Dak., ND	1889	39	Peach Garden State
Ohio	Columbus	Ohio, OH	1803	17	Buckeye State
Oklahoma	Oklahoma City	Okla., OK	1907	46	Sooner State
Oregon	Salem	Oreg., OR	1859	33	Beaver State
Pennsylvania	Harrisburg	Pa., PA	1787	2	Keystone State
Rhode Island	Providence	R.I., RI	1790	13	Little Rhody
South Carolina	Columbia	S.C., SC	1788	8	Palmetto State
South Dakota	Pierre	S.Dak., SD	1889	40	Coyote State
Tennessee	Nashville	Tenn., TN	1796	16	Volunteer State
Texas	Austin	Tex., TX	1845	28	Lone Star State
Utah	Salt Lake City	Utah, UT	1896	45	Beehive State
Vermont	Montpelier	Vt., VT	1791	14	Green Mountain State
Virginia	Richmond	Va., VA	1788	10	Old Dominion
Washington	Olympia	Wash., WA	1889	42	Evergreen State
West Virginia	Charleston	W.Va., WV	1863	35	Mountain State
Wisconsin	Madison	Wis., WI	1848	30	Badger State
Wyoming	Cheyenne	Wyo., WY	1890	44	Equality State

*The standard abbreviation is given first. The second abbreviation should be used with ZIP code.

†Popular names taken from *The World Almanac and Book of Facts 2008.*

United States Presidents *(6 weeks)*

(Memorize Presidents in Order)

No.	Name	Born / Died	Years in Office	State of Birth	State of Residence When Elected
1	**George Washington**	1732–1799	1789–1797	Va.	Va.
2	**John Adams**	1735–1826	1797–1801	Mass.	Mass.
3	**Thomas Jefferson**	1743–1826	1801–1809	Va.	Va.
4	**James Madison**	1751–1836	1809–1817	Va.	Va.
5	**James Monroe**	1758–1831	1817–1825	Va.	Va.
6	**John Quincy Adams**	1767–1848	1825–1829	Mass.	Mass.
7	**Andrew Jackson**	1767–1845	1829–1837	S.C.	Tenn.
8	**Martin Van Buren**	1782–1862	1837–1841	N.Y.	N.Y.
9	**William Henry Harrison**	1773–1841	1841	Va.	Ohio
10	**John Tyler**	1790–1862	1841–1845	Va.	Va.
11	**James K. Polk**	1795–1849	1845–1849	N.C.	Tenn.
12	**Zachary Taylor**	1784–1850	1849–1850	Va.	La.
13	**Millard Fillmore**	1800–1874	1850–1853	N.Y.	N.Y.
14	**Franklin Pierce**	1804–1869	1853–1857	N.H.	N.H.
15	**James Buchanan**	1791–1868	1857–1861	Pa.	Pa.
16	**Abraham Lincoln**	1809–1865	1861–1865	Ky.	Ill.
17	**Andrew Johnson**	1808–1875	1865–1869	N.C.	Tenn.
18	**Ulysses S. Grant**	1822–1885	1869–1877	Ohio	Ill.
19	**Rutherford B. Hayes**	1822–1893	1877–1881	Ohio	Ohio
20	**James A. Garfield**	1831–1881	1881	Ohio	Ohio
21	**Chester A. Arthur**	1830–1886	1881–1885	Vt.	N.Y.
22	**Grover Cleveland**	1837–1908	1885–1889	N.J.	N.Y.

No.	Name	Born/Died	Years in Office	State of Birth	State of Residence When Elected
23	**Benjamin Harrison**	1833–1901	1889–1893	Ohio	Ind.
24	**Grover Cleveland**	1837–1908	1893–1897	N.J.	N.Y.
25	**William McKinley**	1843–1901	1897–1901	Ohio	Ohio
26	**Theodore Roosevelt**	1858–1919	1901–1909	N.Y.	N.Y.
27	**William Howard Taft**	1857–1930	1909–1913	Ohio	Ohio
28	**Woodrow Wilson**	1856–1924	1913–1921	Va.	N.J.
29	**Warren G. Harding**	1865–1923	1921–1923	Ohio	Ohio
30	**Calvin Coolidge**	1872–1933	1923–1929	Vt.	Mass.
31	**Herbert Hoover**	1874–1964	1929–1933	Iowa	Calif.
32	**Franklin D. Roosevelt**	1882–1945	1933–1945	N.Y.	N.Y.
33	**Harry S. Truman**	1884–1972	1945–1953	Mo.	Mo.
34	**Dwight D. Eisenhower**	1890–1969	1953–1961	Tex.	N.Y.
35	**John F. Kennedy**	1917–1963	1961–1963	Mass.	Mass.
36	**Lyndon B. Johnson**	1908–1973	1963–1969	Tex.	Tex.
37	**Richard M. Nixon**	1913–1994	1969–1974	Calif.	N.Y.
38	**Gerald R. Ford**	1913–2006	1974–1977	Nebr.	Mich.
39	**James E. Carter**	1924	1977–1981	Ga.	Ga.
40	**Ronald Reagan**	1911–2004	1981–1989	Ill.	Calif.
41	**George Bush**	1924	1989–1993	Mass.	Tex.
42	**William J. Clinton**	1946	1993–2001	Ark.	Ark.
43	**George W. Bush**	1946	2001–2009	Conn.	Tex.
44	**Barack Obama**	1961	2009–	Hawaii	Ill.

Index

Page numbers for illustrations are indicated by a *p* and printed in *italic type.*

A

B

C

D

E

F

G

H

I

J

K

L

M

N

O

P

Q

R

S

T

U

V

W

Y

Scripture Index

Credits

Credits are listed from left to right, top to bottom on a page. If all photos on a page are from the same source, the credit is listed only once. Materials provided by the publisher (ABB) is credited only to clarify location of other photos. Abbreviations used: AA—Animals Animals; CB—Corbis; CI—Corbis Images; CC—Corel Corporation; ES—Earth Scenes; GI—Getty Images; GR—The Granger Collection, New York; IS—istockphoto.com; NAS—National Audubon Society Collection; NGIS—National Geographic Image Sales, PR—Photo Researchers, Inc. All map/globe images throughout the book are adapted from Mountain High Maps® copyright ©1997 Digital Wisdom Inc.

Front cover—Karim Hesham/IS, Rick Hyman/IS, Javier Garcia/IS, Alexander Hafemann/IS; back cover—Hedda Gjerpen/IS, David Ciemny/IS; title page—Karim Hesham/IS; backgrounds throughout book—textures CB, world map Peter Zelei/IS; vi—CB, CB, Y. T. Wong/IS, CB, CB; 6—Pool/Reuters/CB, John Van Hasselt/CB, Francois G. Durand/GI; 7—GR; 10—Ricky Hyman/IS, Richard Sobol/AA, CB, ABB, Dale Walsh/IS, Brian Chase/IS, David Butow/CB SABA, James Hager/Robert Harding World Imagery/CB, Stockbyte, CC, CB, CC, TH Foto-Werbung/PR, CI, CC, Dusko Matic/IS, CC, Eric Isselée/IS, CB, CC, CC, CB, CB, CC, Marcel Boehmelt/IS; 11—Georg Gerster/PR; 12—Jane Sweeney/JAI/CB; 14—GR; 15—Tom Hahn/IS, GR; 16—Richard T. Nowitz/PR; 17—Georg Gerster/PR; 18, 20—GR; 22—Frans Lemmens/zefa/CB; 23—CC; 26—Dani-Jeske/ES/AA; 28—CC, GI; 29—GR; 30—CC; 31—GR; 32—Hanan Isachar/CB; 33—CC; 38—GR; 39—Bettmann/CB; 40—Gianni Dagli Orti/CB; 41—Bettmann/CB; 42—Michael Freeman/CB; 44—GR; 50—CC; 51—John C. Stevenson/AA; 52—Jeffrey L. Rotman/CB; 54-55—CC; 56—Photri Images, J. Gerard Sidaner/PR, Atlantide Phototravel/CB; 57—Photri Images; 58—David Weintraub/PR, Owen Franken/CB, AFP/GI; 59—Mehmet Biber/PR; 60—CC; 61—Murat Taner/GI, Catherine Ursillo/PR, DEA/G. Cigolini/GI; 62—AEP/GI; 65—David Ciemny/IS; 66—GR; 68—Lindsay Hebberd/CB; 69—Hubertus Kanus/PR; 70—CB; 72—GR; 73—Bettmann/CB; 74—Steve Raymer/NGIS, AFP/GI; 75—Simon Fraser/PR, Atlantide Phototravel/CB, Alison Wright/PR; 80—CB, David Samuel Robbins/CB; 83—GR, James Davis Eye Ubiquitous/CB; 84—CC; 85—Bettmann/CB; 87—GR; 88—Michael S. Yamashita/CB; 89—Michael Flippo/IS; 90—CC, CC, CI; 92—David Turnley/CB; 93—Uwe Halstenbach/IS; 94—Bettmann/CB, Dusko Matic/IS, Bob Krist/CB; 95—Jose Fuste Raga/CB; 96—Bettmann/CB, JP Laffont/Sygma/CB, Bettmann/CB; 97—CB; 98—Craig Hansen/IS, Free Agents Limited/CB; 100—Jose Fuste Raga/zefa/CB; 104—Photri Images, Eric Isselée/IS, CC, CC, CI, CC, CB, CC, Jupiterimages, CC, CC, CC, Eric Isselée/IS, Jupiterimages, Mark Evans/IS, CC, CI, CI, Peter Johnson/CB, Adobe, Alain Couillaud/IS; 105—Holger Mette/IS; 107—O. Alamany & E. Vicens/CB, CC; 108—GR; 111—Patrick Robert/Sygma/CB; 112—Bettmann/CB, GR; 113—Domin Domin/IS; 114—CC, Photri Images, GR, Photri Images, Fred J. Maroon/PR, Photri Images; 116—CC; 117, 119—GR; 121—Oversnap/IS, 122—Hermanus Karel/IS; 123—Michael Freeman/CB; 124—Klaas Lingbeek-van Kranen/IS, Bettmann/CB; 126—Bruno Morandi/Robert Harding World Imagery/CB, CC; 127—GR; 128—Georg Gerster/NAS/PR; 129—GR; 132—Stapleton Collection/CB; 136—Frans Lemmens/zefa/CB; 137—Photri Images; 138—Atlantide Phototravel/CB, Robert Holmes/CB; 139—Lloyd Cluff/CB, Adrian Beesley/IS; 140—Candace Feit/Reuters/CB; 141—GR, Nigel Cattlin/PR; 142—Art Wolfe/PR, Tom McHugh/NAS/PR; 143—Frank van den Bergh/IS; 144—Jacques Pavlovsky/Sygma/CB, Martin Harvey/CB; 145—Heinrich Sanden/dpa/CB; 146—CC; 147—Gerard Lacz/AA; 148—Tom & Pat Leeson/PR, Dirk Freder/IS, Adobe; 149—Nico Smit/IS; 150—Hubertus Kanus/PR; 152—STR/epa/CB, Emily Riddell/Grant Heilman Photography, James P. Blair/NGIS; 153—Dave G. Houser/CB; 156—CB, Marko Heuver/IS, Adam Woolfitt/CB, CC, CB, CI, CC, CB, CB, CB, CB, CC, MRusty/IS, Merce Bellera/IS, CB, CB, CC, CB, Zyuzin Andriy/IS, Jeremy Voisey/IS, CB, Asier Villafranca Velasco/IS; 158—Bettmann/CB, Gianni Dagli Orti/CB; 159—Bettmann/CB; 160—Ted Spiegel/CB; 161—CC, CB; 162, 166—GR; 174—GR, Jason Kandel/IS; 175—George Haling/PR; 177—GR; 178—Bettmann/CB; 180—John Ross/PR, GR; 181—Richard T. Nowitz/CB; 184—GR, Bettmann/CB; 185—CB, ABB; 186—Bettmann/CB; 187—Historical Pictures Archive/CB; 189—GR; 190—Cristian Santinon/IS; 191—Gerard Rancinan/Sygma/CB, Helena Shlyapina/IS; 192—Bettmann/CB; 193-194, 196—GR; 200—Hulton-Deutsch Collection/CB; 202—ImageStateRM/Fotosearch, GR, GR; 203—GR, GI; 204-206—GR; 207—Bettmann/CB, GR; 208—Bettmann/CB; 209—GR; 210—Allan Ramsay/GI, GR; 211—GR; 212—Bettmann/CB, GR; 213—GR, ImageStateRM/Fotosearch, GR; 214—Bettmann/CB; 215—CB, Grand Tour/CB; 216—Owen Franken/CB, Quentin Bargate/Loop Images/CB; 217—CC; 218—Andrew Brown/Ecoscene/CB; 219—David Ball/CB, GR; 220—Paul Thompson/Ecoscene/CB; 223—CI; 225—Patrick Ward/CB; 226—Bruce Gordon/PR, Paolo Koch/PR; 227—CI, Neil Beer/CB; 228—David Ciemny/IS; 229—Charles O'Rear/CB; 230—Peter Turnley/CB, Wolfgang Kaehler/CB; 232—Alinari Archives/CB, CC, CB; 233—Stefano Bianchetti/CB, Bettmann/CB; 234—Domenico Pellegriti/IS, CI; 235—Atlantide Phototravel/CB, CB; 236—CC, Diane Stamatelatos/IS; 237—Gian Berto Vanni/CB; 238—Frank Lukasseck/CB; 239—Frank Lukasseck/CB, Bettmann/CB; 240-241—GR; 242—CB; 243—GR; 244—C.I.C.R. Vernier Jean Bern/Sygma/CB, CB; 245—W. Geiersperger/CB; 246—Anna Dorothea Lisiewska/GI; 247—Bettmann/CB; 248—Bettmann/CB; 250—Russ Kinne, Inc./AA, GR, Underwood & Underwood/CB; 251—CC, Robert Estall/CB; 252—Paul Almasy/CB, GR; 253—CC; 254—Robin Laurance/PR; 255—GR; 256—Danny Lehman/CB; 257—CC; 258—Bettmann/CB; 259—CB, CC; 260—Jorn Georg Tomter/GI, George Holton/PR, Peter Lilja/ES/AA; 268—Bettmann/CB, GR, GR; 270, 271—GR; 272—GR, Bettmann/CB; 274—Peter Turnley/CB; 275—Hulton-Deutsch Collection/CB, Peter Turnley/CB; 276—Bob Krist/CB; 279—Jeremy Edwards/IS, Bernard Bisson/Sygma/CB; 280—Ayzek/IS; 281—Doug Allan, OSF/ES/AA; 282—CC, CB, Win Initiative/GI; 283—CC, AFP/GI; 284—Andrii Gatash/IS; 285—Courau/Explorer/PR, Puchan/IS; 286—CC, Hubertus Kanus/PR; 287—Russell Young/JAI/CB, Bettmann/CB; 288—Walter Bibikow/GI, Aldo Pavan/Grand Tour/CB; 290—Alexander Hafemann/IS, CC, Bob Krist/CB, Sergey Korotkov/IS, David H. Lewis/IS, Alan Toepfer/IS, CC, Tom McHugh/PR, Robert Cumming/IS, CC, CB, CC, CC, CC, RainforestAustralia/IS, CC, DNY59/IS, CI, Pjjones/IS, CC, Stephen Patterson/IS; 291—GR; 294—James Bowyer/IS, Paul A. Souders/CB; 295—CB; 296—Gary Bell/zefa/CB, Paul A. Souders/CB, Tom McHugh/PR; 297—DEA/P. Jaccod/GI, Stock Connection RM/Fotosearch; 298—CB; 299—Paul A. Souders/CB, CB, CB; 300—Jack Fields/PR; 301—Panoramic Images/GI, Ray Hems/IS, William E. Ferguson; 303—Travel Pix/GI, Jochen Schlenker/Robert Harding World Imagery/CB; 304—Hubertus Kanus/PR; 305—Photri Images; 306—Seth Resnick/Science Faction/CB; 307—Momatiuk/Eastcott/CB, Eric and David Hosking/CB, Bettmann/CB; 308—GR, Norbert Wu/Science Faction/CB, CB, CB; 323—CI; 324—Tissa/IS; 325—Alexander Hafemann/IS, Debra James/IS, Ranjan Chari/IS; 336—Xiaoping Liang/IS; 338—CC; 343—Eliza Snow/IS; 344—Brue/IS.